Regional Development Theories & Their Application

Regional Development Theories & Their Application

Benjamin Higgins
Donald J. Savoie

Transaction Publishers
New Brunswick (U.S.A.) and London (U.K.)

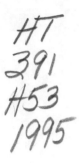

*HT
391
H53
1995*

Library of Congress Catalog Number: 93-45849
ISBN: 1-56000-160-7
Printed in the United States of America

Library of Congress Cataloging-in-Publication Data

Higgins, Benjamin Howard, 1912-
    Regional development theories and their application / Benjamin Higgins, Donald J. Savoie.
        p.   cm.
    Includes bibliographical references and index.
    ISBN 1-56000-160-7
    1. Regional planning.   2. Regional disparities.   3. Regionalism.
I. Savoie, Donald J.   II. Title.
HT391.H53   1994
338.9—dc20
                                                                93-45849
                                                                    CIP

Contents

Part III: Looking Back—Looking Ahead

List of Abbreviations

ACOA	Atlantic Canada Opportunities Agency
ADA	Area Development Agency
ADIA	Area Development Incentives Act
AEP	Atlantic Enterprise Program
ARDA	Agriculture Rehabilitation and Development Act
CCP	The Country Centres Project
CDE	Centre for Development of Entrepreneurs
CES	Commonwealth Employment Service
CIDA	Canadian International Development Agency
CRDE	Centre de recherche en développement économique
DILGEA	Department of Immigration Local Government and Ethnic Affairs
DIST	Department of Industry, Science and Technology
DREE	Department of Regional Economic Expansion
DRIE	Department of Regional Industrial Expansion
DRIPP	Développement régional intégré Petit Goave-Petit Trou de Nippes
DURD	Department of Urban and Regional Development
EAGGF	European Agricultural Guidance and Guarantee Fund
ERDA	Economic and Regional Development Agreement
ERDF	European Regional Development Fund
ESF	European Social Fund
FEDNOR	Federal Economic Development Northern Ontario
GDA	General Development Agreement
HRAC	Hunter Regional Association of Councils
IADB	Inter-American Development Bank
IMRA	Inner Metropolitan Regional Association
MSERD	Ministry of State for Economic and Regional Development
NEP	New Economic Policy

NRPB	National Resources Planning Board
OECD	Organization for Economic Co-operation and Development
OEMA	Outer Eastern Municipalities Association
RDD	Regional Development Division
RDG	Regional Development Grant
SUDENE	Superintendency for the Development of the Northeast
TVA	The Tennessee Valley Authority
UNCRD	United Nations Centre for Regional Development
WD	Western Development Department
WSROC	Western Sydney Regional Organization of Councils
WTID	Western Transportation Industrial Development

Preface

The objective of this book is to introduce the reader to the major theories of regional development by providing a readable, readily comprehensible summary of them; to show their strengths and weaknesses by considering their application—or lack of it—in several development projects and programs, in both industrialized and developing countries; and to suggest ways in which regional development theory, plans, policies and programs could be improved. In choosing both theories and case studies we have been, necessarily, highly selective. In Part I, on theory, we have concentrated for the most part on "received doctrine." We have selected the theories that seem to us most basic and fundamental, and presented them in their pure, classical form, in accordance with the writings of the principal authors of each theory. We have not, in other words, endeavoured to cover recent articles in professional journals revising, criticizing, updating these classic theories. The literature is much too voluminous for that. The reader, once having grasped the basic ideas, will be in a position to consult further literature on whatever subjects have captured his interest. In the chapter on "Recent Literature on Regional Development," we do not discuss systematically recent literature on the theories already treated in the earlier chapters, but rather deal with *new* ideas and controversies that have arisen in the last decade or so.

In Part II, presenting our case studies, the United States and the United Kingdom are obviously important countries where experience with regional development can teach us significant lessons; and Canada is an important country where regional development is concerned. Both authors have been deeply involved, in one way or another, in Canadian regional development. Both have lived in the United Kingdom, and one has been involved in regional policy there. The other has lived for years in the United States and has been involved in regional planning in that country. Australia is included because one author has lived for years in that country, is well acquainted with regional policy there, and because it is an interesting case, with sharp contrasts to the other three.

As for the Developing Countries and the Least Developed Countries, the case analyzed are all ones in which Benjamin Higgins spent long periods as member of a team charged with preparing a regional development plan. In our opinion, such first-hand experience is crucial as a basis for writing about regional development in such countries.

ix

Part III contains suggestions for improving both theory and practice of regional development, and indicates how concentration of analysis on the regional level can improve the social sciences as a whole.

The reader will no doubt see that Benjamin Higgins' hand looms large indeed in this book. He took the lead in writing the great majority of the chapters. I enjoyed immensely working with him on this book, as I have on every initiatives I have been fortunate enough to have worked with him over the past ten years. His sense of humour, his vast experience in field work, his ability to simplify complex issues, his zest for life, his curiosity and thirst for new knowledge are all the things that one enjoys about Ben. I had the good fortune of spending a few weeks on his ranch in Australia in February 1993 to work on this book.

Donald J. Savoie

Part I

Theory

1

Introduction

This book has three objectives: to provide a readable, readily comprehensible survey of the literature and current discussion in the fields of regional economics, regional development, regional policy and planning; to lay the foundations for improved economic and social policy, formulated and implemented at the regional or community level; and to demonstrate that the social sciences, and particularly economics, can be more effective instruments for discovery of truth and acquisition of new knowledge, and thus for solution of current economic and social problems, if major emphasis is laid on analysis at the regional and community level, rather than putting the emphasis exclusively on analysis at the national (macro) level and at the (micro) level of the industry, enterprise (firm), household and local government.

It is our contention that societies and economies cannot be well understood without analyzing the multi-faceted interactions, feedbacks, and overlaps among spaces, structures, and societies. "Countries," nations, nation-states, and national economies are in fact collections of spaces (regions), each with its own society and its own economic, social, political and power structure. The degree to which these spaces are integrated into a unified national economic, social, political and administrative system varies a great deal from country to country, and these variations go a long way in explaining differences in performance (economic, social, and political) from country to country. Where performance is unsatisfactory, more often than not, intervention is required at the regional and community level, and not just at the macro or micro levels. In other words, regional analysis is not a "branch" of, or field apart from, other social sciences; rather, it is an *integral and integrating* component, a catalyst, a synapse, for the social sciences as a whole.

In the past, the separate disciplines comprising the social sciences have tended to view "regional analysis" in different ways. Anthropologists, by and large, did not think of themselves as conducting "regional analysis," although the societies they studied necessarily occupied particular spaces, and were influenced by the physical environment. In recent years, however, as anthropologists were more and more frequently included on regional development planning teams, the profession became more aware of the contribution it can make to analysis and policy defined in regional terms. Sociologists, naturally enough, have been interested in differences in social structures from region to region, and in the causes and effects of these differences. They have shown concern regarding regional disparities. Political scientists conducting regional analysis have tended to concentrate on such matters as relationships among governments at federal, state or provincial, and local levels, revenue sharing, distribution of taxing and spending powers among levels of government, and problems of public administration arising from regional disparities and efforts to reduce them.

When urban and regional economics began to develop as a separate field in the 1950s and 1960s, most economists entering that field thought of it as a distinct branch of their discipline. As regional development planning became a more and more important aspect of the international development effort, in the late 1960s and early 1970s, and as regional disparities became a matter of growing concern in many industrialized countries as well, urban and regional economists began to see that their field was in fact a vital part of the economics discipline as a whole. Except for the greater emphasis on the physical environment, geographers, and especially economic geographers, have applied to regional problems a methodology barely distinguishable from that followed by urban and regional economists.

The degree to which recognition of the integrating function of regional analysis requires changes in the methodology of particular social sciences varies from branch to branch. Anthropology is based on on-the-spot study of particular *societies*, which regional analysis also entails. However, as a rule, the anthropologist does not devote detailed attention to analysis of the physical environment with which the society of a particular space interacts, let alone making recommendations for changing that environment so as to improve the society. Comparisons of one society with another are too seldom made, and generalizations leading to policy conclusions even more seldom. Geographers, on the other hand, while making major contributions to regional analysis, tend to err in the other direction; they are keenly aware of the physical environment but underemphasize the social and cultural structure, including the political framework and administrative problems. Sociologists today, when they enter into regional analysis, usually do so in a comprehensive fashion, but seldom include in their analysis such purely economic factors as market structures, distribution of monopoly power, impact of monetary, fiscal, and foreign trade policy. Political scientists also tend to pay little attention to these factors, and to socio-cultural factors.

There is need for some degree of division of labour among the social sciences; but regional analysis, if it is to be effective, cannot afford to leave out anything of importance. By definition, regional analysis must adopt a multidisciplinary approach, which is why it is uniquely placed to play a major role in weaving together the various strands of the social sciences into an elegant but strong fabric.

Scope: Space as a Strategic Variable in Socio-Economic Analysis

Mainstream economics has traditionally considered space in four ways:

1. Although much of mainstream (neo-classical) economics explicitly or implicitly assumes that space is homogeneous, and therefore abstracts from spatial considerations altogether, when working at a level closer to reality, mainstream economists do recognize that different spaces have different resource endowments, physical and human. These differences create opportunities for geographic specialization, according to comparative advantage. Recognition of the existence of these opportunities gives rise to the theory of interregional and international trade.

2. Similarly, while much of mainstream economics abstracts from transport costs and assumes, implicitly or explicitly, completely costless and instantaneous mobility of all factors of production, at a higher level of reality it is recognized that the different resource endowments of different regions, which provide a basis for interregional trade, also entail the existence of distances between spaces. Transport costs and limited mobility must therefore be taken into account in any analysis that purports to be realistic enough to provide a basis for policy recommendations. Nonetheless, much neo-classical analysis treats transport costs and immobilities essentially as nuisances that detract from the elegance of the analysis, and neither is the subject of thorough analysis in most of the mainstream literature.

3. Since neither people nor resources are spread evenly through space, there are necessary choices and decisions to be made as to what economic activities should be carried out where. Proximity to markets (people) and to resources, production costs, and transport costs will be considerations in these decisions. More recently, access to information and to innovations have been added to the list of considerations. The aggregation of these decisions will determine the location of industry and other economic activities, and thus the location of population, the location and size of cities, the urban hierarchy. These very complex interactions gave rise to the theory of location, which became one of the most abstract, one of the most abstruse, and one of the least satisfactory branches of neo-classical economics.

4. The boundaries of political units are defined in space: nation-states, states and provinces, municipalities, districts. These units have varying degrees of power in various fields of policy: monetary, fiscal, trade, foreign ex-

change, wage-price regulation, land use, and so on. Thus in the analysis of public policy, neo-classical mainstream economics was obliged to recognize the existence of differentiated spaces. As a rule, however, it did not take account of specific social, cultural, or political differences among these spaces.

It is fair to say, however, that mainstream economics, whether neo-classical or Marxist, or even Institutionalist, never dealt adequately with space as such. It is one of the principal aims of this book to fill this gap, at least in part. We shall argue that the failure of neo-classical economics to deal adequately with space springs largely from three fundamental tenets, seldom explicitly stated, and even less frequently defended:

1. The free market actually works in such a way as to bring an optimal allocation of resources, to bring rapid, painless, and essentially costless adjustment to change, and to assure an acceptable distribution of income.
2. There is a basic harmony of interests among social groups, communities, regions, and nation-states.
3. In the absence of misguided government interference, the degree of actual mobility in the real world would be such that the assumption of complete, costless and instantaneous mobility would do no great violence to reality.

With these assumptions or beliefs, regional analysis becomes simply uninteresting. A free market with sensible monetary and fiscal policy to maximize the level and rate of growth of national income would maximize the welfare of all social groups, regions, and countries. Regional disparities could not persist. If yields per man/hour in growing rice in Texas were several times as high as in India (as they are), Indian rice-growers would move to Texas until productivity was equalized in the two regions. Differences in productivity and incomes among sectors would also tend to disappear, as they have done to a considerable degree in Australia. The overlap between disadvantaged sectors and disadvantaged regions, so evident in developing countries and present in industrialized ones as well, could not persist. Indeed, "regions" would have little meaning. They would be artificial subdivisions of national economies, and any intervention in the market in the name of regional policy would be at the cost of a reduction of efficiency in those national economies. Implicit or explicit in the standard neo-classical analysis is a "natural" tendency of unhampered economies toward equilibrium, and to return to equilibrium if disturbed. In the extreme version, this "equilibrium" is even one with full employment and stable price levels. In other versions (Milton Friedman) "full" becomes "natural," the amount of unemployment consistent with stable prices, or a stable rate of inflation.

On the whole, Marxists have paid little more attention to space than the neo-classical economists. When they do, it is usually in the guise of some variant of the "dependency theory," with space in the form of a "centre" where the international monopoly capitalists have their headquarters, and a "periphery" in the form of regions or countries where abide the people they systematically exploit. In this theory, interregional or international disparities persist because the capitalists, who have the power, want them to persist, to keep wages down and profits up. Thus regions or spaces are defined in terms of the interregional and international power structure, and the distribution of income that results from it.

It is our contention that the real world is very different from the pictures painted by either the neo-classical or Marxist schools, and that space plays a far more vital role in economies and societies than either school allows. Among the factors which lead us to this view, to be elaborated below, are the following:

1. All societies live in particular places; cultures are defined in terms of space. This simple fact has been recognized by other social scientists, but seldom explicitly by economists.
2. These spaces are almost always smaller geographically than a nation-state. There is hardly any country, with the possible exception of some of the smallest island nations, which is so homogeneous as to be regarded as a single society or culture.
3. In most countries, there are sharply differing or even conflicting interests among various societies occupying various spaces within them. Most apparent are cases like Tamils in Sri Lanka, Sikhs in India, Basques in Spain, Welsh and Scotch in the United Kingdom, Québécois and Acadiens in Canada, Indians in Mexico. But there are more subtle conflicts among societies/spaces in almost every country in the world. In Canada, for example, there is scarcely a region or province that does not have its own cultural and social characteristics and its own special interests, which are often in conflict with those of other provinces and regions.
4. Economic and social interests of particular societies in particular spaces are closely tied to the dominance of particular *sectors* of economic activity and the consequent *structure* of the economy and society. A commonality of interests arises only when people live and make their living in the same *sector* and in the same *place*. Sugar cane growers and cutters in Fiji, for example, are not much interested in promoting the welfare of sugar cane growers and cutters in nearby Queensland. People seldom develop loyalties to *sectors*.
5. People do, however, develop strong loyalties and attachments to *spaces*. Family, friends, institutions, landscapes, climates, a general sense of belonging and of knowing how to behave in a particular society,—these exercise a very strong pull on most normal people. And this pull means that mobility could never be costless, instantaneous, and painless even if

transport were free, and if houses, churches, hospitals, schools, power plants, etc. could be transported, instantaneously and costlessly along with the people. Many people have a passionate desire to go on living and earning their living where they are; and that desire is a factor that must be given its proper weight in the calculation of the impact of any policy on the welfare of a particular society.

6. Most people do not think of "welfare" in terms of nation-states. They may have enough national pride to be pleased when they read that the per capita income of their country has surpassed that of a neighbouring country; but their pleasure in that fact is not likely to be overwhelming if they live in a retarded region, and if many of their family and friends are unemployed, ill housed, impoverished, and unable to get satisfactory schooling or medical attention. Where social welfare is concerned, much smaller spaces than the nation-state must be used as the criterion.

7. As the result of a combination of "market failure" and "government failure," each compounding the effects of the other, the market in fact does not work well. There is no assurance that a general rise in national income will quickly solve the economic and social problems of particular social groups, societies, sectors, or regions. Each problem must be tackled where it exists, *ad hoc*, with measures appropriate to each case.

8. There is a limited sense in which there is a "harmony of interests" in a national economy and national society. If farmers are prosperous they will buy more agricultural implements and machinery, and that is good for the steel industry. But there are obvious conflicts as well. If the agricultural equipment is inefficient but highly protected, the farmers would be better off if the restrictions on imports were removed; but then both the implement industry and the steel industry would suffer.

9. These conflicts tend to be translated into spatial terms, because there is an overlap between technological dualism or pluralism and regional dualism or pluralism. Conflict between wheat farmers and the steel industry becomes conflict between the wheat region and the steel region. Poverty, or relatively low incomes, occurs when too many people are engaged in a particular sector in a particular place: sugar in Haiti or Cuba, textiles in the eastern townships of Quebec or the southeast of Australia, rice in Bangladesh or Sri Lanka, millet in Senegal or Mali. Such problems cannot be solved by sectoral policies alone. Making rice farmers in Texas and Australia more productive will not help rice farmers in Java. The task of getting people out of sectors they should not be in must be undertaken at the regional level.

10. There is also an overlap between structural adjustment and regional development. This fact has been most obvious in countries with "moving frontiers:" the United States, Canada, the former USSR, Argentina, Brazil. The changes in the product-mix, the socio-economic and occupational structure, went hand-in-hand with the movement of population into new *spaces*—that is, with regional development. The regional struc-

ture, the economic structure, and the social structure all move together. But all countries have experienced such change in varying degrees. Even in Australia, which has had a relatively stable regional structure for a large, regionalized country of recent settlement, the postwar minerals boom has developed principally the Pilbara and other parts of the Northwest, making the Pilbara the richest region of the Bureau of Statistics' 60. The impact on the national economy and the national society is quite different from the discoveries in the nineteenth or early twentieth centuries, in the backyards of the established metropolitan centres. So, too, mineral discoveries in Alberta and Saskatchewan have changed the face of the Canadian prairie provinces; they are no longer simply "the wheat economy."

There is throughout the world today more fluidity in the location of economic activity than ever before and, consequently, more rapid and more unpredictable changes in patterns of regional development: the continued movement toward the southeast of UK despite all efforts to halt it; the converse move away from Paris; the return to the biggest metropolitan centres of Japan after a decade of "polarization reversal;" the movement to the south of Italy, the east of Malaysia, the north and northeast of Brazil. The speed of diffusion of innovation is also unprecedented. It is not possible to understand what is going on in any of these national economies without knowing what is going on in the various regional economies of which they are composed.

11. Far from there being a trade-off between policies to develop particular regions and efficiency of the national economy, there is a strong complementarity between the two. The complementarity has several interlocking aspects:

a) Countries with high and rapidly growing per capita income tend to have small and diminishing regional disparities; countries with large and increasing regional disparities tend to have low and slowly growing per capita incomes.

b) Countries with large regional gaps tend to have very unfavourable trade-off curves between inflation and unemployment; countries with small regional gaps tend to have low combinations of inflation and unemployment.

c) Slow-growth regions tend to have economic fluctuations of greater amplitude, with shorter booms and longer depressions than high growth regions, which tend to have greater stability, with longer booms and shorter depressions.

d) Long-run growth rates tend to be highest in countries undergoing long-run regional convergence, as a result of the operation of a "ratchet effect;" that is, when regions take turns at being the high-growth region, the slow-growth region of one period becoming the high-growth region of the next, and no region moving from slow-growth to decline.

12. There is no evidence of a general movement toward "equilibrium" in a free market economy, whether in the sense of regional balance or any

other sense, and especially not in the sense of "equilibrium" with full employment without inflation. On the other hand, Gunnar Myrdal's concept of "cumulative causation," economies moving cumulatively away from equilibrium whenever a disturbance occurs, is also not universally supported by experience, whether in terms of regional convergence or divergence or any other concept of equilibrium. Rather, what appears to happen is an alternation of movements toward and movements away from equilibrium. Theories of economic fluctuations depend upon such alternations.

In short, our argument is that designing policy to assure good performance of national economies requires thorough understanding of the behaviour of the regional economies of which they are composed, and formulating policies for each region on the basis of that understanding. Such understanding will not be gleaned through stubborn pursuit of standard methodology of either neo-classical or Marxist economics. It requires making regions (spaces) basic units of analysis, studying the societies of each space on the spot, determining who the actors are, who really informs the development of the economy of each space, what their aims are, and how they strive to achieve them, and building explanatory models based on those observations.

Method

From Aristotle to Karl Popper, philosophers have reiterated formulations of "*the* scientific method."[1] In his book on *The Joy of Science*, Carl J. Sinderman, a biologist, offers this formulation of "the classical scientific method":

1. formulation of a hypothesis
2. accumulation of relevant data through observation and experimentation
3. possible modification of the hypothesis based on interpretation of the data
4. further observation and experimentation to verify the revised hypothesis
5. synthesis of all available data
6. statement of a concept

Sinderman goes on, however, to exclaim: "What a beautiful blueprint for action!...What a fraud! There is no single scientific method;...Reality, for most professionals, is far sloppier than the neat textbook 'scientific method,' and follows no single pathway."[2] His "sloppy method" entails:

1. evolution of ideas and insights
2. evolution of experimental design
3. evolution of data analysis
4. evolution of syntheses

Sinderman is, of course, quite right. One can be too fussy about scientific method. Methods varying a good deal in detailed content can contribute to the advance of knowledge. Provided he or she knows what scientific method is, a scholar can afford to be a bit sloppy. Today's scientist never really works alone. There are always others interested in the same field of inquiry. It is the aggregation of all the work done in each field that advances knowledge, not the work of any one individual.

Nor is "sloppiness" the special preserve of the social sciences. The line between "soft" and "hard" sciences is not all that easily drawn.[3] Robert Persig quotes Einstein as saying: "The supreme task...is to arrive at those universal elementary laws from which the cosmos can be built up by pure deduction. There is no logical path to these laws; only intuition, resting on sympathetic understanding of experience, can reach them...."[4]

Paul Feyerahand states his view of the current position of philosophy of science regarding "scientific method" as follows: "The only principle that does not inhibit progress is: *anything goes*...There is no idea, however ancient and absurd, that is not capable of improving our knowledge...even the most advanced and apparently secure theory is not safe...the knowledge of today may become the fairy tale of tomorrow and...the most laughable myth may eventually turn into the most solid piece of science...."[5]

Our concern here, therefore, is not with the degree to which regional analysis follows the rules of scientific positivism, or with the extent of its ability to predict. Natural scientists seldom follow these rules rigorously either, and some would argue that it is a good thing that they don't.[6] Progress is faster without rigorous adhesion to "the scientific method" and "ability to predict" is always limited. Rather, we are concerned in a quite pragmatic way with the usefulness of regional analysis as a basis of regional policy, and more broadly and more importantly with the potential of regional analysis as an approach to economic and social theory, policy and planning.

Regional Analysis

Regional analysis is an amalgam of several contributing disciplines, notably economics, geography, and political science; and to a lesser degree sociology, anthropology, and physical sciences like geology and climatology. With one important exception to be noted below, no distinctive methodology has been developed for "regional" analysis. Members of each discipline, when tackling regional problems, apply, perhaps with slight modification, the broad methodology of their own discipline. Essentially, all these methods are "scientific." They begin with observation, proceed to postulating hypotheses regarding causal explanations of observed phenomena, then to empirical testing of these hypotheses, generalization from those hypotheses that pass the tests and are also consistent with other received doctrine, and sometimes to conclusions regarding policy. The proportion of the total scientific effort devoted to each of these stages of analysis varies a good deal from one discipline to another. For example, the ratio of description to abstract theory is higher in geography or anthropology than it is in economics. Consequently, the methodology of "regional analysis" as a whole is something of a hodge podge, and tends to be somewhat "sloppier" than the methods of the contributing disciplines. This defect helps to explain the difficulty of integrating regional analysis into a single, systematic body of thought; but it does not prevent regional analysis from constituting a solid foundation for policy and planning, any more than the similar situation in "medical science," which is also an unsystematical amalgam of other sciences, prevents it from being a useful basis for medical practice.[7]

The *scope* of regional analysis is, almost by definition, broader than that of any one of the disciplines contributing to it. This greater breadth is not merely the result of aggregating several disciplines. It is also, and more importantly, the consequence of the fact that regional analysis does not deliberately exclude any of the subject matter of the component disciplines, but adds to *each* discipline considerations of *space* in a manner not usual for each separate discipline.

Regional analysis is concerned with aspects of space which cannot be handled in terms of transport cost, resource endowment, and class structure alone. Some of these include:

1. The spatial multiplier. Events taking place in one space have an impact on events in other places which cannot be adequately explained in terms of market forces or class struggle alone. Political, socio-cultural, and purely physical forces play a role. Examples are the impact on Montreal of opening the Toronto airport to transatlantic traffic, the construction of the Welland and Erie canals and the St. Lawrence Seaway; the impact on Minaus, Brazil, of smuggling rubber clones to London and then to Southeast Asia, or the construction of Brasilia, and the consequent opening up of the Brazilian centre.
2. Space and time. This relationship is much more than transport costs, involving communications, personal contacts, interest costs, and so on.
3. The relationship of space to the diffusion of knowledge and information, indivisibilities and externalities. (Fall-out from Chernobyl, export of London fog to Holland through use of high smoke stacks, and so on.).
4. Polarization and cumulative causation. Recognition of the heterogeneity of space leads to the conclusion that polarization and cumulative movements away from equilibrium are more likely than smooth and rapid "adjustment" and movements toward "equilibrium."

5. The overlap between spatial heterogeneity, occupational structures, socio-cultural disparities, and political action and expression identified with defined spaces. Fishermen are not a major social group on the desert or the prairie, and they play a bigger role when they are not only fishermen but also Basques, Acadiens, or Gaspésiens.

The Distinctive Methodology of Regional Analysis

The disciplines contributing to regional analysis, we contend, are about as scientific or as sloppy, as positive or as dependent on value judgements, as any other science. The fact that it is an amalgam of several disciplines makes it difficult to construct synthetic theories incorporating elements of all of them. However, such general theories are not really necessary for professional *practice* in the field—formulation of regional policy and preparation of regional plans—no more than a "general theory of health" is necessary for the practice of medicine, or a "general theory of three-dimensional form" is necessary for the practice of architecture. We are prepared to go further and state the claim that there is one unique feature in the methodology of regional analysis and practice which makes it more suitable for its purpose than most social sciences are for theirs. This element is that when it comes to formulation of regional policy and preparation of regional plans, the regional analyst, whatever his basic discipline, feels obliged to go into the field and study the target population and its behaviour in relation to its physical environment on the spot. He consequently acquires a much more profound knowledge of the people with whom he is concerned, their problems and potential, than social scientists who generalize from presumed *universal* laws of human behaviour. By diagnosing maladies on the spot, with the "patient" present, he or she can be much more precise in his or her prognosis and much more effective in prescription. The anthropologist, of course, also studies societies and their environment on the spot; but the anthropologist usually considers his job finished when he or she can describe the culture and its functioning; for the regional analyst, that is just the beginning. Of course, regional analysts can make mistakes. But they are likely to make fewer and less egregious errors than those who prescribe policies or make plans for national economies and societies on the basis of macro-models, or of micro-models constructed on tautological or simplistic "laws" of behaviour (maximization of utility, maximization of profits), alone.

Regional Analysis as a Method for Social Science

Thus far, we have been talking of regional analysis which, as a field of scientific inquiry, is created by slicing off specialized parts of various disciplines, and then gluing together the slices to make another discipline. However, there is another way of looking at regional analysis, a way that becomes increasingly attractive with the growing dissatisfaction with social science, using traditional methodology and with the usual definitions of scope, because of its inability to deal with today's social problems. That way is to regard regional analysis as a distinct social science methodology in its own right.

When with the "marginal revolution" of the 1870s economists set out to make their discipline a rigorous, mathematical, pure science, it was inevitable that it would be the methodology of physics, and especially of mechanics, that they took as their model. Physics was the queen science of the time. One of the implications of that methodology was the assumption that social scientists, like natural scientists, are dealing with a single universe, subject to laws that are true always and everywhere. To construct a single-universe economics, it was essential to have basic rules regarding the behaviour of individuals from which laws regarding the functioning of entire economies could be derived. In the search for such rules, the behavioral assumptions of economics became increasingly simplistic and tautological. Nonetheless, with considerable ingenuity, economists made substantial progress in explaining the functioning of economic systems, so much so that many of their colleagues in other disciplines, including political science and sociology, made the great mistake of following in the same methodological path.[8]

During World War II and the reconstruction period that followed it, the faith in the standard methodology of the social sciences seemed warranted. The war economies of the Allied Nations were well managed; full employment was maintained without inflation or foreign exchange crises. The reconstruction period was weathered without the feared onslaught of renewed massive unemployment. It seemed that with the Keynesian revolution, together with the advances in statistical method and econometrics and in the statistics themselves, and the high-speed computer, economists, at least, and perhaps other social scientists too, could pursue the methodology of physics effectively, and produce "laws" that would serve as the basis for effective policy. And then in the mid 1950s, this world began to fall apart. Unemployment and inflation appeared side by side, and even increased together. Balance of payments crises and unstable foreign exchange rates appeared even in the most advanced countries. The problem of developing underdeveloped countries seemed impossible to solve. Conflict among regional groups cropped up everywhere. Something had gone sadly wrong, and social scientists no longer seemed to have the answers.

One response to this situation was a wide-spread decision to abandon macroeconomic planning for growth of national income, with expected trickledown effects, as the major device for promoting development. Government after government opted for disaggregation in space. Growth poles became a fad, and regional planning became a key component of national development planning.

But regional planning requires regional analysis, and in the process, regional analysis was upgraded too. Moreover, much of regional planning and analysis has to be done on the spot. As regional planners and analysts worked in various regions throughout the world, on the spot, they made an important discovery: most theories constructed on the foundation of assumptions of universal individual behaviour were either invalid or useless.

Regions and Nations

However, an important branch of political science operating largely outside the strict "scientific method," has had some success in delineating and describing the forces which have shaped regional groups and cultures, and which have motivated these groups to assert themselves more and more. We have come to realize that the sovereign nation-state is not the final stage of political development. All over the world, and not only in countries with federal constitutions, distinct regional interests are being expressed, loudly and sometimes forcibly. The attachment of people to particular regions, as distinct from the nations in which these regions happen to exist today, as a result of accidents of history and geography, is stronger than most of us had realized; the overlapping of space with differences in language, culture, and special interests is a more important factor in the social and political life of nations than is the weight attached to these factors in political theory. Today such regional considerations have come to the forefront of political debate in Canada, the United Kingdom, France, Spain, Italy, Greece, West Germany, the former Soviet Union, eastern Europe, Australia, and virtually all of the less-developed countries. Moreover, while other elements are involved as well, there is a close relationship between the political and the economic aspects of regionalism.[9]

Political scientists have produced a spate of books and articles on regionalism in national politics and national identity. An important conclusion is that there is a very close relationship between forms of government and political culture.[10] The stability of political institutions is developed in such a way as to coincide with the cultural characteristics of the local population. This realization, for example, contributed substantially to the acceptance in all federations of a flexible non-legalistic arrangement labelled cooperative federalism.[11] In addition, we have now come to accept the idea that British or other western forms of government are not appropriate for all developing countries.

Organization

This book has three parts. In part one, we present a comprehensive look at the various theories that have been put forward to explain regional disparities or to promote regional development. It is a broad sweep beginning with Adam Smith and concluding with a review of the most recent literature including studies on the spatial division of labour.

In part two, we report on the efforts of four countries in regional development. We can learn a great deal more about the merits of any one country's regional development policy by comparing the experiences of different countries rather than by focusing on just one. We study the United States, Great Britain, Canada and Australia. The four countries have common institutional roots, three have a federal form of government and the fourth is moving towards closer economic integration with Europe. We know that there has been a marked shift to the right since the early 1980s. After her 1979 election victory, Margaret Thatcher introduced sweeping changes to her country's public policy agenda. Her efforts to privatize the "commanding heights" of British industries, deep cuts in public spending and other new measures such as the contracting out of government services to the private sector soon found favour with Ronald Reagan, Brian Mulroney and Bob Hawke. Still, there have been over the years—and continue to be—sharp differences in how the four countries attempt to deal with regional disparities. In reporting on these differences, we adopt two approaches. In the case of the United States and Australia, we study specific initiatives in a highly detailed fashion. In the case of Canada and Britain, we study the evolution of the regional development policy with some reference to specific programs. The two approaches complement each other and provide the basis for an assessment of the extent to which the theories presented in part one influenced not only regional development policies but programs as well.

Part three does this by examining the application of the theories to government policies and programs. There are, of course, a variety of ways economic theories can influence public policy. Our main concern is to consider how theories assisted regional policy-makers and regional development planners to improve the outcome of measures taken to encourage the development of particular regions. We conclude the study by suggesting ways to strengthen regional development strategies and programs.

Notes

1. Aristotle, *Politique*, texte établi et traduit par Jean Aubonnet (Paris: Société d'édition Les Belles Lettres), undated. See also Karl Popper, *The Logic of Scientific Discovery* (New York: Harper and Row, 1965); Benjamin Higgins, *What Do Economists Know?: Six Lectures on Economics in the Crisis of Democracy*

(Melbourne: Melbourne University Press, 1951) and *What Do Economists Know Now?* (Perth: University of Western Australia Press, 1973).

2. Carl J. Sinderman, *The Joy of Science: Excellence and Its Rewards* (New York: Plenum Press, 1985), pp. 4–5.

3. Richard Blandy, "Soft Science," *The Economic Record*, Giblin lecture, vol. 61, no. 175, 1985, pp. 693–706.

4. Robert Persig, *Zen and the Art of Motor Cycle Maintenance: An Inquiry into Values* (Bodley Head: Great Britain, Corgi Edition, 1977).

5. Paul Feyerahand, *Against Method: Outline of an Anarchistic Theory of Knowledge* (London: New Left Books, 1975), pp. 10–11 and 52.

6. Mark Blaug, "Kuhn vs Lakatos or Paradigms vs Research Programs in the History of Economics," in *Method and Appraisal in Economics*, S.J. Latsis, (ed.) (Cambridge: Cambridge University Press, 1976).

7. See among others, Harry Richardson, "A Review of Techniques for Regional Policy Analysis," in Benjamin Higgins and Donald J. Savoie (eds), *Regional Economic Development: Essays in Honour of François Perroux* (London and Boston: Unwin Hyman, 1988).

8. Tom J. Courchene, "Avenues of Regional Adjustment: The Transfer System and Regional Disparities," in M. Walker (ed.), *Canadian Confederation at the Crossroads* (Vancouver: The Fraser Institute, 1978); Tom J. Courchene and James R. Melvin, "A Neoclassical Approach to Regional Economics," in Benjamin Higgins and Donald J. Savoie (eds), *Regional Economic Development: Essays in Honour of François Perroux* (London and Boston: Unwin Hyman, 1988).

9. See, among others, Ernest Mandel, *Late Capitalism* (London: New Left Books, 1975) and André Gunder Frank, *Latin America: Underdevelopment or Revolution* (New York: Modern Reader Paperback, 1970).

10. See Alan C. Isaak, *Scope and Method of Political Science* (Homewood, Ill.: The Dorsey Press, 1967).

11. Cooperative federalism takes many form. It was first used in the United States in 1938 in connection with the New Deal, in Canada, in 1963, to describe federal-provincial programs in health care, in the Federal Republic of Germany in 1966 at a meeting of the Freiheir-Von-Stein Association, and the list goes on. Wherever the term is employed, it invariably emphasizes the role of states and local government. In an address to the nation, President Richard Nixon explained cooperative federalism as "A co-operative venture among governments at all levels...in which power, funds, and authority are channelled increasingly to those governments which are closest to the people." There are numerous studies on cooperative federalism. See, for example, Samuel H. Beer, "The Modernization of American Federalism," in *Publius*, vol. 3, no. 2, pp. 49–75. See also Aaron Wildawsky (ed.), *American Federalism in Perspective* (Boston: Little, Brown and Company, 1967).

2

Geography, Culture, and Regional Development

Ever since the publication of Adam Smith's *Wealth of Nations* in 1776, there have been attempts to explain the wealth or poverty of nations in terms of soil, climate, and abundance or paucity of natural resources. These attempts have failed, because they cannot deal with the special cases. The countries with the highest GNP per capita today are Switzerland and Japan, neither of which is considered "rich in natural resources," or have particularly good climates. But if the resource endowment does not explain the differences in GNP, then differences in quality and quantity of human resources must. Major emphasis has been laid on that elusive factor of production called "entrepreneurship;" but differences in managerial, scientific, engineering, technical, and labour skills have also been stressed. But why should the people of some countries be smarter, better educated and trained, more innovative, more adventurous, and more skilled than the people of other countries? The answer is because they have different cultures, and some cultures are more favourable to economic development than others. But surely this is a very incomplete answer. Why should entrepreneurship flower in some cultures and wither in others, for example?

If geography and culture together explain the wealth or poverty of nations, will they not explain regional disparities within one nation as well? Offhand, one might expect that within one country, the regions where most of the people live would be more or less equal in resource endowment; otherwise, people would move to the regions where the resources are. To some extent, that is true; but, nonetheless, there is more difference in geography between southern and northern United States than there is between neighbouring countries in Europe. Similarly, one would expect some degree of cultural homogeneity within one country. But it is worth remembering that as late as 1880, the gap between the per capita income of the richest region in the United States (the Far West) and the poorest (the Southeast) was 400 percent. Since a gap of such magnitude could hardly be explained by the resource endowment, we must conclude that differences in human resources—cultural differences—played a role. May not these cultural differences, whatever they were, be still there in vestigial form? Are some of the differences in geography and culture still operative?

Geography

Differences in soil, climate, and resource endowment are the simplest explanation of regional disparities. In the United States, however, this explanation has never had much currency. It could not explain the wide regional gaps that existed in 1880, let alone the dramatic regional convergence that followed. There has been, it is true, a substantial literature on the effects of *exhaustion* of the resources of a particular region, "mining" the soil and the forest and strip mining the minerals. Professor John H. Cumberland explains the deterioration of Appalachia in such terms.[1] Similar statements were made regarding the exhaustion of the Masabi Range, a copper mine in northern Minnesota, which was one of the reasons for launching the Upper Great Lakes Regional Commission.[2] On the whole, however, few economists, economic historians, or historians have sought to explain regional disparities in the United States in terms of the resource endowment alone.

Partly because regional gaps have proved more recalcitrant than in the United States, and partly because of the enormous influence Harold Innis and his staples theory exerted on Canadian economic historians, historians, and economists, and perhaps because of Frederic Turner's ideas about the influence of the frontier, the story is quite different in Canada. There is also the fact that Canadian development has left Canada much more dependent on the export of natural resources than the United States. Thus James P. Bickerton writes, "The application of the staples model to the case of the Maritimes led to the widely accepted thesis that the economic stagnation of the region within Confederation was the outcome of inexorable technological changes that left its resource endowment marginal to the pattern of growth in twentieth century North America."[3] Professor E.R. Forbes, however, thinks that the staples thesis, if anything, contributed to the misunderstanding of the Maritimes: "The view of Canada's history as the story of the development of a series of staples for export...contributed only slightly more (to understanding of the Maritimes). Accounts of the fur trade touched on the Maritimes only in the earliest period; those on the timber trade largely petered out with confederation. Harold Innis' *Cod Fisheries* devoted but two of fifteen chapters to the Atlantic fishery after 1867, and studies of the wheat economy ignored the Maritimes entirely."[4]

Forbes thinks the same of the application of Turner's frontier thesis to the Canadian case. The thesis, he says, states that from the ever-moving frontier

"came a dynamic for social and material progress, democracy and nationalism. It was a thesis which with a few adjustments for differences in westward
movement could readily be applied to Canada. The thesis has tremendous
appeal to those who could still see themselves or their region as close to the
frontier stage. After all, it implied that they were progressive, democratic and
represented the essence of the nation. But it was difficult for Maritimers to
perceive themselves as part of a frontier society. The Maritimes were the only
provinces lacking huge territories in the process of settlement or other forms
of primitive development."[5]

There is, however, another school of thought which sees a rich resource
endowment as a positive hindrance to development. Some years ago, in
Canberra, the Pacific Council on Trade and Development was discussing "the
Singapore miracle." Helen Hughes, Director of the Australian National
University's National Centre for Development Studies, broke in impatiently
and exclaimed, "That is no miracle! Singapore is not *cursed* with rich natural
resources and a vast hinterland!"

There is truth in both points of view. In the past, countries with temperate
climates and abundant natural resources have tended to develop more rapidly
than others. On the other hand, countries that have developed on the basis of
their natural resources, tend to go on doing so, and to put insufficient emphasis on science, technology, education and training, and human resource development in general. As a consequence, leaders in development tend to become
laggards. Countries which are relatively small or which lack natural resources
have no choice but to follow the human resource development route, and sometimes deliver spectacular performance by doing so. Switzerland, Japan, Fin-
land, Singapore and Hong Kong are cases in point.

Any economy that continues to develop will arrive sooner or later at the
point where further improvement in levels of welfare requires drastic structural change. Some countries or regions, perhaps, face this need more than
once. If technological progress happens to coincide with repeated new resource discovery related to the newest technology, as has been the case in the
United States and Canada, the structural change needed for continued growth
may take place through a shift from one natural-resource-based pattern of
output and employment to another. The really difficult cases are those where
growth on the basis of a particular set of natural resources nears its end, while
no saviour in the form of new resource discovery and technological change
appears on the horizon. For in these cases further development requires a sharp,
discontinuous quantum leap from a natural-resource-based to a human-resource-based pattern of development.

The substitution of skills for natural resources is never an easy affair. It is
particularly difficult where a relatively rich natural resource base, in compari-

son to the size of the population, has made the development of increasingly advanced and ever-more-widely applicable skills seem unnecessary. Australia faced this problem when the good land gave out in the mid 1920s. The forty years that followed were a period of near stagnation when industrial import replacement proceeded painfully behind a high protective tariff wall. Now a new kind of growth has begun, partly on the basis of newly discovered mineral resources and partly on the basis of recently created or imported human resources. Argentina, New Zealand and Uruguay, facing the same problem at about the same time, were less lucky; there is as yet no assurance that these economies are clearly on the road to a new pattern of economic development.

The need for the leap from natural-resource-based to human-resource-based development may come at any level of per capita income, depending on the wealth of the natural resource endowment in relation to population. Canada, being richly endowed in natural resources, has come a long way without moving very far from the natural resource base. Natural resources still account for some 46 percent of Canadian exports. Many of the remaining exports are resource-based. The Canadian pattern of growth, maintaining an export sector still based on natural resources, while gradually shifting the labour force from farm to factory and office, has worked reasonably well. But this form of development has gone just about as far as it can go, if Canada is to maintain its position among nations in terms of economic development, let alone to narrow the gap between Canada and the United States. There remain relatively few people to get off the farms, out of the forests, and away from the mines; and the natural resource endowment as we now know it, and the existing technology, does not provide in itself the basis for transferring labour out of the primary sector. Transferring low-productivity people out of the primary sector will require the development of high-productivity occupations not directly tied to the resource base.

It is too seldom realized that this situation may arise even if there are still natural resources left to exploit. When we talk of "economic development," we talk of raising the general level of welfare by creating new jobs where man-year productivity is above the present national average. Frequently, the average output of resource-based-employment—high as it may be in comparison to the average of other countries or of the same country in the past—is fairly close to the present national average for all occupations. Accordingly, it is below what the national average will be if economic development continues. It applies to most of the resource-exploitation and direct resource-processing activities in Canada. The frontier mining region of Quebec yields man-year output below the national average, for example. Canada in recent decades has experienced one of the slowest rates of increase in output per unit of input of all advanced countries. Development in the form of "more of the same" will no longer do.

The United States was also "cursed with rich natural resources and a vast hinterland." However, in the American case the resources were so diversified and so wide spread among the various regions of the country, as to permit a unique frontier history, which allowed advantage to be taken of virtually every new advance in technology. "The frontier" in the United States moved, not only west, but quite a way north and a long way south as well. The Great Plains were virtually unique in their capacity to incite people to move. Urbanization and industrialization were spread to every major region of the country, "from sea to shining sea" and from Mexico to Canada. The Argentine pampas were a rival, but they were not attractive enough to create scores of great cities in the interior. Brazilians moved south on or near the coast, but the interior outside of Brazilia is still largely unsettled. Canadians moved "from sea to shining sea," but they could not move very far south without finding themselves in the United States, and there was little to lure them north except adventure. Most Australians stayed in their six capital cities on the coast, leaving "rich squatters" to exploit the good land, the multi-national corporations to exploit the mines, and leaving the interior empty—a very different pattern of settlement to that of the United States.

As a consequence, American society is imbued with "the frontier spirit"; Americans are more enterprising, more adventurous, more mobile, more individualistic, more suspicious of government and more trusting of free private enterprise and "the market" than their Canadian neighbours, and considerably more than their counterparts in Australia.[6] Which brings us to the consideration of culture as an element of regional differences.

Culture

If rich natural resources and a vast hinterland are a "curse," it follows that regional disparities are to be explained in terms of human resources, or cultural factors. For example, the lag of the Southeast behind other regions in the United States has been attributed to values and attitudes that are inimical to entrepreneurship. The old South was a "large man's frontier" from the beginning, and plantation society did not produce the kind of entrepreneurship that could bring rapid structural change. As Professor William H. Nicholls of Vanderbilt University has put it: "In the South as in most underdeveloped countries, the dominant agrarian values long supported a scale of social prestige which placed the land owner, the religious leader, the military leader and the political leader at the top and the man of business down the line. As a result, much of the South's business leadership has been furnished, if at all, from such minorities as the migratory Yankees, and South Highlanders who have been reared in other traditions. The resulting dearth of indigenous business leadership has also protected the large landowner (and even certain industrialists) from new forces which will inevitably weaken his political and economic hold on his rural community, reduce the cheap labor supply so essential to his comfortable way of life, and increase the general public concern for improving the lot of his less privileged neighbors."[7]

The "old Southwest" (Alabama, Mississippi, Louisiana and Tennessee), from the Revolution to the Civil War, was a "large man's frontier" too. With the invention of the cotton gin in 1793 southern planters turned their eyes westward to new sources of land for large scale commercial farming. The small farmers who first opened up the area were simply bought out, and moved farther west. With the fall of the small independent farmer, the "old Southwest" was ruled by owners of large cotton plantations; for a while, "cotton was King."[8] The comparative advantage of cotton was so marked—or the disadvantage of other lines of production so apparent—that the South, including the "old Southwest," alone of all major regions in the United States, came close to constructing an economy based on monoculture.

In terms of enterprise the reaction to military defeat was one of withdrawal from competition and retreat to the "superior" culture of the South. To quote Professor Nicholls again: "The Agrarians' indictment of Industrialism charged that through it science was applied to make labor intense, mercenary, servile and insecure, instead of something to be performed with leisure and enjoyment; to create overproduction, unemployment, and greater inequality in the distribution of wealth which could lead only to the super-state; to destroy that relation of man to nature which is conducive to a flourishing religion and vital creative arts; to develop relations between man and man unfavourable to such amenities of life as good manners, hospitality, family life, and romantic loves; and to accelerate the tempo and stability of life by a never-ending race between material goods, human wants, and human effort."[9]

Nicholls also quotes Cash regarding the tendency for the South "to wrap itself in contemptuous superiority, to sneer down the Yankee as low-bred, crass, money-grubbing, and even to beget in his bourgeoise soul the kind of secret and envy of all."[10] Slavery and *latifundia*, never important in the North, were other factors. Douglas North maintains that the relatively undemocratic society associated with the plantation economy of the South explains the striking lag of education investment in the South behind that of the Midwest and Northeast in the period 1815–1860.[11]

The Midwest had a very different culture. The Great Plains developed on the basis of family farms. In contrast to the South, the West developed a variety of export products, which in turn stimulated a variety of subsidiary industries. Distribution of property and income was relatively equitable; the West was the "small man's frontier" par excellence. And the westerner looked upon education as a capital investment with a high rate of return. Today, with its excellent universities, it has its share of hi-tech industries and sophisticated services.

In Quebec a similar retreat took place after the conquest. Some of the richer and better educated French retreated the whole way back to France, depriving French Canada of much of its economic and political élite. France itself showed little concern for the fate of her former colonists once the colony itself was lost. Far from helping them to rebuild their economy after a damaging war, France even renounced its debts to the colony. But the impact of defeat seems to have been more profound. No longer in control of their own land, and finding themselves for one reason or another at a disadvantage in competition with the British conquerors, the French seem to have withdrawn from competition as the American southerners were to do a century later. Like them, they withdrew into their traditions and cultivated a local nationalism, consoling themselves for their failure to participate fully in the economic life of the province by assuring themselves that they did not wish to do so anyway. They preferred the gentility and humanity of their own life, their own faith, values, and culture to the vulgar materialism of the victors. As time went by these attitudes became formalized and ritualized. Ideologically, if not in fact, there was a "return to the land," as there was in the American south.

So persuasive was this ideal of a serene, agrarian society led by the Church and a cultivated élite indifferent to wealth that many French Canadians began to think that Quebec really was like that. Thus in 1898 Sir John Bourinet, Clerk of the House of Commons in Ottawa, Honourable Secretary of the Royal Society of Canada, Doctor of Letters of Laval University, wrote: "As a rule, the *habitant* lives contentedly on very little. Give him a pipe of native tobacco, a chance for discussing politics, a gossip with his fellows at the church door after service, a visit now and then to the county town, and he will be happy. It does not take much to amuse him, while he is quite satisfied that his spiritual safety is secured as long as he is within the sound of the church bells, goes regularly to confession, and observes all the *fêtes d'obligation*. If he or one of his family can only get a little office in the municipality, or in the "government," then his happiness is nearly perfect."[12]

J.P. Beaulieu of the Quebec Department of Industry wrote in a similar vein in 1952, although showing more appreciation of the industrialization which was then taking place: "Quebec, barely half a century ago, a picturesque region in a vast country, over most of its extent farm lands alternated with forest, rivers, villages and freshly cleared colonization centres. This was Quebec little changed from pioneer days with the old ways kept alive from one generation to the other by the rural population. Quebec today is a dominant factor in the Canadian nation. On its skyline the tall chimneys have increased in number and intense activity overflows from plants, factories and workshops."[13]

And here is Prime Minister Pierre Trudeau, writing at the time of the asbestos strike in 1956, in which he was deeply involved: "C'est pourquoi, contre une ambiance anglaise, protestante, démocratique, matérialiste, commerciale et plus tard, industrielle, notre nationalisme élabora un système de défense où primaient toutes les forces contraires: la langue française, le catholicisme, l'autoritarisme, l'idéalisme, la vie rurale et plus tard le retour à la terre."[14]

This French-Canadian philosophy, complete with its "back to the land" component, did not prevent Montreal from becoming Canada's major industrial centre, nor did it prevent Quebec from industrializing just as fast as Ontario. But this pervasive philosophy among Francophones may well have had something to do with the underrepresentation of French Canadians in Montreal's industrial, commercial, and financial activities. It has something to do too with the fact that until after World War II, Quebec had no real trade unions but had instead *syndicats catholiques*; and why instead of a Chamber of Commerce devoted to expansion of business enterprise, francophone Montreal had an *Association des Patrons* devoted to the philosophical principles of *Rerum Novarum* and *Quadragesimo Anno*.

What the province of Quebec lacked then was indigenous entrepreneurship. French Canadians as a group were insignificant in entrepreneurial activity associated with industries in their own province. Industrialization was carried out by "foreign" entrepreneurs, such as English Canadians, Jews, Americans, and others who were a "sub-dominant" élite in French Canadian society, whatever they may have in their own. Why was entrepreneurial activity taken over by "foreigners"? The school of historians at the University of Montreal explained the whole matter in terms of conquest. The economic inferiority of the French Canadian community, they say, is the fatal consequence of being placed in servitude as a vanquished nation, conquered and occupied, reduced to the status of a minority in a country which they did not share. As is so often the case in economic development, a "vicious circle" then appeared. Debarred by defeat from full participation in the economic life of the country, French Canadians retreated into their traditions and nurtured French Canadian "nationalism." They comforted themselves with the superiority of their values and their civilization to those of the rest of Canada. As Monsignor Paquet wrote in 1902, "Our mission is less to manage capital than to preserve ideals; it consists less of lighting the fires of the factories than of maintaining and spreading the luminous fires of religion and thought."[15] In one of its manifestations, this set of attitudes took the form of a "return to the land" movement. As early as 1895, Paquet, the leading bishop, stated that agriculture is the normal estate of man here below, that it is on the farms that man is in most direct relationship with God, and that only through agriculture could French Canadians "accomplish the grand destinies indubitably reserved for them by Providence."[16]

The conclusion seems to be that French Canadian incomes, on the average, lagged behind those of the rest of the country because French Canada did not provide its own entrepreneurs; entrepreneurship—and to a considerable degree, capital as well—came from outside. Frontier theory would explain this lack of entrepreneurship, by pointing out that Quebec was originally settled by *grands seigneurs* and peasants, not by commercial farmers. The physical environment was such as to create only one real city, on the border of Ontario, and economically dominated by English Canadians. There were few "log-cabin-to-riches" stories among French Canadians. Projecting this analysis, we would conclude that this lag could be closed only when conditions were such as to change French Canadian attitudes, so that a larger share of the entrepreneurial function in Quebec is carried out by French Canadians themselves. This transformation, of course, is precisely what took place in the 1970s and 1980s.

"Culture" is also invoked to explain the retardation of the Maritimes. As Bickerton puts it: "...the by-now-accepted explanation for Maritime underdevelopment based on geography, technological change, and lack of resources was supplemented and reinforced by claims of a regional parochialism and conservatism that led to such deficiencies as lack of entrepreneurship and initiative and an irrational resistance to change." Culture was thus recruited in the effort to explain the historic failure of Maritime firms to diversify, invest in new technologies, or take the necessary risks in establishing or expanding manufacturing ventures. A variation of this type of explanation points to a lack of adequate entrepreneurship as a residual factor in explaining Maritime underdevelopment."[17]

Ernest Forbes, however, thinks "we do not know enough about the maritimes following confederation to accept the stereotype of a conservative, backward, risk-avoiding, unprogressive society. It is not the purpose of this paper to develop a new myth of a dynamic and progressive Maritimes. What I am trying to show is that we really know little about the Maritimes in the post-confederation period...With repetition in so many books on so many topics, the stereotype has come to be accepted as historical 'fact.'"[18]

Interactions of Culture and Environment

The development of any region is the outcome of the reactions of its population to their environment. Lack of natural resources may prove to be a blessing, if the culture of the people is such that their "response" to this "challenge" (to use Arnold Toynbee's famous expression encapsulating all of history) is the development of entrepreneurship; managerial, scientific, and technical skills; a pervasive work ethic and an extraordinarily disciplined and loyal labour force, as in the case of Japan. An abundance of natural resources can be a "curse," if as a consequence the people become timid, lazy, unenterprising, and rooted in habit, custom, and tradition. Canada is a case in point.

In his study of the Canadian economy, prepared for the government of Canada and the Business Council on National Issues, Professor Michael Porter of the Harvard School of Business Administration, issues some dire warnings.[19] Canada, he says, has done well during the last thirty years, largely on the basis of its natural resources, but now finds itself at the crossroads. Abundant resources and proximity to the United States has made possible an enviable economic performance. But these same factors have led government, enterprises, trade unions, and citizens in general to adopt a set of strategies, policies, and attitudes that leave Canada's economy poorly armed to react to the competitive realities. Already Canada is facing difficulties in the changes of economic space and the intensification of competition. If present trends continue, the standard of living seems condemned to deteriorate. However, this scenario is not inevitable. Canadians have the elements of a solution in their own hands—if they will mend their ways and put them to good use.

There are some fundamental deficiencies in the Canadian economy. Most serious of these is the weak performance where increase in productivity is concerned: 0.4 percent average between 1979 and 1989. Canada shares with the United States the lowest rung on the ladder among the Group of Seven members of the OECD. For increase in productivity in manufacturing, Canada has the worst record of the members of the Group of Seven. Canada's labour costs have increased more rapidly than those of the majority of industrialized countries. The high level of unemployment is another alarm signal. The low level of investment in machines and the increase in national debt are further signs of weakness.

Canada is remarkably dependent on exports. Within the Group of Seven, only Germany has a ratio of exports to GNP higher than Canada's 25 percent. Moreover, 46 percent of Canada's exports are natural resources; when metals, forest products, and transport equipment are added, the figure comes to 82 percent. Exports of machinery are very weak. Some 45 percent of manufacturing is controlled by foreigners. There are few sophisticated industries. Services account for 68 percent of GDP and 70 percent of employment; within the Group of Seven, only the United States is more dependent on the services sector. Unfortunately, relatively few of these services is of international standard. Canada is on the lowest rung of the Group of Seven ladder for exports of services.

In Porter's opinion, Canada cannot count on its long shared frontier with the United States to maintain its standard of living. Its economy must be strengthened internally, to make it more competitive. To begin with, it must develop more intense rivalries *within* the country if it is to compete on world markets. It must develop its human resources. Its illiteracy rate of 24 percent is inexcusably high for an advanced country. More than 30 percent of Canada's young people leave school before finishing secondary school. It must develop more of the sharply focused competence (compétence de pointe) that is necessary for competitive advantage. Canada's institutions of tertiary education are not turning out enough people with genuinely high professional and scientific skills, and expenditures on training by employers is half that of the United States and one quarter that of Germany. Expenditures on R & D are the second lowest in the Group of Seven. Canada is classed lowest of all the countries in OECD in the search for and adoption of new technologies. Neither the general consumer nor enterprises in Canada demand high quality or new products that would be a stimulus to innovation. In sum, Canada is confronted at the present time with an unprecedented challenge, on which depends its economic viability and its future prosperity.

In effect, Porter is demanding that Canadians become different people, more like Americans or Germans. In other words, he is asking for revolutionary cultural change. It is more likely that, so long as her "rich resources and vast hinterland" hold out, Canadians will go on exploiting them in the same old way, until the threat to the standard of living of her citizens becomes a good deal more visible than it is now.

It is obvious that physical environments and cultures are interrelated. The physical environment may determine whether a particular society devotes itself to fishing, agriculture, or grazing, and the culture will vary accordingly. As societies become more industrialized and more urbanized, the direct impact of the physical environment on the culture becomes more subtle and more complex, but it is still there. The question that preoccupies us most in the present context, however, is: Are there some cultures that favour development and others that are inimical to it? Can regional disparities be explained in these terms? It is clear that these questions are just as pertinent to regions as to nations, provided only that cultural differences among regions exist, as they surely do. The answer to the questions is, however, clearly of great importance. There can be little doubt that the social framework does influence behaviour in a manner influencing development. But in almost any society we will find some customs, values, and institutions which encourage development, and others that inhibit it. We are therefore constrained to ask, "Just how integrated are the societies of particular countries or regions? Is it possible to eliminate or overcome the social *obstacles* to development without changing the society as a whole?"

Can Development Take Place Without Social Change?

It seems clear enough that development with no social change whatsoever is extremely unlikely. We must still ask, however, whether development can take place without fundamental social change, provided a small but powerful and capable élite makes a concerted effort to generate development. The Schumpeter theory seems to say "yes" to this question; but Schumpeter was speaking of relatively integrated societies of early twentieth century Europe and North America, where social conditions favoured economic expansion; and during the great depression of the 1930's, Schumpeter himself became pessimistic about the future of capitalist development. What of the very different social frameworks of the Northeast of New Brunswick, Gaspésie, and Appalachia? Will it be enough to create a few entrepreneurs in order to assure development, and can the entrepreneurs be created in such societies?

Social psychologist James Abegglen, for one, maintains that entrepreneurship can be generated, and development can ensue, without a wholesale transformation of the society, even when the society has long been both traditional and stagnant. He argues that the spectacular industrialization of Japan after the Meiji restoration of 1868—the classical case of conversion of a traditional Asxian society into a modern industrial one—was accomplished, not by scrapping the feudal structure, but by using it. The industrialization of Japan took place essentially within the framework of feudal society, through the transfer of the feudal system from farm to factory. According to Abegglen: "The development of industrial Japan has taken place with much less change from one kind of social organization and social relations of preindustrial Japan than would be expected from the Western model of the growth of an industrial society...At repeated points in the study of the factory, parallels to an essentially feudal system of organization may be seen—not, to be sure, a replication of the feudal loyalties, commitments, rewards, and methods of leadership but a rephrasing of them in the setting of modern industry...It would seem from this study, then, that the very success of the Japanese experience with industrialization may well have been a function of the fact that, far from undergoing at total revolution in social structure or social relationships, the hard core of Japan's system of social relationships remained intact, allowing an orderly transition to industrialization continuous with here earlier social forms."[20] Even today, vestiges of the feudal system contribute to the extraordinary discipline of the Japanese industrial system.

Will Rapid Economic Development Automatically Bring the Necessary Social Change in its Wake?

We are not yet entirely out of the woods. A determined élite with power and prescience can launch economic growth without first transforming the society; there are cases on record, like Japan, which seem to illustrate the manner in which economic-development-followed-by-limited-social-change can take place. But we are in danger of circular reasoning here. Japan may be a case in which the social-cultural barriers were less inimical to development than they seemed to be before the leaders of the society determined to industrialize their economy. What of all the countries that have not developed? Is it only development-minded leadership that is missing? Can the necessary social changes be expected to follow, at least, if a big push is undertaken on the purely economic front? What of truly primitive societies? May not the socio-cultural obstacles in some of these prove insurmountable, despite a committed leadership?

There is growing evidence that the answer is "no" even to this question. If the economic effort is big enough, and is accompanied by appropriate training and demonstration effects, even the most primitive of societies can be quickly transformed, and quite painlessly. The evidence to this effect is provided mainly by a series of "revisits" by anthropologists, who have returned to societies previous studied in a stagnant and traditional state, after some massive outside shock has transformed the society. Perhaps most famous of these revisits is Margaret Mead's return to Manus, which led to her description of the transformation of Manus' society as a consequence of the occupation of the island by American troops during World War II.[21] The demonstration effect of having on the island a number of American GI's considerably in excess of the local population resulted in the Manus' culture jumping 2,000 years in ten. Why should not a well-construed economic development program—national or regional—have a similar effect?

It does not appear that there is a reason to fear any generalized and mysterious "socio-cultural obstacles to development." Rather, it is a matter of understanding individual societies so as to know how to strengthen dynamic forces for change and modify resistance to change. In broad outline, Clifford Geertz stated the situation neatly twenty-five years ago: "The issue properly stated, however," he wrote, "is not whether every aspect of society must change, or nothing but the economy itself must change in the process of economic rationalization; clearly neither of these extreme positions is defensible. Rather it is: What must change and what need not?"[22]

Notes

1. John H. Cumberland, *Regional Development: Experience and Prospects 2, United States of America* (Paris and the Hague: Mouton, 1971), p. 91.
2. *Ibid.*, pp. 115–16.
3. James P. Bickerton, *Nova Scotia, Ottawa and the Politics of Regional Development* (Toronto: University of Toronto Press, 1990), pp. 12–3.

4. Ernest R. Forbes, "In Search of a Post-Confederation Maritime Historiography 1900-1967," in Bercuson, D.J. and Buckner, P.A. (eds), *Eastern and Western Perspectives* (Toronto: University of Toronto Press, 1981), pp. 48-9.
5. *Ibid.*
6. Benjamin Higgins, *The Frontiers as an Element in National and Regional Development* (Moncton: Canadian Institute for Research on Regional Development, 1991), *passim*.
7. William H. Nicholls, *Southern Traditions and Regional Progress* (Chapel Hill: University of North Carolina Press, 1960), pp. 34-5.
8. Douglass C. North, *The Economic Growth of the United States, 1790-1860* (Englewood Cliffs, New Jersey: Prentice-Hall, 1961), pp. 68, 123, 128-33.
9. Nicholls, *Southern Traditions and Regional Progress*, pp. 34-5.
10. *Ibid.*, p. 48.
11. North, *The Economic Growth of the United States, 1790-1860*, pp. 9 and 133. In 1840 the ratio of pupils to white population was 5.72 percent in slave-holding states and 2.13 percent in the non-slave-holding states. In the former states 7.46 percent of the white population was illiterate, in the latter, 2.13 percent. In 1950, with about half the white population of the north, the slave-holding states had less than 1/3 as many public schools, 1/4 as many pupils, 1/20 as many public libraries.
12. Sir John Bourinet, *Canada* (New York: G.P. Putnam and Sons, 1898), pp. 438-9.
13. J.P. Beaulieu, *Province of Quebec Industrial Expansion Publication* (Quebec: Office provincial de publicité pour le ministère de Commerce et Industrie, 1952).
14. Pierre E. Trudeau, *La province au moment de la grève de l'amiante* (Montreal: Les Éditions Cité Libre, 1956), p. 12.
15. Louis-Adolphe Paquet, "La terre canadienne," *Études et appréciations*, vol. 1 (Québec: Imprimerie Franciscaine Missionnaire, 1918), 3-12; and "La vocation de la race française en Amérique," *Discours et Allocutions*, vol. 1 (Québec: Imprimerie Franciscaine Missionnaire, 1915), p. 187.
16. *Ibid.*
17. Bickerton, *Nova Scotia, Ottawa and the Politics of Regional Development*, p. 14.
18. Forbes, "In Search of a Post-Confederation Maritime Historiography 1900-1967," pp. 60-61.
19. Michael Porter, *Canada at the Crossroads: The New Competitive Realities* (Ottawa: Canadian Council of Chief Executive Officers, 1991).
20. J.C. Abegglen, *The Japanese Factory* (Glencoe, Ill.: Free Press, 1963), pp. 129, 131 and 134.
21. Margaret Mead, *New Lives for Old: Cultural Transformation* (New York: Morrow, 1956). See also D. Lerner, *The Passing of Traditional Society: Modernizing the Middle East* (New York: The Free Press, 1958).
22. Clifford Geertz, *Peddlers and Princes: Social Development and Economic Change in Two Indonesian Towns* (Chicago: University of Chicago Press, 1963), pp. 147-56.

3

Entrepreneurship and Regional Development

Perhaps no concept has played so great a role in development theory as "entrepreneurship:" the capacity to introduce new technologies and new products, to develop new resources, improve business organization and management; the ability to bring to life innovations of all kinds; and to bring together the required land, labour, capital and management in an efficient and dynamic enterprise to make innovations succeed. Once again, entrepreneurship has been analyzed and discussed mainly in the context of development of national economics and societies; but the concept has certainly been no stranger to the theory of regional development. To the degree that subnational regions have distinct economies and societies, the need for entrepreneurship to promote development is just as pressing at the regional level as at the national level. The lack of entrepreneurship in some regions and its concentration in others has been cited as an explanation of regional disparities in a good many countries—Brazil, Colombia, India, Indonesia, Malaysia, Thailand, Nigeria—and Canada—to name but a few.

The presence or absence of entrepreneurship in a particular country or region is frequently attributed to the culture of the society that inhabits it. We are learning that cultural differences among regions can persist even in highly industrialized countries, including—one might even say especially—some within the former Soviet Bloc. Regional differences in supply of entrepreneurship should come as no surprise. As little as two decades ago the role of the Roman Catholic Church in Quebec, and the Québécois culture more generally, was frequently cited as a cause of lack of French Canadian entrepreneurship, and the consequent lag in economic development of French Canada. But there is an element of hen-and-egg circularity in much of the discussion of entrepreneurship. Do entrepreneurs bring development or does development bring forth entrepreneurs? As we survey various theories of entrepreneurship, we must bear this question constantly in mind.

Theories of Entrepreneurship

With the theory of entrepreneurship we move to interdisciplinary analysis. Not that the literature on the role of the innovating entrepreneur in improving technology, accumulating capital, and generating economic growth is the product of teamwork among social scientists. On the contrary, it is almost wholly the result of "lone-wolf" endeavours, with the synthesis of economic, socio-cultural, and political elements taking place in a single mind. But it is interdisciplinary in the sense that it explains economic behaviour, at both micro and macro-levels, in terms of socio-cultural, psychological, and political variables. For that reason, the theory has attracted attention, and contributions to the literature, from sociologists, historians, political scientists, and anthropologists as well as from economists. By the same token, it is one of the "grand theories" we wish to test and apply in the context of regional development.

The Weber-Tawney Thesis

While it is far from being "operational," and while it can hardly be said to have been "applied" during the development decades, the Weber-Tawney thesis regarding the rise of capitalism remains important for the enormous influence it has had on social thought. Translated more broadly into a theory of the relationship between a society's ideological framework and entrepreneurial endeavour, it remains highly germane to today's development problems, whether at the national or the regional level.

Max Weber's explanation of the "rise of capitalism" is at once most fascinating and most controversial. The reason for capitalistic development in the sixteenth century is that the Reformation provided the proper philosophical and ethical setting for the "capitalist spirit" to flourish. The impulse to acquisition is common to all times and all places, but Roman Catholicism held in check the pursuit of profit and the accumulation of wealth which characterize capitalism. The problem is not the advent of capitalistic activity but the appearance of the sober bourgeois society in which capitalism reached its apex. Even contemporary society gives us a clue to the rise of this middle-class society, Weber argued, for in countries of mixed religion, we find a dominance of Protestants among entrepreneurs, owners of capital, and high-grade labour. It was also true that the more highly developed districts were those which gave most support to the Reformation, finding its creed more suitable to aggressive and progressive ways of life.

The spirit of capitalism is typified by Benjamin Franklin's "philosophy of avarice." Acquisition of wealth becomes an end in itself. In the Middle Ages, such ideas were considered as the lowest kind of avarice; after the Reformation, such conduct became highly respectable. At the beginning of modern times, it was not the existing entrepreneurs who represented the capitalistic spirit, for they were bound by traditionalism: fixed profits, limited interest rates, just wages, and just prices. It was in the lower middle class that the spirit was strongest. This spirit, and not new streams of money, stimulated the rise of capitalism. The chief reward for making money was the feeling of having done the job well.

This concept is to be found in Luther's doctrines under the name of the "calling," the idea that each individual is "called" to do a certain job and to do it as well as possible. The highest form of moral conduct is the fulfilment of duty in worldly affairs. The ideal of monastic asceticism was extended to worldly life; one should not indulge in luxury. Yet Luther was opposed to monopoly and to usury, and cannot be regarded as the apostle of capitalism. The real enemy of Catholicism was Calvinism. In order to become one of the "chosen," one must work hard and spend little. One must accept one's lot as part of God's scheme. The intensity of worldly activity alone dispels doubts as to one's being among the "elect." Pietism was a similar doctrine of predestination which influenced the ascetic movement. Methodism was an Anglo-Saxon movement corresponding to Pietism. In practice, the reasoning of the Baptist sects becomes equivalent to Calvinism.

The net result was to justify the pursuit of wealth, provided that happened to be one's "calling." Poverty was not required, but the pursuit of riches must not lead one to reckless enjoyment. Profits are as holy as wages, and interest is not wrong unless wrung from the poor. The cardinal sin is idleness. As for labourers, only when they were poor did they remain obedient to God, but remaining obedient they attained eternal happiness in another world. Thus the Reformation gave to the entrepreneur and to the capitalist a clear conscience to pursue profits to the best of their ability. In condemning expenditure, it provided the basis for capital accumulation. The profits of this era were not absorbed into the life of a new nobility but were reinvested. On the other hand, the new spirit justified a marked class distinction and forbade open dissatisfaction on the part of oppressed labour.

This explanation of the rise of capitalism was introduced to English readers by R.H. Tawney. Although essentially the same as Weber's, his treatment is more general and develops the thesis in relation to its historical setting. Like Weber, Tawney points out that the Catholic Church opposed usury and emphasized the sin of avarice. The outbursts of commercial activity in the fifteenth century made the older teaching an economic anachronism. (It will be noted that Tawney is more inclined than Weber to say that the Reformation stimulated a movement already under way). Catholic teaching was an effective barrier to capitalistic development despite its neglect in practice. Tawney attributes less positive and more negative influence to Luther than does Weber. Luther, he says, was opposed to the accumulation of wealth, usury, monopoly, high prices, speculation, and the luxury trade with the East. But Calvin's teaching was most characteristic and most influential of the new doctrines. He saw economic life with the eyes of a peasant, and recognized frankly the need for capital, credit and banking, and large-scale commerce and finance. Thrift, diligence, sobriety, and frugality are the Christian virtues, and profits and interest are not necessarily evil gains.

While few social scientists today believe that levels or rates of development can be explained by formal religion alone, there remains a rough rank-correlation between dominant religion and per capita incomes (Protestant, Catholic, Communist, Muslim, Hindu-Bhuddist, Animist and Pagan, etc.). More important, many social scientists believe that development is aided and abetted by a generally-held ideology of a sort that provides a unifying force and encourages entrepreneurship—as the Communist ideology did yesterday and as the 18th—19th century Liberal ideology has done in the past.

Schumpeter: Entrepreneurship as The Mainspring of Development

Joseph Schumpeter's career encompassed the neo-classical and Keynesian periods and approaches; and to these schools of thought he added something unique of his own, based partly on his knowledge of other social sciences than economics, and partly on a range of experience unusually wide for his generation, including a term as Minister of Finance in Austria and a sojourn as Professor of Economics in Japan. Out of this experience came a basic theory of entrepreneurship essentially interdisciplinary in scope.

Joseph Schumpeter ranks among the all time greats in the history of economic thought. He has special interest for this survey of economic thought because virtually alone in his generation of economists his main interest was in economic development. The German edition of his *Theory of Economic Development* was published in 1911, and throughout his career, he continued to elaborate and refine his theory.[1] His eclectic and synthesizing approach was no doubt partly due to his wide range of experience. He leaned heavily on Marx, sharing his conviction that economic fluctuations and growth are inseparably intertwined. Schumpeter's own theory was largely concerned with entrepreneurship, innovations, and their institutional setting. His ideas on these elements of development have become stock in trade for all development economists.

Schumpeter maintained that the most important part of private investment is determined by such long range considerations as technological change. He stressed innovation as the mainspring of this type of investment. Any "doing things differently," that increases the productivity of the bundle of factors of production available is an innovation. The entrepreneur is not the inventor; he is the man who sees the opportunity for introducing an innovation, a new technique or a new commodity, an improved organization, or the development of newly discovered resources. The entrepreneur raises the money to launch the new enterprise, assembles the factors of production, chooses top managers and sets the organization going. Schumpeter believed that growth is associated with booms and recessions, because successful innovations tend to bring "clusters of followers," with investment financed largely through new credit, resulting in a boom; then when the new plants are in place, debts are repaid and the money supply contracts just as output increases, prices fall, and the recession sets in. However, Schumpeter did not feel that deep depressions like that of the 1930s were necessary; like other neo-classicists, he believed such depressions represented mismanagement of the monetary system.

In Schumpeter's system, the supply of entrepreneurship is the ultimate determining factor of the rate of economic growth. This supply in turn depends on the "social climate," a complex phenomenon reflecting the whole social, political, and socio-psychological atmosphere within which entrepreneurs must operate. It would include the social values of a particular country at a particular time, the class structure, the educational system, the attitude of society toward business success, and the nature and extent of the prestige and other social rewards, apart from profits, which accompany business success in the society. A particularly important factor in "climate" is the entrepreneur's understanding of the "rules of the game," the conditions under which he must operate. Sudden changes in the rules of the game are particularly deleterious to an increasing flow of enterprise. In general, the climate is appropriate when entrepreneurial success is amply rewarded, and where there are good but not too good chances of success. There must be a risk and a challenge to bring forth true entrepreneurial endeavour, but there must be some chance of high rewards.

In contrast to Marx, who thought of "capitalists" as a "class" almost in the sense of caste, a group to which workers could not aspire, an essential aspect of Schumpeter's vigorous capitalist development is rapid circulation of the élite. Since entrepreneurs are usually social deviants in some degree, the society may oppose them, accepting them only after they have proven successful. The Schumpeterian entrepreneur is untraditional and ambitious; success in the innovational process must lead to the top of the social ladder if not for oneself, then at least for one's son or grandson, as it did in nineteenth-century Europe.

Capitalism, however, produces, by its mere working, a social atmosphere that is hostile to it, and this atmosphere, in turn, produces policies which do not allow it to function. Thus Schumpeter explained the depth and duration of the Great Depression of the 1930s in terms of the labour legislation, social security, public works spending, progressive tax structure, public utilities regulation, and other New Deal policies introduced in the middle and late 1930s.

These constituted a change in the "rules of the game" so drastic as to discourage enterprise and thus retard investment.

Schumpeter was an extremely independent thinker, and something of an enigma. He has sometimes been taken for an apologist for private enterprise, but that is not quite true. Schumpeter admired and enjoyed the kind of society produced in capitalist countries, yet he stated explicitly that the socialist formula is superior to the capitalist one. His development theory as such is neutral. The crucial role of entrepreneurship and innovation in economic development is not tied to the capitalist system. Socialist countries have need of new techniques, new products, new resources, and new organizational systems; and the men who see and seize the opportunity to introduce these new "ways of doing things differently," bring together the factors of production and organize them into effective enterprises, play a significant role in economic progress in any society and tend to be rewarded for this role one way or another. Indeed one of the most fascinating subjects for analysis is the comparative roles of entrepreneurs in capitalist and in socialist societies. Unfortunately, apart from his insistence on the right "climate," Schumpeter does not tell us how to create entrepreneurs where they do not exist.

Veblen, Ayres, and the Institutionalists

A school of thought which has been more optimistic about entrepreneurship, and which anticipated the contemporary approach to development theory in their insistence on looking at the facts and in doing so in an interdisciplinary manner, are the American Institutionalists. The founder of this school was Thorstein Veblen, who had an enormous influence on a whole generation of American economists. With the Keynesian revolution and the increasing application of mathematics to economic problems, the Institutionalists lost for a while their prestige among "mainstream" economists. But with the resurgence of interest in development the Institutionalists are enjoying a renaissance, and some economists trained in the "main stream," like Myrdal, Galbraith, Neale, and others are now identifying themselves as "institutionalists."

We are more concerned here with the Institutionalist theory of growth than with their protest against neo-classical economics and the society of the late nineteenth and early twentieth centuries, but the two are inter-related. Veblen was writing at the time of the American "robber barons," when American capitalism was at its most vigorous, most lusty, most brutal, most uninhibited and irresponsible. At the same time most teachers of economics in the United States at the time treated the free enterprise system as almost literally divine. Veblen found the combination hard to swallow.

Veblen began by attacking the very fundamentals of neo-classical theory. In his famous first book, *The Theory of the Leisure Class* published in 1899, he challenged the hypothesis that economic behaviour is rational. Whereas the neo-classical economist, echoing eighteenth and nineteenth century liberal philosophy, saw men as both rational and spiritual beings, to Veblen men were not yet far removed from the jungle, filled with what Vilfredo Pareto called "résidues"—remnants of superstitious fears, tribal myths, tabus, ceremonial rites, and magic. Where the neo-classicists saw essential harmony in society, Veblen saw conflict and coercion. The entrepreneur is not so much concerned with improving resource allocation as in copying his neighbour, emulating those still richer than he, coercing those that are weaker, and conspiring to increase his power. He is concerned, not with producing, but with "making money," which is an entirely different thing. "Man's behaviour in respect of using and handling and 'making' money is varied, irrational, complicated, and often confused—confused as dreams of primitive magic are full of confusion," as a contemporary institutionalist, John Gambs, put it.[2]

Already in his first book Veblen's cross-disciplinary approach, which has remained an essential feature of Institutionalism, appears. He looked at primitive societies such as the American Indians, the Ainus of Japan, and the Australian aborigines, and found no "leisure class." Then he looked at the Polynesians, the ancient Icelanders and the shoguns of Japan, and found a well-defined leisure class. But these leisure classes were not always "idle"; they did not work much, but they were very busy seizing wealth from others. In time these leisure classes became rich and powerful enough to become respectable, and so their means of acquiring wealth became respectable too. Veblen thought that the financiers and industrialists who comprised the European and American leisure class of his day were much the same. In his second book, *The Theory of Business Enterprises* published in 1904, Veblen went even further, describing businessmen as the saboteurs, rather than the motivating force, of the economic system. Machines produce goods, he argued, while entrepreneurs produce profits, by controlling, restricting, and manipulating production, and speculating on the results. He compared the "captains of industry" to watchful toads, ready to devour any innocent spider or fly that came their way. Veblen had more admiration for machines than for captains of industry.

For one whose blast against the establishment was so powerful, Veblen's own proposals for revolution seem rather tame. He was of two minds about Marx; he admired his work, but found his conclusions wrong. The facts do not bear Marx out, he said, especially with regard to increasing misery of the working class. The Hegelian dialectics on which Marxist theory rests is being replaced by Darwinism, and evolutionary concept of society. Nor is it true that the institutions of private property under free competition have worked to the detriment of the material interests of the average member of society. On the contrary, recent decades have brought a significant increase in creature comforts to the average human being. What Veblen wanted rather than socialism was a technocratic society. His admiration for machines spilled over into an admiration for the men who make them, the scientists and engineers. Machines impose a discipline on men, strengthen their productive propensities, and make possible an industrial republic run by engineers. It was this limited kind of revolution that Veblen proposed in his last books, especially *Engineers and the Price System (1921)* and *The Technicians and the Revolution (1921)*.

Veblen, then, was at the opposite pole to Schumpeter where entrepreneurs are concerned. Where Schumpeter had only limited respect for inventors, and reserved his special admiration for the innovators, the entrepreneurs who take over where scientists and engineers leave off and create new enterprises, Veblen admired the inventor and had no faith in the entrepreneur. But if entrepreneurship is not the mainspring of growth, how does growth take place?

For Veblen as for the Classical School the rate of economic progress was also the outcome of a contest; but not a race between technological progress and population growth bringing diminishing returns, but a conflict between technological progress and irrational, magical, and ceremonial resistance to technological change—socio-cultural obstacles, if one chooses. Here Veblen identifies one of today's major development problems: science and technology are the forces of progress; cultural lags, superstitious fears, ceremonial patterns, ingrown conservatism of thought and action are the opponents of progress.

This concept of the growth process was enlarged and refined by a disciple of Veblen, the late Clarence Ayres, of the University of Texas. Of his work Joan Robinson was to write, after dismissing a series of attempts by other economists to explain development, "there is a less well-known theory that seems more promising."[3] Like Veblen, Ayres saw development as a race between technological progress and the inhibiting role of ceremonial patterns and tradition, particularly as embodied in religious institutions. Western Europe's headstart in industrialization is explained by the withdrawal of the Romans, which left Western Europe essentially a frontier society, with a technology inherited from older civilizations, but without the social arteriosclerosis associated with deeply imbedded traditional institutional power: "It is doubtful if history affords another instance of any comparable areas and population so completely severed. That Western Europe was the seat of a great civilization in the centuries that followed was due altogether to that endowment no important part of which was ever lost; that it was of all the great civilizations of the time incomparably the youngest, the least rigid, less stifled than any other by age-long accumulations of institutional dust, more susceptible to change and innovation was due to the unique severance. Almost certainly it was this composite character which made the civilization of medieval Europe the parent of industrial revolution."[4]

By the same token, the ever moving frontier played an important role in the later development of the United States. By definition, a "frontier" is a region into which people come from an older centre of civilization, bringing with them the tools and materials of their older life; and while they also bring their traditional values and folkways, these are weakened by a frontier environment. "Existence on the frontier is, as we say, free and easy. Meticulous observance of the Sabbath and the rules of grammar are somehow less important on the frontier than 'back home'."[5]

For Ayres even more than Veblen himself, technological progress was an essentially biological process. Machines breed machines, almost "untouched by human hand." Once a certain collection of tools is in existence, they are almost certain to combine in new patterns so as to breed new tools: "Thus the airplane is a combination of kite and an internal combustion engine. An automobile is a combination of a buggy with an internal combustion engine.... What is presented to the public as a 'new' invention is usually itself the end-product of a long series of inventions. Granted that tools are always tools of men who have the capacity to use tools and therefore the capacity to use them together, combinations are bound to occur. Furthermore, it follows that the more tools there are, the greater is the number of potential combinations."[6] Here we have an explanation of the tendency for economic development to become cumulative and for stagnation to lead to retrogression.

Thus Ayres, like Veblen, was at the opposite end of the spectrum from Schumpeter with respect to the role of the entrepreneur. The Classical School admired entrepreneurs, industrialists, and inventors but had little use for absentee landlords. Schumpeter didn't much mind landed aristocrats—they gave the entrepreneurs something to aspire to—but his special admiration was reserved for the "captains of industry," the innovators. Even scientists and engineers were, for Schumpeter, run-of-the-mill, and only the innovators who organized new enterprises were deserving of really high rewards. But for Veblen and Ayres there are always plenty of people around ready to make "a quick buck." The captains of industry may even impede progress, and thus entrepreneurs deserve no particular award. For Schumpeter the entrepreneur is a delicate hothouse plant that needs nurturing with palatable monopolies; for Veblen and Ayres he is just a tough robber baron that needs watching.

One other aspect of institutionalism is important for a theory of economic development: its methodology. The institutionalist approach had two facets:

the insistence on a stern empirical approach, on what Veblen called "the opaque fact," in contrast to the delicately woven but transparent cobwebs of abstract theory of the neo-classical school; and the insistence on a cross-disciplinary or multi-disciplinary analysis. Since in their view social behaviour is a *Gestalt* or pattern—a seamless web—it is futile to try to separate something called "economic behaviour" to the exclusion of all other aspects of a particular culture which determine how people behave, in the market place or anywhere else. As John Gambs puts it: "Institutionalists have taken economics out of the realm of pseudo-physical science, which is where standard economics seems to want to put it, and have placed it squarely into the biological sciences. They have made—or at least, valiantly tried to make—its doctrines conformable with those of anthropology, ethnology, psychology, genetics—disciplines that have bothered standard theorists less."[7] In this regard the institutionalists were undoubtedly right. All economists today admit the importance of quantitative analysis, and all those who have seriously tackled the problems of developing countries admit the need for knowledge outside the scope of standard economics in order to understand the development process.

Unfortunately, the institutionalist theory of development is little more operational than the Weber-Tawney thesis or the Schumpeter theory. It belongs to the category of theories, like the classical, Marxist, neo-classical and Schumpeterian theories, which maintain that development will take place automatically, given the right socio-cultural and political framework, and not otherwise. The idea that "machines breed machines" is a useful one; more generally, as the Director General of UNIDO once remarked in conversation with one of the authors, it suggests that "the important thing is to get something going." Introduce a new agricultural or manufacturing technique, put a factory in a small city, build a road or a powerplant, and other things will happen. No doubt: but we need something more precise than that as a basis for plans and policies.

Everett Hagen: Gradualism

Everett Hagen is rather pessimistic regarding the generation of entrepreneurship and development. His ideas had their genesis in his dissatisfaction with his own discipline while he was economic advisor in Burma.[8] He came to regard standard economic models as inadequate to explain economic growth, and concluded that broader social and psychological considerations were pertinent. He proceeded to examine the factors which cause a traditional society to become one in which economic growth is occurring, and in carrying out this objective, attempts to integrate anthropology, sociology, and psychology—especially psychoanalysis—into a single weapon of analysis.

To understand why some traditional societies enter in economic growth sooner than others, he maintains, we must understand the internal structure and functioning of these societies, for both the barriers to growth and the causes of growth seem to be largely internal rather than external. The traditional society is dual or triple, consisting of the "peasantry and other simple folk, the élite classes, and the trader-financier." This traditional society leads to a particular type of uncreative and non-innovational individual behaviour. A member of traditional society is uncreative because he sees the world as an arbitrary place rather than one subject to analysis and control. His unconscious processes are both inaccessible and uncreative. Interpersonal relations are solved on the basis of "ascriptive authority;" and people avoid anxiety by resort to authority. However, out of traditional society emerge some creative individuals, particularly the "anxious innovator."

Technological change is difficult in traditional society. Who will introduce it? The urban craftsman does not have the capital and cannot obtain the credit for such a venture because bankers "do not customarily look upon him as worthy of credit except on a pawnshop basis." A member of the élite, on the other hand, would not set up a modernized textile enterprise because it would be demeaning himself. In a peasant society, large-scale enterprise can be introduced only be foreigners. An isolated deviant with the necessary creative imagination will be hemmed in by social pressures tending against cumulative innovation and change.

Because traditional society is so resistant to change, the forces that disrupt it must be powerful ones. The change comes about if and when members of some social group perceive that their purposes and values are not respected by groups in the society whom they respect and whose esteem they value. Such social disaffection is most readily apparent when a group migrates to a new society. However, there are only four types of events that result in withdrawal of status: a change in the power structure; derogation of institutional activity without change in the power structure; contradiction among status symbols, and nonacceptance of expected status in migration to a new society.

A classic example is the threatened élite of Meiji Japan who responded to their fear of colonial domination by modernizing Japan. Another example is found in the sultans of Bali, who, upon Indonesia's gaining its independence, became entrepreneurs. Nowhere had the Dutch system of indirect rule maintained feudalism more intact than in Bali. Before the war, Balinese enterprise was limited to trading conducted by Javanese Moslems plus a few Chinese and Dutch. The aristocracy, with the sultans themselves at the top of the social ladder, depended heavily upon their salaries as civil administrators paid to them by the Dutch. Few were truly wealthy in terms of their own landholdings. By the same token, however, Balinese society was less detraditionalized than was Javanese society, because the Dutch played such a small part in the Balinese economy. The revolution left it with stronger internal dynamics of its own. The social position of the sultans was unimpaired by independence, but with their civil service salaries gone they faced one transcendent problem: to repair their financial position to match their social position. Moreover, with the growth of central government in Djakarta they ceased to be true rulers; to that extent their social status was impaired as well.

Using their social status to help amass capital, the aristocracy went directly into industry—bicycle assembly, tire recapping, ice manufacturing, weaving, shoe manufacturing, and soft drink bottling, as well as transport, domestic and foreign trade, tourist traffic, and hotel keeping. They seemed to be moving back easily toward the way of the merchant princes of precolonial days. A leading young nobleman entrepreneur was heard to say "They've taken the government away from us; all right, we'll capture the economy."

Hagen comes close to saying that economic development takes place where the socio-cultural conditions are appropriate for it and cannot take place otherwise, and that the transition "typically occupies a period of several generations." It is hard to see what would be left for the economic adviser to do if he accepted this sort of theory of growth. Clearly, Hagen belongs to the Weber-Tawney-Schumpeter tradition where entrepreneurship and development are concerned. If this school of thought is right, we must satisfy ourselves with being "social astronomers," observing and predicting rather than planning or formulating policy,—unless we can "engineer" the whole social "climate" in an effective manner, including the political system itself. But social psychologist David McClelland, although Hagen leans on his work to a considerable extent, reaches very different conclusions. "Psychological analysis of this type," he says, "requires a far greater discipline, a far greater concern for operational precision—than Professor Hagen shows, if it is not to be laughed out of court." Hagen's dynamics "leaves at least this clinical psychologist breathless...." Neither Hagen nor his theory has much to offer those working with the Burmese or the Sioux, except to tell them to be patient." McClelland adds, "I strongly suspect that in the Burmese case the Communists will have a chance to prove that it needn't take so long, for they 'naively' reject Freudian pessimism and espouse a Skinnerian optimism about the infinite educability of human beings through ideological reform."[9]

Instant Entrepreneurs? Motivating Economic Achievement

The conclusions of Harvard psychologist David McClelland and his colleague David Winters could hardly be more different from that of Hagen: if development is hampered by a lack of entrepreneurship, it is possible to create entrepreneurs, within a short space of time, by appropriate training of carefully selected individuals, without operating on the rest of the society at all.

In choosing methods for inducing technological change, many social scientists set store by the simple device of demonstration, which has substantial results over the last two decades. But demonstration alone does not always succeed, say McClelland and Winter.[10] Some very poor fishermen in Kakinada, Andra Pradesh, India, for example, were provided with nylon fishing nets by the government. These nets were stronger and held more fish than the fishermen's own primitive nets. Some men caught more fish with the new nets but stopped fishing when they had caught their usual number, while others fished longer but used the extra income to buy more liquor. Technical advance does not always produce the values and attitudes necessary to produce development. The purely economic tools to promote development (investment and technological advance) work too slowly. These tools should be supplemented by psychological education to accelerate development.

The authors concede that many modern attitudes will be fostered simply by a man's working in a factory and living in a city; he must be on time to catch a bus, he must participate in the orderly routine procedures which govern the flow of work in a factory. But how does the factory get going in the first place? How can one motivate an entrepreneur to launch an enterprise?

McClelland and Winter emphasize the importance of opportunity. In a limited or contracting world, competition becomes a sin against one's fellows: increasing competitiveness may in fact lower collective output, rather than if cooperation is stressed. On the other hand, improved economic opportunities plus incentives can stimulate very rapid industrial growth. They suggest that attempts to change entrepreneurial activity might well concentrate on enhancing the incentives and constraints of the situation, such as closing off some possibilities through land reform, but creating other opportunities instead.

While vigorous economic activity can be successfully encouraged by a policy of changing incentives alone, it can only succeed if the "target population" (entrepreneurs, managers in public enterprises) have the appropriate interests. Men naturally seek to maximize their interests, but what are they trying to maximize?—income, growth of the firm, leisure? A fisherman of Kakinada who is trying to maximize leisure may choose to work shorter hours; a businessman from the same area may prefer to keep tight control of his company, rather than to expand its capital base; a money-lender may choose to lend funds at 24 percent annual interest to finance elaborate wedding ceremonies rather than to set up a business. In order to understand and predict action, one must know the interest, strategy, time perspective and perceived environment of the individual. If they do not have this appropriate structure, the structure must be changed so that they will respond to changed situations in certain ways.

Observing that reform movements have usually affected minority groups which have thought of themselves as superior to the masses around them, and which have often had high achievement motivation and entrepreneurial success, McClelland and Winter suggest that the same kind of dedication might be created among a band of entrepreneurs whose achievement motivation has been directly influenced, and that a specific short term educational input in a segment of the population could have far reacting economic effects. On this premise some motivation training courses were programmed by the Center for Research in Personality at Harvard University. A course was conducted at the port of Kakinada.

The Kakinada project was carried out in collaboration with the Small Industries Extension Training Institute (SIET) (an instrument of the Indian government strategy to promote transitional industry and to encourage decentralization of industry.) The SIET Institute, was oriented towards encouraging small factories in small cities. Frequently wealthy Indians are neither interested nor competent at business, being inexperienced in getting things going. In cities such as Kakinada, much capital was tied up in prestige possessions such as gold or jewellery and in money lending to farmers at high rates of return. A key problem for SIET was to draw this "frozen wealth" into productive investment; the Institute therefore entered enthusiastically into the training scheme.

The achievement-motivation course was designed for self-development, presenting methods for achieving a self-directed change in motivation. The participants learned to view job situations, problems, and possibilities in terms of achievement. A continuing theme was that participants could initiate and control change by setting reasonable goals for change in themselves, in their firms, and in their area. They were encouraged to understand the needs of others and to help them in solving their problems; the idea was that businessmen should work together to develop their city.[11]

Fifty-two men were enrolled, and divided into four courses, with three matched groups of controls. They practised realistic goal setting. Group discussion helped and cooperative behaviour increased. One man, for example, decided to sell off part of his plant (he had overinvested in machinery) and to use the proceeds to operate on a more realistic scale. He then offered his power permit to another participant who was held back by lack of electric power. Since the group included a bank manager and a money-lender, different combines were arranged to provide capital.

A review of subsequent activities of the participants showed that two thirds were active either in promoting their own business or planning to establish new ones; small groups helped each other, and in certain instances combined to start new enterprises, something that was almost non-existent in the control groups. It was also noted that the men seemed more imaginative, and that many seemed to have a changed perception of risk; seeing the same things as involving less risk, as something they could handle. The men seemed more inclined toward more risky, long term investments (as compared to money-lending) providing more employment. The Kakinada course participants provided almost twice as many new jobs per entrepreneur during the subsequent two year period after the course than did the controls.

In summing up, McClelland and Winter stated that the course participants showed more active business behaviour, worked longer hours, made more definite attempts to start new business ventures, made more specific investments in new fixed productive capital and employed more people. Finally they tended to have relatively large percentage increases in the gross income of their firms. Thus by measures of all the basic aspects of the entrepreneurial function they had become improved entrepreneurs.

This study suggests a conclusion radically different from that of Hagen, and closer to that of James Abegglen: given a firm commitment on the part of the political élite, and given a clear understanding of the socio-economic requirements for development, no major transformation of the society is needed. It is a matter rather of operation on a small set of strategic factors. Proper education and training of the leading actors in the drama, especially of entrepreneurs, but perhaps also in some cases managers, scientists, technicians, trade union leaders, etc. will be an essential element of the process; but this training need not take generations, but only a few years, months, or even weeks.

A Hen-and-Egg Problem?

There is clearly a wide range of views among social scientists regarding entrepreneurship and development. At one extreme are those that argue that entrepreneurship is needed for development, and that it is a rare, delicate hot house plant, requiring careful nourishment with juicy monopolies. At the other end of the spectrum are those who argue that it is only necessary to get something going—a major resource discovery, a new road, a factory—and entrepreneurs will spring up under every tree, or even in the desert. Between these extremes is a majority who say "it depends." But on what? Here is an area where more research is clearly needed, especially at the micro-level.

Anthropologists on Entrepreneurship

The role of entrepreneurs in development, and the relationship of the socio-cultural environment to entrepreneurial activity, is a subject which has attracted the attention of anthropologists as well as of other social scientists.

Thus anthropologist Clifford Geertz found a social climate conducive to entrepreneurship in east and central Java, as well as in Bali—within limits. But whereas the Balinese entrepreneurs were aristocrats, in Java they were mainly upper-middle class Moslem reformers and to a lesser extent skilled craftsmen. Geertz describes them as the same sort of religious, highly serious, petty businessmen who have appeared in the earlier phases of economic revolution in many countries, such as the New England Puritan, the Dutch Calvinist, reformists who believed in the virtue of hard honest work and saving. Indeed a conversation between Geertz and a Moslem reformer entrepreneur has a familiar ring: "I asked him what he thought the reason for his success was, especially since most Javanese don't do very well in business. He said it was very simple: 'all he does is work and pray, work and pray; and it only takes a few minutes to pray.... When we are not selling we are working at something else. We are not like people in the market who between their attempts to sell something just sit there and waste time. We work continually...there are two equal things in Islam; this world and the next, and nothing else, so that if you work hard and pray that's all you need do.' He said that in his opinion everyone is given an equal chance. Thus those who are poor are poor mainly because they are lazy, stupid or sinful...while those who are rich are rich because they work hard and are clever."[12]

Economic development in Java seemed to be taking the classical form we have known in the west. But Geertz also sounded a note of caution. The development activities he described were essentially small scale. The smaller enterprises were expansions of craft activities, the larger ones usually development of trading activities, still linked to the *pasar* (bazaar) and operating within trading patterns that were "individualistic, speculative, marvellously intricate," but limited in foresight and scale of operation. Geertz himself could see no easy route by which these Javanese enterprises could grow gradually into modern large-scale industries; such a change would need a long step forward in education and experience.

The second edition of Raymond Firth's well-known study of Malay fishermen contains a new chapter on "Modern Development—a restudy after twenty-three years," which presents the results of two revisits, one in 1947 and the second in 1963 (the original study had been based on observations made in 1930-40).[13] Firth's area, in northern Kelantan, remains one of the most retarded in all of Malaysia, and one least touched by modernization and economic progress. Nonetheless, Firth found significant differences, particularly during his second revisit. From the economic point of view, the most significant change was the rise of relative cost of the nets, the basic capital stock of the fishermen. The result of this change was an increase in the share of the return from the catch going to the net owners, and a proportionate decline in the share of workers. Firth makes the following observations in this regard: "Two points are noteworthy about this situation. One is the flexibility of the Malay entrepreneurs in taking advantage of a rise in the proportion of capital investment in the undertaking, to increase not merely the gross takings of capital but also the proportionate takings. The second point is that relations of 'labour'—the ordinary crew men—to the entrepreneurs were essentially of the same social and economic order as before, manifested by grumbling about the smallness of their earnings but by no more effective protest."[14]

In 1963 Firth found "radical technical change" in his area. The population had expanded substantially, the rail link of the capital city of Kelantan (Kota Bharu) with the west coast had been rebuilt, the road system had been substantially improved, and internal air services established. Cheap interurban taxi services had greatly increased the mobility of the population. Moreover, after several years of independence, Kelantan "in common with the other states was being administered by active, forward-looking Malayan officials with a direct and permanent stake in the country, and much closer local contacts than had even the best-equipped British officials."[15] (p. 304) Local open-air cinemas had been added to the shadow play, there were radios in one house in ten, and western medicine had been added to the faith healer. But most important, a technological revolution had taken place in the form of motor fishing boats, using ice for preserving the fish, with a greatly improved market situation. This situation led to a further increase in the relative importance of entrepreneurs and capitalists, and a further deterioration in the economic and social position of the simple fishermen. Firth summarizes his finding as follows: "Two characteristics of the economy at this point may be emphasized. The first is that Malay entrepreneurs had shown initiative and energy in appreciating the advantages of the new technology, and financial acumen in organizing their capital and credit resources to this end. This offers an interesting comment on an observation made by Yamey that a topic of considerable practical importance is the response in a peasant economy to a new source of finance, and the type of calculation made by investors. The second point is that in so doing they had widened the gap between themselves and the ordinary Malay fishermen."[16]

Firth was impressed by the fact that the fishermen had "the good judgement," once they had decided to motorize, to go all the way to inboard diesel motors, rather than starting with an "intermediate technology" in the form of less powerful and less efficient outboard motors.[17] Presumably because the ability to go further to sea brought heavier catches, there was also a shift from weaker cotton and ramie nets to nylon.

Particularly interesting is the change in the nature and status of entrepreneurs: "In 1940 the entrepreneurs in the area were of two kinds, the lift-net experts and the major fish dealers. The latter had some investment in fishing equipment but on the whole these two sectors were independent. The lift-net expert might, with a little exaggeration, have been described as the economic aristocrat of the fishing community, was for the most part possessed of what was then considerable capital, and receiving the respect of his fellows. By 1963 the economic aristocrat was rather the large-scale fish dealer who attempted to take over the ownership of the fishing equipment and employed the fishing experts as technical manager or foreman."[18] Finally, "the new entrepreneurs were spoken of as *Orang Kaya* or rich men. Not only were they much more wealthy they were also much more economically powerful than their forerunners of a generation earlier."[19] Firth had the impression too that the social distance between the new entrepreneurs and the people of the villages was greater than before.

A series of studies with an intent very similar to our own was carried out by Dr. T.S. Epstein in two villages in the State of Mysore in South India. The two villages, Wangala and Dalena, belong to the same culture area, the same ward and the same regional economy. They are only some eight miles apart, as the crow flies, although there are no direct links between them, each being connected by road and track to the regional centre at Mandya, some six miles from each village. The two villages, however, show striking differences, particularly in their reactions to the introduction of irrigation in Wangala. Wangala became a wet village while Dalena remained a dry one; and it is particularly the reactions to this difference in economic development that Dr. Epstein wished to study. The original field work was carried out in 1954–1956, and resulted in a book entitled *Economic Development and Social Change in South India*.[20]

Fifteen years later Dr. Epstein had the occasion to revisit the villages, and published a second book reporting the changes over a decade and a half. The interesting aspect of Epstein's findings is that more entrepreneurship appeared in the village that remained dry than in the village where irrigation was introduced.

The impact on Wangala is summarized as follows: "Wangala's social and political system continued to operate along customary lines hardly affected by the economic development which succeeded the introduction of canal irrigation. In my earlier report I argued that Wangala's traditional economic, social and political system had survived because of the unilinear nature of Wangala's economic growth—agriculture remained the dominant economic pursuit of villagers—and because of the flexibilities which operated within the limits of the traditional system. This I contrasted with the much more drastic changes that had taken place in the dry land village I studied. The burst of entrepreneurial effort in Dalena is summarized as follows: As soon as Dalena men began to respond to the new opportunities which arose in the regional economic expansion, each new effort perpetuated the village's economic diversification. Dalena entrepreneurs, having been conditioned to operating in the wider economy, were thus quick to take to black market dealings when rationing and shortages during the war made these very profitable. A number of the wealthiest villagers in 1955 were supposed to have made their fortunes in this way. The black market in paddy and ragi induced Dalena's patel to establish a flour mill at a nearby rail junction, which was a roaring business during the war. His younger brother, Kempegowda, was keen also to profit from such enterprise and wanted to open a flour mill and cane-crusher in Dalena itself."[21] The intervening 15 years had brought new opportunities to Wangala and Dalena of two types: expert advice and help in improving the cultivation of customary crops; increasing demand for small-scale cane-crushing facilities, as a consequence of rapidly rising crisis for jaggery (crude sugar).

Dr. Epstein describes in some detail the activities of an outside small-scale entrepreneur, Ramakrishna from Mandia, who was the first farmer ever to use a tractor to plough virgin land in Wangala. He was able to rent the tractor from an agricultural research and training station some six miles from Mandya. His innovation led to a "cluster of followers;" Dr. Epstein found "a number of Wangala farmers use tractors for ploughing and bulldozers for levelling their lands."[22]

Epstein provides evidence of "the Protestant ethic" among leading entrepreneurs in the two villages. The income elasticity of demand for consumption goods, Epstein found, was low, and with rising incomes savings increased substantially. These were invested in various new activities including purchase of more wet land, pumps, rice mills, cane-crushers, etc.. But whereas Tugowda of Wangala invested in shrines and temples to raise his ritual status, Lingowda of Dalena spent money financing his son's election campaign. The horizons of Dalena's entrepreneurs continued to expand much more rapidly than those of Wangala's entrepreneurs. Lingowda's continued economic advance depended on his contacts with the administrative officials in influential positions and farmers in neighbouring irrigated villages; he therefore saw clear-cut advantages in having his son enter politics. Here then is an example of political change induced by economic change at the community level.

Indeed Epstein's Lingowda is reminiscent of Geertz' Javanese entrepreneur: "When I discussed with him his business ventures and enquired which of his sons he thought would continue in his footsteps after his own death, he told me that he kept advising his children to remain a joint entity even when he himself was no more, otherwise the wealth which their household had managed to accumulate would soon be dissipated and none of them would be left with very much. He stressed over and over again the importance of reinvesting funds in business enterprises rather than spending all the profits lavishly on unnecessary consumer goods."[23]

The recent anthropological literature is replete with such stories of entrepreneurial endeavour at the village level. Yet it is clear that this sort of petty entrepreneurship is not what Schumpeter had in mind. He was thinking of "captains of industry," the Rockefellers, the Goulds, the Henry Fords, and of major innovations such as steam, the internal combustion engine, electricity. Can the small-scale entrepreneurship at the community level, as described by the anthropologists, if repeated often enough, serve as the "engine of growth" of an entire society and a national economy? Or do these activities belong to the category of "clusters of followers," while the true entrepreneurs remain in the metropolitan centres, as suggested by both the dependency theory and the theory of growth poles? This is the sort of question which we feel is best studied at the community level. What are the ramifications of "innovations" such as motorizing fishing boats? What are the channels of transmission of such innovations from the centres to the individual?

Notes

1. Joseph Schumpeter, *The Theory of Economic Development* (Cambridge: Harvard University Press, 1934.)
2. John S. Gambs, *Beyond Supply and Demand* (New York: Columbia University Press, 1946), p. 18. The standard work on Veblen is Joseph Dorfman, *Thorstein Veblen and His America* (New York: The Viking Press, 1934). A lively shorter treatment can be found in Robert L. Heilbroner, *The Worldly Philosophers* (New York: Simon and Schuster, 1972).
3. Joan Robinson, *Economic Philosophy* (New York: Doubleday, 1964), p. 112.
4. Clarence, E. Ayres, *The Theory of Economic Progress* (Durham: University of North Carolina Press, 1944), p. 137.
5. *Ibid.*
6. *Ibid.*, p. 133.
7. Gambs, *Beyond Supply and Demand*, p. 10.
8. Everett E. Hagen, *On a Theory of Social Change: How Economic Growth Begins* (Homewood, Ill.: The Dorsey Press, 1962).
9. David C. McClelland, "A Psychological Approach to Economic Development," *Economic Development and Cultural Change*, April 1964, p. 324.
10. David C. McClelland and David C. Winter, *Motivating Economic Achievement* (New York: The Free Press, 1973), p. 30.
11. *Ibid.*, p. 150.
12. Clifford Geertz, *Peddlers and Princes: Social Development and Economic Change in Two Indonesian Towns* (Chicago: University of Chicago Press, 1963). pp. 147–156.
13. Notes on Raymond Firth, *Malay Fishermen: Their Peasant Economy* (London: Routledge and Kegan Paul, 1966).
14. *Ibid.*, p. 304.
15. *Ibid.*
16. *Ibid.*, p. 315.
17. *Ibid.*, p. 306.

18. *Ibid.*, p. 343.
19. *Ibid.*, p. 345.
20. T.S. Epstein, *Economic Development and Social Change in South India* (Manchester: University of Manchester Press, 1962).
21. T.S. Epstein, *South India: Yesterday, Today and Tomorrow* (London: Macmillan, 1973), p. 58.
22. *Ibid.*, p. 59.
23. *Ibid.*, p. 205.

4

Interregional and International Trade

Until quite recently economists regarded spatial differentiation essentially as a nuisance, an inconvenient roadblock on the route to discovery of universal laws, true always and everywhere, and derived from assumptions of universally similar human behaviour. When they did admit that different societies, inhabiting different spaces, had widely differing endowments of natural and human resources, and that some spaces were much more attractive to new enterprises than others, so that rates of industrialization and urbanization also differed, they preferred to allow into their models differences in the physical environment, while retaining the assumption of universal human behaviour, rather than to cope with the more complex problems arising from behaviour that differs from time to time and from place to place. As also indicated in chapter one, there were two main products of these limited efforts to cope with space: the theories of interregional and international trade, which, when linked to the base industry concept and the export multiplier, yielded a sort of theory of regional growth; and location theory.

Interregional and International Trade

What really interested the classical economists, from Adam Smith to Stuart Mill, was international trade, which was thought to be an "engine of growth." The same was true later of the neo-classical economists, from Jevons and Edgeworth through Marshall to Samuelson. Yet, it was clear that the same heterogeneity of space which gave rise to international trade could also give rise to interregional trade. Some economists were logical enough in their analysis to draw attention to this fact. A few even found the theory of interregional trade a convenient way of approaching the theory of international trade. As early as 1752, it was pointed out that the theory of international equilibrium applied also to regions within the same country.[1] Adam Smith recognized that if all factors were perfectly mobile, the factors would move rather than goods and services; and since he believed such mobility to exist only within single neighbourhoods, he implicitly recognized that factor immobility could give rise to trade among regions of the same country.[2] John Stuart Mill reiterated this view.[3] Moving into the neo-classical period, Cairnes related interregional trade to his concept of "non-competing groups,"[4] and J.S. Nicholson regarded interregional trade arising from internal immobility of factors of production as the general case.[5]

The person who thoroughly entrenched interregional trade into modern neo-classical theory, however, and made it ever since an integral part of general equilibrium theory, in 1933, was the Swedish economist Bertil Ohlin, in his classic work *Interregional and International Trade*. Virtually all subsequent work on the subject owes a debt to him, and his analysis makes a good peg on which to hang our own. Let us not forget, however, that our interest is different from Ohlin's. He was not primarily interested in regional analysis, regional development and its relation to national development, or regional disparities. He was interested mainly in international trade theory as a device for explaining conditions under which trade took place and the distribution of gains from trade; and as a guide to foreign trade policy. We shall make no attempt here to provide a comprehensive survey of general theories of international trade, but shall limit ourselves to those aspects of interregional trade theory which are relevant to regional analysis.

Classical and Early Neo-Classical Theory of Comparative Advantage

The classical economists contended that the volume and pattern of trade between two regions or two countries depends on the amount of labour required to produce various commodities in each region. To take David Ricardo's famous example, suppose that a certain amount of labour will produce 20 bolts of cloth or 10 tuns of wine in the United Kingdom, and 10 bolts of cloth or 20 tuns of wine in Portugal. If there are no restrictions on trade, and transport costs are not exorbitant, the United Kingdom will specialize in textiles and Portugal in wine. Trade will take place at a rate of exchange of 1 bolt of cloth for 1 tun of wine, since the amounts of labour entailed in the producing country are the same, and transport costs are the same in both directions. In effect, Portugal and the United Kingdom are exchanging 1 person-day of British labour for 1 person-day of Portuguese labour. In this example, and in any other case where trade takes place, both countries or regions are better off than they would be if each tried to produce both commodities.

An important extension of the classical theory is the demonstration that trade is still mutually beneficial even if one region is more efficient at the production of all commodities, provided the superior productivity is more marked in some industries than in others. It is hard to imagine the United Kingdom being superior to Portugal at producing wine, but we can suppose that Portugal could introduce a modernized textile industry, so that the same amount of labour would produce 25 bolts of cloth instead of 10; whereas the United Kingdom textile industry is reluctant to change its ways. It will still pay Portugal to specialize in wine, and import its cloth; it can get cloth much more cheaply (in person-days) by exporting wine than by producing cloth at home.

Since the whole analytical system of the classical economist was built on the labour theory of value, it was natural and consistent of them to make differing labour costs the basis for interregional and international trade. But curiously enough, while attacking the labour theory of value in general, and emphasizing marginal utility and the demand side of the "demand = supply, price = marginal cost" equation, neo-classical economists continued to analyze interregional and international trade in terms of labour costs until well into the 1930s. P.T. Ellsworth, in a well-known book on international economics published in 1938, in illustrating "the modern classical position," uses as an example Ohio and neighbouring Pennsylvania.[6] Ten days of labour will produce 20 tires or 10 bolts of cloth in Ohio, 10 tires or 20 bolts of cloth in Pennsylvania. So Ohio specializes in tires and Pennsylvania in cloth, and they exchange tires for bolts of cloth on a one-to-one basis. Some neo-classical economists even tried to justify building trade theory on a real-labour-cost foundation. The famous Harvard economist Frank Taussig, for example, argued that capital costs (interest rates), and wages for the same kind of labour, did not vary much from country to country; and that prices equal costs of units produced at the margin, where there are no rents.[7]

It is possible to doctor the labour theory of value, allowing for cost of labour "embodied" in capital, regarding types of labour with different wage rates as different factors of production, allowing for increasing and decreasing costs, allowing for the possibility of producing a given commodities with varying factor proportions, and so on. To approach reality, simplifying assumptions such as those limiting analysis to cases of only two regions (or countries), each with two factors of production and producing only two commodities, and stipulating complete mobility of factors of production and unrestricted movement of goods and services, must be dropped. By the time all this has been done, it is clear that any "real cost" theory is not only unrealistic but unwieldy and inconvenient, "an especially clumsy and even dangerous tool."[8] However, it nonetheless contains elements of truth, and if we are to reject it, we must be sure that the theory that replaces it is better. Ellsworth continues: "...what is wanted is a theory of international trade which is based on a thoroughly modern theory of value (instead of the discarded labor-cost theory), and which is direct and realistic instead of awkwardly roundabout and unreal. Such requirements appear in large part to be met by the analysis furnished by the Swedish economist Bertil Ohlin."[9]

Ohlin's Theory of Interregional Trade

Ohlin's great contribution was to take the theory of interregional and international trade out of its position of rather peculiar and indefensible isolation and bring it into the generally accepted general theory of equilibrium, in which "everything depends on everything." He begins with interregional trade, as the general case, and then proceeds to international trade as a particular type of interregional trade with certain peculiarities of its own, such as a high degree of immobility of factors of production among nations, restrictions on international movements of goods and services, and the existence of more than one currency. In fact, he pursues generality even further, and begins by pointing out the similarity of occupational specialization by individuals and geographic specialization by regions. Individuals have different endowments of capabilities, and are better at doing some things than others. It is sensible and profitable for them to specialize in the things they are good at. In the same way, different regions have varying endowments of natural and human resources, and because of varying economic histories, they also have different stocks of plant and equipment in existence and varying capacities to save and invest. These differences result in varying costs of production and varying demand for particular goods and services, and thus to varying prices. The differences in costs and prices among regions create opportunities for mutually beneficial trade among regions. They can also, however, result in differences in level of welfare among regions, if there are barriers, natural or manmade, to movement of either factors of production or of goods and services among regions.

Here is a proposition of fundamental importance for regional analysis, and we shall revert to it, in one form or another, again and again in the course of this volume. Theoretically, differences in standards of living among regions could be eliminated, even if limits to movements of goods and services existed, making it difficult for a poor region to export the goods in which it has a comparative advantage, so long as there was perfect mobility of factors of production. People could move to the richer regions, or capital to the poorer regions to take advantage of relatively low wage rates, thus making wages higher. But perfect mobility does not, and basically cannot exist. As Ellsworth puts it: "It may be stated at the outset that the chief obstacle to movements of both labour and capital is psychological in nature. Human beings dislike change, and the changes involved in breaking home ties, leaving secure employment and a familiar environment for a strange locality and an uncertain economic future, are painful to make.... Owners of capital are likewise reluctant to transfer their wealth across national and regional boundaries to places where it is no longer under their direct supervision, and where the 'real or fancied insecurity' is greater. To this psychological obstacle must be added another, the financial cost of moving. This often, in the case of labor, though rarely with capital, constitutes an obstacle of the first importance."[10]

It might be noted in passing that when Ellsworth says that financial costs of moving capital are "rarely" an obstacle to its movement, he is obviously thinking of capital in the form of money, or liquid capital. When an enterprise has built up plant and equipment in a particular region, the cost of moving it to another region may indeed be "an obstacle of the first importance" to moving the enterprise to another region. If the entrepreneur wants to move, he has two choices: sell the enterprise for what he can get and establish new plant and equipment in the other region; or wear out his machinery without replacing it (which could take years), sell it for scrap and sell his buildings for what he can get, and reinvest in the other region. Neither decision is one that entrepreneurs make lightly.

Interregional Trade and General Equilibrium Theory

Interregional trade, then, results from differences in factor-endowment among regions, plus some degree of immobility of factors among regions. (Ellsworth, following Ohlin, includes among the simplifying assumptions made in the first stage of his analysis that factors of production are perfectly mobile within regions but immobile between them. Note that this assumption is essentially a definition of economic regions: a region is a geographic area within which factors of production are completely mobile. Taken literally, this definition would make regions rather small. An alternative approach would be to establish scales of mobility and define "region" as an area within which there is some arbitrarily chosen degree of mobility.)[11] The differences in availability of factors of production among regions give rise to differences in costs and thus to different prices. But what determines the differences in prices? The answer, in effect, is the whole global economic system.

Ohlin answers the question in these words: The starting point for such an investigation is the fact that all prices of goods as well as of industrial agents are ultimately, in each region, at any given moment, determined by the demand for goods and the possibility of producing them. Behind the former lie two circumstances to be considered as known data in the problem of pricing: (1) the wants and desires of consumers, and (2) the conditions of ownership of the factors of production, which affect individual incomes and thus demand. The supply of goods, on the other hand, depends ultimately on (3) the supply of productive factors, and (4) the physical conditions of production...[12]

Ohlin is here assuming perfect competition throughout. In a more realistic analysis relative prices would be affected also by the relative degrees of monopoly power exercised in the production of various goods and services in various regions, and these would have to be taken into account.

As we shall see more fully below, the level of prosperity in any region depends a good deal on its volume and pattern of trade with other regions, including regions outside as well as inside the country. It follows that the level of social welfare in any region, too, depends on the functioning of the entire global economic system, a fact that makes adjustment of regional economies to change, and the formulation of policies to cure regional maladies, extremely difficult.

In approaching the analysis of regional variations in price structures, Ohlin is insistent on a full-cost approach.[13] The only sensible approach is: ... to take a complete cost account in different countries (or regions) for the commodity in question and to examine to what extent the cheapness of production in one country is due to low wage expenses, low interest expenses, low transportation expenses, etc. Then the next step is to go behind these cost items and examine their relation to quantity of labour employed, the wage level, the quantity of capital employed, the interest level, etc.; in other words, the relations of the cost items to the price system in each country.

Abstract Nature of the Theory

Interregional or international trade is thus an extremely complex phenomenon, and economists usually resort to complicated mathematical models to handle it. Even so, they find it necessary to make a host of simplifying assumptions to get started on an analysis of the phenomenon. All sciences make such abstractions; but trade theory makes rather more of them than is common even in other branches of economics, and it is extremely rare that all of the simplifying assumptions are dropped. As a consequence, much of the literature on trade theory retains an atmosphere of abstraction and unreality that makes it daunting for non-economists, and even for some economists. And yet the theory as a whole nonetheless contains large elements of fundamental truth. We shall concentrate on these truths, as they affect regional analysis, and shall not attempt an exposition of the refinements of interregional and international trade theory.

Equalization of Commodity and Factor Prices

We are interested in regional disparities and in the way in which regional structures affect the welfare of various national societies, the "wealth and poverty of nations." Thus we have a special interest in two arguments made in the interregional trade literature, unfortunately arguments that have been conducted in some of the most highly abstract terms ever devised by economists:

1. that trade tends to bring convergence of regional price structures, and
2. that trade tends to equalize prices of factors of production, and so to iron out differences in levels of income and welfare among the populations of different regions.

The first of these is easier to swallow, and more obviously "contains large elements of fundamental truth." If there were no restrictions on the movement of goods among regions, prices could not for long differ by more than transport costs; if there were no transport costs, prices would be the same in all regions. Moreover, each region would produce *only* commodities for which it had a comparative advantage. All goods would be exported and imported, and no commodity would be produced for an internal market alone.

The effects of price equalization on regional welfare is, however, ambivalent. The price of fish and petroleum may both be the same (apart from transport costs) in the province of Nova Scotia and the province of Alberta. But if in one person-day Alberta produces "x" barrels of oil worth $1,000, and Nova Scotia produces "y" kilograms of fish worth $100, the people of Alberta are going to be considerably better off than the people of Nova Scotia.

Equalization of Factor Prices

The proposition that trade tends to equalize factor prices among regions is more open to doubt. If it were true, the only policy that would be needed to equalize incomes of people, in particular occupations in every region of the world, would be free trade. It is obvious that centuries of trade among regions and nations have not equalized incomes in this way, and show no sign of doing so. Ardent champions of free trade and a free market, however, can always argue that the reason for the failure to achieve equalization is that the market has not been, and is not, allowed to work; rather, it is hampered by all manner of ill conceived and misguided intervention.

The proposition is buttressed by a daunting array of simplifying assumptions. The classic article setting forth the argument and providing a mathematical proof was written by Paul Samuelson and published in the *Economic Journal* in 1948.[14] Among his simplifying assumptions (explicit and implicit) are the following:

1. There are only two countries, each producing the same two commodities with the same two factors of production.
2. Pure competition prevails throughout in both countries (no firm is able to influence the price of anything it buys or anything it sells).
3. Technology and information are perfectly mobile, so that the techniques of production and access to information are identical in the two countries.

4. Production isoquants are well behaved; that is, in both countries the factors of production can be combined in whatever proportions the entrepreneurs choose, for both commodities.
5. There are no costs of transportation.
6. Factor endowments are not greatly unequal in the two countries.
7. There is perfect mobility of all factors of production (both in space and by occupation) within each country (or region).

Under these conditions the equalization of price ratios requires equalization of the cost of production ratios, which in turn requires the use of the same technology and factor-proportions, and the equalization of factor prices. Each region or country will concentrate on the production of the commodity which requires more of the relatively abundant factor of production, export that commodity, and import the one requiring more of the relatively scarce factor.

Despite the unreality of the underlying assumptions, there can be little doubt that trade tends to reduce disparities in factor prices as well as in commodity prices. In effect, trade makes the abundant factor in each country more scarce, and raises its price; and it makes the scarce factor more abundant, and lowers its price. Complete equalization, however, would require not only that the formal assumptions conform to reality, but that in each region demand is concentrated on the commodities requiring large amounts of the abundant factor. That could happen only as the result of the most unlikely of accidents. There is little reason to suppose that free trade alone can eliminate disparities among regions or nations.

The Marxists, of course, argue the exact opposite: interregional and international trade becomes the very vehicle by which the capitalists at the centre exploit the people on the periphery.

Economies of Scale

One of the reasons why the theory of equalization of factor prices does not work out in the real world is that not all production isoquants are "well behaved."[15] To be able to choose any combination whatsoever of factors of production to produce whatever good or service one likes, all factors of production would have to be perfectly divisible. Many of them are not: electric furnaces, rolling mills, assembly lines, turbines. These have to achieve a certain scale to be efficient, and costs of production per unit decline as output increases, until the optimal scale of production is reached. There are "economies of scale." This fact limits competition; new firms cannot enter the industry unless they are capable of attaining the requisite scale of production, and find a market for their output. Thus industries in regions where population is large and concentrated, providing a large internal market, have an advantage over regions where population is small or dispersed. It is also an advantage to be first in the field; additional firms will have more difficulty in reaching the requisite scale. Moreover, there is a "learning curve" for enterprises as for individuals. Mistakes are likely to be made at the beginning, but if these are survived, management will be better able to achieve continuous improvements in techniques and organization.

Imperfect Competition

The pure competition assumption is also highly unrealistic. Throughout much of the world market some degree of monopoly or "imperfect competition" prevails. Economies of scale are a contributing factor. With imperfect competition, prices can be above average cost per unit, and costs can be above what they would be at the optimal scale of production. In a "world of monopolies" relative prices reflect, among other things, relative degrees of monopoly power. Other things being equal, regions with enterprises exercising a high degree of monopoly power will be better off than those with enterprises with only a low degree of monopoly power (in the case of enterprises operating under pure competition, zero monopoly power). As Lawrence Towle points out, the degree of monopoly power exercised by the industries of a particular region is partly a matter of historical accident: "One country...may gain a decisive advantage over other countries by mere accident. The industry may have started up in one locality because the individual or individuals responsible for its birth just happened to settle there. Once the industry has been launched, external and internal economies and technological knowledge may develop so fast that other localities are unable to get the initial toehold necessary to compete on even terms with the leader."[16]

It should also be noted that changes in technology or in tastes can change a "leader" into a laggard, as happened with the Atlantic provinces of Canada, with the famous wooden sailing ships, its fish exports, and later its coal and steel industries.

How much exercise of monopoly power benefits or injures particular regions is a matter of fact, not of theory. Towle thinks that the injury is limited. He points out that many of the goods entering into interregional and international trade are produced under conditions approaching pure competition: cereals, animal products, natural fibres, natural rubber, sugar, coffee, cocoa, lumber. But with the increasing importance of trade in manufactured or processed goods, and of specialized services, plus the growing role of the multinational corporations (MNCs), the proportion of interregional or international trade characterized by pure competition is surely shrinking. On the other hand, two things can be said: with the divorce of management from ownership, fewer and fewer corporations are operated so as to maximize profits or to raise prices as far as possible above average cost (managers are interested in outselling rivals, maximizing growth of the firm, while avoiding stockholders' revolts and excessive fixed debt); and with the increasing speed of the spread of new technology and information, monopoly positions become ever harder to maintain. We shall return to these important considerations below.

The Gains From Trade

We have seen that according to classical and neo-classical theory all partners in interregional and international trade gain from it. Trade—especially free trade—results in a more efficient allocation of resources in all regions, resulting in higher total output and higher real income. In a sense, trade makes available to all regions factors of production that are scarce in some of them. The question as to how these gains are distributed among trading partners is another matter, and an extremely complex one. Resource endowment, natural and human, level of technology, degrees of monopoly power, structures of demand, size of internal markets, geographic location and transport cost— indeed, the whole manner in which the global economy functions—will determine how well or badly each region fares from its trade. Concrete answers cannot emerge from the theory of general equilibrium; to obtain an answer for a particular region, it is necessary to study it empirically.

The Terms of Trade

How much a given region gains from trade with other regions (inside and outside the country) depends not only on the volume of trade and the balance of trade (value of total exports minus value of total imports), but on the ratio of its export prices to its import prices, or terms of trade. A region that can sell at high prices, relative to costs, and buy at low prices, relative to internal costs of producing the same commodities, obviously gains more from trade than a region facing the reverse situation. In the real world, because of the vagaries of demand for particular commodities, and sharp shifts in costs of producing them and in world supplies of them, terms of trade are highly volatile, a matter of concern to regions and to nations as a whole. Sudden changes in the degree to which monopoly power is exercised to the full can also have dramatic effects on terms of trade, if the commodity is a major export of some regions and a major import of others. The sharp increases in OPEC oil prices in 1973 and 1978 provide abundant evidence of this fact. Terms of trade can have a significant impact, positive or negative, on the rate of development of particular regions, through their effect on the capacity to import.

Some contemporary neo-Marxists (the dependency theory school) have gone so far as to make deteriorating terms to trade a major part of the explanation of the continuing underdevelopment of less-developed countries. The developing countries, the argument goes, export foodstuffs and raw materials, which operate under conditions approximating pure competition. Consequently, their export prices are low, and relative to other commodities become lower and lower. The industrialized countries export manufactured goods, which are produced under conditions of imperfect competition. Accordingly, their prices are high, and relatively become higher and higher. Thus, the terms of trade of developing countries have a constant tendency to deteriorate, while those of industrialized countries tend to become more and more favourable. The same argument is applied to less-developed and more advanced regions.

We shall consider this argument in some detail below, where we deal with the theory of dependency and unequal exchange. At this point, let us merely report our findings: there are developing countries and retarded regions where the argument seems to fit; but when less-developed countries *as a group* are compared with industrialized countries *as a group*, exactly the reverse of the argument emerges, according to United Nations and World Bank data of the past 25 years (the terms of trade of less-developed countries have improved, those of industrialized countries have deteriorated); and there are logical flaws in the argument when presented as a general theory. We can certainly agree that *if* terms of trade of a particular region deteriorate, and if that event is not offset by an improvement in volume of exports (lower export prices will expand sales), so that capacity to import is maintained, the region's rate of growth is likely to decline. That proposition, however, applies to advanced and retarded regions alike. To decide what is likely to happen in a particular region, its entire structure of employment, production, exports and imports must be studied.

The Economic Base Theory

Closely related to theories of interregional trade is the economic base theory. It states that the development of any region, and particularly the development of its urban centres, is a function of the growth of its "base industries." These, by definition, are export industries. They are not attracted to a particular region or city in order to exploit the market of that region or city. They are attracted because the location provides a favourable base from which to export to other regions; the location promises a comparative advantage to the base industry. In the case of "smoke-stack industries" proximity to sources of natural resources is often the determining factor. The steel industry of the United States settled in Pittsburgh because of proximity to coal mines, and also to iron and industrial water. Pulp and paper mills settle near forests, aluminum mills near sources of hydro-electric power. Scientifically-oriented enterprises settle where there are research institutes, universities, specialized consulting firms, and other sophisticated services. As services and scientifically-oriented ("hi-tech") industries come more and more to dominate metropolitan centres, and as both become more footloose, access to the most modern information and communications systems, and amenities which make a city attractive to top-level managers, scientists, engineers, and technicians, become increasingly important factors in the location of economic activity. In the case of sophisticated services like consulting, top-level banking, (trading desks), stock markets, insurance, and specialized accounting or legal services, access to clients on the one hand and to information and technology on the other are major considerations, which is why one finds the head offices of such enterprises in New York, Boston, Hartford Connecticut, Toronto, Montreal, Sydney and Melbourne, rather than in Austin Texas, Buffalo, Toledo Ohio, Victoria B.C., Darwin or Hobart.

Whatever the reason for its choice of location, the base industry, once established, attracts a labour force, and other enterprises which service the base industry and its employees. Houses and other buildings must be constructed, retail outlets established, various services provided. The various enterprises feed on each other, and as the centre grows, new types of enterprise come in. All, however, depend fundamentally on the bases industry; without its presence nothing else would be there. And since the base industry is by definition an export industry, everything going on in a region and in its urban centres depends ultimately on what is going on in other regions.

The Export Multiplier

The effect on any region of what is going on in other regions, as a result of the impact of events outside the region on its exports, is formalized under the heading of the "export multiplier theory." The original concept of the multiplier, as introduced by Richard Kahn and elaborated by John Maynard Keynes in his famous *General Theory of Employment, Interest, and Money* was formulated in terms of the impact of an increase in investment on income, and thus, indirectly, on employment. How big that impact is depends on the magnitude of the "leakages" in the second and third and subsequent rounds of spending of income. The principal leakages are savings, payment of taxes, and imports; these are uses of income which do not increase further the incomes of other residents of the same region. If "Y" is income, "k" is the multiplier, "I" is investment, "S" is saving, "T" is taxes, "M" is imports, and "Δ" the mathematical symbol meaning "increase in," we can express the multiplier principle as follows:

$$Y = k.\Delta I = \frac{1}{\Delta S/\Delta Y + \Delta T/\Delta Y + \Delta M/\Delta Y}$$

It did not take long for economists to recognize that the same principle can be applied to any other increase in incomes of a region which does not arise simply from respending of income already earned by residents of the region. One of the more obvious sources of increased income in a region, through actions taken by people outside the region, is increased purchases of the region's exports. If exports are denoted by "X," we can substitute "X" for "I" in the equation above and we have the "export multiplier." Since increases in savings, taxes, and imports combined seldom absorb more than two thirds of an increase in regional incomes, the expression above might be 1/0.66 = 1.6.

The process of expansion does not stop with the multiplier in the strict sense of the term, as defined above. The increase in consumer spending through the multiplier process stimulates increased investment in the region as well. The impact of increased consumer spending on investment is called the "accelerator." Interactions between accelerator and multiplier constitute the "super-multiplier." The value of the super-multiplier can be several times as high as the value of the multiplier alone. It can be measured in terms of either income or employment. It is easier to measure the super-multiplier than it is to measure either the multiplier or the accelerator by itself, because one need only compare the total increase in income or employment with the initial increase. In his 1960 work, Isard gives employment multipliers for Wichita Kansas,[17] ranging from 2.6 to 3.5. The important point is that an initial increase in exports for any region can result in very substantial increases in total income and employment.

A Theory of Regional Development?

One of the most forthright efforts to construct a general theory of regional development on the foundation of the base-industry-export-multiplier principle was made by professor Douglass North, noted economic historian at the University of Washington.[18] He begins his well known book on *The Economic Growth of the United States* with this statement: "The gist of the argument is that the timing and pace of an economy's development has been determined by: 1) the success of its export sector, and 2) the characteristics of the export industry and the disposition of the income received from the export sector. He continues: Why does one area remain tied to a single export staple while another diversifies its production and becomes an urbanized, industrialized economy? Regions or nations which remain tied to a single export commodity almost inevitably fail to achieve sustained expansion."[19]

Whether or not a regional economy achieves sustained development, North argues, depends on three factors: the natural endowments of the region; the character of the export industry; and changes in technology and transfer costs. The first of these factors determines how growth begins in any region. If the factor endowment results in a clear-cut comparative advantage in one industry, production will be concentrated in that industry at the outset. If on the other hand there are a good many commodities for which comparative advantage is not too much less than in the leading sector, development of the region is likely to lead to diversification.

How strong the spread effects from the base industry to other economic activities within the region depends on the character of the base industry. For example, if the initial export industry is a plantation product, with increasing returns to scale, and concentration of income in the hands of the landowners, the economy is likely to get stuck with the initial export and fail to expand or diversify. The landowners will spend their incomes on imported luxury goods, the workers and peasants will limit their spending to home-grown necessities. A society of small farmers (North argues) has more chance to diversify and grow, because the population will demand a wide range of products, some of which can be produced within the region. North also argues, on the basis mainly of North American experience, that plantation societies, with their marked inequality of incomes, will be uninterested in spending money for education or research not directly related to the staple export, while regions with a more equitable income distribution will be more interested. In the United States, both the farmers of the West and the industrialists and financiers of the Northeast were prepared to invest in education. The planters of the South were not. Another element is the amount of investment social overhead required by the export industry. Finally, North argues, changes in technology and transport may completely alter a region's comparative advantage, in either direction.

North sums up his argument as follows: "The *successful* economy grows because the initial developments from the export industry lead to a widening of the export base and growth in the size of the domestic market. Growing demand in the domestic sector leads to an ever widening variety of residentiary industries.... In the *unsuccessful* economy, the increment to income from expansion of the export industry leads to an increase in the supply of that export commodity, but not to broadening of the export base nor growth in the size of the domestic market. Income flows out of the area with little more than expansion of the export industry as a result."[20]

As a description of what actually happened in the growth of various regional and national economies, North's thesis is very useful. The United States fits very well North's model of the "successful economy," while Brazil fits his model of the "unsuccessful economy," at least up to the last three decades or so. The American leading exports of each era led to diversified production, geographic spread of industrialization and urbanization, and appearance of new exports without total disappearance of old ones. Until about 1930, however, this scenario was less applicable to the South than to other major regions. Brazil's economic history up to about 1960 was one of "boom and bust" in one sector and region after another, without spread effects or diversification in any significant degree, and without much spread of urbanization and industrialization. Australia and Canada fall in between. Despite its usefulness in describing what happened in some cases, however, the base-industry-export-multiplier theory has serious limitations as a general theory of regional development.

Critique of the Base-Industry-Export-Multiplier Theory

There are several reasons why the base-industry-export-multiplier analysis cannot be accepted as a general theory explaining regional development.

1. The most obvious is that on theoretical grounds it is incomplete; the multiplier principle applies to any increase in income other than respending on consumption of income generated in some other fashion. As we have seen, in its original formulation by Kahn and Keynes it was applied to investment. Investment in any region from outside of it, perhaps to develop newly discovered resources, even if directed towards the internal market, can and does launch a process of regional economic expansion. So does an increase in government expenditures in the region, to subsidize railways or build highways, for example. Such spending has played a major role in regional development, even in the United States. Shifts in consumption functions, so that more is spent and less is saved out of a given income, such as took place in the years following World War II, could also launch a process of expansion. Thus on purely theoretical grounds there is no justification for giving pride of place to increases in regional exports. If exports are to be stressed to the exclusion of other generators of development, there must be empirical justification. By and large such empirical support has not been forthcoming; such studies as there are show rather that behaviour of exports has low predictive value in explaining growth of regional income.[21]

2. The theory does not really explain how development in a region begins; for exports from the region to grow, something must first happen outside the region to generate an increase in demand for the product of the base export industry. Moreover, the argument is circular. Consider the following, where k_1, k_2…are multipliers, X_a are exports of region A and X_b exports of region B, M_a imports of region A and M_b imports of region B, Y_a income of region A and Y_b income of region B:

$$\Delta Y_a = k_1 \cdot \Delta X_a = k_1 \cdot \Delta M_b \dots\dots\dots\dots\dots\dots\dots\dots\dots (1)$$
$$\Delta X_a = k_2 \cdot \Delta Y_b \dots\dots\dots\dots\dots\dots\dots\dots\dots\dots\dots\dots (2)$$
$$\Delta Y_b = k_3 \cdot \Delta X_b = K_3 \cdot \Delta M_a \dots\dots\dots\dots\dots\dots\dots\dots (3)$$

$$\Delta X_b = k_4 \cdot \Delta Y_a = k_4 \cdot k_1 \cdot \Delta M_b \dots \dots \dots (4)$$
$$\Delta Y_b = k_1 \cdot k_4 \cdot k_1 \cdot \Delta M_b \dots \dots \dots (5)$$
$$\Delta M_b = k_5 \cdot \Delta Y_b \dots \dots \dots (6)$$
$$\Delta Y_b = k_1 \cdot k_4 \cdot k_1 \cdot k_5 \cdot \Delta Y_b \dots \dots \dots (7)$$

Equation (5) is already a bit peculiar. One doesn't usually think of an increase in imports as the cause of a rise in regional income. There is a sense in which it could be true: if the imports are financed by capital inflow, regional income might indeed increase. Importing is a way of consuming more than a region produces—for a while. But then we need an explanation of the capital inflow, and the base-industry-export-multiplier by itself does not provide it.

More damaging is equation (7) which says that the increase in regional income in B depends on the increase in regional income in B. Again, there is a sense in which this relationship could hold, one that we shall discuss below under the heading of "cumulative causation." Economic movements do have a tendency to become cumulative, and an initial increase in regional income can provide the incentive for decisions, especially investment decisions and government spending decisions, that could make income grow more. But it is also true that such movements have a tendency to take a cyclical form, and initial increases in regional income can give way to declines. We shall discuss regional fluctuations, as well, further on. But it is clear that the "b-i-e-m" theory, while not exactly wrong, is far from complete. We must consider a lot of factors besides regional exports, and we must track down the fundamental factors which generate expansion in all regions, if our theory is to be complete.

3) There are other problems with the "b-i-e-m," as well. Apart from its poor performance as a predictor of growth, Harry Richardson stresses two: "Firstly, there are serious difficulties in measuring the economic base, especially the problem of how to distinguish between basic and service activities…. Thirdly, urban base analysis suffers from theoretical drawbacks so weighty that one might argue that a division into basic and non-basic sectors is meaningless."[22]

With regard to the first of these weaknesses, Richardson points out that to begin with, in order to describe or measure the base industry exports of a region, we must first have a definition of the "region." Here we stumble into a veritable hornet's nest of problems, as we shall see below. Of course, when the "region" is a political or administrative unit like a state or province, its borders are defined. But whether such units make sense for economic analysis of the sort involved in the "b-i-e-m" theory is open to debate.

Even more sticky is the problem of deciding what are base activities and what activities are in the region essentially to serve the base industries and the population these have drawn to the region. Perhaps in a "steel town" or a "pulp and paper town" in the early stages of its development the distinction is fairly clear. But today most of the people in any urban region are engaged in services, and services as well as goods can be exported. In the small city of Moncton, New Brunswick, the University is an exporter of educational services; most of the students and most of the users of research products come from outside the Moncton region. Retail shopping centres are also exporters; people come from as far away as the province of Prince Edward Island to shop in Moncton. The fact is that most enterprises, whether producing goods or services, serve both an internal and an external market, and any division into non-basic and basic industries must be to some degree arbitrary. For that reason, too, we cannot avoid the problems of defining "base industries" merely by resorting to "export industries" instead.

These criticisms do not mean that exports are unimportant for regional growth, nor that the export multiplier does not operate. And once a region is defined, we can determine and even measure the volume of its exports. What we cannot do is make a rigorous distinction between "base" or "export" industries and others, and explain regional growth in terms of this distinction.

Conclusion

Where does this bird's eye-view survey of interregional trade leave us? What we have seen most clearly is that we are able to explain in an *ad hoc* pragmatic way, patterns of location and interregional trade, and their impact on regional development, *after the event*. We can list the factors involved and perhaps rank them according to their importance in determining the course of events. However, we do not have, and we are unlikely soon (if ever) to have a general theory that can *predict* what *will happen* to a particular region. To do that, we will have to take a long, hard look at the region itself, and at other regions with which it is related, and analyze carefully what we see.

Readers who were hoping for simple recipes for regional development should not be too discouraged by this conclusion. We shall see as we go along that there are quite a few partial theories that are very helpful in formulating policy and making plans for regional development. We shall see also that there is an accumulation of empirical knowledge about regional development upon which we can draw.

Notes

1. David Hume, "On the Balance of Trade," *Political Discourses*, 1752, reprinted in A.E. Monroe (ed.), *Early Economic Thought Selections from Economic Literature Prior to Adam Smith* (Cambridge, Mass.: Harvard University Press, 1948), p. 327.

2. Adam Smith, *The Wealth of Nations* (New York: P.F. Collier, 1902).

3. John Stuart Mill, *Principles of Political Economy: With Some of Their Applications to Social Philosophy* (London: Longmans, Green, 1865).

4. J.E. Cairnes, *The Character and Logical Method of Political Economy* (New York: Kelley, 1888).

5. J.S. Nicholson, *Principles of Political Economy*, 2nd edition, A and C Black, 1901–3 (3 vols; Vol. 1 is London, first edition; Vol. 2, 1897, p. 294).

6. P.T. Ellsworth, *The International Economy* (New York: Macmillan, 1958).

7. Frank Taussig, *International Trade* (New York: Macmillan, 1928), pp. 67-8 and chapter six.

8. Ellsworth, *The International Economy*, p. 84.

9. *Ibid.*, p. 86.

10. *Ibid.*, p. 123.

11. *Ibid.*, p. 89.

12. Bertil Ohlin, *International and Interregional Trade* (Cambridge, Mass.: Harvard University Press, 1933), p. 582.

13. *Ibid.*

14. Paul Samuelson, "International Trade and the Equalization of Factor Prices," *The Economic Journal*, vol. 58 (LVIII), June 1948.

15. See also the work of Paul Krugman notably Paul Krugman *Geography and Trade*, (Cambridge, Mass: The MIT Press, 1991) and "Increasing Returns and Long Run Growth," *Journal of Political Economy*, Vol. 94, no. 4, pp. 1002-37.

16. Lawrence Towle, *International Trade and Commercial Policy* (New York: Harper and Brothers, 1956), p. 188.

17. Walter Isard, *Methods of Regional Analysis: An Introduction to Regional Science* (Cambridge, Mass.: M.I.T. Press, 1960), p. 192.

18. Douglass North, *The Economic Growth of the United States 1790–1860* (New York: Norton, 1966).

19. *Ibid.*, p. 1.

20. *Ibid.*, pp. 6-7.

21. Harry Richardson, *Elements of Regional Economics: Location Theory, Urban Structure, and Regional Change* (Baltimore, Md.: Penguin, 1969), p. 166.

22. *Ibid.*, p. 166.

5

Circular and Cumulative Causation

This chapter, and the next one, are devoted to general theories of development which were originally formulated to explain the development and under-development of whole societies and national economies; but which have been applied to the explanation of chronic regional disparities as well. They resemble each other in arguing that a free market, in and of itself, does not guarantee steady growth, or dynamic equilibrium, either throughout time or throughout space. Far more likely, the arguments run, is that market economies, left to themselves, will generate disequilibrium, imbalance, uneven development, and growing inequalities among regions and social groups.

To understand the contribution of these theories to regional analysis, it is necessary to look at each of them as a whole. Their specific application to regional development, regional interactions, and regional gaps does not stand on its own. Successful application depends on the appearance in specific spatial form of more general phenomena observed at the level of national economies and societies. Whether or not these phenomena appear in the form of regional interactions is a question of observed fact; the answer cannot be deduced directly from the conclusions reached regarding national economies from the general theories.

This statement sounds more complicated than it really is. Let us illustrate it with an example or two. The theory expounded in the next chapter states that under certain conditions, which occur almost always in colonial regimes, and quite frequently in neo-colonial and other regimes as well, development of the national economy divides into two distinct sectors: one, the "modern" sector, is capital-intensive, with advanced technology, and a high level of output per person-year; the other, the "traditional" sector, is labour-intensive, uses a simple, traditional technology, and has a low level of output per person-year. This phenomenon is called "bi-modal production," or "technological dualism." A national economy will be relatively highly developed and prosperous if the modern sector predominates. It will be relatively underdeveloped and poor if the traditional sector predominates.

73

Assuming that this theory is scientifically established, does it also explain regional disparities? Obviously, it does if the modern sector is concentrated in one or two regions, while the traditional sector is concentrated in others. If, on the other hand, both modern and traditional sectors are even distributed through-out space, the theory of bi-modal production or technological dualism cannot explain regional disparities. So the answer depends on the facts. The observed facts are, of course, that where significant regional gaps are found, marked differences among regions with regard to occupational structures, product-mix, technology, and factor proportions are nearly always found too. In other words, the blend of modern and traditional economic activities varies from region to region, with corresponding differences in per capita output and in-comes. Bi-modal production, technological dualism, and "regional dualism," are virtually the same thing. Consequently, the theory of bi-modal production and the question as to whether it is right or wrong is extremely important for regional analysis.

The "dependency theory" presented in the chapter 9 states that the interna-tional capitalists, who run the non-socialist world, have both the will and the power to hold peasant incomes and wages down in order to keep their profits up; and also the power to buy cheap and sell dear in less developed countries. At home (in the "Centre," the Industrialized Capitalist Countries) the capital-ists face stronger trade unions, and stronger left-of-centre political parties, and find it expedient to share a bit more of their profits with the workers, reluctant though they may be to do so.

If *this* theory is true, does it explains regional gaps *within* national econo-mies, as well as the international gaps between ICCs and LDCs? Again, the answer depends on the facts. If the relative bargaining power of the capitalists on the one hand, and of governments (to the degree that they are not merely "creatures" of the capitalists), peasants and farmers, and workers on the other, were evenly distributed throughout space in every country in the world, then the dependency theory could not explain regional disparities, even if the theory were validated as an explanation of *international* disparities. There is clearly some interrelationship between the applicability of the dependency theory at the regional level and the applicability of the theory of bi-modal production. That is, capacity of capitalists to exploit workers and peasants is more likely to vary significantly from region to region within the same country if various regions are producing different things in different ways, than it will if every region is producing the same things in the same ways. In any case, a good many neo-Marxists and radical political economists have maintained that the poorer regions in any capitalist country are those that are the most readily exploited by the international capitalists; they are occupied by social groups that are particularly weak in bargaining power.

∠ Applicability at the regional level is more difficult to test for the dependency theory than it is for the theory of technological dualism. One must have a measure of relative bargaining power that is independent of the results of differences in bargaining power. To measure bargaining power by incomes, health, education, housing or other social indices would be circular reasoning and thus scientifically illegitimate. It is not easy (although not altogether impossible) to devise independent measures of bargaining power and attach numbers to them. Nonetheless, the dependency theory has a good many vigorous and able exponents, and if the theory is both correct and applicable at the regional level, it has enormous implications for regional analysis, regional policy and regional planning. It is therefore incumbent upon us to examine it thoroughly.

The third set of theories, concerned with circular and cumulative causation, feedback effects, economic fluctuations and movements away from equilibrium, have perhaps had the most impact on economic thought of all the new theories introduced since World War II. To these theories we now turn.

Circular and Cumulative Causation

A major component of the foundations of the neoclassical system of economic thought is the notion that free market economies tend to move towards "equilibrium," to stay in equilibrium once established and to return to "equilibrium" if temporarily dislodged by some "shock" emanating "from outside the system." This notion was borrowed from physics, without much empirical evidence that economic systems are similar enough to those in the world of nature to warrant the use of the same concepts. However, in the skilled hands of the neoclassical economists, pure logic can demonstrate the necessity of the principles regarding equilibrium, once the basic assumptions of the neoclassical system, and especially the behavioural assumptions, are accepted.

The neoclassical economists have never been altogether comfortable when compelled to recognize the existence of heterogeneous space, and the implications of the equilibrium principles for the distribution of economic activity, employment, and incomes in space were never very clearly spelled out. Nevertheless, the basic idea was certainly that the free market would bring "equilibrium," and an optimal allocation of resources, throughout space as well as time. Regional disparities are an affront to neoclassical economists. Their suspicion always is that where regional gaps occur, it is because some misguided government is delaying or obstructing the movements of labour, capital and technology that would eliminate them, through some inappropriate and unwarranted intervention in the free market.[1]

In recent decades there have been challenges to the idea that a free market always tends to establish and maintain equilibrium, quite distinct from those emanating from the neo-Marxists and radical political economists. Far from a market system generating forces that will return it to equilibrium when disturbed, the new argument maintains, it is more likely to generate a process of cumulative causation that will carry it further and further *away* from equilibrium.

One of the first and most influential presentations of this new idea came from the very heart of the neoclassical establishment itself. In the April 1946 issue of *Econometrica*, Evsey Domar of M.I.T. published his seminal article, "Capital Expansion, Rate of Growth and Employment," presenting his "knife-edge theory;" dynamic equilibrium, or steady growth with full employment and no inflation, is about as difficult as balancing the world on a knife-edge, so stringent and improbable are the conditions that must be met. Two years later Sir Roy Harrod of Oxford published his book, *Towards a Dynamic Economics*, providing a more extensive treatment of a similar idea; that a market economy, once disturbed from equilibrium, will tend to move even further from it. In 1950 Sir John Hicks, also of Oxford, brought out his book on *The Trade Cycle*, which leaned heavily on Harrod's book. Hicks states that when he read it "everything began to fall in place," and adds, "I could have kicked myself for not having seen it before."[2] In 1955, Benjamin Higgins published an article entitled "Interaction of Cycles and Trends," in *The Economic Journal*, which carried the Hicks analysis one step further.

Finally, in 1957, Nobel Laureate Gunnar Myrdal published his book on *Economic Theory and Under-developed Regions*, which applied the principal of circular and cumulative causation specifically to the problem of regional disparities. Myrdal was himself a product of the neoclassical tradition, and particularly of his mentors Knut Wicksell and Gustav Cassel. His earlier works, which established his world-wide reputation, were very much in that tradition. As he widened and deepened his experience, however, he found himself—as he himself expressed it—increasingly swimming "against the stream."[3]

Let us take a brief look at these related theories, and see what light they cast on problem of regional development.

Domar's "Knife-edge"

In the economics literature one encounters frequent references to the "Harrod-Domar thesis," as though the arguments of these two economists, demonstrating the essential instability of a market economy, were virtually identical. In fact they are quite different. Domar's theory is cast in terms of the mechanics of a market economy at the macro-level, and states the conditions necessary, in an essentially tautological fashion, for steady growth of such a national economy, with full employment and without inflation. Harrod is concerned with reactions of individual entrepreneurs and investors to the outcome of the interplay of market forces, and the effects of these reactions on subsequent outcomes in the market. His theory rests upon a particular set of behavioural assumptions.

Domar assumes that some national economy is growing steadily with full employment and stable prices, and asks what conditions must be met for it to stay like that. He uses the following symbols: Y_d is the level of effective demand, or national income; accordingly, ΔY_d is the (annual) increase in national income; I is investment, ΔI, the (annual) increase in investment; Y_s is the level of effective supply, or total annual output of goods and services, with full employment and full use of capacity; K is the stock of real capital; σ is the marginal propensity to save (proportion of increases in national income saved) and $\frac{1}{\sigma}$ is therefore the Keynesian multiplier relating increases in national income to increases in investment; a is the incremental output: capital ratio, relating increases in national output to increases in net investment. ($\Delta Y_s /I$).

We then have the following equations:

Level of effective demand $Y_d = I \cdot \frac{1}{\sigma}$ .... (1)

Level of productive capacity $Y_s = \alpha K$ .... (2)

Equilibrium condition $Y_d = Y_s$ or $I \cdot \frac{1}{\sigma} = \alpha \cdot K$ .... (3)

Increment of demand $\Delta Y_d = \frac{\Delta I}{\sigma}$ .... (4)

Increment of capacity $\Delta Y_s = \Delta K = I$ .... (5)

Equilibrium condition $\Delta Y_d = \Delta Y_s$ or $\frac{\Delta I}{\sigma} = \alpha I$ .... (6)

Growth rate of investment $r = \frac{\Delta I}{I} = \alpha \sigma$ .... (7)

Thus for steady growth,

The growth rate of demand must be $\frac{\Delta Y_d}{Y_d} = \frac{\Delta I/\sigma}{Y_d} = \frac{\Delta I}{I} = \alpha \sigma$ .... (8)

Thus steady growth requires investment to grow at the same percentage rate as national income, and that rate must be equal to a specific figure, the marginal propensity to save X the incremental capital: output ratio. Starting with full employment and stable prices, if investment falls below this required figure, unemployment will occur; if investment rises above this figure the result will be inflation. Since there are no automatic forces in a market economy that could assure that these equilibrium conditions are met, even if, by some miracle, a national economy enjoys a period of steady growth with full employment and stable prices, this happy state of affairs almost certainly will not last, unless the economy is astutely managed through monetary, fiscal, and other policies.

Since the Domar theory is completely general, it applies to regional economies as much as to national economies. However, as formulated by Domar,
the theory applies to closed economies, not engaged in trade or capital movements outside its borders. Since regional economies are, almost by definition, more open than the national economy of which they are a part, it is
even more essential to consider influences from outside its borders than is
the case with national economies. Within its own framework, however, given
its simplifying assumptions, the Domar thesis is a useful reminder of the
difficulty of attaining steady growth, stable prices, and full employment in
any regional economy.

Harrod's Cumulative Causation

Harrod posits a certain type of universal entrepreneurial behaviour, whereby
investment decisions (and presumably related other decisions as well) are based
on a certain anticipated rate of growth. Harrod casts this growth in terms of
national income. While in industrialized countries the increasingly sophisticated business community does pay a good deal of attention to forecasts of
national income, and of national rates of unemployment and inflation as well,
no doubt expectations as to what will happen to their own sales play an important role in their decision-making. These will, of course, be influenced by
what happens in the economy as a whole, but they will also be affected by
factors specific to each enterprise. Harrod, of course, is well aware of all these
factors, but to keep his analysis simple he uses growth of national income as a
kind of shorthand or blanket term to cover all of them. Harrod also assumes
that if things turn out exactly as expected, the investment decisions of the last
period will be repeated in the next. If growth exceeds expectations, investment will be increased; and if growth is disappointing, investment will be
diminished.

Harrod's basic equation is GC = s: where G is the growth during a unit of
time, $\Delta Y/Y$; C is net capital accumulation in the period (including goods in
process and stocks), divided by the increase in output in the period, $I/\Delta Y$; and
s is the average propensity to save, S/Y. Thus the equation is really a restate-
ment of the truism that *ex post* savings equals *ex post* investment; it could be
written:

$$\frac{\Delta Y}{Y} \cdot \frac{I}{\Delta Y} = \frac{S}{Y} \leftrightarrow \frac{I}{Y} = \frac{S}{Y} \leftrightarrow I = S$$

Harrod's second fundamental equation, $G_w C_r = s$, expresses the equilibrium conditions for a steady advance. G_w, the "warranted rate of growth," is
the value of $\Delta Y/Y$ that barely satisfies entrepreneurs; C_r, the "capital require-

ments," is the value of $I/\Delta Y$ that is needed to sustain the warranted rate of growth. It will be noted that s is the same in both equations. Thus in dynamic equilibrium (stable value of $\Delta Y/Y$), $G_w C_r = GC$; the actual, or *ex post* value of I/Y, equals the equilibrium value, which is a subjective phenomenon. Moreover, G must equal G_w and C must equal C_r. For if G exceeds G_w, then C will be below C_r; that is, entrepreneurs will consider the amount of capital accumulation inadequate to sustain the increase in total output and will increase their orders for capital goods (and conversely). But then G will depart still further from G_w in the next period, and a cumulative movement away from equilibrium will set in. Thus: "Around the line of advance which, if adhered to, would alone give satisfaction, centrifugal forces are at work, causing the system to depart further and further from the required line of advance."[4]

There are two possible interpretations of Harrod's argument that if G exceeds G_w, C must be below C_r, and vice versa. If $G_w C_r = GC = s$ by assumption, then the proposition follows by mere arithmetic. Harrod's presentation, however, suggests that he thinks $G_w C_r$ must equal GC for economic and definitional reasons, in much the same way that *ex post* savings *must* equal *ex post* investment. It is hard to see that such is the case. It is clear enough that G and C must vary inversely with a given I/Y or C. But why should the equilibrium ratio of (*ex post*) savings and investment to income (i.e., the ratio that satisfies entrepreneurs, or $G_w C_r$ = equilibrium $\frac{I=S}{Y}$) be continuously equal to the actual ratio of savings and investment to income (GC, or *actual* $\frac{I=S}{Y}$)?

Harrod's main argument does not depend upon the equality of GC and $G_w C_r$ anyhow. It depends rather on the acceleration principle (or better, on the "relation"). For if G exceeds G_w, what this really means is that the rate of increase in total spending is greater than is necessary to call forth the current rate of investment, and consequently investment will increase. By definition, if the rate of investment is above the equilibrium level, C_r is below C. Such a situation would be inconsistent with an excess of GC (actual $I/Y = S/Y$) over $G_w C_r$ (equilibrium $I/Y = S/Y$), since investment cannot be simultaneously above and below the equilibrium level, but it would be quite consistent with an excess of $G_w C_r$ over GC. That is, C – C_r may exceed G_w – G; entrepreneurs may consider actual investment low, not only relative to the actual rate of increase in consumer spending, but also relative to the level of income. In this case there would be a double incentive to increase investment in the next period. The movement away from equilibrium when G > G_w, and *in addition* GC > $G_w C_r$, will be greater than if G > G_w but GC = $G_w C_r$.

Harrod anticipates the criticism that his formulation gives too much weight to the acceleration principle, and he suggests that the criticism could be met by rewriting the first equation GC = s – k, where k is investment not due to the current increase in orders for output. It is not quite clear how much investment is meant to go into k and how much into C. C would presumably not include primary investment induced by innovations—let us say, building of automobile factories in the early stages of the automobile long wave, or "Kondratieff." But would the petroleum refineries, rubber plantations, and roadside restaurants brought into being by the automobile Kondratieff go into C or into k? Harrod says k will include "capital outlay which no one expects to see justified or not justified in a fairly short period."[5] How long is that? As will appear below, it is not a matter of indifference how investment is distributed between C and k.

Another problem arises in connection with C and C_r. The "relation" usually expresses the extent to which investment increases as a consequence of increases in demand for the final products of plant and equipment of a given type. For the "relation" to operate in the economy as a whole (without any change in the period of investment, which is not closely related to rates of consumption, and which Harrod excludes from this part of his analysis), there must be a change in the rate of consumer spending. The relation might be expressed as $I = r \cdot dC_n$. Harrod argues throughout as though an increase in income necessarily entailed an increase in consumption, and also as though an increase in investment would always bring with it an increase in consumption. Why else would the increase in investment, $C_r \Delta Y$, resulting from an excess of G over G_w, (excess of C_r over C) carry the system *further* from equilibrium?

Harrod's point is, it will be remembered, that the greater investment brought about by $C_r > C$ will raise G still further above G_w. In the context of his argument, this proposition must mean that the increase in investment in the next period will bring with it an increase in the rate of expansion of consumer spending $\Delta C_n / C_n$. Now, if the increased investment is deficit financed, it is quite likely that the increase in rate of expansion of consumption that accompanies an increase in investment, $\frac{d}{dI}(\frac{dC_n}{C_n})$, will be positive; for then the multiplier will operate on the increase in I and so raise consumer spending substantially. But in most of Harrod's argument, savings and investment are always equal; if entrepreneurs consider their investment too low, they also consider their saving too low. An increase in investment financed by an equal and simultaneous increase in saving will not raise income at all, and consumption will actually fall. In this event, investment in period 2 will be too high, rather than still too low, and will be reduced rather than raised in period 3, and so on. The initial excess of G over G_w would in this case set up a series of damped fluctuations, and in the absence of a new disturbance, the system would tend toward a new equilibrium with the actual $\frac{I=S}{Y}$ equal to the equilibrium $\frac{I=S}{Y}$, and so with $G = G_w$ and $GC = G_w C_r$.

The manner in which new investment is financed is crucial to Harrod's analysis. Unless he can demonstrate beyond a shadow of doubt that it is *impossible* for enough of an increase in investment to be financed by new savings to make $\frac{d}{dI}(\frac{dC_n}{C})$ zero or negative, he can argue that an initial divergence of G and G_w *may* start a cumulative movement; but he cannot argue that it *must* start a cumulative movement.

Harrod's third fundamental equation is $G_n C_r$ may or may not be equal to s; here G_n is the "natural rate of growth" or "that steady rate of advance determined by fundamental conditions."[6] What G_n really seems to be is the rate of increase in output at full employment, given the rate of population increase and the rate of technological progress. A better term would have been "potential rate of growth"; there is nothing very natural about full employment. It will be noted that, whereas Harrod seems to feel that $G_w C_r$ must equal GC, he stresses the possibility that $G_n C_r$ may not equal GC, by making $G_n C_r$ equal, or not equal, to s.

With the introduction of G_n, Harrod is able to develop a theory of increasing underemployment for advanced economies. If G_w exceeds G_n (as it well may when population growth tapers off, or the rate of improvement in technique or discovery of new resources tapers off), G will also tend to lie below G_w, C will be chronically above C_r, and the economy will be chronically depressed. (After all, G can exceed G_n only in the recovery phase of the cycle.) Conversely, in a rapidly expanding economy (where population growth, or technological progress, or geographic expansion is at a high level) there will be a chronic excess of G_n over G_w, and also of G over G_w, and thus a chronic excess of C_r over C, and a perpetual tendency for an inflationary boom to develop. We might call economies of the former type "deflationary gap" economies and of the latter type, "inflationary gap" economies. We shall have something to say later on as to whether or not underdeveloped countries are, by definition, "inflationary gap" countries as well. Harrod's general conclusion about the "virtue of saving" should surprise no one; it is a "good thing" in an "inflationary gap" economy, and a "bad thing" in a "deflationary gap" economy.

The causal relation between G_w and s is one of many problems that could have been made clearer by an elaboration of the central concept, G_w. The term "warranted rate of growth" is not a very happy one for what Harrod seems to have in mind. Nor is "the line of entrepreneurial contentment"[7] a very clear-cut definition of G_w. In his *Economic Journal,* article of March, 1939, he defines G_w as "that rate of growth which if it occurs, will leave all parties satisfied that they have produced neither more nor less that the right amount;" it is the rate that "will put them in the frame of mind which will cause them to give such orders as will maintain the same rate of growth." Thus G_w is subjective, but not, apparently, *ex ante*; it is the rate of growth that makes entrepreneurs satisfied with what has happened, rather than a plan for the future.[8]

Although reference to the article makes Harrod's concept of G_w a bit clearer, it still does not tell us what Harrod thinks are the determinants of G_w; and what determines G_w is obviously all-important, for C_r depends on G_w; it is, indeed, defined in terms of G_w. G and C cannot be changed except as a result of entrepreneurial decisions, and these decisions depend on G_w. Thus what happens in Harrod's dynamic economy depends ultimately on G_w. Harrod nowhere presents an analysis of the determinants of G_w, but in the course of his discussion he does indicate the following relationships:

G_w varies (1) inversely with C_r (capital requirements); (2) directly with s (the average propensity to save); (3) inversely with the volume of public works; (4) inversely with the volume of investment, that is, independent of the current rate of growth, k; (5) directly with the rate of interest r (since k and C_r vary inversely with r, and s probably varies directly with r).

The first of these relationships is arithmetic. Given s, G_w must vary inversely with C_r, just as G varies inversely with C. There are no clues to entrepreneurial behaviour here. The second relationship has already been discussed; it, too, seems to be a matter of definition rather than of business behaviour. Relationships (3) and (4) really amount to the same thing. Public works are one kind of investment that need not depend solely on the current rate of growth of income and that may, therefore, be included in k. Since $G_w C_r = s - k$, by definition, any increase in k must, other things being equal, be accompanied by a reduction in G_w. The fifth relationship is a product of several others:

1. s varies directly with r, and since G_w varies directly with s, G_w varies directly with r.
2. k varies inversely with r, G_w varies inversely with k, and therefore, G_w varies directly with r.
3. C_r varies inversely with r, G_w varies inversely with C_r, and therefore, G_w varies directly with r.

The relationship between s and r is a true causal relationship; s(r) is a savings function with psychological meaning: savings depend on the interest rate. The same is true of the k(r) function, which is really the marginal efficiency of capital schedule: investment depends on the rate of interest. The C_r (r) function is the period of investment, which also has meaningful content: as the interest rate falls, the capital-output ratio will be increased. But G_w (r) has no meaning of its own whatsoever; given the other relationships, the dG_w/dr is given by definition. Thus not one of these G_w relationships is a truly causal one, with meaning in terms of entrepreneurial behaviour.

Finally, Harrod adds two refinements. If d represents the fraction of income needed for capital involved in lengthening the production process ("deepening"), then $G_w C_r = s - d$. If inventions are capital saving, d is negative, and the equilibrium rate of growth is enhanced. Thus any tendency toward chronic underemployment resulting from $G_w > G_n$ will be aggravated by capital-saving inventions. Harrod thinks falling interest rates might tend to lengthen the period of production and so keep d positive.

In his fourth chapter, "The Foreign Balance," Harrod points out that when we move to an open economy, the appropriate equations are $GC = s - b$ and $G_w C_r = s - b$, where b is the foreign balance. The equation expresses what is already well known: in a country with chronic underemployment, $G_w > G_n$, a favourable balance of trade on goods and services account helps to reduce the deflationary gap—and conversely for countries with a chronic inflationary gap.

Like the Domar model, the Harrod model can be applied to regional as well as to national economies. Indeed, Harrod's specific introduction of "the foreign balance" into his model makes it more relevant to fluctuations and growth in regional economies than the Domar model. His concentration on entrepreneurial decision-making, their expectations regarding growth of the economy in which they operate, and whether or not they are likely to be pleased with what actually happens or are foredoomed to disappointment, also gives us helpful clues to the growth, stagnation, or decline of particular regional economies. It is because of this greater usefulness in understanding regional economies that we have accorded Harrod's model so much more space than Domar's. Both models, however, lead to the conclusion that once a regional economy strays from the path of steady growth, with full employment and no inflation, there is little reason to expect automatic market forces to bring it back to that path. Far more likely is a cumulative movement away from it, in the absence of well-chosen and effective policies.

Daniel Hamberg demonstrates mathematically what is really apparent intuitively: the Domar and Harrod models become identical if, in Harrod's terms, $G_w = G_n$.[9] That is, if the economy is on the full-employment, full-capacity path and this is what entrepreneurs like, then both Domar's and Harrod's conditions will be met if income and investment continue to grow at the same constant rate, equal to G_n. But there is no assurance that such will be the case. Entrepreneurs may not be happy with growing excess capacity or swelling inventories, or even with a chronic excess of orders over capacity production; but they can be content for a long time with chronic inflation, chronic underemployment, or both. In advanced countries and regions, many businessmen identify their own prosperity with a high level of employment in the economy as a whole. In underdeveloped countries, this identification is much less common.

It is worth noting in passing that the conditions laid down by Harrod and Domar are by no means the only ones that must be met for steady growth. If wages are too high in relation to prices, profits are squeezed, investment falls, and with it income and employment. If wages are too low in relation to prices, there is a "shift to profits," the propensity to consume falls, investment follows, and income and employment fall again. Other distortions of the price structure can also bring trouble. If interest rates are temporarily too low in relation to wage rates, investment may be excessively concentrated in capital-intensive projects and techniques, building up a structure of capital that will prove to have too high a capital-output ratio and so be unprofitable when interest rates rise again. Anticipations regarding prices, wages, profits, etc., must be fulfilled, or else windfall losses and gains must precisely offset each other and factors of production must be completely mobile. *Ex ante* (planned) and *ex post* investment must both exceed *ex ante* savings by a constant percentage amount. Technological progress and resource discovery must be steady and neutral, population growth must be constant. Indeed when all the ways in which "lapses from steady growth" may occur are taken into account, it is a wonder that recent growth in industrialized countries has been as steady as it has been.

Gunnar Myrdal's Theory of Cumulative Causation

Myrdal begins his exposition of the principle of cumulative causation, not with an economic illustration, but with a sociological one. He quotes the Bible (St. Matthew xxv; 29): "For unto everyone that hath shall be given, and he shall have abundance; but from him who hath not shall be taken away even that which he hath." He then proceeds to the case of the American Blacks, drawn from the famous book by his wife Alva and himself, *The American Dilemma.* "In its simplest form the explanatory model can be reduced to two factors: "white prejudice," causing discrimination against the Negro in various respects, and the "low plane of living" of the Negro population. These two factors are mutually inter-related: the Negroes' low plane of living is kept down by discrimination from the whites while, on the other side, the Negroes' poverty, ignorance, superstition, slum dwellings, health deficiencies, dirty appearance, bad odour, disorderly conduct, unstable family relations and criminality stimulate and feed the antipathy of whites for Negroes. White prejudice and low Negro standards thus mutually "cause each other."[10]

Thus for Myrdal circular and cumulative causation is not a characteristic of the economy alone, but a deeply engrained characteristic of human society as a whole. The whole concept of "stable equilibrium" is "a false analogy" when applied to social reality. A particular social process may be stopped, social forces might temporarily balance each and bring change to a halt for a while, an economy may stagnate; but "there is no such tendency towards self-stabilization in the social system."[11]

In the third chapter of his book Myrdal turns to "The Drift Towards Regional Economic Inequalities in a Country." At the outset of the chapter he states again that "the principle of interlocking, circular inter-dependence within a process of cumulative causation...should be the main hypothesis when studying economic under-development and development." Suppose that a factory which is a town's main employer burns down, and that it would not pay to rebuild it in the same place, Myrdal postulates. The firm goes out of business and its workers become unemployed. Incomes and demand fall, causing other businesses which formerly sold to the firm and its employees to discharge workers, adding to the unemployment. The town becomes less attractive to outside businesses and workers who were contemplating moving into it. In time, businesses established in the town and workers living there will increasingly find reasons for moving out. This emigration will further decrease incomes and demand, leading to bankruptcy and still more unemployment. "A process of circular causation has so been started with effects which cumulate in the fashion of the vicious circle."[12] As Benjamin Higgins stated in the first edition of his book on *Economic Development*: "The road to development is paved with vicious circles." Myrdal also makes the point that the emigration from the dying town will have adverse effects on the population structure; it will be the younger, better educated, more dynamic and ambitious adults who will move out, leaving behind older and less highly skilled adults, and children of parents living on unemployment insurance or welfare, or parents who have no hope of employment elsewhere.

The cumulative process, of course, can work in both directions. If instead of a factory burning down a major enterprise decides to locate in the town, a cumulative process of expansion will occur. Total employment and spending will rise, stimulating other firms to expand and attracting other enterprises to locate there.

The same sort of principle applies with respect to the entire regions: "The main idea I want to convey in this book is that the play of the forces in the market normally tends to increase, rather than decrease, the inequality between regions. If things were left to market forces unhampered by any policy interferences, industrial production, commerce, banking, insurance, shipping, and indeed almost all of those economic activities which in a developing economy tend to give a bigger than average return—and, in addition, science, art, literature, education and high culture generally, would cluster in certain localities and regions, leaving the rest of the country more or less in a backwater."[13]

Very often, Myrdal states the agglomerative attraction and polarization of particular centres and regions have their origin in historical accident: something got started there, and not in other places and then the whole cumulative process of expansion got under way. We can see in Myrdal's argument, once

again, the importance of *moving* frontiers in the reduction of regional disparities. By attracting enterprise and economic activity to one region after another
the moving frontier diffuses the cumulative expansion to region after region—
in the American case, as we have seen, eventually spreading it throughout the
whole country.

Expansion of one region may have either favourable of unfavourable effects on other regions. Myrdal calls these "spread effects" and "backwash
effects" respectively: "It is easy to see how expansion in one locality has "backwash effects" in other localities. More specifically the movements of labour,
capital, goods and services do not by themselves counteract the natural tendency to regional inequality. By themselves, migration, capital movements,
and trade are rather the media through which the cumulative process evolves—
upwards in the lucky regions and downwards in the unlucky ones. In general,
if they have positive results for the former, their effects on the latter are negative. The localities and regions where economic activity is expanding will
attract net immigration from other parts of the country. As migration is always
selective, at least with respect to the migrant's age, this movement by itself
tends to favour the rapidly growing communities and disfavour the other."[14]

In some regions backwash and spread effects may balance each other for a
period, giving an appearance of "equilibrium." However, Myrdal insists, "This
condition is not the equilibrium of neoclassical theory, but rather stagnation.
It is not a steady state; any change in the forces at work can launch a cumulative process upwards or downwards.[15]

When Myrdal was Executive Secretary of the United Nations Economic
Commission for Europe, he organized a study of regional development and
underdevelopment in Europe. The results, which were published in the *Economic Survey of Europe in 1954*, were highly interesting: (1) regional gaps
were large in the poorer countries, small in the richer ones; (2) regional gaps
are increasing in the poorer countries, diminishing in the richer ones. In those
days Italy, Turkey and Spain, along with Greece, Yugoslavia and Portugal,
were still regarded as underdeveloped countries. In such countries, with regional inequality defined as the proportion of the population living in regions
where the average income was less than two thirds of the national average, the
gap was about 33 percent, compared to some 10 percent in such countries as
Norway and France, and only "a few percent" in Great Britain and
Switzerland.[16]

In addition, in the countries where regional gaps were large they were also
increasing; where gaps were small they were diminishing. Myrdal comments:
"A large part of the explanation for these two broad correlations may be found
in the important fact that the higher the level of economic development that a
country has already attained, the stronger the spread effects will usually be....

The neutralization of backwash effects, when a country reaches a high level of development where the spread effects are strong, will itself spur on economic development, and so becomes an important factor in the cumulative process. For with the extinction of abject poverty on a large scale goes a fuller utilization of the potentialities of the human resources in a nation.... In contrast, part of the curse of a low level of development in a country is the fact that the spread effects there are weak."[17]

Myrdal believed that the free market works better at high levels of development than it does at low levels; that is, there is more chance that spread effects will outweigh backwash effects. But he also believed that the more advanced countries are more likely to introduce an effective welfare state, including measures to reduce regional inequalities and thus keep the upward cumulative movement going: "The more effectively a national state becomes a welfare state—motivated in a way which approaches a more perfect democracy, and having at its disposal national resources big enough to carry out large-scale egalitarian policies with bearable sacrifices on the part of the regions and groups that are relatively better off—the stronger will be both the urge and the capacity to counteract the blind market forces which tend to result in regional inequalities; and this, again, will spur economic development in the country, and so on and so on, in circular causation."[18]

With these views, it is not surprising that Myrdal agreed with the dependency theorists that international trade and investment can have backwash effects in the poorer countries, just as interregional trade and investment can have backwash effects on the poorer regions. It also is no surprise that he was an advocate of a managed economy, more or less along the lines of the Social Democrats in his own country.

Notes

1. Tom Courchene and James Melvin, "A Neoclassical Approach to Regional Economics," in Benjamin Higgins and Donald J. Savoie (eds), *Regional Economic Development: Essays in Honour of François Perroux* (London and Boston: Unwin Hyman, 1988). See also Courchene, *Economic Management and the Division of Powers* (Toronto: University of Toronto Press, 1986), pp. 169–92.
2. Hicks, John R., *A Contribution to the Theory of Trade Cycle* (Oxford: Clarendon Press, 1950), p. 7.
3. Gunnar Myrdal, *Against the Stream* (New York: Vintage Books, 1973).
4. Roy Harrod, *Towards a Dynamic Economics: Some Recent Developments of Economic Theory and Their Application to Policy* (London: Macmillan, 1948), p. 86.
5. *Ibid.*, p. 79.
6. *Ibid.*, p. 87.
7. *Ibid.*, p. 88.
8. Harrod also explains in his article that he uses "the unprofessional term warranted instead of equilibrium," because the equilibrium is a "highly unstable

one." Stable or unstable, the term "equilibrium" conveys more meaning than "warranted."

9. Daniel Hamberg, *Economic Growth and Instability* (New York: W.W. Norton, 1956).

10. Gunnar Myrdal, *An American Dilemma: The Negro Problem and Modern Democracy* (New York: Harper & Row, 1962), p. 16.

11. *Ibid.*, p. 13.

12. *Ibid.*, p. 23.

13. *Ibid.*, p. 26.

14. *Ibid.*, p. 27.

15. *Ibid.*, p. 33.

16. *Ibid.*, p. 33.

17. *Ibid.*, p. 34.

18. *Ibid.*, p. 51.

6

Growth Poles and Central Places

Of all the concepts utilized since World War II in the formulation of regional policy and preparation of regional development plans, none generated so rapid a rise in popularity, nor so early and so complete disillusionment, as "growth poles." During the late 1960s and early 1970s, there was scarcely a developed or a developing country that did not make use of the concept in formulating its development policy. In the form in which it was usually applied, the notion of growth poles made regional development seem so simple. "All you have to do is" to push or pull some industries into some urban centre in a retarded or disadvantaged region, through construction of infrastructure, and incentives or regulations for private investment, and then sit back and watch the "spread effects" of this investment eliminate the gap between that region and the more prosperous and dynamic ones in the same country.

The earlier concept of "central places" did not undergo the same rise and fall of interest, and was scarcely applied as a tool of regional policy at all. The reason for this difference is simple. Central place theory is concerned with the manner in which development of a region generates forces which create an urban centre, as a market place and a provider of services for the agricultural and industrial activities of the region. Thus to create a central place in a retarded or disadvantaged region, one has to know how to develop the region in the first place, a much more complex and difficult task, and one requiring much more, and more continuous intervention than creation of a growth pole in accordance with the more simplistic versions of the growth pole theory. Perhaps one could say that central place theory began as an abstraction and remained just that, and was gradually expanded and refined, without becoming sufficiently operational to be attractive to policy makers. Thus it remained theoretically sound, if not a great deal of use. Growth pole theory, as we shall see, started as and remained a highly abstract portion of a wider general theory, in the mind and writings of its creator, François Perroux. In the hands of Perroux's disciples and of workaday regional planners, desperate as they were

89

to have something workable in practice, growth pole theory became something quite different, conceptually operational but in most real world situations, simply wrong.

Whatever the true nature of the interactions among urban growth, regional economic expansion, and national economic development, it is clear that such interactions are a major aspect of the economic development process, and that they must be understood if we are to understand that process as a whole, thoroughly enough to formulate sound policies and construct effective plans. This chapter is devoted to theories related to these interactions. We begin with growth pole theory, because once that is sorted out, putting central place and other theories in their proper place within a more general theory becomes a relatively simple task.

Growth Poles

Growth pole theory is irrevocably associated with the works of the late professor François Perroux, and it is appropriate that we begin our own survey with them. Perroux was a prolific writer, and remained so right up to his death at the age of 86, as the volume of essays in his honor shows.[1] There can be no question of attempting to cover the evolution of Perroux's thought as a whole in this chapter; readers who want such a survey might turn to the volume already cited. Here we shall present only the bare bones of his theory of growth poles, as the basis for demonstrating how his ideas were distorted and misapplied, and for indicating how the theory might be made both more analytically sound and more applicable in policy formulation and planning.

Perroux's notions about interactions in space first came to the attention of English-speaking social scientists through a lecture delivered at Harvard in 1949, and published in the *Quarterly Journal of Economics* in March 1950.[2] The article was entitled "Economic Spaces, Theory and Applications." Coming so soon after the war, it is not surprising that it expressed concern about European reconstruction and about mounting tensions—already— among European countries. Perroux thought that a false concept of space— territorial, "banal," "geonomic"—was contributing to these tensions. The idea of space as "a container," holding a defined group of people ("the contained") gave rise to territorial demands and conflicts, including protectionism. It was essential to think instead in terms of abstract economic space, spaces as "fields of force," or as space defined by a plan or as homogeneous aggregates, rather than space defined in terms of points, lines, surfaces or volumes. It should be noted that when Perroux spoke here of "space defined by a plan," he was thinking of plans made by private enterprises, not of regional development plans in the usual sense. Since a firm might buy and sell all over the world, its "planning" space need not be geographically contiguous. "The topographical zone of influence of Michelin in France is inscribed in a region, but its economic zone of influence, like that of all large firms, defies cartography.[3]

In the 1950 article the term "growth pole" or "growth centre" does not actually appear, but Perroux does speak of "poles" and "centres," and it is clear that he thinks of them as concentrations of economic activity and as generators of growth. His idea that growth is always polarized (concentrated in particular centres or poles), leading to dominance and dependence, is also present in the article, although not yet spelled out in any detail.

Five years later Perroux published another article in English, although in a French journal, *Économie appliquée*, entitled "A Note on the Notion of Growth Pole," where the main outlines of his growth pole theory are drawn.[4] A more thorough exposition of the theory was contained in his 1961 book *L'Économie du XXe siècle*. Even in the 1955 article, however, the basic concept of growth poles as constellations of dynamic, innovating enterprises, often but not always in urban centres, and generating "effets d'entraînement" (propulsive effects) upstream and downstream, positive (spread effects) or negative (backwash effects) is already present.

Karen Polenske observes: "As a number of previous reviewers, such as Darwent (1969) and Hermansen (1972) have noted, Perroux never made a clear distinction between a growth pole and a growth centre."[5] That neglect was one of the reasons for the confusion surrounding the understanding and the application of Perroux's growth pole theory. He also failed to provide a clear distinction between a growth pole and a development pole. His last effort to do so did not help much, particularly for those who wanted operational concepts as a basis of policy making and planning: "The *growth pole* is a set that has the capacity to induce the growth of another set ("growth" being defined as a lasting increase in the dimensional indicator); *the pole of development* is a set that has the capacity to engender a dialectic of economic and social structures whose effect is to increase the complexity of the whole and to expand its multidimensional return."[6]

In 1969, as part of an exercise to outline a strategy for the development of Quebec, Benjamin Higgins, Fernand Martin and André Raynauld endeavoured to introduce greater clarity into the growth pole concept, and related concepts, while at the same time making them somewhat more operational.[7] Since Perroux defined a development pole as an aggregation of propulsive industries, they considered it convenient to begin the series of concepts and definitions with "propulsive industry." They defined an industry B as "propulsive" with regard to industry A if:

Criticism

$$I_A = f(I_B) \text{ and } \frac{\Delta I_A}{\Delta I_B} > 0 \quad \dots \dots \dots \dots \dots \dots \dots \dots \dots \dots \dots \quad (1)$$

where I_A is investment in industry A and I_B is investment in industry B. We might also express this relationship as

$$I_A = a \cdot I_B \text{ and } \Delta I_A = a \cdot \Delta I \quad \dots \dots \dots \dots \dots \dots \dots \dots \dots \dots \quad (2)$$

In other words, contrary to the original formulation of Perroux, it is not possible to discern propulsive industries by their relative rate of expansion. If a propulsive industry is a particularly powerful generator of spread effects, or if the other industry is a strong reactor, it is possible for the rate of expansion in the "growth industry" A, to be higher than the expansion of the propulsive industry, B, even though it is the propulsive industry that generates the expansion process. With t as time, if:

$$a > 1, \text{ then } \frac{dI_B}{dt} < \frac{dI_A}{dt} \quad \dots \dots \dots \dots \dots \dots \dots \dots \dots \dots \quad (3)$$

Since a "development pole" is defined as an aggregation of "propulsive industries," it follows that its rate of growth *may be lower* than the growth of cities whose expansion depends basically on investments initially taking place in the development pole.

Investment in a development pole affects other cities and regions in various ways. The impact may be expressed in terms of investment, income, employment, population, level of technology, etc. For the moment, however, we shall measure the impact in terms of welfare, W . We shall also assume for convenience that welfare can be measured by per capita income, modified however one wishes by use of social indicators or shadow prices, to take care of objectives regarding income distribution, education, health, nutrition, environmental protection, etc., which are not accurately reflected in national income figures with standard methods of national accounting.

Development Pole

"Development pole" is then conveniently defined in terms of the elasticity of welfare of a peripheral region W_r, to investment in an urban centre. We shall consider that each region r is composed of an urban centre u and a peripheral region r. Thus:

$$r = u + r \quad \dots \dots \dots \dots \dots \dots \dots \dots \dots \dots \dots \dots \dots \quad (4)$$

we will then say that u is a development pole if,

$$\frac{\frac{\Delta W_r}{W_r}}{\frac{\Delta I_u}{I_u}} = \frac{I_u}{W_r} \cdot \frac{\Delta W_r}{\Delta I_u} > 0 \quad \dots \dots \dots \dots \dots \dots \dots \dots \dots \quad (5)$$

That is, investment in the pole generates growth (of welfare) in the entire peripheral region. If the expression in equation (5) is greater than unity, the city is a "dominant" development pole. A 5 percent increase in investment in the pole brings a more than 5 percent increase of income in the peripheral region. If it is greater than zero but less than one, the city is a "sub-dominant" development pole. Once again, if the sum of the a's relating to investment in the development pole to investment in other cities in the system is greater than one, the growth of the development pole will be lower than the growth of the region as a whole.

Growth Centre

We will define a city j as a growth centre if:

$$\frac{\frac{\Delta I_j}{I_j}}{\frac{\Delta I_u}{I_u}} = \frac{I_u}{I_j} \cdot \frac{\Delta I_j}{\Delta I_u} > 0 \dots\dots\dots\dots\dots\dots\dots\dots\dots\dots\dots \quad (6)$$

that is, the percentage change of investment in the city, as a result of investment in the development pole, is positive. If the expression in equation (6) is greater than unity, the city is a "strong" growth centre. If it is greater than zero but less than one, we will describe the city as a "weak" growth centre. Implicitly, there is some multiplier relationship between investment in the city j and income, employment, population growth, technological progress, etc., in the city, so that expansion will take place in terms of all these variables, whenever investment in the city increases.

Propulsive Region

It is possible that the initial force for expansion is generated, not in a city but in a non-urbanized region, with agriculture, forestry, fishing, or mining as the principal economic activities. A region is "propulsive" if:

$$\frac{I_r}{I_u} \cdot \frac{\Delta I_u}{\Delta I_r} > 0 \dots\dots\dots\dots\dots\dots\dots\dots\dots\dots\dots \quad (7)$$

that is, with a positive percentage change of investment in the region there will be a positive percentage change of investment in some urban centre or centres. If the expression in equation (7) is greater than unity, (the percentage increase in investment in the urban centre is greater than the percentage increase of investment in the region) we will say that the region is a "strong" propulsive region. If it is greater than zero but less than one, we will say that it is a "weak" propulsive region.

Because of the relationship between migration and investment we can also conclude that if the region is propulsive, and using P for population,

$$\frac{P_r}{P_u} \cdot \frac{\Delta P_u}{\Delta P_r} > 0 \dots\dots\dots\dots\dots\dots\dots\dots\dots\dots\dots\dots\dots\dots\dots\dots \quad (7a)$$

that is the percentage increase in population of the urban centre will exceed the percentage increase in population of the region itself.

Centre of Attraction

There remains the question of the impact of growth of a development pole or a growth centre on the population density of the surrounding region. A city is a centre of attraction if:

$$\frac{I_u}{P_r} \cdot \frac{\Delta P_r}{\Delta I_u} < 0 \dots\dots\dots\dots\dots\dots\dots\dots\dots\dots\dots\dots\dots\dots\dots\dots \quad (8)$$

that is expansion in the urban centre generated by investment in that centre leads to a reduction of population in the peripheral region. If the elasticity expressed by equation (8) is greater than minus one (greater than unity in the negative direction) the city is a "strong" centre of attraction, and if it is between zero and minus one, it is a "weak" centre of attraction.

It is apparent that a city may be both a development pole and a centre of attraction. That is, expansion of the city may raise the level of per capita income or per capita welfare in the peripheral region by reducing the population pressure in the region, permitting larger holdings of land per family, improvements in agricultural techniques, etc.

If the elasticity of equation (8) is positive, we will say that the city is a *diffusion centre* (to avoid calling it a "repulsive city"). In this case investment in the city increases population density in the peripheral region.

Probably most people, or at least most politicians, will be most pleased when a city turns out to be both a development pole and a diffusion centre. That is, investment in the city will raise per capita incomes, employment, etc., in the peripheral region, but will raise population densities there as well. Some people are always unhappy if rural-urban migration is the only way of raising the level of welfare of the rural population. Some people dislike even migration from small towns to large cities. However, unless one attaches a high shadow price to rural or small town life as such, a development pole which is also a centre of diffusion is not obviously preferable to a development pole which is a centre of attraction. There may, of course, be diseconomies of scale in terms of pollution, congestion, etc., but these factors need separate analysis.

How Many Development Poles?

A somewhat complicated conceptual problem is whether or not to allow for two-way interactions among cities in the definition of development poles.

Perroux himself was adamant on this point. He insisted that the interaction must be uni-directional and non-symmetrical. If two cities generate favourable interactions on each other, then in Perroux's terminology, neither of them is a true development pole.

Similarly, if:

$$\frac{\Delta I_A}{\Delta I_B} > 0 \text{ and also } \frac{\Delta I_B}{\Delta I_A} > 0,$$

both industries acting upon each other, neither is a true "propulsive industry." There may be two cities in one region, both of which generate spread effects to the region, but which do not sustain each other's growth. For both of them to be developed poles, in other words, the relationship between them must be essentially competitive rather than complementary.

At first blush, this definition seems inconvenient and unnecessarily restrictive. Yet if we permit a city to be defined as a development pole provided that its expansion has positive effects somewhere, even though the city may itself be responding to investment in another city, the concept of development pole becomes virtually meaningless, and it is almost impossible to distinguish development poles from growth centers. Any city might then be a development pole. One possibility would be to define a city as a development pole if the expression in equation (5) is greater than one for the impact of investment in the city on the rest of the region, while the elasticity of the response of that city to investment anywhere else in the region is less than one. The inconvenience of this definition would be that we might end up with no development poles in a particular regional or national economy, even though one or two large cities were in fact generating positive and substantial effects on the growth of employment, per capita income, etc., elsewhere in the economy.

Thus a true development pole must have some true propulsive enterprises, which generate spread effects through investment which is not to any significant degree a reaction to investment and related growth which has already taken place elsewhere in the system.

Thus, $\frac{\Delta I_A}{\Delta I_B} > 0$ but $\frac{\Delta I_B}{\Delta I_A} = 0$, and a development pole contains a collection of enterprises of the B type, which are *sui generis* innovating enterprises. In reality any city will have *some* enterprises which expand in reaction to events elsewhere in the region. But while we may not wish to insist that:

$\frac{I_r}{I_u} \cdot \frac{\Delta I_u}{\Delta I_r} = 0$ for the city to be a "pole," we must insist that it is "low," perhaps less than 0.5. The essential characteristic of a development pole is the domination of its economy by innovating enterprises of the B type, which make investments in terms of the future, and not in response to recent growth of their markets.

With these definitions, there must be at least one development pole or one propulsive region in every system, if growth is to take place in that system. Natural-resource-based development will be generated by a propulsive region, with the causal flow from the rural areas to the cities. Human-resource-based expansion will be generated by development poles. Historical experience indicates clearly that higher levels of welfare are attained through human-resource-based development than through natural-resource-based development. It also indicates that sooner or later every economy, whether national or regional, must make the shift from natural-to human-resource-based development if continuing growth is to be assured. However, the propulsive region or development pole need not be inside the borders of any particular region, or even inside the borders of the country. Regional and national borders are sometimes political or historical accidents. Several cities may serve simultaneously as development poles for the same region. Nor is the level of welfare necessarily higher within the development poles or the propulsive regions than it is in the growth centres.

In this analysis, we have treated "growth pole" and "development pole" as alternative expressions for the same phenomenon. In our view, the concept is too fragile to permit a distinction between "growth" and "development" in this context. We could, of course, define "development" as growth plus structural change, or growth that brings widely distributed improvement in social welfare, as is done in other contexts; but in the context of interactions in space we feel that such distinctions overburden the concept, and make it just that more difficult to convert into a useful operational tool.

Note also that in the set of definitions laid down above Perroux's *dictum* regarding "banal" or "geonomic" *versus* economic space is deliberately ignored. The reason is simply that development poles defined in terms of Perroux's abstract economic space—fields of force scattered about the globe— can never be an operational tool for regional policy making or planning. This way of defining development poles does not mean that we can ignore the *fact* that in reality the spread effects generated by a particular urban centre may not be felt primarily in the peripheral geographic region of which it is the center, but may be diffused throughout the world. Conversely, a geographic region's true generator of spread effects may lie outside its borders; the "development pole" for the retarded northeast region of New Brunswick, Canada may not be Moncton or even Halifax, but Montreal, Toronto or even Boston. Walter Prescott Webb, it will be recalled, spoke of the whole of the New World as a development pole (or perhaps a propulsive region) for the whole of Europe throughout a "three hundred years' boom."[8] Perroux himself recently reiterated his point that even today Latin America's true development poles lie in Europe rather than within Latin America itself.[9]

All this may be true as a description of fact, and it was probably necessary for Perroux to underline the point in order to counter simplistic and unrealistic models in which it was assumed, explicitly or implicitly, that *all* spread effects of investment in a development pole are felt within its "own" geographic region or hinterland. No doubt Perroux wanted to get away from the concept of cities as "central places," essentially market towns *created by* their peripheral region. However, the inclusion of "economic space" in the concept of "development pole" makes it virtually useless from a policy point of view. Add "economic space" to "development pole" and what do we have? A statement that within the global economy there is a network of interrelations and interactions, "effets d'entraînement" flowing mainly from cities to other cities or to rural areas, but in part from rural areas to cities, and taking the form of movements of goods, natural resources, capital, people, technological knowledge and skills.

It is, of course, extremely useful to have empirical knowledge as to what these flows are for any country or region. But when spread effects are generated from centers outside the geographic area of control of the authority wishing to accelerate growth of a retarded region, the knowledge can affect regional development policy only in very roundabout ways. Suppose the Malaysian government discovers that investments in Tokyo, Bangkok, Singapore and London will result in some spread effect trickling down to the Malaysian northeast. What then? The Malaysian authorities are not going to undertake investments in these cities as a device for improving economic and social conditions in their own northeast.

When planners or politicians talk of the creation or expansion of growth centers or development poles as a device for raising productivity and incomes in a retarded region, they are not talking of investing in several major world centers outside their own country. They are usually not even thinking of investing in cities within the country but completely outside the region. No one talks of making Toronto a stronger "development pole" in order to solve the problem of the Atlantic provinces. Some people do talk of making Montreal a stronger development pole to solve problems in Quebec of which it is the major urban center. If we are concerned with reducing regional disparities, concentration on growth centers or development poles within the geographic region towards which the policy is directed is almost always justified; it is rare indeed that investment in a development pole outside the retarded region will have more impact on income and employment in the retarded region than in the pole itself, or even in its own peripheral region. Investment in Toronto is far more likely to increase than to reduce gaps between Ontario and the Atlantic provinces, and investment in Montreal may very well widen the gap between Montreal and Gaspésie. There are usually leakages all along the way, and the more remote the region from the pole, the more leakages there are and the less likely is investment in the pole to reduce gaps between a retarded region and more prosperous regions. It is conceivable that some kind of investment in Tokyo will raise income and employment in Gaspésie, but it is likely to raise income and employment in Montreal more.

If we are to retain the concept of growth centers and development poles as building blocks in the preparation of regional and national development plans, then we must put aside for the moment the concept of economic space, and consider quite simply the relationship between investment in an urban center and the creation of income and employment in the larger geographic region of which the urban center is a part. That does not mean that relations with other parts of the world will be ignored, but only that these relations will not be considered part of "development pole" policy. We have to choose between retaining the concept of development pole as a major instrument of development policy, and the concept of development poles being set in economic space rather than in geographic space.

Need For Uni-directional and Non-symmetrical Interactions

While Perroux's concept of economic space thus turns out to be a nuisance *when combined with the concept of development pole policy*, the same cannot be said for his insistence that relations between a propulsive enterprise and other enterprises, and thus between a development pole and its region, must be uni-directional and non-symmetrical. As we have already seen, this restriction is necessary to make sense out of the concept of development pole. In other words, a propulsive enterprise must be one in which some investment is taking place which is not "induced;" that is, it is not related to recent increases in profits or sales. It is here that the relationship between Perroux and Schumpeter comes in. A propulsive enterprise is an innovating enterprise. Investments are made in anticipation of future success of the innovation, not because of past success of a routine operation. What Perroux did was to put Schumpeter's concept of innovations into space, pointing out that innovating, propulsive enterprises tend to be concentrated in certain urban centers. This concentration of propulsive enterprises makes these urban centers development poles. Moreover, Schumpeter's concept of "clusters of followers," who appear after the success of the innovation is clear, together with his concept of secondary effects, is closely akin to Perroux's "effets d'entraînement;" here again, Perroux has put the Schumpeter concept into space, specifying where the clusters of followers and expansion of related enterprises takes place.

A simple equation will serve to illustrate the point. Let Y be income, k_s the supermultiplier, I_i induced investment, I_r investment in discovery and exploitation of new resources, K the stock of known natural resources, I_t investment in discovery and application of new technology, and T the level of technology. Then in any economy:

$$\Delta Y = k_s \cdot [I_i(Y) + I_d(K) + I_t(T)]$$

Now what the development pole concept does is to put these growth forces into space. $I_d(K)$ will occur mainly in propulsive regions. $I_t(T)$ takes place in development poles. Induced investment might take place anywhere, but it will take place in growth centers as well as in propulsive regions and development poles; and as pointed out above, if the growth center is a strong reactor, its growth may be faster than that of the development pole itself.

In reality we will find few enterprises which are engaged exclusively in research and innovation; some of their investment will be induced, related to past increases in profits and sales. Thus to distinguish propulsive enterprises from others we shall have to define propulsive enterprises as those where at least x percent of their investment are in research and development leading to innovations. By the same token, no city consists of propulsive enterprises alone, and we should have to define a "development pole" as a city where y percent of the enterprises are propulsive. No doubt the x and the y could be determined empirically in any particular country; but the concept of development pole begins to become a bit blurred.

Centers of Attraction vs. Centers of Diffusion

This formulation brings us back to another and fundamental aspect of the development pole concept: the distinction between development poles that are centers of attraction and those that are centers of diffusion. We have known for a long time that technological progress, resource discovery, and structural change are at the core of the development process. The development pole concept has the merit of allocating these aspects of growth in space. Cities are necessary both to the process of technological progress and to structural change, since industries and services, and particularly sophisticated industries and services, are concentrated in cities. But is there nothing more to growth pole theory than that? If all development poles were centers of attraction, the growth of cities would simply be an adjunct of structural change; the primary sector is in the countryside, the secondary, tertiary and now the quaternary sectors are in cities. Technological progress is generated in cities and structural change moves people to cities, so that development is accompanied by relative growth of the urban sector.

Would the development pole concept be worth retaining if it involved no more than that? Note that in the process described in the preceding paragraph, it is development that creates the poles, not the poles that generate the development. Perhaps innovators like to live in cities, but it is not clear that they all like to live in large cities, nor that they would stop innovating if policy were designed to diffuse industrial and service activities. Here the policy proposal "Make Halifax-Dartmouth a development pole in order to resuscitate the Atlantic Provinces" means simply, "Make some industrial and service investments in Halifax-Dartmouth in order to draw people to the city from the countryside, and let's hope some of the investments will lead to innovations." To say that is to say no more than "Let's try to raise productivity of the Atlantic Provinces." It is likely to mean in practice, "Let's move some of the development investment from Toronto to Halifax-Dartmouth." But it is obvious that if developmental investment is redistributed, income and employment will also be redistributed. The concept of a "pole" as the generator of development has disappeared.

And so we come to "development poles—centers of diffusion." It is likely that most politicians, and perhaps even most planners, when they speak of creating development poles to turn a retarded region into a prosperous one, really have in mind creation or expansion of urban centers that will raise incomes and create employment for people where they are, elsewhere in the region, and do not have in mind solving the problems of the peripheral region by emptying it.

Should we then confine the concept of development pole to those urban centers which are also centers of diffusion, as well as having "y" percent of its enterprises propulsive, and generating increases in income and employment in the region as a whole through investment in these enterprises? Certainly, we would then have a clear definition of development poles. But how many such urban centers exist? Historically, regions have created cities, not the other way around, and the number of cases in which investment in a pole raises income, employment *and population* in the peripheral region are probably rather rare.

Perroux's General Theory

In order to understand completely Perroux's theory of growth poles and development poles, it is essential to understand that it is just one facet, although an important one, of his running battle with the neoclassical system.

Neoclassical economics implies that the market will bring, among other pleasant things, an essential harmony in the distribution of economic activity through space, a kind of Pareto optimum of spatial equilibrium. It was precisely this comfortable conclusion that Perroux denied, contending that the natural tendency was towards polarization, dominance, and dependence, which was likely to become cumulative. Here Perroux's theory bore some resemblance to Harrod's theory of growth,[10] with its cumulative movements away from equilibrium once equilibrium is disturbed, or Myrdal's concept of cumulative causation.[11]

Perroux had a general theory of development, one that he worked on for decades and never completed. The most complete statement is probably his 1975 book.[12] But the last and perhaps the best statement of this general theory is his chapter in the volume of essays in his honour.[13] It is not an easy general theory, and in some ways is more unfamiliar in concept, terminology, and mathematics than was Keynes' *General Theory* when it first appeared. The paper is made all the more difficult by the fact that it really is an outline of a book. At any rate it makes it clear that for Perroux the concept of growth poles is only one part of a much bigger and much more complex system. As noted above, Perroux was quite emphatic that he was not talking about spread effects in "banal" geographic space, let alone increases in income and employment in the immediately surrounding region of some urban center selected as a growth pole. Yet it is in this form that the concept was applied by disciples of Perroux who found themselves in the position of having to put together regional and national development plans.

Perroux's own theory was imperfectly understood and still more imperfectly applied. But applied it certainly was. Many more governments have stated officially that they were pursuing a growth pole strategy, at least in the urban and regional aspects of their development policy, than have claimed to be guided by any other philosophy, apart from laissez-faire; it became the guiding principle for regional planning in France, Belgium, Italy and Quebec as early as 1960, and in the decade that followed spread to Spain, the United States, Japan, Latin America, Africa, and Asia.

It is worth repeating that, as initially presented by Perroux, the theory was too complex, too abstract, and too non-operational to be used as a basis for planning. Indeed to apply the pure theory of Perroux would require global planning, if we take into account Perroux's insistence on planning transmission lines and receptors as well as generators of growth. Perroux's economic space, in which spread effects are felt, is global. He argues, it will be recalled, that Latin America's true growth poles still lie in Europe and, to some degree, in the United States. Such a concept is useless for regional planning which is confined to a single country. As a consequence, economists who found themselves involved in practical regional planning simply discarded the pure theory of Perroux. They converted it into a totally different theory which treated growth poles as urban centers, and spread effects as being generated in a particular geographic space, namely the region adjacent to the urban center itself. Once this happy doctrine is accepted, it is possible to imagine that by pushing and pulling new enterprises (mostly industrial enterprises) into urban centers of retarded regions, it is possible to reduce regional disparities, decentralize urbanization and industrialization, and accelerate national development all at once. It did not take long for this pleasant version of the growth pole doctrine to spread to developing countries and to be applied there as well.

It is here, of course, that the mistake was made. There are, to be sure, conditions under which industrial investment in a city will lead to increased income and employment in its peripheral region. In general, these conditions are that the industries in the city are natural-resource based, and that the natural resources required are found in the peripheral region. When the concept of growth poles was first introduced, it should be remembered, many industries in Western European cities were still natural-resource based, and many cities were based primarily on these industries. For such urban centers, the simplified theory of growth poles may hold. But there are many situations in which this theory—let us label it the Boudeville version of the original Perroux doctrine—simply does not hold at all.[14] One of the situations in which this theory does not hold is in the case of the propulsive region, in which it is the expansion of economic activities in the hinterland which generates growth of its urban center, rather than vice versa. Another is where the urban center is too small and too unsophisticated in its economic activities to generate significant spread effects of any kind, as in the case of a small town with a cannery or some jaggery mills. A third is where industries are natural-resource based, but the natural resources are found outside the peripheral region. And the fourth, most common among major metropolitan centers today, is the situation in which the propulsive enterprises in the city are based not on natural resources but on human resources. In such cases, industry consists of scientifically oriented manufacturing and quaternary services; there is no link to the peripheral region at all, because the enterprises operate in a worldwide economic space.

The Boudeville version, however, simply took no account of these cases, which are certainly in the majority, until it had become abundantly clear that the application of this simple version of the theory was not working. In effect, the adherents to this theory behaved as though growth pole theory and economic base theory were essentially the same. We learned in time the falsity of this premise. We found that it was indeed possible, although not easy, to lure new enterprises into urban centers designated as growth poles in retarded regions. Snaring them required a combination of investment in infrastructure, relocation of government enterprises, and incentives to private enterprise. But in most cases the hoped-for and expected spread effects to the rest of the region did not appear.

Before we learned this bitter lesson, however, and once the door was opened to Boudeville's revisionism, all manner of policies regarding urban growth and regional development were justified as application of the growth pole doctrine. The urban centers labelled "growth poles" ranged in population from many millions to a few thousand. In Japan growth poles were vast industrial complexes requiring hundreds of million of dollars of investment in each. In Mauritania the small, sleepy town of Kaedi on the Senegal River, with about 10,000 population, was treated as a growth pole that could generate spread effects to the countryside. Such effects would come from the linking of the stable, grain-growing agriculture of the Senegal River Valley with the seminomadic livestock cultivation of the Sahel, using grain surpluses (when there were any) to fatten livestock in feedlots before slaughtering them in Kaedi's small but very modern abattoir. The Economic Development Administration in the United States worked with growth centers as small as 500 people, mere villages in remote hill country consisting of exhausted mines and marginal farmland.

It is a long march from Perroux's own theory to giving a capital grant to Volvo to make Halifax into a development pole, generating propulsive effects, in the form of higher employment and incomes, throughout Canada's provinces. Indeed, Perroux is quite specific that it is "untenable to reduce the theory of development poles to a mere instrument of regional policy." One cannot implant any old kind of productive activity anywhere one wishes, in any kind of environment. A rational policy involves both the choice of the motor and the management of the environment. Moreover, Perroux continues, "Clearly, the market, full as it is of monopolies and various imperfections, is not up to these two tasks."[15] In today's mixed economy, communication between public and private sectors is constant; the ideal solution to its problems is offered by the multilevel planning of (Janos) Kornai (of Hungary) and Liptak.

Statements such as these, together with Perroux's related theory of dominance/dependence, which is well analyzed in Karen Polenske's chapter in the Higgins/Savoie volume,[16] make Perroux sound as though he were a radical political economist. But while Perroux was a heretic in relation to his more purely neoclassical colleagues, in politics he was right of center in the French political spectrum. He was conservative enough to have run into severe difficulties during the leftwing student riots in Paris in 1968, including the loss of his editorship of the Journal *Tiers monde* of which he was the founder. Perroux was certainly interested in politics at both the national and the international levels. Like Keynes, he wrote a good many "essays in persuasion." He had limited faith in the free market, and believed that dynamic capitalist economies need some degree of planning and management. Nonetheless, his political philosophy was basically eighteenth and nineteenth century liberal.

Professor Ducarmel Bocage states at the end of his book on Perroux, "Professor Perroux is one of the greatest and most original thinkers of our time."[17]

In his well-known book on *The Growth of Economic Thought*, Professor Henry W. Spiegel characterizes Perroux as "the only living economist who developed a theoretical system rivalling conventional equilibrium analysis."[18]

The usual kind of input-output (I-O) matrix identifies flows among sectors or industries and does not identify interactions in space. But if we could ascertain not only to what sectors or industries a particular sector or industry sells and from what sectors or industries it buys, but also *where* the purchases and sales take place, would we not be on the way to identifying urban centers that already are, or could become, true development poles? The answer must be a resounding "No!" Indeed, it is in retrospect most unfortunate, as Niles Hansen, José Ramon Lasuen, and Tormod Hermansen have pointed out, that Perroux not only permitted his disciples to use input-output analysis as a form of empirical testing of growth pole theory, but also aided and abetted them in this activity. It is difficult to understand now how Perroux could have allowed himself to be thus misled. Hermansen suggests that Perroux, as well as Hirschman, was unduly impressed by Chenery and Watanabe's comparative analysis of interindustry matrices in the United States, Italy, Norway, and Japan, presented to the Econometric Society in 1956. The truth is that commodity flows are only a part, and probably a relatively unimportant part, of all the interactions embraced in Perroux's original model. Hermansen believes that "the choice of Leontief-type interindustry input-output tables as the main tool for empirical testing and application in planning" has been "a major source of confusion." He adds: "Basically, the difficulty stems from the fact that whereas Perroux originally aimed at a truly dynamic theory of development and therefore adopted the Schumpeter theory and framework as one of his cornerstones, the Leotief-type formalization of industrial interdependence is of an essentially static character. And because the latter theory is operational and the former not, or at least not to the same degree, there has been a strong tendency, particularly in planning oriented literature, to attribute to the development pole theory a much stronger input-output bias than it had originally."[19]

Niles Hansen has pointed out that the excessive reliance on input-output analysis in applying growth pole theory has unduly restricted the usefulness of the concept and improperly restricted the concept of key industries to large industries with large matrix-multiplier effects.[20]

Lasuen puts the blame for this distortion of development pole theory squarely on the shoulders of the French school. By restricting its analysis to the interindustry technique, he writes: "It has drained the growth pole concept of its original temporal and dynamic meaning and recharged it with static and/ or comparative static content. The heavy use of input-output technique has shifted the school's attention away from Perroux's original translation of Schumpeterian development. They have failed to develop the point that the activity creating a growth pole was essentially a sectoral and a geographical disturbance not because of its bigger than average size, nor because of its higher multiplier, but because it was an *innovation.*"[21]

We agree with Lasuen and the others that the role of development poles as centers of innovation and diffusers of scientific and technological advance is more important than their roles as buyers and sellers of goods.

Yet nothing we have said in this section should be construed to mean that input-output matrices located in space are totally useless for determination of growth pole policy. On the contrary, if it is known not only what a propulsive industry buys and what it sells but also where it buys and sells, it is possible to locate at least some of the industry's spread and backwash effects (although not all of them). At least such an exercise might be a protection against merely assuming that spread effects will take place in the peripheral region of the urban center where the industry is located, when in fact the industry is operating in an economic space mainly or entirely outside that region.

Having arrived at this point, we are brought back once again to the fact that it is virtually impossible to formulate an operational concept of development poles, and at the same time retain Perroux's dictum that, for an industry to be propulsive, the interactions between it and other industries must be unidirectional and non-symmetrical. If we take this dictum literally, there will be almost no development poles in the world, since the most important diffusers of technological progress are also ardent receivers of innovations made elsewhere. So if we want to retain the concept of development poles as generators and diffusers of innovation and at the same time to retain the concept of dominance of development poles over dependent cities and regions, we are forced to accept some arbitrary rule regarding the ratio of developmental investment (based on innovation, resource discovery, and expected population growth) to induced investment (based on recent increases in sales due to events taking place elsewhere and on innovations introduced elsewhere). The whole business becomes a bit messy.

On the other hand, we get into a mess equally quickly if we do not accept Perroux's dictum. For if we allow an urban center to be treated as a development pole, if it has any spread effects whatsoever in any place whatsoever, any hamlet can be a development pole. We become unable to distinguish between Tokyo and Utsumi (Who knows? One of the fishermen in that charming village may design an improved net!) or between Paris and Saint Tropez. The snowmobile, which has been imitated the world over, was developed by M. Bombardier in a village of the eastern townships of Quebec. Cities of all sizes are in various degrees innovators and adopters, takers of initial risks and part of the cluster of followers, sources of developmental investment and of induced investment. No clear lines of distinction can be drawn. The whole matter of whether these cities should be categorized as development poles or growth centers or neither becomes moot: all cities qualify more or less for any of the labels. It is hard to see how the concepts can be at once made clear, simple, and operational in a sense that is useful for planning regional development. The all-important innovating function of propulsive industries gathered in an urban center and operating in a wide economic space seems irreconcilable with the concept of development poles which generate spread effects to their own surrounding regions; and the idea of development poles which operate in economic space is a concept of little use to the regional planner.

Conclusions on Growth Poles

What remains of the growth pole concept? Perhaps most participants in the recent debate would agree on the following conclusions:

(a) Development involves polarization.
(b) Growth poles are accordingly a "good thing," a source of dynamism in the economy, which generate spread effects *somewhere*, but not necessarily in their own peripheral geographic region.
(c) The principal role of growth poles is as a source and a diffuser of innovations.
(d) Therefore growth poles should be encouraged to form and to play this role, even if it involves some degree of domination/dependence relationship.
(e) A policy of selected decentralization, or creation of "pôles d'équilibre," is not in conflict with this Perroux-style growth pole policy.
(f) Since investment decisions in propulsive industries are risky and discontinuous, temporary subsidization can be justified in the same way that protection of "infant industries" is justified. Growth pole strategy might be regarded as infant industry strategy set in space and time, and should involve nurturing healthy infants for strictly limited periods, together with refusal to run life-support systems for doddering geriatrics.
(g) There may be cases when small and middle-sized cities can serve as growth poles.
(h) What is excluded from a Perroux-style growth pole strategy is pushing and pulling enterprises at random into retarded and disadvantaged regions when the conditions for generation of spread effects are not present— in other words, the kind of growth pole strategy that was in fact pursued in many countries during the 1960s and 1970s.

Central Place Theory

The concept of a central place, as we have said, is the very opposite of the concept of growth poles. Instead of the urban centre generating spread effects to its economic or geonomic space, in the form of diffusion of technology and increases in income and employment, in central place theory the peripheral region generates spread effects to the urban centre. Indeed, the urban centre is the creation of the region, as the source of required services and as the market for its products, whether for direct consumption, for further processing, or for export to other regions. The existence of a central place implies the existence of a "propulsive region," as defined above. Thus, the "central place" and "growth pole" theories are not really opposing doctrines. Once we have arrived at the concept of *systems of interactions in space*, it becomes apparent that a particular urban centre may be both central place and growth pole, within a complex system of feedback relationships. We shall return to this point below.

Readers who are interested in the history of thought regarding theory of urban-regional relationships may wish to go back to von Thünen's *Der Isolierte Staat*, published in 1826. Here can be found some of the basic ideas and hypotheses that have remained in central place theory ever since. Von Thünen conducted his analysis on the assumption that the economic unit involved consisted of a completely homogeneous land surface, and demonstrated that the ideal form of development would be a metropolitan city at the centre and with concentric rings of various types of land use around this central city.[22]

While there is a scattering of earlier literature, however, most of today's discussion of the location of cities, urban structures, and interactions of growth of cities and development of regions takes off from the work of Walter Christaller and its elaboration by August Lösch.[23] In introducing his concept of central place, Christaller wished to abstract from all factors other than pure space that might influence the location of economic activities, and thus of cities. He therefore followed Von Thünen in assuming that each economy under consideration consisted of a single flat, homogeneous plain, with people of uniform tastes and productive capacities spread evenly throughout it. Under these conditions, he concluded, the optimal or equilibrium configuration of economic activity would be a pattern of contiguous hexagons, each with its own urban centre, as in Figure 6.1. In this structure of development all space is occupied and utilized; and for these conditions, aggregate transport costs from all parts of each hexagonal region to its urban center would be minimized. The circular pattern makes total transport costs even lower, but wastes space. However, not all of these urban centres are the same. Some kind of regional products require larger markets than others, and some kinds of services to the regions require concentration in larger centres than others. Thus a hierarchy of urban centres emerges; all urban "places" are "central," but some are more central than others.

Christaller made some effort to verify his theory empirically. He provided data on the average size of urban centres at various positions in the urban

FIGURE 6.1

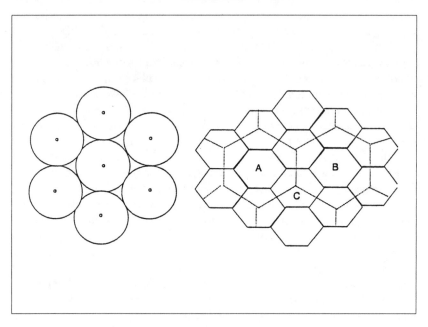

Theoretical shapes of tributary areas. Circles leave unserved spaces, hexagons do not. Small hexagons are service areas for smaller places, large hexagons (dotted lines) represent service areas for next higher-rank central places.

TABLE 6.1

Central Place Population	Towns Distance apart (km.)		Tributary Areas Population (Sq.km.)	Size
Market hamlet (Marktort)	7	800	45	2,700
Township center (Amtsort)	12	1,500	135	8,100
County seat (Kreisstadt)	21	3,500	400	24,000
District city (Bezirksstadt)	36	9,000	1,200	75,000
Small state capital (Gaustadt)	62	27,000	3,600	225,000
Provincial head city (Provinzhauptstadt)	108	90,000	10,800	675,000
Regional capital city (Landeshauptstadt)	186	300,000	32,400	2,025,000

hierarchy of South Germany, their populations, their distance apart, and their tributary areas, as follows:[24]

Christaller was of course aware that in the real world other factors than mere distance and centrality influence the location and size of cities. But he considered these factors of fundamental importance, no matter what the physiography of a region may be. He argued that they dominate topography in the distribution of urban centres even in mountain areas. He also contended that to explain the location of a city by the importance of the river on whose banks it grew up is like saying that if there were no rivers there would be no cities.[25]

Christaller also recognized that the rank of any particular city within its hierarchy is not a function of its population size alone. Smokestack-industry towns have smaller zones of influence than cities of equal population which are centres of innovation, telecommunications, and other sophisticated services. Christaller, writing when he did, used number of telephones per thousand population as an index to measure degree of centrality. Today's equivalent might be teleports, access to computer networks, etc. Wholesale sales per capita have also been used as an index of centrality, and number of automobiles entering the city per week from outside its metropolitan region.

John Ullman makes the point that central place structures are distorted from the Christaller (or Lösch) ideal by such factors as existing transportation routes and industrial structures. But there is obviously a chicken-and-egg feedback relationship here. Why are the airlines, roads, and railroads where they are, if not to serve existing urban centres? Leslie Curry converts the existence of such feedback mechanisms into a criticism of central place theory: "The major difficulty in writing central place theory is that the elements comprise a system without really independent variables so there are no fundamental determinants to use in understanding the logic. The locations of centers are suitable to a given road net while the roads can be understood relative to the places they connect. Centers are the focus of routes, and crossroads suitable for the establishment of centers."[26]

Lösch's "Demand Cones"

Lösch conducted his analysis within a framework limited by two simplifying assumptions: (1) pure competition; no firm earns more than "normal" profits (no "excess profits"); (2) movements of consumers through space in order to acquire goods are minimized. He added to Christaller's analysis the concept of "demand cones" of varying heights and diameters over different areas. With the further assumption that purchasing power is evenly distributed through space, he verified Christaller's conclusion that the optimal pattern of settlement consists of urban centres of varying sizes, each serving a region (zone of influence, range of goods) hexagonal in shape, the smaller hexagons being "nested" in larger ones. He derived a pattern of transportation routes from the same analytical framework. An urban hierarchy emerges that is in effect qualitative as well as quantitative. Larger centers will provide a wider range of goods and services, will have more transportation links and intersections, a more complex telecommunications network, etc.

A simplified version of "Lösch's 'demand cones'" has been provided by Gunnar Olsson, presented here in Figure 6.2. O is a central place providing goods to other places. Transportation costs are determined by distance alone. Consequently the price of goods provided in centre O increases with the distance from O. Beyond place B, consumers will buy their goods in some other centre than O. Thus OB is the "range of goods" provided by O. OA is the demand (value of sales) which just yields a normal profit. At C the firms in O make a loss and will cease to provide the goods. At D the firms make an excess profit and, accordingly, under pure competition, D is not an equilibrium position. New firms will enter or old ones expand. The "threshold" or equilibrium position is given by the triangle OAB.[27]

FIGURE 6.2
Variations in Demand With Variations in Distance

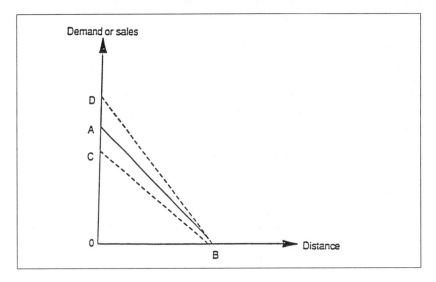

Current Status of Central Place Theory

The question of how urban hierarchies are formed and what determines the pattern of urban structures is an intriguing one, and a complex one. It has analogies in other disciplines, such as physics, biology, statistics, and management science. It is therefore to be expected that the "central place game" is one that regional scientists love to play. They can apply refined mathematics and econometrics, systems analysis, organization theory, decision and choice theory, linear programming, and cybernetics to their hearts' content. And apply them they do, at both the purely theoretical and the empirical level. Consequently, the literature on central place theory continues to mount. But what does it amount to?

Considerable success has been achieved in relaxing the simplifying assumptions of Christaller and Lösch and still getting results in terms of urban hierarchies, transportation networks, and the like. Brian Berry and William Garrison have shown that both the assumption of pure competition (no excess profits) and the assumption of uniform distribution of purchasing power through space can be dropped from the central place model, and the logical necessity of a hierarchical urban structure still be derived from it, and verified empirically.[28] Conclusions regarding the structure of the transportation system (and by implication, at least, of the telecommunications system, can also be analytically derived and empirically tested. In other words, central place theory is gradually becoming more realistic, and factual knowledge about urban structures is being steadily accumulated. Both Berry and Olsson have managed to link the rank-size rule to central place models.[29] Olsson also links urban structures to the second law of thermodynamics (entropy) and to the biological principle of allometric growth (relating growth of a particular organ to the growth of the entire body).[30]

Conclusions on Growth Poles and Central Places

Despite the ingenuity, the sophisticated techniques, and the borrowing from other sciences, we are a little closer today to a general theory of either growth poles or central places, that could be applied always and everywhere to solution of urban and regional problems, than we were thirty-five years ago. The factors determining the interactions among cities and regions in any real situation are enormously complex, and there is no substitute for analysis of them as they are and on the spot, before formulating policy or constructing plans. Growth pole and central place theory are springboards, jumping off points, which help us to get started on the study of particular cities and regions and which tell us some of the things to look for. Neither general theory will tell us, by itself, what will be the impact of luring the Volvo plant to Halifax N.S. or of installing an I.B.M. plant in Bromeau, Province of Quebec.

In today's world nearly all urban centres are in some degree growth poles and in some degree central places. They generate spread effects to other cities and regions and absorb spread effects from other—not necessarily the same— cities and regions. Cases where the most significant interactions take place between the urban centre and its immediate geographic hinterland are relatively rare, especially in industrialized countries. For large cities in industrialized countries, the "hinterland," in both the growth pole and the central place sense, is mainly *a system of cities*, and the cities in such a "hinterland" may be scattered all over the world.

In short, the simplified models of growth poles and central places that have been constructed to facilitate their application to policy and planning are in fact self-defeating. They leave out too many of the factors which determine what actually happens in real world cases, distorting, redirecting, offsetting, obfuscating, even nullifying the basic factors dealt with by the models. Recognition of this fact does not mean that we should throw away the models. The basic forces are there, and are powerful. But we must add to the models the other powerful forces which are operating in each particular case.

Notes

1. Benjamin Higgins and Donald J. Savoie, ed. *Regional Economic Development: Essays in Honour of François Perroux* (London and Boston: Allen & Unwin, 1988).
2. François Perroux, "Economic Space: Theory and Applications," *Quarterly Journal of Economics*, vol. 64, 1950, pp. 89–104.
3. *Ibid.*, p. 96.
4. François Perroux, "A Note on the Notion of Growth Pole," *Économie Appliquée*, 1955, nos 1 and 2.
5. Karen Polenske, "Growth Pole Theory and Strategy Reconsidered: Domination Linkages, and Distribution," in Benjamin Higgins and Donald J. Savoie (eds.), *Regional Economic Development: Essays in Honour of François Perroux* (Boston: Allen & Unwin, 1988), p. 93.
6. François Perroux, "The Pole of Development and the General Theory of the Economy, in Benjamin Higgins and Donald J. Savoie (eds.), *Regional Economic Development: Essays in Honour of François Perroux* (Boston: Allen & Unwin, 1988), p. 49.
7. Benjamin Higgins, Fernand Martin, and André Raynauld, "Les orientations du développement économique du Québec, (HMR Report), (Ottawa: Department of Regional Economic Expansion, 1970), chapter 5. This chapter was republished with little change in *La revue européenne des sciences sociales (Cahiers Vilfredo Pareto)*, and again in revised and refined form under the title "Development Poles: Do They Exist?" in the volume edited by Anthoni Kuklinski entitled *Polarized Development and Regional Policies*.
8. Walter Prescott Webb, *The Great Plains*, (Boston: Ginn and Co., 1931).

9. François Perroux, "The Transnational Firms and South America," *Revue de la Défense Nationale*, April 1978.
10. Roy Harrod, *Towards a Dynamic Economics: Some Recent Developments of Economic Theory and Their Application to Policy* (London: Macmillan, 1948).
11. Gunnar Myrdal, *Economic Theory and Under-developed Regions* (London: Gerald Duckworth, 1957).
12. François Perroux, *Unités actives et mathématiques nouvelles* (Paris: Dunod, 1975).
13. Higgins, Savoie, *Regional Economic Development*.
14. For those unacquainted with Boudeville's work, the best introductions might be in *French Regional Polarization and Planning* (Paris: Pion, 1976) and in "Functional Regional Analysis: An Elementary Exposition on Some Selected Topics," in *University of Toronto Lectures*, J.H.P. Paelinck and A. Sailez (eds.) (Paris: Association de science régionale de langue française, 1977). See also Anthony Kuklinski, *Polarized Development and Regional Policies: Tribute to Jacques Boudeville* (The Hague, Paris and New York: Mouton, 1981).
15. Higgins, Savoie, *Regional Economic Development*, pp. 54 and 56.
16. *Ibid.* Chapter 4.
17. Ducarmel Bocage, *General Economic Theory of François Perroux* (New York and London: University Press of America, 1985).
18. Henry Spiegel, *The Growth of Economic Thought* (Englewood Cliffs: Prentice Hall, 1971).
19. Tormod Hermansen, "Development Poles and Development Centres in National and Regional Development: Elements of a Theoretical Framework?," in *Growth Poles and Growth Centres in Regional Planning*, Anthony Kuklinski (ed.), (The Hague, the Netherlands: Mouton, 1972), vol. 5.
20. Niles Hansen, (ed.), *Growth Centers in Regional Economic Development* (New York: The Free Press, 1972).
21. José Ramon Lasuen, "Urbanization and Development—The Temporal Interaction Between Geographical and Sectoral Clusters," *Urban Studies*, 1973, vol. 10, pp. 163-88.
22. J.H. von Thünen, *Der Isolierte Statt in Beziehung auf Nationalökonomie und Landwirtschaft*, Stuttgart: Gustav Fischer; reprint of 1826 edition.
23. Walter Christaller, *Die Zentralen Orte in Suddeutschland*, English translation by C.W. Baskin, *Central Places in Southern Germany* (Englewood Cliffs, New Jersey: Prentice-Hall, 1966). See also August Lösch, *The Economic of Location* (New Haven: Yale University Press, 1954).
24. Christaller, *Centreal Places in Southern Germany*.
25. John E. Ullman, *Potential Civilian Markets for the Military-Electronics Industry: Strategies for Conversion* (New York: Praeger Publishers, 1970).
26. Leslie Curry, *A Theory of Political Exchange and Economic Reasoning in Political Analysis* (Englewood Cliffs, N.J.: Prentice-Hall, 1968).
27. Gunnar Olsson, "Central Place Systems, Spatial Interaction and Stochostic Processes," in B. Berry, *Spatial Analysis: A Reader in Statistical Geography* (Toronto: Prentice-Hall, 1968), pp. 178-80.
28. Berry, *Spatial Analysis*.
29. *Ibid.* See also Olsson, "Central Place Systems, Spatial Interaction and Stochostic Processes," pp. 199-201.
30. Olsson, "Central Place Systems."

7

Location Theory

Location theory can be as intellectually challenging, as indeterminate as to outcome, as much fun, and about as relevant to regional development as a game of chess. Few branches of economics have generated as much ingenuity, nor have been as abstract, frustrating, and unproductive as location theory. The literature is massive, much of it highly mathematical, most of it abstruse, and accordingly impossible to summarize in short compass. Here we shall not even try. Rather, we shall give some illustrations of the kind of thing location theory is, summarize the outcome—or lack of outcome—and let it go at that.

The Hotelling Model

A favourite starting point for writers on location theory is the model introduced in 1929 by Harold Hotelling.[1] Imagine two sellers of ice cream on a beach. People are scattered evenly along the beach. The two sellers and their ice creams are absolutely identical in the eyes of all the potential clients; there is no reason to walk farther than the nearest seller to buy ice cream. Thus either seller will maximize his sales and his profits if he locates his stand so as to be nearest to the largest possible number of potential clients. Both sellers charge the same price (or near enough the same that no client will bother to go past one seller and walk to the other). The sellers first set up their stands at points A and B, leaving seller "A" with a sheltered market "a" and seller "B" with the sheltered market "b," and the market between points A and B divided according to any price differential; if prices are exactly the same it will be divided evenly between the two sellers (Figure 7.1).

Each seller assumes that both the price and the location of his rival are fixed. It suddenly occurs to "A" that if he moves his stand next to "B's," as in stage two of the diagram, he can take over the entire market except for the small section "b." But "B" is no fool; he promptly moves just the other side of "A" and takes over the entire market to the west of his new position, as in stage three of the diagram. This game is one that two can play, and they do, until

115

they arrive at the position shown in the final stage of the diagram, side by side at the centre of the beach, dividing the market evenly between them. This position is the product of a competitive market under duopoly conditions. It is not, however, an optimal situation from society's point of view. Clients near either end of the beach have to do a quite unnecessary amount of walking to get their ice cream. The socially optimal position would be the one shown in the diagram as M, with each seller located one quarter of the way along the beach from either end, and the total market again divided between them. If they can come to an agreement, they can choose location M, and perhaps raise their prices a bit as compensation for the greater convenience to their customers.

There can be no doubt that some such phenomenon takes place where convenience of the location for potential customers is the primary consideration in choosing a site for operations. Many cities have competing department stores side by side, or nearly so, at their centres. Most readers have probably seen intersections with rival service stations on each corner. If the market area is a city in the shape of a circle and there are four competitors instead of two, this solution is the one that will arise from Hotelling's assumptions.

We can relax the assumption that neither competitor expects changes in price or location of rivals, and allow one firm to settle first. It will choose the centre of the straight line or circle, to maximize access to customers, and if a rival sets up shop he will do so beside the original firm, or on an opposite corner. Once such a location is determined (still assuming that customers regard the two firms and their wares as being equally desirable) prices must be nearly equal too; otherwise, customers would walk the few extra steps to the shop with the lower prices.

In the real world, unfortunately, location decisions are much more complicated. Even if we continue to ignore for the time being the importance of differences in production and transport costs for choices of location, but allow for a variety of "rational expectations" on the part of each competitor regarding reactions of the others, we are soon in trouble. For example, if both ice cream vendors attribute to their rival as much common sense and aggressive-

FIGURE 7.1

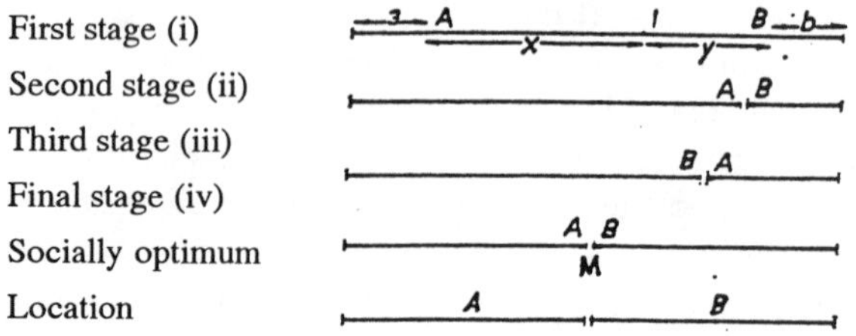

First stage (i)	
Second stage (ii)	
Third stage (iii)	
Final stage (iv)	
Socially optimum	
Location	

ness as they have themselves, and one settles initially at a point like A or B, the other will not move next to him, because he knows that his rival can jump over him and start a senseless, irritating, and in the real world possibly expensive, series of moves, until the final stage is reached. He may therefore move to somewhere near, but not at the centre, hoping his rival will then not bother to move, and perhaps cut his prices a bit to lure more customers to him. In short, *we cannot know* what will happen in terms of either location or prices, without knowing precisely what each competitor *expects his rivals to do* in various circumstances. We are stuck with what has been called the "I think that he thinks that I think that he thinks" analysis, which is indeterminate.

Then there is the fact that rival sellers are rarely identical in the eyes of all potential customers. If one ice cream vendor is a lovely girl in bikini and the other an ugly man in overalls, a good many potential male customers will be influenced by that fact. People start with a certain firm or product, become used to it, and can't be bothered changing for a minor difference in price or convenience of location. Also, the analysis becomes more complicated as one moves from two competitors to three or more. Abba Lerner and Hans Singer, in a well known joint article[2] argued that with three competitors there is no equilibrium solution, and instead there is total instability of location, or chaos. Another consideration is that with the divorce of management from ownership, many enterprises strive to maximize sales or revenues rather than profits, leading to different decisions regarding both location and prices. Still another consideration is that any move involves uncertainty as well as costs, providing a strong temptation for enterprises to just stay where they are.

Thus far our analysis has been conducted in terms of demand. Much of the location theory literature, however, concentrates rather on the combination of transport and production costs, assuming demand to be more or less given. Alfred Weber went so far as to argue in effect that location is determined primarily by transport costs alone.[3] He saw no reason for processing costs to vary significantly from one location to another. However, there are two kinds of transport costs: costs of transporting raw materials and energy to the plant, and costs of transporting finished products from the plant to the market. When inputs are more or less evenly dispersed in space they have no influence on location. When they are concentrated in particular places they exert a force of attraction, particularly if the inputs are heavy and lose weight during the production process (coal). If the raw materials are not weight-losing, the enterprise is more likely to locate near the market. These are sensible propositions, but Weber's critics have maintained that they are much too simple. For example, the possibility of substituting one input for another (electricity for coal) affects location decisions, and the minimum-transport-cost site depends on the scale of production and the choice of technology.[4]

It is obvious that if the market for a particular good or service is taken as a constant, with buyers distributed in a certain way over a defined space and with a given demand curve, enterprises will be attracted to sites where the combination of costs of producing and costs of delivering that good or service to the market is minimized. However, that simple statement does not take us very far towards an ability to predict where a particular enterprise will settle. To make such predictions, we need a good deal of empirical information as well. Production costs include land (sites), other natural resources, plant and equipment, labour, energy, and various services. The precise nature of these various factors of production, and the proportions in which they are combined, vary enormously from one industry to another, and the predominant considerations in location decisions vary accordingly. Steel industries usually locate near sources of coal (or cheap hydroelectric power) and, if possible, near iron and industrial water as well, to avoid transport costs of these heavy, weight-losing inputs. For the aluminum industry, in contrast, cheap power is so important that the chief raw material, bauxite, is hauled thousands of miles to sites with cheap and abundant hydroelectric power (waterfalls). The garment trades often settle in large cities like New York because they provide a plentiful supply of cheap female labour. There is no general rule. We cannot say "Enterprises tend to settle near sources of cheap raw materials"—or cheap labour or cheap land or cheap power or cheap capital. We can say only, "It depends, particularly on the proportions in which these factors of production are required." The importance of transport costs also varies enormously; it is a lot cheaper to transfer $100,000 worth of consulting services than $100,000 worth of turbines.

Edgar M. Hoover, one of the leading writers on location theory of his generation, put the matter this way: The most obvious basis for the distribution of industries and people is the disposition of natural resources. Clearly it is better to grow oranges in Florida and wheat in Kansas than the other way around; it is almost equally clear that New York's harbor and its "water-level" route to the interior predestined growth of a great seaport. Simple and direct relations to natural resources, however, do not take us far in accounting for most locations. They give no convincing explanation for the concentration of automobile manufacturing in Michigan or of the woolen manufacturing in Massachusetts.[5]

Perhaps most exaggerated in the public mind is the importance of cheap labour for the location of industry in certain regions, especially today with the growing concern about competition from developing countries in the field of manufacturing. Hoover has this to say on that subject: "Locations with high wage rates do not necessarily attract job seekers or repel employers. The employer is interested essentially in low processing costs, which depend on labour

TABLE 7.1
Some Statistical Ratios Pertaining to the
Fabricated Structural Steel Industry in 1939

	Average wage ($)	Wages to value added (%)	Cost of materials to value added (%)	Cost of fuel and power to value added (%)	Wages, cost of materials, fuel, and power to final product value (%)
Alabama	936	27.25	131.17	1.94	68.79
United States	1,340	42.37	149.50	2.66	76.64

productivity and also on how the local labour supply lends itself to low over-head, i.e., good utilization of fixed investment, and to improvements in production techniques. The best labour supply from the employer's standpoint is often found in places with relatively high wage rates."[6]

Similarly, Melvin Greenhut states that "low wages are not necessarily low labour costs."[7] He follows this statement immediately, however, by an example that shows in one particular case that wages low relative to productivity were a major factor in locating a steel plant in Alabama.

Personal Preferences

As "smokestack industry" is replaced in importance by scientifically oriented, "hi-tech" industry, industry becomes increasingly "footloose" or mobile. Accordingly, the factors we have been discussing thus far become less important, and personal preferences of managers, scientists, engineers and technicians become more important. Such people are interested in things like the presence in a particular centre of universities and research institutes; good climate and pleasant surroundings; cultural amenities like symphony orchestras, opera, ballet, and live theatre; having interesting and creative people as neighbours; and being where the action is.

Writing forty years ago, Hoover already took note of the importance of these personal preferences: "Everyone has some preference as to consumer location, i.e. where he would like to live and spend his income. For all but an envied minority there is also the question of producer location, i.e. the best place to earn an income.... Most people come to prefer the kind of environment in which they have been living rather than some other social, racial or institutional atmosphere; unfamiliar climate and landscape, or change from urban to rural living or vice versa."[8] This basic conservatism about where people live and work is a major factor governing mobility, which, as we have already noted above and will return to again, is a key factor in regional analysis.

Harry Richardson makes the point that many enterprises are where they are because the founder was born there and wanted to stay there.[9] He mentions Ford in Detroit and Morris at Cowley (Oxford), and Boots and Players at Nottingham; and he notes that "personal factors such as proximity to home and family and locational preferences feature prominently in the result of location surveys." Greenhut devotes a whole chapter to "personal contacts" and another to "purely personal considerations," and cites many cases where site-selection was governed primarily by one or the other.[10]

It is apparent that location of economic activity is a very complicated affair. Hoover even suggests that it is stochastic, a matter of chance or law of probability: A good analogy is the scattering of certain types of seeds by the wind. These seeds may be carried for miles before finally coming to rest, and nothing makes them select spots particularly favorable for germination. Some fall in good places and get a quick and vigorous start; other fall in sterile or overcrowded spots and die. Because of the survival of those which happen to be well located, the resulting distribution of such plants from generation to generation follows closely the distribution of favorable growing conditions. So in the location of economic activities it is not necessary to have both competition and wise business planning to have a somewhat rational locational pattern emerge; either alone will work in that direction.[11]

A General Theory of Location?

If Hoover's analogy is apt, can we really hope to have a general theory of location that is complete, realistic, operational and applicable? The answer is: probably not. There have been a good many attempts to produce one, but none yet satisfies these criteria of a satisfactory general theory. One of the most heroic efforts, and one of the most cited books on the subject is that of August Lösch.[12] It is a monumental work; but it ends up being hopelessly abstract, and no one yet has succeeded in re-working it to the point where the result meets the criteria laid down above. Among the simplifying assumptions laid down are: industrial raw materials distributed evenly through space and identical transportation facilities everywhere, so costs are the same at all points over a homogeneous plain; an even distribution of population over that plain; identical consumer tastes and preferences everywhere; and freedom of entry into all industries, pure competition, and identical production functions for all competitors. Tord Palander, Swedish economist who wrote one of the most important book on location theory of the 1930s, basing his criticism on the original German edition of Lösch, made it clear that such attempts at a "general" theory are hopelessly inadequate. Not only must a "general" theory take account of local differences in demand and in the supply of factors of production, but any attempt to integrate location theory into the Walras-Pareto-Cassel general equilibrium theory is self defeating; that theory requires zero transport costs and complete mobility of all factors of production. In such a theory, space disappears, and Lösch's "homogeneous plain" becomes a single point, with the entire market at that point.[13]

Greenhut, in his final chapter, presents a "non-mathematical formulation of a general theory."[14] That might seem like a boon to a non-mathematician, but making the theory non-mathematical does not really make it less complicated. His model includes eight variables on the demand side, and twenty-three on the cost side, plus three (unquantifiable) "purely personal factors." Such a model could not be specified, let alone tested empirically, and in proceeding to a mathematical model Greenhut simplifies it a great deal.

Richardson sums up his view of the general theory of location in these words: "As yet, no fully satisfactory general theory of location has been developed. It is not difficult to outline some of the main factors affecting spatial economic activity and to demonstrate their influence in a broad unsystematic fashion, but such an approach fails to develop any rules for explaining the structure of the space economy. One of the main troubles is that the simplest methodology for development of a determinate theory is that of general equilibrium analysis, yet the concept of general equilibrium is not very appropriate to an understanding of the geographic basis of production, consumption and trade.... Even if some kind of equilibrium could be assumed to exist, it would be difficult to predict the consequences of a disturbance of that equilibrium.... A model capable of doing this requires great precision in setting up its assumptions and specifying constraints within which it operates. It would demand quantification and would, therefore, need to be operational."[15] Neither his 1978 book nor his 1988 contribution to the volume on *Regional Development: Essays in Honour of François Perroux* suggest that Richardson thinks that the situation regarding a general theory of location has improved very much since.[16]

Theory of Interregional and International Trade and Location Theory

Several writers have made the point that a truly general theory of location would not only be required to integrate location theory with theory of prices, production, employment and distribution, but with the theory of interregional and international trade as well. Already in 1933 Bertil Ohlin was very clear on this point. He states that among his objectives is: "...to demonstrate that the theory of international trade is only part of a general localization theory, wherein the space aspects of pricing are taken into full account, and to frame certain fundamentals of such a theory as a background for a theory of international trade, wherein the influence of local differences in supply of factors of production and transportation costs within each country is duly considered."[17]

Ohlin did not quite succeed in pulling all this off. It is a formidable task. Richardson thinks that the best way of attempting it, is "by grafting locational aspects on to an interregional trade model rather than by abandoning the latter."[18] More power to him.

Notes

1. Harold Hotelling, "Stability in Competition," *The Economic Journal*, vol. 39, March 1929. See also Harry Richardson, *Elements of Regional Economics: Local Theory, Urban Structure, and Regional Change* (Harmondsworth: Penguin, 1969), p. 81 and *Urban Economics* (Hillsdale, Ill.: Dryden Press, 1978), p. 59.
2. Abba Lerner and hans Singer, "Some Notes on Duopoly and Spatial Competition," *Journal of Political Economy*, vol. 45, 1939, pp. 145-86.
3. Alfred Weber, *Theory of Location of Industries* (Chicago: University of Chicago Press, 1929).
4. Richardson, *Urban Economics*, pp. 54-5.
5. Edgar Hoover, *The Location of Economic Activity* (New York: McGraw-Hill, 1948), p. 3.
6. *Ibid.*, p. 3.
7. Melvin Greenhut, *Intermediate Income and Growth Theory* (Englewood Cliffs, New Jersey: Prentice-Hall, 1961), p. 216.
8. Hoover, *The Location of Economic Activity*, pp. 4-5.
9. Richardson, *Urban Economics*, p. 63.
10. Greenhut, *Intermediate Income and Growth Theory*, chapters 9 and 10.
11. Hoover, *The Location of Economic Activity*, p. 10.
12. August Lösch, *The Economic of Location* (New Haven: Yale University Press, 1954).
13. Tord Palander, *Beiträge zur Standordtheorie* (Uppsala, Almquist and Wicksells Bergrycken, A.B., 1935). See also Walt Isard, *Location and Space-Economy* (New York: M.I.T. Press & Wiley, 1956), pp. 52-3.
14. Greenhut, *Intermediate Income and Growth Theory*, chapter 12.
15. Richardson, *Elements of Regional Economics*, pp. 101-2.
16. Benjamin Higgins and Donald J. Savoie, *Regional Economic Development: Essays in Honour of François Perroux* (London and Boston: Unwin Hyman, 1988).
17. Bertil Ohlin, *International and Interregional Trade* (Cambridge, Mass.: Harvard University Press, 1933, p. 582.
18. Richardson, *Elements of Regional Economics*, p. 103.

8

Bi-Modal Production and Regional Dualism

The theory of bi-modal production, or "technological dualism," was initially formulated to explain why countries that have experienced a good deal of modernization of production techniques, and spectacular expansion of their modern export sectors, have nonetheless left the bulk of their populations in poverty. The term "technological dualism" was the one originally used for this theory; the expression "bi-modal production" was invented only after the earlier term was thoroughly entrenched in the literature. That sequence was unfortunate because, despite efforts to distinguish "technological" from "cultural" dualism, the confusion of the two remained. The theory of cultural dualism is associated particularly with the name of Jan Boeke, a Dutch economist who spent thirteen years in Indonesia as a government official, before becoming Professor of Economics at Leiden. As one of the few well-trained economists with experience in developing countries, Boeke exerted a good deal of influence in the 1950s, becoming the focal point of a whole school of "oriental economics" in Holland. His theory has been regarded by critics as an apology for colonialism, but that interpretation is not quite fair. His thought was rather that the kindest thing the colonial powers could do for indigenous people was to leave them alone, to develop within the limits of the internal dynamics of their own culture, instead of destroying that culture by excessive contact with the Western world.[1]

The theory of technological dualism, with its rejection of Boeke's cultural dualism, emerged from discussions among economists, anthropologists, sociologists and political scientists associated with the Massachusetts Institute of Technology Indonesia Project in the latter half of the 1950s. Basic to the theory is the population explosion that followed European settlement wherever it took place in the colonies, as a result of improved public health and the maintenance of law and order (prevention of wars among neighbouring tribes, kingdoms, or sultanates). Also basic is the idea that technology in the modern sector became increasingly capital intensive as time went by, so that its capacity to absorb a growing labour supply is limited. (In Indonesia, after three hundred and fifty years of Dutch rule, only seven percent of the labour force had been absorbed into the modern sector). Consequently, most of the increasing population must make a living as best it can in the traditional sector; population pressure on the land becomes severe, and the result is shared poverty in the traditional sector.

The theory of bi-modal production or "technological dualism" was presented as an explanation of underdevelopment in general, but it was quickly recognized that it was also an explanation of regional disparities, or regional dualism, because of the tendency of enterprises using advanced technology to be concentrated in some regions, and of enterprises using retarded, old-fashioned, traditional techniques of production to be concentrated in other regions.

In industrialized countries, of course, the terms "traditional" and "modern" can have somewhat different meanings from those typical in developing countries. "Traditional" can refer to the "smokestack" industries that grew up in the late nineteenth and early twentieth centuries, like iron and steel, textiles, automobiles, and the services common to the same period. "Modern" can mean high-technology manufacturing like electronics, computer hardware and software, biological engineering, and sophisticated services. The same principles apply however; the regions where the "modern" sector in this sense is concentrated will be relatively rich, and the regions in which this kind of "traditional" sector is concentrated will be relatively poor—as we are witnessing today in the contrast between the Great Lakes region, and New England or the southeast of the United States, or the contrast between the Atlantic provinces and the "golden triangle" of Ontario in Canada.

The story of technological dualism is told by Figures 8.1 and 8.2. In both figures the vertical axis measures capital K and land L. For convenience we assume that land and capital are used in fixed proportions, which is not too unrealistic an assumption in either the modern or the traditional sector, but dropping this assumption would make no significant difference to the main argument. On the horizontal axis we are measuring labour and time; as time goes by the labour force grows, capital is accumulated and output increases. The curves in each figure are "isopods," showing various combinations of labour with land-and-capital that will produce a given output. As we move upwards from 0_1 to 0_2, etc., we are moving to higher levels of output. The curves marked EE' are expansion paths, showing how the actual combination of labour with land-and-capital, and actual total output, move through time.

Given the fixed technical coefficients and increasingly capital-intensive nature of the modern sector, only a small section of the increasing population can be absorbed into that sector. Most of the increase in population is compelled to find its livelihood in the traditional sector. The end result is a high level of output per-man-year in the modern sector, although not necessarily high average incomes for industrial workers. In the traditional sector the result is sharing a limited output among increasing numbers, and consequent poverty.

While this analysis provides the essence of the theory of the technological dualism, there are other elements in it. The process of expansion under colonialism, according to the argument, not only led to technological dualism, but detraditionalized indigenous society, depriving it of much of its internal dynamics. In particular the gradual assumption by Europeans of responsibility for all aspects of management in the modern sector prevented the natural evolution of effective indigenous entrepreneurship. Moreover, in many cases, the neglect of education by the colonial power led to a marked decline in levels of education in many developing countries.

The theory of technological dualism is largely backward looking, a theory of history. It explains why concentration of development efforts in a modern export sector, despite spectacular growth of that sector, failed to bring prosperity to the mass of the population. It tells us how we got where we are, rather than suggesting a path to be followed to get somewhere better. It is probably true, however, that most "dualists" thought of the solution as a "Big Push" designed to accelerate expansion of the modern sector (without neglecting opportunities to raise productivity in the traditional sector), to the point where significant structural change could take place. But a change in policy, emphasizing investment and job creation in the lagging region does not invalidate the theory. The explanation of the past remains the same.

The terms "modern-traditional" were conceived as technical terms, a convenient shorthand for describing conditions in the two major sectors. In retrospect, some term other than "traditional" might have been preferable, since it is easy for readers to slip into the attitude of thinking that the term implies that the society of the sector is "traditional" in the sense of being more or less untouched by colonialism and contact with the modern sector. Even Jan Boeke was saying just the opposite of that; and certainly in the M.I.T. version the essence of the argument is that contact of indigenous cultures with imported European cultures led to modification, and essentially retrogression (involution) of the indigenous culture. It is only the technology that must remain traditional for the theory to hold. It is the agricultural revolution, much more than the industrial revolution, which has failed to touch the lives of the masses of the populations of developing countries. Perhaps "technologically advanced" and "technologically retarded" sectors would give rise to less misunderstanding, awkward as they are as terms to be frequently used. By the same token, the theory is essentially one of interactions between the two sectors.

It was understood from the beginning that dealing with underdeveloped economies with a two-sector model was a convenient abstraction. It was rec-

FIGURE 8.1
Traditional Sector

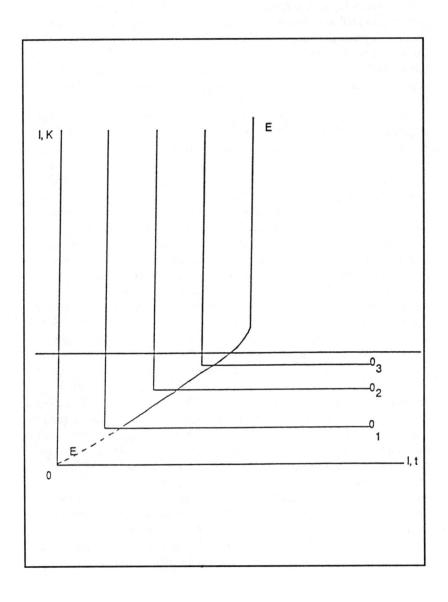

FIGURE 8.2
Modern Sector

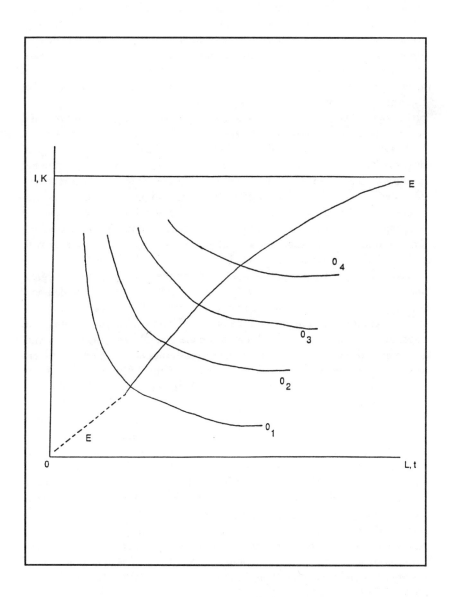

ognized that there were intermediate economic activities, such as smallholder'
rubber and copra in rural areas or "opelettes" and "jeepneys" (small busses) in
the cities, which did not fit well into the "modern-traditional" dichotomy.
However, the proportion of the population engaged in such activities was so
small that there was a danger of distracting attention from the core phenomenon of developing countries, and making the analysis unnecessarily cumbersome, by introducing a third, "transitional" sector.[2] I did introduce a
"transitional" sector, which certainly complicated the diagrammatic analysis,
and I am not sure it was worthwhile. The question here is whether or not
astute policy can convert the small transitional sector into an instrument for
dynamic growth of the economy as a whole. That question is largely an empirical one. This question also bears on the role of the "informal sector," and
we shall return to it below under that heading.

The theory of regional dualism is derived from the theory of technological
dualism. The argument is that poor regions are those in which the traditional
sector is concentrated, and rich regions those where the modern sector is concentrated. The historical process of creating rich and poor regions is identical
to the process which created the modern and traditional sectors. Nor need the
poor regions be basically resource poor; very often they are the regions which
were initially rich in resources and where, accordingly, population growth
and involution has been concentrated.

Oswaldo Sunkel puts considerable stress on the overlap of technological
and regional dualism. The internal process of polarization can be seen as a
growing division between modern dominant and advanced economic activities, social groups and regions on the one hand, and backward, marginal and
dependent activities, groups and regions on the other. In fact, the geographic,
economic, social, political and cultural centres of modernity and development
are closely associated with the rise and fall of the activities linked more
closely—directly or indirectly—to the developed countries. This is the case
of regions, cities or ports which are subject to the direct influence of the investments and expansion of the traditional export activities, and also of those
other cities or regions which, either because they are administrative centres or
areas producing inputs for the export sector and are able to capture part of the
income generated in the export sector and redistribute it to other regions and
social groups. When this polarization of population corresponds to the decline
of economic activity in traditional export and/or agricultural activity, it leads
to acute and growing spatial imbalances. We might in this respect, recall that
some of the most underdeveloped areas of Latin America today are precisely
zones which once were regions of exceptional wealth, social prestige, political importance and cultural splendour: the Northeast of Brazil; the areas of
precious metals in Mexico, Peru, Bolivia, Brazil and Chile; the nitrate fields

of Chile; henequén fields of Yacatan; the abandoned banana fields of Central America, and the old coffee and cocoa plantations of Brazil.[3] One might add Appalachia and the Great Lakes regions and the Atlantic provinces and Gaspésie-Bas-St. Laurent in Canada.

Is bi-modal production the explanation of regional disparities? The theory of technological dualism was advanced to explain why large-scale investment and substantial technological advance in underdeveloped countries, especially under colonial (or neo-colonial) regimes, failed to bring a tolerable level of prosperity to the majority of the population. If the theory is correct within its own framework, and if at the same time the modern sector is concentrated in some regions and the traditional sector in others, the theory is also an explanation of regional dualism.

But *why should* such concentration take place? Basically, the neoclassical theory says that it shouldn't. Any tendency for high-technology, high-productivity economic activities to agglomerate in some regions and low-technology, low-productivity in others will, according to that theory, bring into play countervailing forces which will restore balance, or spatial equilibrium. The mere fact that in many countries the modern and traditional sectors do overlap with leading and lagging regions is not final proof that the overlapping is inevitable. The neoclassical faithful can always say that the mere existence of regional disparities are proof of misguided and injurious government intervention. The only reason that regional gaps do not disappear is that government is preventing the free market from doing its job.

There is also the question as to the degree in which a theory advanced to explain underdevelopment in Third World countries can be applied without modification to industrialized ones. There can be no doubt that, as a matter of actual fact, regional disparities in industrialized countries are related to differences in occupational structure, product-mix, and level of technology. But why should such differences exist? There would seem to be less reason for their persistence in industrialized countries than in developing ones, given their generally superior levels of science and technology, education and training, transport and communications, information, political institutions and administration. Can it be that government policy is even worse in industrialized countries than in underdeveloped ones?

There is also the fact, which needs explanation, that the curves of regional per capita income and other social indicators, are not only capable of converging under some circumstances, but of crossing. Thus in Brazil, the Northeast, for some decades now the country's major problem region, was once its richest. Harry W. Richardson has raised the question as to whether such a phenomenon may not occur in the United States, the once lagging Southeast and Southwest not just catching up but becoming the country's richest, while the once industrially powerful Great Lakes region, and perhaps even New England, become relatively poor: The key question is whether regional per capita income will stabilize close to equality (i.e. an approximation to neoclassical equilibrium) or whether they will cross over, with the four lower income regions (South Atlantic, East South Central, West South Central and Mountain) becoming progressively richer than the four regions of the Northeast and Midwest.[4] Benjamin Higgins has suggested that Quebec, not so long ago the region that gave most cause for concern in Canada, may soon be Canada's richest province, what with the present dynamism of its younger French Canadian entrepreneurs and its current rapid growth, combined with Ontario's difficulties as a result of its ties with the Great Lakes "smokestack industries," and the troubles Alberta and British Colombia face with their natural resource development.[5]

It cannot be said that we have a tight, generally accepted theory to explain regional dualism. The theory of bi-modal production certainly gives us some valuable clues as to what to look for, but it does not really explain why regional gaps must appear, nor why there must be convergence, or a crossover. There is, however, a paradigm that purports to explain the inevitability of regional dualism in a capitalist system: the theory of dependency.

Notes

1. Jan Boeke's major work was *Economics and Economic Policy in Dual Societies* (New York: International Secretariat of the Institute of International Relations, 1953). See also "Three Forms of Disintegration in Dual Societies," *Indonesie*, vol. vii, no. 4, April 1954, pp. 278–285; and "Western Influence on the Growth of Eastern Population," *Economia Internazionale*, vol. viii, no. 2, April 1954, pp. 358–369. For an extensive exposition and criticism of the theory of cultural dualism, see Benjamin Higgins, *Economic Development: Problems, Principles, and Policies* (New York: W.W. Norton, 1968), chapter on Cultural Determinism. This volume also contains a more extensive treatment of technological dualism.
2. Benjamin Higgins, "The Employment Problem in Development" in Eliezer Ayal *Micro-Aspects of Economic Development*, New York, Macmillan, 1976b. (In this chapter, I did introduce a "transitional" sector, which certainly complicated the diagrammatic analysis, and I am not sure it was worthwhile).
3. Oswald Sunkel, "Transnational Capitalism and National Disintegration in Latin America," in *Social and Economic Studies*, Girvan, N. (ed.), vol. 22, no.1, 1973, Special Number on Dependence and Underdevelopment in the New World and the Old, pp.140-41.
4. Harry Richardson, "Regional Policy in a Slow Growth Economy," in G.J. Demko, editor, *Regional Development Problems and Policies in Eastern & Western Europe*, (London: Croom Helm, 1984), pp. 258–81).
5. Benjamin Higgins, *The Rise and Fall? of Montreal* (Moncton: Canadian Institute for Research on Regional Development, 1986). See also Benjamin Higgins and Donald J. Savoie, *Regional Economic Development: Essays in Honour of François Perroux* (London and Boston: Unwin Hyman, 1988), p. 198.

9

Dependency and Uneven Development

The "dependency theory" has been one of the major products of what may be broadly termed neo-Marxist thought, or radical political economy, since World War II. Much of it has been generated in Latin America, and the dependency school is associated with the United Nations Economic Commission for Latin America, and with the names of economists who have written in and about Latin America: Raul Prebisch, Osvaldo Sunkel, Fernando Cardoso, Celso Furtado, André Gunder Frank. However, the school has by no means been confined to Latin America, but include Africans like Samir Amin and Europeans like Johan Galtung, Stuart Holland, and Frances Saunders. Like many of the theories that we have already discussed in this volume, the dependency theory is concerned with underdevelopment in general, with poverty, and with disparities among social groups. It has been applied more frequently to differences among nations than to regional gaps; but, like other theories, it has been extended to the explanation of regional disparities.

In its purest form, dependency theory argues that continued underdevelopment and poverty in less developed countries, and in lagging regions, is not the result of the failure of international capitalism but of its success in keeping wages and peasant (or small farm) incomes down in order to keep profits up. (Rising peasant or small farm incomes would exert upward pressure on industrial wages, since poor peasants and farmers are a "reserve army" of cheap labour on which capitalists can draw for industrial expansion). The theory has been applied both to developing countries as a whole and to relatively poor regions in industrialized countries. On the international scene, dependency is linked to colonialism and neo-colonialism, and some writers have attributed lagging regions in economically advanced countries to a species of "internal colonialism."

The Theory

Let us begin by conceding to our "dependentista" colleagues that their theory contains large chunks of truth, particularly that portion of it which is concerned with the impact of colonialism and neo-colonialism on LDCs.

It is not difficult to show that differences in levels and patterns of development in today's LDCs can be explained in large measure by colonial history. In varying degrees and in different ways the colonial administrations destroyed indigenous entrepreneurship; fostered industrialization at home, restrained industrial expansion in the colonies, and encouraged industrial exports to the colonies; limited the modern sector to resource exploitation and large-scale (plantation) agriculture and services related to these activities; launched a population explosion wherever Europeans settled, by improving public health, discouraging inter-tribal or inter-sultanate wars and maintaining law and order; neglected education of indigenous populations (and of imported slaves); and left behind a legacy of anti-capitalism, anti-liberalism, and anti-Westernism that complicates both the relations of LDCs with ICCs and the definition of economic ideologies and policies at home. Even differences in patterns of development since independence reflect in large degree differences in the impact of colonialism in terms of these five variables. All that being so, why not explain more recent experience of LDCs in terms of the impact of neo-colonialism and economic imperialism, along similar lines? The radical political economists, of course, (let us call them "Rads" for short) do just that.

Much of the literature on "dependencia" is historical or descriptive, consisting in large measure of accounts of widening gaps between rich countries and poor countries, and between rich and poor within LDC's, both before and after independence. The economic history of LDCs is seen as a continuum from early colonial days until the present. The analytical framework is not very elaborate and consists mainly in the application of Marxist categories to present-day LDCs. But one element of the theory is clear at the outset: to treat post-independence history as an extension of colonial exploitation, one must be prepared to argue that political independence as such makes no real difference in the economic status of LDCs. That is precisely what the "Rads" do. International capitalism, especially in its latest guise of multi-national corporations (MNCs) is no respecter of borders, they argue, and nation-states have become units of no great importance. The whole global economy is one system, whereby capitalists the world over exploit workers and peasants, and to a lesser degree the lower middle classes, the world over. In that analytical framework, for example, the energy crisis of 1973 and since is seen, not as exploitation of North Americans and Europeans by Arabs, but as exploitation of workers and peasants the world over by American, British, Dutch, French and Arab capitalists working in unison to maximize their profits.

Some of the "Rads" would probably admit that the day of the "gunboat in the harbour" is past. But according to them that makes little difference; for the ruling élites of the LDCs, recognizing the economic, technical, scientific and cultural transcendence of the ruling élites of the ICCs, find it to their advantage to become junior partners in the international capitalist system. They join the foreign capitalists in exploiting their own workers and peasants. The major spoils go to the capitalists at the "Centre," the ICCs, but the capitalists of the Periphery, in the LDCs, share in the spoils nonetheless.

Most of the dependency school are quite adamant in rejecting theories of dualism. The current quarrel between "dualists" and "dependentistas" does not, however, relate to the description of current economic and social conditions in LDCs. The "Rads" do not deny that developing countries are typically split into two clearly distinguishable sectors, which correspond in large measure with advanced and retarded regions, which overlap also with distinct social and economic classes. What then, lies at the base of the "Rads" vehement attack on the theory of dualism? There seem to be two major pillars of their arguments:

1. The concept of dualism, with its division into "modern" and "traditional" sectors, suggests that there are two economic systems operating in (non-socialist) LDCs, whereas in fact there is only one, international capitalism, which makes the decisions for the whole (non-socialist) world and determines the outcome in social, economic and political terms.
2. Whereas standard or "Dualist" economists tend to suggest that the continuing poverty and growing gaps in LDCs reflect failure of development policies adopted by government of LDCs, either because the wrong development models were chosen or because they were inefficiently applied, the truth is that the current situation in LDCs reflects the success of the policies imposed by international capitalism. In other words, there is sharp disagreement between the "Rads" and the Dualists with respect to the intent behind development plans and policies.

One of the clearest statements of the first argument is presented by Samir Amin, based on his analysis of economic history of Africa. "The colonial system organizaed the society so that it produced on the best possible terms from the point of view of the mother country, exports which only provided a very low and stagnating return to labor. This goal having been achieved—and it must now be analyzed in theoretical terms—we have to conclude that there are no traditional societies in modern Africa, there are only dependent peripheral societies."[1]

A somewhat stronger statement is provided by André Gunder Frank: "Each of the two parts is supposed to have a history of its own, a structure, and a dynamic largely independent of the other. Supposedly, only part of the economy and society has been importantly affected by intimate economic relations with the outside world; and that part, it is held, became modern, capitalist and relatively developed precisely because of this contact. The other part is widely regarded as variously isolated, subsistence-based, feudal, or precapitalist, and therefore more underdeveloped.

I believe on the contrary that the entire 'dual society' thesis is false and that the policy recommendation to which it tends will, if acted upon, serve only to intensify and perpetuate the very conditions of underdevelopment they are supposedly designed to remendy.... The expansion of the capitalist system over the past centuries effectively and entirely penetrated even the apparently most isolated sectors of the underdeveloped world. Therefore, the economic, political, social and cultural institutions and reltions we now observe there are the produces of the capitalist system no less than are the seemingly more modern or capitalist features of the national metropoles of these underdeveloped countries."[2]

But if there are no traditional societies, how do the "Rads" explain the appearance of marginal groups, untouched by progress? We come now to the second argument, which has not been so precisely presented as the first one. So far as we can gather, the essence of the theory consists of the following points:

1. International capitalism is organized so as to maximize profits.
2. The advanced technology and the ultimate power is in the hands of the capitalists of ICCs (and particularly of the direction of MNCs.)
3. The capitalists of LDCs need the technology, equipment, managerial skills, markets, etc., of capitalist of ICCs. They, therefore, join hands with them in exploiting indigenous workers and peasants, concentrating themselves on relatively low-technology, less capital-intensive activities, serving as junior partners in enterprises run by capitalists of ICCs. The big profits go to capitalists of ICCs (and especially MNCs) and are seldom reinvested in LDCs.[3]
4. The workers and peasants are more important as sources of labour than as consumers. It, therefore, pays the capitalists to keep worker and peasant incomes down and keep raw materials and foodstuffs cheap, to avoid upward pressure on wages in the industrial sector.
5. The workers and peasants have no power of their own, and governments of LDCs, as "creatures" of capitalism do whatever is needed to keep them poor.
6. The economies of LDCs are thus mere extensions of the economies of ICCs, all dominated by an international capitalist hierarchy with the MNCs at the top. The LDCs are dependent upon the ICCs for technology, capital equipment, finance, markets, and entrepreneurial, administrative and scientific skills. They are, therefore, trapped in a stage of development which is based on exports of raw materials and foodstuffs and import of capital goods.

Varieties of Dependence

The truth is that there is not "a" dependency theory but several dependency theories. Clearly, the sort of "dependence" that springs from a high ratio of exports and imports to gross national product—an "open" economy—is in itself a very different phenomenon from loss of national sovereignty to foreign multinational firms. The United Kingdom in the nineteenth century, Japan in the early twentieth and West Germany in the mid twentieth, all had very open economies; but their positions in the world power structure hardly conformed to any normal concept of "dependence." Nor does concentration of exports in one or a few commodities necessarily mean lack of international bargaining power. As between the OPEC countries and Western Europe, who "depends" on whom? When we come to countries such as those of the Commonwealth Caribbean or the Lebanon, where imports of consumers goods are financed by capital inflow (one Caribbean island country has imports equal to 120 percent of GDP) dependence is more obvious. Some of the Caribbean island states have also depended on large-scale emigration to ICCs to keep numbers down, as Ireland did in the nineteenth century. Here "dependence" has clear cut meaning. The countries concerned cannot maintain their present standard of living without continued inflows of capital and outflows of people, and their bargaining position is weak. But these are special cases; few LDCs are in this position today.

Dependence on foreign technology is different in quality again. Every country has the choice of rejecting imported technology and being content with whatever standard of living indigenous technology will bring, as China essentially did between her rift with Russia and the recent reforms. "Inflow" of technology, in contrast to inflow of capital, does not help directly to close either the investment-savings gap or the foreign exchange gap. On the contrary, its impact effect is to aggravate both. There may be cases, such as Haiti or Indonesia (i.e. Java and Bali) where population pressure on the land is so severe that even maintaining present levels of welfare is impossible without importing the technology which would permit rapid industrialization, or sharp increases in agricultural productivity, or both. In such cases the country concerned may be truly "dependent" on imported technology. But once again only a minority of LDCs are in so precarious a position.

Underdevelopment due to dependence may occur where a narrowly based export sector offers the sole avenue to wealth and power. Such seems to be the case in Zambia, for example. Lacking industrial entrepreneurs of her own, and with no important class of large-scale and wealthy landowners, and being very underdeveloped in indigenous technology and skills, it becomes attractive to exploit the copper with foreign capital and technology. "Nationalization," by acquiring 51 percent of the stock in the mines and thus establishing parastatal enterprises, provides opportunities for government officials to participate in the management, acquire a modicum of power and a high income (often, it seems, substantially higher than their nominal salaries). However, since the local government officials lack the specialized training and experience that would provide them with the level of expertise enjoyed by the foreign managers, scientists and engineers—and know it—all important decisions are made by foreigners. Meanwhile, the opportunities for fame and fortune provided by the mining enclave diverts the few Zambians with some training away from projects designed to develop the rural sector, where most of the population seeks its livelihood. Moreover, in such a situation, it is easy for foreign firms and governments to persuade the government officials that foreign aid should be directed towards projects such as roads, railroads, power plants, and training schemes which are needed for expansion of the mining sector.

Dependency and Regional Disparities

If the dependency theory were extended to the explanation of regional disparities, while retaining its simplest form, it would say: "The international monopoly capitalists, best represented today by the multi-national corporation, want to keep workers and farmers poor in lagging regions, and have the power to do so. By preserving poverty and unemployment in retarded regions they maintain a constant reserve army of cheap labour for transfer to the more prosperous regions, where the capitalists prefer to operate their more dynamic and profitable enterprises, to meet their needs for capital accumulation and expansion of production in the richer regions. Regional disparities within a capitalist country are just an expression of internal neo-colonialism."

Actually, however, this kind of oversimplified statement seems to be less common among neo-Marxists or radical political economists who have turned their attention to regional problems than among those who have concentrated their attack on international rather than interregional disparities. Indeed, as the special issue on uneven regional development of *The Review of Radical Political Economics* indicates, the explanation of regional gaps as a form of internal neo-colonialism seems to be rejected by most "Rads" in favour of a more complex theory of uneven development. The reason for the difference between "Rads" tackling regional gaps and those addressing international disparities is not altogether clear. Could it be that "Rads" operating at the regional level, like all regional analysts, are analyzing smaller units, than their colleagues dealing with national economies or individual enterprises from afar, and so are less prone to stray far from reality?

Not that "Regional Rads" have a markedly greater sympathy and admiration for "capitalists" than the "International Rads." A fairly typical statement is one by Neil Smith, Columbia University geographer, who writes: "Capital is like a plague of locusts. It settles in one place, devours it, moves on to plague another place. Better, in the process of restoring itself after one plague the region makes itself ripe for another. At the very least, uneven development is the geographical expression of the contradictions of capital."[4]

A similar brand of language is used by J. Hinderink and M. J. Titus. Dependency theory, they say, seems to indicate "a potentially positive role for small centres;" but "with the prevailing national power structure of most Third World countries and in the present international political and economic framework they are seen as 'vanguards of exploitation'." Indeed, "capitalistic exploitation and integration is seen as a unilinear and causative process of progressive impoverishment of peripheral areas." These particular authors come to no firm conclusion about the role of small urban centres in regional development; "generalizations about the role of small centres...are hard to make."[5]

Such passages certainly sound like statements of dependency theorists like Gunder Frank and Samir Amin to the effect that developing countries (and in this context lagging regions) would be better off if they cut themselves off from the capitalist world altogether, became independent of it, and relied solely on whatever investment, and whatever technology, they could muster up from their own resources, within their own borders. But most regional "Rads" are not actually arguing that the depressed regions are those that have had too much investment and too much technological progress. They are arguing the opposite. Smith goes on to argue, like Myrdal and Perroux, that capitalistic market economies tend to lead to polarization of investment and technological advance, so that *wealth* is concentrated, not only in the hands of the capitalist class, but in particular places as well. Underdevelopment in some cities and regions is merely the opposite side of the coin to development in others. Cities are "the most accomplished geographical expression of the centralization of capital." Even the geographic landscape is a product of capitalistic development rather than a gift of nature. But Neil Smith's capitalists are not all-powerful. They are constantly threatened by rising wages, transport costs, and rents. Thus they are constantly on the lookout for new locations that are cheaper, and will not hesitate to move when they find them, no matter how disastrous the impact of their move on the people of communities they desert. Thus instead of a tendency towards spatial "equilibrium," a market economy under capitalism brings instability, disorder, and repeated disruption and restructuring of geographic space. Smith's solution to this chaos, however, is not that each community should be totally independent and self-sufficient, like a medieval village, but that the entire economy and the entire society should be subject to orderly, rational planning.

Stuart Holland of Sussex University ends up in much the same position as Smith. Despite the rather aggressive title of his book (*Capital versus the Regions*) Holland's analysis is more balanced than that of many "Rads."[6] He is not advocating revolution so much as more effective use of government pow-

ers to influence and regulate decisions of private enterprise regarding location, especially those of multinational corporations. In other words, he wants
more private investment in underdeveloped regions, not less.

In his preface, Holland indicates his reasons for writing his book: "This
book is about capitalism and the regions. In itself, this is more surprising than
it should be. Too much regional theory abstracts from the system in which
regional problems occur, failing to see the underlying causes of regional imbalance in capitalism itself."[7]

He attributes this abstraction in part to the fact that the first generation of
regional economists were imbued with neoclassical ideas of a self-balancing
market economy, and that economics between the wars was focused on macro-
economic theories of employment. While Myrdal and Perroux stressed the
imbalance generated by a capitalist economy, they failed to loosen the hold of
self-balance theories, particularly in the United States. The apparent success
of Keynesian theory during and immediately after the war strengthened the
idea that regional problems could be solved by relatively modest types of
intervention in the market, such as incentives and subsidies to firms: "This
combination of Keynesian and neo-classical theory has increasingly been challenged by the stubbornness of regional problems in mature capitalist economies. It has become clear that the causes of regional inequality are deeper that
the superficial analysis of frictions and imperfections in neo-classical self-
balance models would have us believe. It is also clear that indirect state intervention to improve infrastructure or concentrate incentives in growth-pole
centres does not reverse the cumulative imbalance of Myrdaliam or Perrouxial
models of regional growth."[8]

Holland's opening chapter is devoted to theories of regional self-balance.
Classical and neoclassical economics, he says, paid little attention to the regional distribution of economic activity; that matter was supposed to be taken
care of by migration of labour to areas where wages were highest and by
migration of capital to areas where returns to investment were highest. He
proceeds to a critical appraisal of the works of Alfred Weber, Lösch ("Regional Metaphysics") and Ohlin. Like many others, he regards Walter Isard as
the father of regional science, and treats Isard's writings as "the apotheosis of
technique." He thinks regional scientists are getting nowhere: "They fail to
appreciate that their reasoning is almost entirely circular, and that in genuinely scientific term it is a cul-de-sac leading nowhere. To make any progress
they must reverse their method, adopt a more divergent approach, and abandon their most cherished self-balance or equilibrium assumptions."[9]

In his second chapter, Holland turns to theories of regional imbalance, notably those of Karl Marx, Gunnar Myrdal, and François Perroux. Marx's regional theory has been unduly neglected, he says. In fact, Marx anticipated

much of the theory of Myrdal and Perroux. At the end of the chapter, Holland provides an interesting summary of his views on theories of regional self-balance and imbalance: "Much of this text is an extension of imbalance or disequilibrium theory, and an attempt to demonstrate that the trend to regional inequality is intrinsic to capitalist economic growth. In this sense the analysis is an extended consideration of both the scope and limits of the theory of regional imbalance. Essentially it corroborates main elements of Marx's analysis of capital versus the regions as well as some of the postwar work of Myrdal and Perroux."[10] But Holland also recognizes limits to imbalance theory: "One is basic and should be borne in mind in considering the analysis of forces working for imbalance in capitalist economies. This is the role of the State in offsetting observable trends to disequilibrium in the spatial distribution of resources or the trend to monopoly in interfirm competition. Myrdal saw 'the Welfare State' as intervening through development policies to offset the cumulative disequilibrium process which he analyzed. Perroux focused his recommendation for State intervention in growth-pole policy. Marx died before the rise of the modern capitalist State, which undertakes the role of umpire, regulator and planner of resource distribution. He also died before union bargaining strength and relative labour shortages in particular regions and countries increased the real wages paid to organized labour and offset the tendency to falling profit through under-consumption. Both the role of the modern capitalist State and rising regional incomes through trade-union bargaining power had acted to offset these imbalances between regions which otherwise would have occurred through the long-run working of the market."[11]

Obviously, this is not the language of a pure, die-hard, old-fashioned Marxist. A government that is "umpire, regulator, and planner" is a far cry from a government that is a mere creature of the monopoly-capitalist class. Government officials who can make plans and introduce regulations to reduce regional disparities by enforcing decisions different from those that the capitalists would make if left entirely on their own, are not merely "learned handmaidens" of capitalism.

Holland also notes that, because of various social welfare programs, income per capita varies less from region to region than gross product per capita, in the industrialized countries of Europe and North America. He also takes note of the long-run tendency towards regional convergence as development takes place, citing Jeffrey Williamson. He then asks: "why should we worry about any underlying trend to imbalance through the free working of modern capitalism, or bother to up-date and extend the imbalance theory of Marx, Myrdal, or Perroux?"[12] He gives several answers to his own question. The rise of meso-economic power in national economies (in the form of large, monopolistic corporations) means that private enterprise is increasingly able to escape the impact and intent of national regional policies. The fact that many of these corporations are multi-nationals, as well, aggravates this trend. True, one result of this trend is that capital does move to low-wage regions and low-wage countries, but this movement does not bring smooth elimination of regional disparities: "Capital is not moving in the incremental shuffle beloved of perfect-competition theorists, but strides the world in seven-league boots, overstepping problem regions in both developed and less-developed countries.... Expressed differently, there are new dimensions to regions inequality in a capitalist system which can only be traced by following the location pattern of the new capitalist leaders in the meso-economic sector."[13]

The long third chapter on imbalanced growth and trade reviews models of economic fluctuations and growth of the Domar, Harrod and Hicks type, admits that interregional trade may reduce regional disparities, but maintains that the export base theory of regional development is misleading in several respects. There is nothing very distinctive in the treatment in this chapter. Much of it could have come—and, indeed, some of it has come—from within the neoclassical establishment itself. Chapter 4 on migration and imbalanced resource use refers to historical experience, mainly of South Italy and Southern United States, to demonstrate that neither interregional nor intersectoral migration can always be counted upon to solve regional problems: "The migration process observable in capitalist economies such as the United States and Italy contrasts sharply with the harmonious self-balance assumptions of neo-classical theory. The facts simply do not support a picture in which migrants optimise their potential welfare by moving from regions where jobs or pay are low to high-job and high-pay regions."[14]

Chapter 5 on unequal competition and regional imbalance considers location theory under conditions of imperfect competition. After analyzing the operations of oligopolies Holland states: "The regional implications of such oligopoly theory are elaborated in the following section of this chapter. However, one of the most important is that small LDR (less developed region) firms cannot count upon any inbuilt restraint mechanism to hold back national sector-leading firms located in the MDR (more developed region), and allow them to catch them up in terms of scale, productivity, rate of innovation, and so on. This is not to say that no small, late starting, LDR firms ever catch up with early starting MDR firms. It has already been admitted that size is not a sufficient condition for competitive success.... On the other hand, the mechanism of oligopolistic competition tends to increase rather than close such (regional) disparities, and also can mean that once large firms have started to expand in more developed regions their continued further expansion in those regions will 'backwash' smaller firms in LDRs. The scale of the backwash concerned will clearly depend *inter alia* on (1) the initial national and regional location patterns in early industrialization; (2) the force of other factors contributing to interregional divergence such as centripetal labour and capital flow; and (3) the time-period in which such divergence is not checked or off-set by government policies. However, if that time-period is sufficiently long, a situation may arise in which most of the 'modern' meso-economic firms in the economy are concentrated in the more-developed regions, and most of the 'traditional' micro-economic firms in the less developed (giving rise to re-gional dualism)."[15]

Holland also makes the point that the increasing scope of the MNCs ren-ders regional development programs ineffective or very expensive. Multina-tionals which can go to Mexico, the Philippines, or Taiwan may need a wage subsidy of 75 percent or more to induce them to locate in a development area in the United Kingdom. He cites evidence from "the U.S. Tariff Commission and other sources" showing that labour costs in Mexico or the Far East range from 5 to 10 percent of U.S. costs, depending on the area and product. Note that he is speaking of costs, not wage levels. With standardized techniques, output per manhour in developing countries quickly reaches American levels. Clearly, the international mobility of the MNCs complicates the task of de-signing effective *regional* development policy. In Marxist language, one could say that the dependence of the peripheral countries of the Third World not only perpetuates poverty within their own borders, but also perpetuates the unemployment and relative poverty in lagging regions of the capitalist coun-tries at the Centre.[16]

Chapter 6 is entitled "Structure versus the Regions." From the title, a reader might hope that the chapter would explain in more precise detail what Hol-land means by "Capital versus the Regions." Instead the chapter presents at great length two propositions, neither of them very original:

1. Per capita income of any region depends upon the structure of its produc-tion and employment;
2. This structure is determined by the decisions of private enterprise, par-ticularly the MNCs. Thus regional convergence will not take place unless the MNCs want to upgrade the structures of lagging regions.

Holland does not deny the possibility that such a thing may happen, but he does deny that it *will inevitably* happen. Stage theories of the kind advanced by Colin Clark, Simon Kuznets, and Walt Rostow are not laws, Holland in-sists. Structural change of the kind described in these models may or may not occur. It depends upon where the MNCs want to locate leading sectors and innovations. Less developed regions cannot catch up merely by expanding their manufacturing sectors. What counts is the relative shares of modern and traditional manufacturing in the expansion. The chapter closes with a rather routine critique of input-output analysis. In short, its content hardly justifies its title.

Chapter 7 deals with spatial concentration versus dispersion. It raises the question as to whether or not there are locational economies of scale. Is concentration justified by the lower costs attaching to putting everything—or at least all modern sector activities—in the same place? His answer to this question is, "It depends: It is apparent that concentration and dispersion need not be mutually exclusive options for a national locational policy. The desirability depends on the kind of firm, the type of production, the distribution of market and supply areas, the nature of the transport system, labour availability and cost, congestion costs, and so on.... The question for locational policy should not be whether but what to concentrate and disperse, where and how much."[17] One can hardly quarrel with this statement.

Holland's final chapter deals with theory, practice and policy alternatives. A good deal of space is devoted to Italy's efforts to solve its North-South problem. Referring to this problem, Holland remarks that regional science is *not* the answer: "Any regional policy which is concerned to make a quantified approach to resolving such imbalance should be guided by a systematic, if flexible, cost-benefit framework. So far too little has been pioneered in this area. The Regional Science school in the United States includes some of the most accomplished mathematicians to have escaped the NASA space program. But since they mainly have been concerned to give algebraic elegance to equilibrium models which assume-away regional imbalance in the first place, their talents have not resulted in major advances in cost-benefit models."[18]

A key section on "harnessing meso-economic power" provides the guidelines for Holland's basic strategy. He accepts the high probability that the giant corporation and the MNC are here to stay, at least in Western Europe and North America, and accordingly concentrates on policies to use them as a vehicle for reducing regional disparities. In a free market, there is every possibility of increased concentration of meso-economic, big-league firms in the more developed regions. State competition policy may drive such firms to expansion abroad rather than in the less developed regions of industrialized countries. It is futile to assume that indirect incentives alone will ensure the growth of small, micro-economic firms into medium-size meso-economic firms in less developed regions. Nor is concentration of industry in selected growth poles a complete solution.

The solution lies rather in detailed micro-economic planning in which all relevant factors are taken into account, supported by effective locational controls so that plans can be implemented. There is need for "new dimensions in regional policy—harnessing big-league meso-economic power through new public enterprise, backed by powers of specific locational controls."[19] It is not a matter of once-over interventions "to patch the market," but of continuous management of the economy; "the macro, meso, and micro factor must constitute a consistent and continuing dimension of regional policies. In short—yes—regional policy forever."[20]

In short, while Holland's somewhat belligerent language and choice of terminology (such as the use of the word "capital" to mean a dominant and aggressive force in society, unconcerned about anything but earning profits and accumulating wealth and power) are suggestive of a Marxist approach, in point of fact other economists could, and some other economists did, arrive at similar conclusions without a trace of Marxist sympathies. François Perroux, whom Holland frequently quotes, was right-of-centre in the French political spectrum, yet he shared many of Holland's views.[21] Gunnar Myrdal, as we have seen above, was just about dead centre in Swedish politics, yet he too shared many of Holland's views. Let us note that the question as to whether problems of regional development can be solved by freeing the market, or whether their solution requires astute management of the national economy and the regional economies of which it is composed, cannot be answered by any exercise in pure theory. It is a question pertaining to facts, and to facts that are not easily pinned down. Virtually every less developed region in the world is in that unhappy condition partly because it has been a victim of ill construed policy, and partly because private enterprise and the free market have not operated in such a way as to make the region more highly developed. Market failure and government failure interact in a cumulative fashion, each compounding the other in a kind of feedback mechanism, so that it becomes difficult to disentangle the two, and to allocate the blame for regional failure. But difficult or not, we must try to do it. There is no other way of arriving at effective policies for dealing with disadvantaged regions.

Radical Political Planners

An interesting recent development in the United States is the invasion of the field of local and regional planning by neo-Marxist or radical political economy thought. A good example of the kind of soul-searching amongst planners which is associated with this invasion is the volume edited by Harvey Goldstein and Sara Rosenberry, presenting the proceedings of "the Conference on Planning Theory."[22] The conference, which was held at Virginia Polytechnic Institute in May of 1978, grew out of the dissatisfaction of graduate students in planning, particularly at Pennsylvania's Department of City and Regional Planning. The result was a series of seminars and colloquia at which, according to the editors, there was a "desire to explore the potential for establishing defensible links between social scientist theory and planning practice. Exploring the relationship between various social theories (including functionalism, structuralism, structural Marxism, Marxist humanism, and pragmatism) and their implied modes of planned intervention became the principal intellectual thrust of the seminars."[23] The international crisis of capitalism, they continue, has led to a "revolution of falling expectations," and planners at all levels have been asked to accept this new ideology and to implement supporting policies. They point to the tensions and conflicts that arise when planners try to be both radical and professional within the existing institutional framework in the United States.

In the opening chapter of the volume, the Feinsteins apply the Marxist paradigm to planning activity. For those acquainted with general Marxist theory, there are few surprises here. Disparate interests among the bourgeoisie compel it to organize itself through the State to plan for its common interest. Through planning the varying interests of different groups of capitalists can be subordinated to the general good of the ruling class. State activities are legitimized in the name of society as a whole while being directed towards the interests of the bourgeoisie. The ruling class needs planning to facilitate accumulation of capital and maintain social control in the face of class conflict. Urban planners are agents of the State and specialize in managing those contradictions of capitalism which manifest themselves in urban form and spatial development. These include inability of the private economy to meet the need for low-cost housing for low-income people. The roots of planning, and more generally of progressivism, is to be found in protection of upper class privilege. But the character of governmental response nonetheless depends on the factual analysis and values of those within it, and the ideology of planners has an impact on government policy at critical moments.

As with Marxism in general, there is, of course, a large element of truth in this theory, although no doubt many American businessmen and bankers who hate both "liberals" and "planners," regarding them as interlopers in their God-given field of decision-making, would be astonished to learn that the planners are merely doing their bidding.

There are, in any case, many shades of opinion in the volume. In his chapter on local planners, Robert Beauregard seems willing to give planners more credit for genuine efforts to reform and improve the society in which they work, not just to stabilize it. He describes the local planner as follows: "Urban and regional planning is performed by individuals whose interests are the built and natural environments, whose activities take place in local political arenas, whose dominant role is that of the technical expert, whose purpose is to give advice to elected officials, and whose ideology is primarily one of liberal reform."[24]

Given the continual crises of the political economy of the United States, Beauregard maintains, conflict is endemic. The values and goals of classes, and even of social groups within classes, are mutually incompatible. Institutions supposedly serving society as a whole serve disproportionately the politically powerful. The State hires planners to deal with urban and regional tensions surrounding the built and natural environments. Local planner then concentrate on two kinds of tensions for technical analysis: those with political salience, and those with little immediate political import for the local state but with technical and ideological meaning for the planners themselves. The planners release some of their own personal tensions by tackling the latter, and also maintain thereby an appearance of professionalism, not only to themselves but to the general public. Consequently, Beauregard insists, the resolution of tensions by planners does not always serve the interests of the State or of the politically dominant class: "Planners have a set of concerns (e.g., the public interest, comprehensiveness, a future-orientation, liberal reform) which may or may not intersect perfectly with the state's interests on any given tension. Given the opportunity for the articulation of these interests, planners will develop resolutions not strictly compatible with accumulation or with the interests of the politically dominant classes. Additionally, planners are generally ignorant of the underlying contradictions which lead to these tensions and thus generally unaware of how certain resolutions favour and others hinder the prevailing political economy."[25]

The sentiment running throughout the volume as a whole is perhaps best summarized by the opening paragraph of the penultimate chapter, by Thomas Angotti: "The 'crisis' in planning theory is not a crisis that stands alone: it is part of the general crisis affecting every aspect of American society. The 'crisis' in planning theory is in fact a manifestation at the ideological level of a genuine and profound political crisis arising out of Vietnam and Watergate in which the role of the state is increasingly exposed to scrutiny and criticism. It also reflects the general economic crisis—the most severe cyclical decline in capitalism since the Great Depression. The crisis affects planning practice in particular because planners are generally wedded to the workings of the state, upon which most depend for jobs."[26]

Conclusions: Dualism Versus Dependency

To take but one example by way of illustration, we are convinced that a Castro-style revolution which would cut off Haiti from the advanced capitalist countries, or which would cut off the DRIPP region from Port-au-Prince, would in the short run, make Haitians, or residents of the DRIPP region, worse off rather than better off. Heaven knows the masses of poor Haitians benefit very little from export of bauxite, coffee, sugar or baseballs to the United States. But they are better off for these exports than they would be with no exports at all, since even the poor benefit to some small extent from imports of vegetable oils, petroleum products, and tools and equipment.

And here, of course, is the crux of the matter. When it comes to specific policy recommendations, the theory of dualism and the theory of *dependencia* do not lead in totally different directions. There is perhaps a stronger implication of desirability of autonomy in the *dependencia* theory. There is certainly an implication of a need to "get the rascals out." But dualists would also insist on the need to get the rascals out where the political power élite is opposed to all the measures and reforms needed for development. There might be differences in opinion as to who the real rascals are, and as to who should replace them. But if a team comprised equally of "Rads" and dualists were assembled to prepare a development plan for a particular region in Algeria, or Haiti, or Cuba,—or Atlantic Canada—we do not believe they would have great difficulty in agreeing on the content of the plan. We might add, however, that we would personally rather have as colleagues in a planning team hard-headed and experienced planners from the socialist countries than most of the neo-Marxist theorists; for most of them—like the Marxist theorists before them—are so busy analyzing the evils of capitalism that they have few solutions for the tough day-to-day problems that plague developing countries and lagging regions.

But here we are in danger of slipping back into the debate about good vs. bad intentions of those with power. More interesting at this point is the debate about interactions of economic development and social change. We believe that there is a sharp difference between the culture and social organization of the wealthy *mulâtres* of Port-au-Prince and that of the peasants in remote mountain *hameaux*, or of Acadiens in Northeast New Brunswick and Scotch Presbyterian in Halifax. Anthropologists not only agree that there are differences, but fear the disruptive effects on any society of efforts to modernize it through new forms of technology, and land tenure, and social organization. To say that few people in LDCs today, and fewer still in LDRs of industrialized countries, are left entirely untouched by modern technology and modern institutions is not to say that they are socio-culturally uniform. Perhaps only a handful of small, isolated primitive tribes remain wholly "traditional;" but many societies of small farmers and fishermen remain traditional enough in their values, attitudes, social organization and institutions to pose serious problems for planners and politicians in settings where some industrialization and some modernization seem necessary to break the vicious circle of poverty. The kind of evidence presented by the "Rads" to disprove the existence of traditional societies—for example, that Indian peasants in Mexico have contacts with urban mestizos—is hardly conclusive. We have many contacts with Arabs but that does not make us culturally Arabs.

We have long been convinced that social-cultural obstacles to change are not the basic cause of underdevelopment; but that does not mean that they do no exist. The debate now centres properly on questions of how easily these obstacles may be overcome, on "what must change and what need not," and on whether economic development and cultural change are a "seamless web" or a "patchwork quilt." Our own view is that any government that really wants development can have it, whatever the socio-cultural framework.[27] Probably the "Rads" would agree, while insisting that no non-socialist government "really wants" development. But not all anthropologists and sociologists would agree, and we would not agree, that development is impossible in a non-socialist state. Recent events, indeed, suggest just the reverse; *continuing* development seems to be impossible in *socialist* states. Here at least is the zone where a meaningful debate might be launched: what are the interactions and feedbacks among the socio-cultural framework, the political system, and economic development?

Notes

1. Amin, Samir, "Underemployment and Dependence in Black Africa," *Social and Economic Studies,* ed. Norman Girvan, Special Number on "Dependence and Underdevelopment in the New World and the Old," vol. 22, no. 1, 1973.
2. André Gunder Frank, "The Development of Underdevelopment," in *Dependence and Underdevelopment: Latin America's Political Economy,* ed. James D. Cockroft, André Gunder Frank and Dale L. Johnson (Garden City, N.Y.: Doubleday, Anchor Books, 1972), pp. 4–5.
4. Neil Smith, *Uneven Regional Development* (New York: Basil Blackwell, 1984), p. 52.
5. J. Hinderink and M.J. Titus, "Paradigms of Regional Development and the Role of Small Centres," *Development and Change,* 1988, vol. 19, no. 3, pp. 401-23 especially pp. 405, 408, 419.
6. Stuart Holland, *Capital versus the Regions* (London: Macmillan, 1976).
7. *Ibid.*, p. v.
8. *Ibid.*
9. *Ibid.*, p. 29.
10. *Ibid.*, p. 54.
11. *Ibid.*, p. 55.
12. *Ibid.*, p. 56.
13. *Ibid.*, p. 57.
14. *Ibid.*, p. 121.
15. *Ibid.*, pp. 134, 144–45.
16. *Ibid.*, p. 152.
17. *Ibid.*, pp. 216–17.
18. *Ibid.*, p. 248.

19. *Ibid., p. 273.*

20. *Ibid.*

21. Benjamin Higgins, "François Perroux," in Benjamin Higgins and Donald J. Savoie (eds), *Regional Economic Development: Essays in Honour of François Perroux* (London and Boston: Allen & Unwin, 1988), p. 46.

22. Harvey A. Goldstein and Sara A. Rosenberry, *The Structural Crisis of the 1970s and Beyond: The Need for a New Planning Theory* (Backsburg, Virginia: Virginia Polytechnic Institute and State University, 1978).

23. *Ibid.*, p. 1.

24. Robert A. Beauregard, "Resolving Tensions: Planning Theory About and for Local Planners," in Goldstein and Rosenberry, (eds), *The Structural Crisis of the 1970s and Beyond: The Need for A New Planning Theory*, p.121.

25. *Ibid.*, p. 131.

26. Thomas Angotti, "Planning and the Class Struggle: Radical Planning Theory and Practice in the Post-Banfield Period," in Goldstein and Rosenberry, (eds), *The Structural Crisis of the 1970s and Beyond*, p. 299.

27. Benjamin Higgins, "Economic Development and Cultural Change: Seamless Web of Patchwork Quilt?," in Manning Nash, (ed.) *Essays on Economic Development and Cultural Change in Honour of Bert Hoselitz* (Chicago: University of Chicago Press, 1976).

10

Regional Science

Regional science was born in the mid 1950s, grew with astonishing rapidity and, some would say, has already achieved maturity—the Wolfgang Amadeus Mozart of the social sciences. The Regional Science Association was founded in December 1954. The *Journal of Regional Science* was established in 1960, and was followed by the *International Journal of Regional Sciences, Regional Science and Urban Economics*, the *Canadian Journal of Regional Science* and similar specialized journals in the same or closely related fields. The First European Congress of the Regional Science Association was held in 1971, and since then two volumes of papers, one European and one North American, have been published each year. French, German, Nordic language sections have been set up, also a Polish committee, an Hungarian section, Australian, Canadian and Japanese associations. A Ph.D. program in regional science was established at the University of Pennsylvania in 1956 and a Department of Regional Science was created there in 1958. Since then, Cornell University has launched a Ph.D. program and postgraduate programs have been introduced at the State University of New York at Binghampton, at Liverpool, Louvain, Queensland and elsewhere.

If there is one name which, more than any other is associated with the birth and growth of regional science, it is Walter Isard, founder of the Regional Science Association, first chairman of the Department of Regional Science at Pennsylvania, whose students occupy prominent positions the world over. In November 1978, at the Chicago meeting of the Regional Science Association, the association presented its first founder's medal to Walter Isard. In his presentation speech, Harvey Perloff, an almost equally famous regional economist, said that the purpose of the first award was "to honor Walter as the founder of the Regional Science Association at its twenty-fifth meeting," and continued, "Very few places in the world today have not been influenced intellectually by the Regional Science Association and Walter Isard."[1] In this chapter, therefore, we shall give pride of place to the writings of Walter Isard.

What is Regional Science?

What are the characteristics of regional "science" that distinguish it from regional economics, regional analysis, regional geography, the study of regional development, regional politics, or other fields of investigation to which the term "regional" might be attached? Use of the term "science" suggests that the work done by those claiming to be "regional scientists" is somehow superior, more true, more profound, a more solid base for regional policy, regional planning, and regional development, than other forms of regional analysis. Is it?

What is presented as regional science in books and learned journals varies a good deal. Taken as a whole, however, regional science may be said to have these characteristics:

1. There is a conscious, deliberate and explicit effort to apply to the analysis of human society the methods of the natural sciences, especially that of physics, and above all, perhaps, that of mechanics. Such an approach implies heavy use of mathematics.
2. There is relatively little purely theoretical analysis, or use of deductive method. Reliance is placed rather on empirical study and inductive method to discover uniformities, truths, or "laws." In this respect it resembles and overlaps with econometrics.
3. For this reason, regional science (again like econometrics) is limited largely to areas of investigation for which good data exist, such as population projection, migration, transport costs, etc.
4. Partly for this same reason, "regional science" seldom studies regions as such. It looks at spaces, sectors, and structures, but seldom at societies. Looking at societies could take them into "soft" sciences like anthropology, sociology, and social psychology where "hard" data of the type needed for their sort of quantitative analysis may not exist. Their interest is less in solving regional problems as such than in disaggregating in space, in order to arrive at a better understanding of how national economies work. They look at particular spaces (such as states or provinces for which statistics are available) as examples, in order to discover relationships, interactions, and "laws" which are universal.
5. Their ultimate aim is to analyze interdependence within systems, by establishing links among sectors, activities, and so on. Their units of analysis are micro- and meso- phenomena. Their major problem, accordingly, is the problem of aggregation, adding up their studies of particular industries, sectors, and spaces so as to construct a system at the macro-level. It is fair to say that, so far, they have not succeeded in this task of constructing macro-models of systems that are a unique product of "regional science."

6. They are happiest when they can apply a principle or law of natural science to an analogous (or supposedly analogous) socio-economic phenomenon, as in their "gravity" and "potential" models.

In essence, regional science is based on the fundamental assumption that in the study of human behaviour we are dealing with a universe that is as deterministic and stable as the universe of "nature," the physical universe. Any changes in behaviour of the particles which compose this universe are themselves the results of known or knowable laws. Once all these laws are known and added together, the behaviour of the entire universe will be known. Any law, once discovered and proven, remains true always and everywhere; mere passage of time cannot make it wrong.

To obtain an overview of how this approach works out, let us begin with Walter Isard's 1960 classic, *Methods of Regional Analysis: An Introduction to Regional Science*. The book presents techniques, tools, and theoretical frameworks for analyzing the following topics: population projection, migration estimation, regional accounts, interregional flows, regional cycles and multipliers, linear programming, gravity and potential models. Each of these topics is discrete, and involves different techniques and tools of analysis. The main emphasis is on gathering the empirical data—anywhere, any time—that will permit statistically significant quantitative analysis. The whole tenor of the argument is that such painful, painstaking gathering together of bits of knowledge will permit, *some* day, putting them together as an accurate picture of the whole universe and how it works. The book reads like the progress report of a research team (which it is—Isard had several collaborators) rather than a monograph or a treatise. There is no pretence that the picture is complete yet, and the long last chapter presents a daunting outline of the research that has yet to be done.

However, Isard does try to weave together, as best he can, what has been established thus far, in his Chapter 12, on "Five Channels of Synthesis." These five channels are: fused interregional comparative cost; industrial, fused framework emphazing urban-metropolitan structure; fused framework incorporating gravity model; values-social goals framework; operational fused framework incorporating values and goals.

Gravity Laws

Of all the "laws" which have been "discovered" by regional science, gravity laws are perhaps the most typical. The basic idea was formulated as early as the 1930s, and the concept is still being elaborated in recent issues of *Regional Science*. An early version was presented by William Reilly, and the concept is sometimes referred to as "Reilly's Law."[2]

In physics, the law of gravity is stated in the following form:

$$F = K \frac{M_1 M_2}{d^2}$$

where F is the force of attraction between two bodies, K is a constant, M_1 and M_2 are the masses of the two bodies, and d is the distance between them. In other words, the force of attraction between two bodies varies directly with their masses and inversely with the square of the distance between them. Reilly took this law and applied it virtually unchanged to the force of attraction between two urban centres. Reilly measured the force of attraction by commercial transactions (sales of goods and services), but the concept could be applied to other interactions between two urban centres, such as volume of passenger traffic between the two cities, number of telephone calls and telegrams, financial transactions, and so forth. Mass is measured by population.

An important change introduced by Jacques Boudeville into the gravity formula of physics was to substitute for the "2" (square) in the denominator a coefficient "x" to be determined statistically (empirically) in each case. This change is an important concession to the complexity and variance of the universe of human behaviour as compared to the relative invariance of the physical universe.[3]

The "law" makes obvious good sense; there is every reason to expect flows of any kind to increase with the "mass," measured by population, of the two urban centres involved, and to diminish with the distance between them. Questions arise, however. How should "distance" be measured? Simply by miles or kilometres, or by the time it takes, and the cost by various means of transport? Because of the growing importance of communications and access to information, "distance" today includes such considerations as availability of telephone, telex, and fax communications, and access to computer chains of various types of specialization. Thus, Carleton University economic geographer Michael Ray found that 90 percent of Los Angeles firms with facilities in the province of Ontario were in metropolitan Toronto, with all its facilities, although Windsor would have been closer in terms of kilometres. Yet only one third of the branches of Buffalo firms established in Ontario were in Toronto. It was more convenient to locate them just over the border, a short drive away. "Distance" is a complicated concept. It is also questionable whether "mass" can be measured by population alone. Per capita income, tastes, and occupational structures certainly have an impact. So does the quality of life in a city, including the quality of its educational system at all levels. The "force of attraction" of a city like Kingston, Ontario, relative to its population, is certainly greater than that of a city like Cornwall, Ontario. The distance between them in kilometres is small, but the distance in other respects is very great indeed.

In approaching the concept of gravity models, Walter Isard adopts what he calls "a rather simple probability point of view."[4] He envisages a region, divided into many subareas, with a certain population P. If the populations of all subareas are substantially alike, and if travel involves no time or expense, we can expect that the share of total trips among subareas will be equal to the share of each subarea in the total population of the region. If the total population is 1,000,000 and the population of subarea "j" is 100,000, "j" should account for 10 percent of the trips made within the whole region from one subarea to another. But, of course, travel does involve time and costs, and the ratio of actual to "expected" trips (based on population alone) will be a function of the distance between any two subareas. Actual trips will depend both on the populations of subareas and on distances between them. The same reasoning can be applied to any kind of flows between urban centres.

Isard illustrates his analysis with the diagram shown in Figure 10.1. Expressed in simple terms such as these, gravity laws make good sense. Isard also shows that the gravity law equation can be derived from a relationship such as that depicted in Figure 10.1.

Stewart called the law "demographic force" and expressed it specifically in terms of population:

$$F = G \frac{P_i P_j}{d^2_{ij}}$$

where P_i and P_j are the populations of two centres and G is again a constant corresponding to the constant in the physical law of gravity. (d_{ij} is again the distance between centre "i" and centre "j"). Continuing his borrowing from physics, Stewart developed two other "laws." One of these is "demographic energy," corresponding to gravitational energy, and expressed:

$$E = G \frac{P_i P_j}{d_{ij}}$$

which is the same as the equation above except that "d" is not squared. The other is called "demographic potential," corresponding to gravitational potential.

It is defined:

$$i^v j = G \frac{P_j}{d_{ij}}$$

where $i^v j$ is the demographical potential produced at point i by the mass (urban centre) j, with mass, measured by population.

These formulations illustrate very well the efforts of regional scientists to discover laws similar to, if not actually identical with, the laws of (Newtonian) physics. A good deal of empirical work has been done to substantiate these

FIGURE 10.1

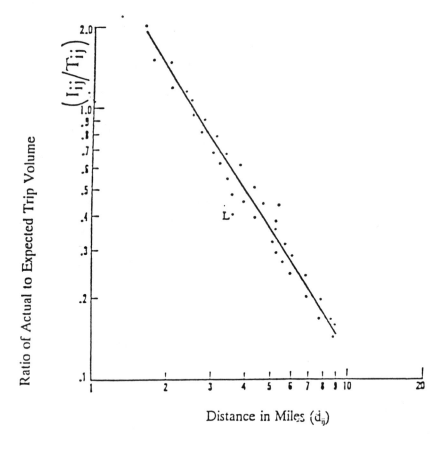

"laws." However, Isard raises some issues with regard to gravity laws. One of these is the question already raised above as to how "mass" and "distance" should be measured when the basic units and actors are human beings. Isard suggests that the measure may have to vary according to the phenomenon studied. For example, if the subject analyzed is migration, employment and per capita income may be a better measure of mass that simple population. If it is potential sales of particular products, total retail and wholesale sales may be a better indicator of "mass" in the relevant sense. Distance, too, can be measured in a variety of ways. Finally, because the units (people) constituting the mass differ from place to place, the masses may have to be weighted to give an accurate measure of relationships among them.

The Urban Hierarchy

One of the subjects that has most interested regional scientists is urban structures; that is, the relative size and importance of cities within one national economy, usually measured by population. One of the simplest and most visible of such structures is "the primate city," where one urban centre so dominates the rest as to stand out alone. This phenomenon is more likely to appear in relatively small countries: Athens in Greece, Dublin in Ireland, Copenhagen in Denmark, Brussels in Belgium. However, Buenos Aires in Argentina and Santiago in Chile are primate cities.

The primate city structure is more likely to appear in individual regions of a large country than in the country as a whole: New York city, Chicago, Atlanta and New Orleans in the United States, the metropolitan centres of virtually all of the Canadian provinces, and the capital cities of all Australian and all Brazilian states. A similar structure, mentioned by Brian Berry, is that of "'dual economies', where one or a few exogenous, colonial, cities of great size, are superimposed upon an indigenous urban system of smaller places, and so on."[5]

The structure that has most intrigued regional scientists is the one which has come to be known as "the rank-size rule." This "rule" may be expressed as:

$$P_r = p_1 / _r q$$

where p_r is the population of a city of rank "r," p_1 is the population of the largest or first-ranking city, and q is a constant.

The equation may also be expressed

$$\log pr = \log p_1 - q\log_r$$

On double log paper, the urban structure appears as a straight line with a slope of -q. In its simplest version (with q = 1) the rule says that the population of the second city will be half that of the biggest city, the third city will have a population one third that of the biggest city, and so on. The same principle can be expressed as a distribution of cities by size, taking the form of a back-to-front J.

The "rule" applies, to some degree of approximation, to a surprising number of countries. Figure 10.2 shows the urban structure for Canada for the three census years 1961, 1971 and 1981, and suggests a high degree of stability in the urban hierarchy.

Why should such a tendency exist? The truth is that we don't really know. One explanation is that it is "stochastic," the outcome of the law of large numbers, or probability. Other phenomena involving large numbers, such as income distribution, show a similar tendency. Another possibility is that it results from "spin-off." As cities grow, diseconomies, as well as economies of scale appear: congestion, pollution, increasing travel time, rising rents, etc. Accordingly, some people and some enterprises move to smaller centres. A third explanation is that it is a simple reflection of varying tastes. Some people like big cities, others prefer middle-sized cities, still others like small cities.

Location Quotients

It is of interest to know the degree to which certain economic activities are concentrated in a certain region or, conversely, the degree to which a certain region is specialized in particular economic activities. The location quotient, which is used to measure such concentration of activity by localities, is among the simpler constructs used by regional scientists. It involves merely comparing a region's share in a particular activity with its share in some macro-measure.

Whether such measures, which in themselves are only reporting and provide no indication of causal relationships or "laws," should really be regarded as regional "science" is perhaps questionable. If we believe the motto of the Econometric Society that "science is measurement" then, perhaps, the location quotient is a part of regional science; but unless relationships of such quotients to some other variables are added, and unless there is a reason to believe that there is a causal connection, it can hardly be regarded as a "law." Nor does the location quotient in itself provide any guidance for regional policy. As Isard points out: "We find in the regional literature suggestions that those industries with location quotients greater than unity represent areas of strength within a region and ought, therefore, to be further developed; and, in somewhat contradictory fashion, that those industries with location coefficients less than unity ought to be encouraged in order to reduce the drain of imports."[6]

FIGURE 10.2
Rank, Size, Rule: Structure of Metropolitan Regions of Canada
1961, 1971 and 1981

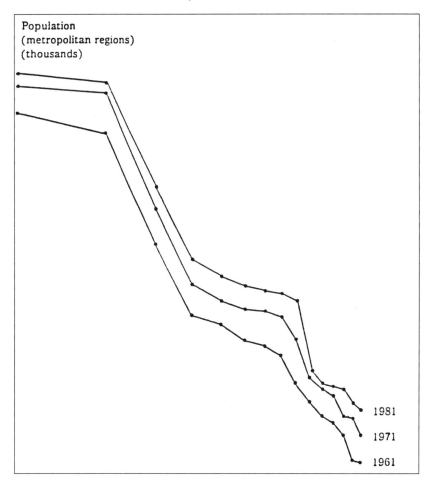

Population
(metropolitan regions)
(thousands)

1981
1971
1961

Interregional Flows

Some knowledge of interregional flows is essential for the formulation of sound regional policy. If the government making policy for a particular region—Esperanza—decides to embark on a road building program in the region to provide employment and generate incomes in Esperanza, thus reducing the gap between Esperanza and Utonia, it is crucial to know how much of the required raw materials, equipment, and high level engineering and technical skills needed to build roads efficiently in Esperanza will have to be imported from Utonia. It is important also to know who owns the means of transport which will carry these flows. It is helpful to have information on flows of bank deposits from region to region, and of flows of other assets and of capital more generally.

The concept of interregional flows is simple enough. Actually constructing matrices or tables of such interregional flows is laborious and difficult, even when the data are available, which they often are not. Today, there is keen interest in interregional flows of technology, innovations, scientific knowledge and research capacity, information, and entrepreneurial talent. Such flows are among the most difficult of all to track down.

The city of Houston has nearly 1,000 miles of underground pipes connecting one industrial enterprise with another, so intricate that it is known as "the spaghetti bowl." Not only final products of one industry, but effluents that would otherwise be wasted and contribute to pollution, become inputs of another industry. Houston, with its high "location quotient" for petro-chemical industries, may be something of an exception; but in many large cities there are relationships among industries which become powerful factors in attracting them all to the same place and in keeping them there. Because of the importance of these interrelationships, "industrial complex analysis" has become a major activity of regional science.

Is Regional Science a Science?

Scholars and practitioners who regard themselves as regional scientists will no doubt regard this excessively brief characterization of their work as a caricature. However, the purpose here is not to summarize the findings of regional science; that would be an impossible task even if the entire book were devoted to it, so massive and so diverse is the literature under that general heading. Rather, the purpose is only to give readers who are not acquainted with this literature some idea of what sort of thing it is, and of how regional scientists go about their tasks. Perhaps, too, the chapter will goad some of them who might happen to read it into reflecting about their field, and even into launching a counter attack, which would be all to the good.

To reiterate, we have seen that regional science has the following characteristics:

1. It is concerned mainly with the spatial aspects of the functioning of macro-economies, and to a considerably lesser degree, of macro-polities and macro-societies. It is not primarily concerned with analyzing and solving the special economic, political, and social problems of particular regions.

2. It does not study in any detail or depth the human behaviour of particular societies inhabiting particular spaces. Rather, it takes over from economics simple, almost tautological assumptions about human behaviour that are regarded as universal, true always and everywhere (maximizing utility or satisfaction, etc.).

3. Unlike standard mainstream neoclassical or neo-Marxist economics, however, regional science does not devote much time or energy to pure theorizing on the basis of these behavioural assumptions. Rather, it is devoted to elaborating and applying tools and techniques of quantitative analysis, with a view to discovering empirical regularities, uniformities, or "laws." It is therefore highly dependent on data.

4. In so doing, it applies constructs of the natural sciences, and particularly of (Newtonian) physics.

5. It makes extensive use of mathematics. (This may not be a distinctive characteristic. Mathematical economic theorists, econometricians, and mathematical geographers use mathematics extensively too. But regional scientists use more mathematics than regional economists and other regional analysts who do not call themselves regional "scientists").

Working in this manner, regional scientists have assembled many bits of empirical knowledge, which approximate "laws" in varying degrees, and which are also useful in varying degrees to regional planners and policy makers. The distinctive activities of "regional scientists," however, do not constitute the whole of regional science, in the sense of scientific inquiry directed towards increasing the store of knowledge about regions (or spaces) and their interactions.

Is it a good idea for social scientists to emulate physicists in their methodology? Something can be learned in this fashion, as the output of regional science shows. There are some regularities and uniformities in the social universe, perhaps even some "laws," and it is of extreme importance to discover these. But it is also important to realize the limitations of a physics-like methodology in the social sciences. The laws of natural science are additive, or cumulative. The laws of Newtonian mechanics have not been disproved by subsequent research; they have been shown to be incomplete, not wrong. But much research in social science is devoted to proving predecessors wrong. Consider the three main revolutions in economics during the past century or so. One of the main aims of the "marginal revolution" of the 1870s was to prove the classical school's labour theory of value wrong. The imperfect/monopolistic competition revolution of the late 1920s and early 1930s proved that earlier neoclassical economists had been wrong in supposing that markets of the real world approximated the perfect competition model; "free" markets, therefore, would not bring an optimal allocation of resources, as previously argued, but misallocation of resources on a colossal scale. The Keynesian revolution of the late 1930s showed that there is no mechanism in a free market economy which tends to move it towards an equilibrium with full employment and no inflation; contrary to the received doctrine of neoclassical economics, maintaining full employment without inflation requires continuous and highly skillful management of both monetary and fiscal policy.

The fact is that the universe of the social sciences is constantly changing. Institutions change, knowledge changes, behaviour changes. And since we do not know, and cannot hope to know, *all the laws of change*, we have to expect that our "Newtonian laws" will change too, and in unforeseen ways. Thus the Keynesian revolution plus the success in fighting World War II without inflation and getting through postwar reconstruction without mass unemployment, led many economists to believe that the Keynesian policy propositions were laws. Given consistent and stable monetary policy, budget deficits would cure unemployment and budget surpluses would cure inflation. But now institutions, and the behaviour of private investors, trade union leaders, bankers and governments have changed in such a way that unemployment and inflation can occur together, and even increase (or decrease) together.[7] The Keynesian prescriptions for fiscal policy are no longer valid. Moreover, private investors have become much more sophisticated regarding the economy and government policy. When an increased budget deficit is projected or announced, they expect interest rates to rise and, consequently, pull in their horns. Instead of decreasing, unemployment increases. The Keynesian law no longer operates.

All this does not mean that regional scientists should stop what they are doing. It means that regional science by itself does not provide us with an adequate basis for regional policy and planning. We cannot be confident that any empirical finding will remain valid forever, at all times and in all places. The findings must be checked and rechecked, not only in other places but at intervals even in the place where they were originally made.

In accepting the founder's medal in November 1978, Walter Isard delivered an address under the title "Notes on the Origins, Development, and Future of Regional Science." In fact, he did not have much to say about the future of the discipline he had created; in effect, he called for more of the same and suggested no sharp changes in direction, methodology, or scope. He did take note of some new problems that regional scientists should tackle, in particular, the declining populations of such metropolitan regions as London, Paris, New York and Tokyo, which at that time he expected to continue. This phenomenon prompted him to say towards the end of his speech: "Hence we now confront an imperative need to develop an economics of decline, notions of decline poles, notions of time paths of infrastructure development relevant for populations declining in absolute numbers...We cannot, of course, use a simple growth model and reverse time..."[8]

He also made a bow towards the methodology of biology, then a popular concept among management scientists, saying, "...we should encourage *paedomorphosis*, a process defined by evolutionary biologists," and emphasize interactive decision making. On the whole, however, he seemed well pleased with the progress of regional science to date: "As a social science, regional science is among those at the top. In fact, there is without doubt less deadwood in our group than in most, if not all, social science fields.... Compare the average quality of the regional science journals to that of the economic journals."[9]

He saw only one danger in the future of regional science: "we are already becoming institutionalized," and, consequently, regional science is losing its dynamism, and will one day be surpassed by some other social science with more youthful vigour.[10]

Five years later, the second founder's medal was awarded to Martin Beckman. He seemed even more content with his chosen field than was Walter Isard. Regional science, he stated, has become a true science. The maturing of any science is usually associated with a small number of major breakthrough, he pointed out, and continued: "In our case these epochal events have been associated with Walter Isard, our founder, and it is only fitting and proper that I would pay homage to him on this occasion.... (There are) two paradigms embraced by us. The newer paradigm is the entropy maximisation concept. It is macroscopic and based on the principle of maximum likelihood in combination with suitably defined constraints. The older principle might be called the behavioural approach. Gravity and potential belong to prehistory when it was still acceptable to reason by analogy with the physical sciences. Such arguments by analogy no longer suffice, at least not among today's regional scientists. The behavioural approach, the other paradigm, is microscopic, and oriented towards utility or profits. It is based on the analysis of maximising behaviour of economic agents."[11]

A few remarks might be made about this statement. First, if regional scientists have given up reasoning by analogy with the physical sciences, they have not given up writing about gravity, potential, migration models, location theory, input-output matrices, and indeed all of the topics covered in Walter Isard's 1960 book. Recent issues of *The Journal of Regional Science* contain articles on all of these subjects; it is just that the treatment of them has become more complex and more sophisticated.

Second, while not wishing to detract in any way from the achievements of regional science to date, it is important to remember that it is not the use of mathematics alone that characterizes a rigorous science. Kenneth Boulding, who has contributed to the regional science literature, as well as to virtually all of the newer and livelier branches of economics, once wisely remarked that mathematics is a wonderful servant but a very bad master. Mathematics are an aid to clear thinking, and sometimes can even lead to unexpected results and discovery of new truths. But good results cannot come out of badly constructed models, no matter how competent the mathematical manipulation of the model may be. Finding the right inputs to build a good model requires observation and thought of a kind different from the use mathematics in and of itself.

Third, despite Beckman's statement, the truth is that regional scientists do not as a rule "analyze behaviour of economic agents." They make assumptions about maximizing behaviour, with regard to utility or profits, as other economists do. They do not observe or study the behaviour itself. What they analyze is the results of this maximizing behaviour, changes in demand for particular products or in consumption, savings and investment as a whole, changing patterns of migration or industrial location. Although they call themselves "regional" scientists, they do not bother to find out if human behaviour differs from one region to another, but, like economists in general, simply assume that it is the same always and everywhere.

Regional science—despite its bows to biology and management science—in the sense in which it is a distinctive discipline, different from other types of regional analysis, pushes the mechanistic model to the limit, making direct use of analogies drawn from classical mechanics. Since physics was still the "queen science" at the time when regional science was born, the use of analogies derived from physics led to such self-congratulatory statement as those of Isard and Beckman cited above. Today, however, not only are the border lines between "mechanistic" and "organistic" sciences becoming blurred, but it is in the more organistic sciences that the more important breakthroughs are occurring.

Whether mechanics is a suitable foundation for a social science like economics is being increasingly questioned, and an increasing number of economists are answering the question with a resounding "No!! "The German Historical School was always opposed to mechanical concepts in economic analysis, and the American Institutionalists followed suit. As John Gambs puts it: "Institutionalists have taken economics out of the real of pseudo-physical science, which is where standard economics seems to want to put it, and have put it squarely into the biological sciences. They have made—or at least valiantly tried to make—its doctrines conformable with those of anthropology, ethnology, psychology, genetics—disciplines that have bothered standard theorists less."[12]

Many "standard" economists seem to have forgotten that Alfred Marshall himself, that giant amongst turn-of-the-century neoclassical economists, was of the same opinion: "The Mecca of the economist lies in economic biology rather than in economic dynamics...Economics is a branch of biology, broadly interpreted."[13]

Herbert Simon, in his acceptance speech for the 1978 Nobel prize in economics, had this to say: " In economics, it has been common enough to admire Newtonian mechanics...and to search for the economic equivalent of the laws of motion. But this is not the only model for a science, and, it seems, not the right one for our purpose...If we wish to be guided by a natural science metaphor, I suggest one drawn from biology rather than physics."[14]

In a penetrating article entitled "Mechanistic and Organistic Analogies in Economics Reconsidered," H. Thorben explains why the mechanistic concept has dominated economics until recently, and why an organistic concept, is more appropriate.[15] The enthusiasm of economists for mechanistic models began with the "marginal revolution" of the 1870s. Thorben quotes W.S. Jevons as speaking of "the mechanics of utility of self-interest," and stating that "economics, if it is to be a science at all, must be a mathematical science;" and cites Léon Walras as declaring, "It is already perfectly clear that economics, like astronomy and mechanics, is both an empirical and a rational science."[16] Irving Fisher's enthusiasm for mechanics let him to construct a physical model "to demonstrate the purely mechanical character of consumer behaviour."[17] Frank Knight considered mechanics as "the sister science of economics." Mechanistic concepts came to dominate, not only static general equilibrium theory, but dynamics, including business cycle theory as well. Thorben sums up his evaluation of mechanical models as follows: "Though it may be a useful vehicle for understanding economic problems, the mechanistic approach implies the fiction that human behaviour is essentially mechanical. This assumption remains highly problematical, or put in another way, 'in the case of celestial mechanics we can neglect the problem of whether planets are moved by angels without causing any trouble at all, for it is only the behaviour of abstract time series of the positions of the planets that we are concerned with. In the case of economic and social systems, however, the (phenomena) with which we deal are moved by people who are not so well behaved as angels, and we forget this fact to our peril.'"[18]

Thorben then moves on to the organistic analogy. He cites Janos Kornai's *Anti equilibrium* (1971) and Kenneth Boulding's *Economics as a Science* as examples of the relatively recent swing to a biological approach. He pays tribute also to systems analysis, which respects Heisenberg's uncertainty principle; "contrary to the mechanistic approach one of the logical consequences of the systems approach is the idea that the observer and the observed influence each other, whereby it is no longer possible to localize uniquely every event and every object in time and space."[19] However, he favours most the model of the Entropy Law, citing Georgescu-Roegen: "The important fact is that the discovery of the Entropy Law brought the downfall of the mechanistic dogma of classical physics...By now, no one would deny that the economy of biological processes is governed by the Entropy Law, not by the laws of mechanics."[20]

Thorben states his own position clearly: "It is the organistic analogy that can deal with the purposive aspects of the economic process."[21] He cites Georgescu-Roegen once more: "It is all right for an economist to rest satisfied with the explanation of a catastrophic crop by some efficient causes triggered by random events. However, the science served by him is ordinarily interested in problems, involving human actions. And so he will not arrive at a penetrating understanding if he refuses to look for the purposes that move men."[22]

In his conclusion, Thorben writes: "First of all it is a well known fact that the main theoretical current of scientific economics have to this day retained the characteristics of a 'mechanistic' system. On the other hand history provides us with periodic attacks against application of the principles of classic mechanics in economics...With the downfall of the mechanistic dogma in physics itself, triggered by the Entropy Law, there is no longer a solid base for arguing that scientific economics should develop in analogy to classical physics and astronomy. At the same time one has to admit that the economic process is an entropic process, which implies that from a physical point of view the economic process cannot be captured in a mechanical analogue. This job is done better by an organical analogue, especially where it leaves room for the analysis of qualitative change and takes into account the purposiveness of human behaviour. Besides, scientific developments in the last three decades in the new fields of general systems theory and cybernetics, may provide the organistic approach with the analytical tools so as to make it a workable alternative instead of the traditional method."[23]

All this does not mean that every construct and concept of regional science which is based on an analogy with mechanics is necessarily wrong. It does mean that regional science can no longer claim to be "more scientific" than other types of regional analysis, based on other concepts, constructs, analogies, or methods. It also means that some of the "laws" of regional science that seemed to be true when first discovered may no longer be true today, because of changes in patterns of human behaviour. The "laws" need to be tested again, to see if they still hold.

Of course, there is nothing to prevent regional scientists from modelling themselves on biology or anthropology or psychology and applying their mathematical techniques to observed human behaviour, with its qualitative changes. But such analysis would be a far cry from what has been typical of regional science in the past. The behavioural assumptions underlying most regional science—if there are any at all, rather than behaviour being *deduced* from its *results* as indicated by statistics at the macroeconomic level—are those of neoclassical economics. Human beings are assumed to maximize utility, or profits, or safety, or liquidity, etc., and in doing so are all assumed to behave in the same fundamental way at all times. But when it is recognized that equally rational human beings, presented with the same set of information and the same market situation, may make directly opposing decisions, the nature of "economic laws" changes drastically, and "laws" are harder to come by.

The old-fashioned neoclassical entrepreneur maximized "his" profits, by determining the output of "his" product that equated marginal cost with marginal revenue. But when the "entrepreneur" is the management of a large corporation today, they have to decide on their product-mix, the technology used to produce the various products, the type of labour force employed, and the location for each branch plant for each product, *simultaneously*. There will, as a general rule, be quarrels among managers themselves; some may favour relatively simple techniques and highly skilled employees, and therefore location in large cities; others may prefer advanced techniques that make skilled labour unnecessary, and locate in small towns with a lot of low-wage women and non-unionized labour. In such a situation the location may be determined by the president's desire to live in an attractive town in the Sunbelt. It is impossible to predict, and almost impossible to describe, such decisions. By analyzing the statistics showing the *results* of past decisions, a regional scientist might measure the probability that certain decisions *would have been made* in the past; but he cannot therefore predict how decisions will be made in the future; there is no reason why a particular management team should make the same decision twice in a row. The techniques of regional science assume implicitly a degree of uniformity of human behaviour, in space and in time, that may not exist.

Notes

1. Harvey Perloff, "Founder's Medal: Walter Isard," in *Papers of the Regional Science Association*, vol. 43, 1979, pp. 5–7.
2. William J. Reilly, *The Law of Retail Gravitation* (New York: Basic Books, 1931).
3. Boudeville, Jacques R. *Aménagement du territoire et polarisation* (Paris: M.-Th. Ge'nin, 1972).
4. Walter Isard, *Methods of Regional Analysis: An Introduction to Regional Science* (Cambridge, Mass.: M.I.T. Press, 1960), p. 494.
5. Brian Berry, *Geography of Market Centers and Retail Distribution* (New York: Doubleday, 1960), p. 160.
6. Isard, *Methods of Regional Analysis*, p. 125.
7. Benjamin Higgins, *Unemployment and Inflation* (New Brunswick, N.J.: Transaction Publishers, forthcoming).
8. Walter Isard, "Notes on the Origins, Development and Future of Regional Science," *Papers of the Regional Science Association*, 1979, vol. 43, pp. 19–22.

9. *Ibid.*

10. *Ibid.*

11. Martin Beckman, "Remarks," in *Papers of the Regional Science Association*, 1985, vol. 57, pp. 3-5.

12. John S. Gambs, *Beyond Supply and Demand* (New York: Columbia University Press, 1946), p. 10.

13. Alfred Marshall, *Principles of Economics* (New York: MacMillan, 8th edition, 1924), pp. xiv, 772.

14. Herbert Simon, "Rational Decision Making," *The American Economic Review*, vol. 69, no. 4, September 1979, pp. 510-11.

15. H. Thorben, "Mechanistic and Organistic Analogies in Economics Reconsidered," *Kyklos*, vol. 35, no. 2, 1982, pp. 292-306.

16. *Ibid.*, p. 294.

17. *Ibid.*

18. Kenneth Boulding, *Economics as a Science*, (New York: Basic Books, 1970), p. 74.

19. Thorben, "Mechanistic and Organistic Analogies in Economics Reconsidered," p. 300.

20. *Ibid.*, p. 302.

21. *Ibid.*, p. 303.

22. *Ibid.*

23. *Ibid.*

11

Recent Literature on Regional
Development Theory

In the field of economic development in general, the period since 1950 has been one of floundering in the theoretical field. Despite the hundreds of thousands of people engaged in the international development effort and the thousands sitting in universities and puzzling over the development problem and what to do about it, no grand new theory has appeared that could rival that of Joseph Schumpeter, or that of Adam Smith or Karl Marx. As our knowledge of the relevant *facts* concerning development of particular countries accumulated, so did our willingness to generalize about the process, and causal factors in it, diminish. We had massive descriptions of the development process in a vast array of countries; but the prescription for policy were all based on very partial theories. The debate took on an "all you have to do is..." "but not in the South!" character. A whole series of panaceas was proposed and then rejected as inadequate as a single prescription for development: the Big Push, Balanced Growth, Unbalanced Growth, Growth Poles, Planned Structural Change, Uncoupling. In the 1970s and 1980s, as disillusionment set in, we were urged to try a number of new approaches: the Unified Approach, the Basic Needs Approach, Bottom Up Development, Entrepreneurship, Another Development/Self Reliance. These were more a set of objectives than new theories of development. Finally, in the 1990s, those of us who have not been put off the development effort altogether, either adopting a "just leave it to the market" approach, or just saying nothing about the development process at all, have finally learned that *we don't need* a grand general theory in order to prescribe policy for particular economies and societies, provided we know enough about the functioning of those particular economies and societies. It is a good thing that the medical profession doesn't await the perfection of a grand general theory of public health before treating individual patients for particular maladies.

A very similar thing has happened in the field of regional development theory. There are endless attempts to describe what is happening in individual

167

regional economies, and even some attempts to explain them. But the global picture of regional development is very confusing. What is happening in some regions seems to be the reverse of what is happening in others. Thus, we have theories of polarization, polarization reversal, and polarization-reversal-reversal; theories of agglomeration and theories of decentralization; diffusion models and theories of clustering; advocacy of small and middle-sized enterprises (SMEs) in small and middle-sized cities (SMCs); long lists of the qualitative advantages of metropolitan centres; factories in the fields; seedbeds and product life cycles.

The point is, however, that *all* these things are valid—somewhere or other. With recent trends in technological advance and in the managerial revolution, decision making has become a much more sophisticated and flexible affair; and there is no reason to expect that the management of one enterprise will make its decisions in the same way that another enterprise does. As Allen J. Scott and Michael Storper put it: "The existing literature of the geography of high technology industry agrees on one point, i.e. that the classical Weberian theory of location with its emphasis on the individual decision maker is unequal to the task of accounting for the emergence and deployment of whole new sectors of production over the economic landscape. Most attempts to explain the spatial pattern of high technology industry have by contrast struggled to gain a systemic view of its concrete development paths in space and time."[1]

When management is concerned, not with maximizing profits but with maximizing growth, within constraints imposed by the need to avoid excessive fixed debt, stockholders' revolts, and take-overs;[2] and when the president, the vice-president for finance with his Wharton School M.B.A., the vice-president for marketing with his Harvard M.B.A., and the vice-president for production with his M.I.T. degree in industrial management all have different views on how to do that; there is no telling how they will decide on the location of a new plant, and no reason to expect that they will make their decision the same way twice in a row. The one thing the vice-presidents often have in common is the desire to be president. Yet, the individual entrepreneur has not disappeared, nor the partnership, and they will presumably keep a closer eye on profits than their corporate colleagues.

The decisions made by the management of a large corporation are in any case much more complex than they were even ten years ago. They do not choose a location for producing a given product with a given technology. The product mix, the technique of producing it, and the location are chosen together. When the products and the technology are such that the products can be produced by a highly mechanized process, utilizing unskilled labour, they may very well choose a small town where labour is unorganized and consists in large measure of women and young people who accept low wages. When they need large inputs of highly skilled labour, especially inputs of scientific, engineering, technical and managerial skills, as in the start-up phase of a new product, they are likely to choose a metropolitan area.

During the 1960s and 1970s, concern was expressed at the seemingly irreversible tendency towards agglomeration and polarization. Only the very large metropolitan centre seemed to have the requisite location factors for the new high-technology industries. As Scott and Storper express it: "The third and last of these currently fashionable accounts of high technology industrial location emphasizes the unique and exogenous locational factors alleged to be necessary pre-conditions of high technology development in particular places. A wide variety of such factors is commonly adduced in the literature: e.g. the presence of universities with major programs in science and engineering, accessibility to international airports, nearby military bases, the local availability of venture capital, a high proportion of technical/scientific workers in the local population, a superior quality of life (we shall have more to say about this at a later stage), and so on."[3]

However, they then add: "In practice, these factors turn out to be little more than *ad hoc* lists hopefully masquerading as analysis. They miss entirely the central problem of the internal evolutionary dynamics of growth complexes..."[4]

Then, towards the end of the 1970s, it was found that there had been a "polarisation reversal."[5] Big cities, like New York and Tokyo, were actually losing population. Fu Chen Lo and Kamal Salih explained this phenomenon in terms of diseconomies of scale, pollution, congestion, high costs of living, high rentals, etc. But now it seems that the big cities are growing again. No one need be surprised at this, once one realizes that all entrepreneurs do *not* behave in the same way, and that at any point of time, they may see the advantages and disadvantages of locating in small middle-sized and large cities differently, *for their own purposes.*

The Spatial Division of Labour

Philippe Aydalot begins his article on "La division spatiale du travail" with this observation: "In the general analysis of the forces which define the spatial inequality of regional development, the location of industry (enterprise) is a major chapter, because it is the enterprise which disposes of the dominant power of decision-making in this domain."[6] He goes on to argue that the problem of location requires a single answer. It is a matter of determining for each agent the optimal location and making explicit the forms of the equilibrium which follow. Space must therefore be heterogeneous. If it were not, location would be a matter of indifference to the enterprise. In most neoclassical theory, space is treated as homogeneous and location is therefore indeterminate. Homogeneity of space follows from the homogeneity of factors of production and the unity of markets.

The tendency is for transport costs to diminish and for products to become less heavy. Aydalot asks: "Is this then the end of theory and the beginning of the era of indeterminacy? All that remains of the structure of space is labour; which, doubtless, one will say, is mobile and tends to become increasingly homogeneous. But such a viewpoint is too hasty; first because men wish to live where they were born, so that space is never completely homogeneous; and also because it is *men* who are displaced, and not the *labour force*...Each environment has its own cost; the cost of reproduction of the labour force is not the same in all locations. The level of wages is only the most visible factor in choice of location. But the enterprise does not seek to minimise its wage cost alone; it seeks also a pattern of social relations which assures the security, regularity and perpetuity of its activity."[7]

Hence, the enterprise will settle in a large city only if the efficiency of production offsets the higher costs. If possible, it will choose technologies that will permit it to employ non-industrial labour, with a low level of unionization and which allows easy social relations. Only if the efficiency of the sophisticated labour force of the large cities is needed, will the enterprise choose them as a location. If the technical processes can be sufficiently mechanized to permit the use of unskilled labour, the enterprise can seek a location where the cost of reproduction of the labour force is low. He concludes this section of his discussion by saying: "One can go further and propose the idea according to which the enterprise chooses a location in such a way as to be able to use an unskilled labour force with a low cost of reproduction, and that it favours for this end techniques which authorise the employment of unskilled labour.... thus, in its choice, the enterprise chooses simultaneously a technique and a *space*: it chooses the technique adapted to the labour force that it wishes to employ; at the same moment, it chooses the location where the labour force is adapted to the technique that it intends to adopt."[8]

Aydalot questions whether "regions" are the right unit to study movements of enterprises. The driving force of such movements is the cost of reproducing the labour force, which in turn is very sensitive to the size of cities. Those enterprises which are able to opt for mass production, mechanization, deskilling, and concentration of capital, develop in urban centres of modest size; those that require a highly skilled labour force will choose the larger cities. French experience, he contends, verifies this theory.[9]

As the average size of cities grows, so does the average cost of reproduction of the labour force which tends to exceed the average increase in wages.

Thus, there is an increasing tendency for enterprises to seek techniques that will permit them to locate in smaller cities.

The Product Cycle

Once one recognizes that different technologies are suitable for cities of different sizes, because of the nature of the labour force available, the way is open for the "product cycle" theory. The idea is that innovation, the introduction of a new product, a new design, or a new process, requires at the R & D phase high powered scientists, engineers, technicians, and managers. These are to be found in large cities. Once it becomes a matter of routine production with highly mechanized techniques, then cheap, unskilled labour can be used, and the enterprise will seek a small town on the "periphery," or even an underdeveloped country, with such a labour force. But the enterprise will not keep its monopoly of the new product, design, or process long. Schumpeter's "cluster of followers" appears on the scene, and competition becomes keen. To keep its competitive edge, the enterprise must find yet another innovation, another new product, design and process. So it's back to the drawing board, back to the R & D phase—and back to the big city.

Niles Hansen gives a good summary of the theory: "In the early phase of a product life cycle, scientific and engineering skills are the key human inputs, and producers depend on external economies. In the growth phase of the cycle, the capital-labor ratio is increased as mass production is introduced and management skills become vital. In the mature phase, the standardized product is manufactured in long, routine production runs. The product cycle theory, as typically presented, predicts that products originate in large urban agglomerations but eventually end up being manufactured in nonmetropolitan areas or foreign export enclaves. Therefore, centres of product innovation must continually renew themselves by creating new, relatively sophisticated products."[10]

Ray Vernon meanwhile observes that: "According to the product cycle hypothesis, firms that set up foreign producing facilities characteristically do so in reliance on some real or imagined monopolistic advantage. In the absence of such a perceived advantage, firms are loath to take on the special costs and uncertainties of operating a subsidiary in a foreign environment. One such strength is an innovational lead."[11]

Stated thus simply, the product cycle thesis seems plausible enough. It is not, however, without its critics. Michael Taylor is quite brutal in his criticism: "There is an appealing logic to this thesis that derives from its simplicity. At the same time, however, simplicity is also its greatest weakness. To the exclusion of almost all other considerations, the core of the model revolves around technological change and its impact on investment decision making.

The foundation of the model is, therefore, technological determinism. Indeed, insofar as they are considered at all, other aspects of the economic system—supply, demand, labour, enterprise, and so on—are subordinated to the technical demands of producing goods of increasing vintage...There are no location-specific advantages for the supply of inputs beyond a vague metropolitan bias in the initial stages of production...Products, as they pass through the cycle, are also seen in isolation and not in relation to the evolution and development of other products, either in a market context of competition and substitution or in an intrafirm context of cross-substitution and the allocation of scarce resources."[12]

Scott and Storper criticize the theory for assuming that "each industrial sector evolves through a cycle of invariant stages. Theses stages are defined as innovation, growth, and maturity."[13] The product cycle model correctly makes the relationship between production organization and location the central pivot on which spatial outcomes turn. Nevertheless, it erroneously ascribes to every production sector an invariant pattern of spatio-temporal development that is, in fact, observable in only a limited number of empirical cases.[14] The relationship of technologies and production organization to markets is much more complex and contingent than the product cycle model allows; for both intra-firm and inter-firm responses to changes in the market vary widely from sector to sector. New technologies may actually reduce the minimal optimal scale of production and bring about significant reskilling.[15] In short, in contradiction to the oversimplified world of the product cycle theorists, what we frequently observe in many cases are radical reversals, changes of course, and unexpected temporal irregularities in patterns of sectoral development.[16]

However that may be, it is apparent that to explain *general* trends towards agglomeration and deglomeration, polarization and polarization-reversal, the advocates of the product cycle would have to prove that not only are the stages invariant, but that an overwhelming majority of firms would have to start and finish their cycles at the same time. Of course, they *could*, especially if they react in the same way to a pervasive business cycle. Schumpeter's theory came close to saying precisely that. On the face of it, however, it seems rather improbable and the general theory would have to be spelled out before it was accepted.

Kelley and Williamson's Computable General Equilibrium Model

Not all economists are trying to explain differences among regions and cities. Some econometricians (or cliometricians) are struggling valiantly to discover uniformities of behaviour among cities and regions of large numbers of countries, using macroeconomic models or, to be more precise, "computable general equilibrium models (CGEs)." An example is Allen C. Kelley and Jeffrey G. Williamson's *What Drives Third World City Growth? A Dynamic General Equilibrium Approach*, which tries to explain city growth within the context of the functioning of national economies of *all* developing countries. The authors begin by outlining the "problem" of Third World city growth: "By the end of the century, the United Nations forecasts urban population growth rate three times those of rural areas. Two billion people, exceeding 40 percent of the Third World population will live in cities; some cities will have reached extremely large size—Mexico City, 31.6 million, Saõ Paulo at 26 million, and Cairo, Jakarta, Seoul and Karachi each exceeding 15 million. Current rates of Third World city growth border on the spectacular, averaging between 4 and 5 percent per annum."[17]

The authors state that the pessimists believe that the Third World countries will be unable to cope with the social overhead requirements of this growth. Optimists view urbanization as the key to alleviation of poverty. The main task of Kelley and Williamson, however, is to isolate the causal factors which explain this growth. Once the growth is understood, it may be possible to do something about it, whether by measures to accommodate it or by policies to alleviate it.

The second chapter outlines the model, and the third, entitled "Fact or Fiction," tests it against experience of forty countries from 1960 to "the present" (about 1983). They divide their period into two: "pre-OPEC" and "post-OPEC," or before and after the oil-price shocks. Their sample contains forty countries with per capita incomes below $500 at 1960 prices, and which have reasonably good data. They converted data for their forty countries into a "prototype," using unweighed averages for each variable. They justify this method because Colin Clark, Simon Kuznets, and Chenery and Syrquin have shown "the existence of a typical pattern of development."[18] There are more than one hundred of these. They proceed to test the model by comparing its predictions with what actually happened. They remark that: "Perhaps 'test' is the wrong word since many of the standard econometric procedures are simply inappropriate when applied to the predictions of a long-run equilibrium model. After all, the data base is weak since several variables have no documentation whatsoever. Furthermore, the model is only a stylized abstraction of what is a very complex social process."[19] Nevertheless, they close their chapter of "Fact or Fiction" with the following conclusion: "We believe that our model has replicated Third World growth, accumulation, distribution, and urban change very closely indeed. That conclusion was not guided by econometric precision, to be sure, but the evidence certainly suggests that ours is a plausible paradigm of long-run city growth, for Third World economies passing through the transition to modernization. Of course, we have no way of knowing whether the structural parameters embedded in the model will remain stable over the next two decades. To the extent that they do, we believe we have an empirically relevant paradigm..."[20]

In the fourth chapter, through the device of short-run impact multipliers, they use their model to test a number of propositions using unbalanced productivity advance "as a vehicle to understand how the economy works," thus revealing their "prejudice that unbalanced productivity advance is *the* central force driving urbanization and city growth during any nation's industrial revolution."[21] Productivity advance favouring modern sectors, they say, "*does* foster urbanization. But in the short-run, the city growth response is constrained "by bottlenecks in housing, labour skills, urban land, and the like."[22] Urban growth seems to be most sensitive to nine variables: prices and productivity change in manufacturing and agriculture, labour force growth, capital accumulation in manufacturing, accumulation of rural and urban housing stocks for the poor, and skills.

Chapter 5 takes a look at the past. Urban growth in the Third World has slowed down since the 1973 oil shock. The slowdown "certainly had nothing to do with retarding agricultural land expansion or labour force growth, since these were pushing in opposite directions." ... "Furthermore—and in spite of all the attention it has received...rising fuel scarcity was nowhere near as important a source of city growth slowdown as was the accelerated decline in the relative price of manufactures."[23] There was nothing unusual about Third World city growth prior to OPEC. Had there been a scarcity of foreign capital, city growth in the Third World would have been much the same. Arable land stock growth did not matter much to city growth. The unbalanced productivity advance, and the unbalanced character of technological progress "is a critical force driving Third World city growth." The chapter closes with these conclusions: "Some key morals have emerged from this counterfactual exercise. First, rapid rates of population growth are not the central influence driving Third World city growth, as a reading of the popular literature would suggest. Nor does it appear that capital transfers to the Third World played a very significant role. In addition, arable land scarcity exerted only a very modest impact in pushing labor to the cities. Second, the most potent influences on Third World city growth appear to have been the rate and unbalancedness of sectoral productivity ad-vance—technological events that have favoured the urban modern sectors, and relative prices. Third, OPEC-induced fuel scarcity has been less important in driving city growth than the state of world markets for manufactures."[24]

Chapter 6 uses the model to make projection to the year 2000. It concludes: "From this perspective we can now see that the city growth problems of the

1960s and 1970s *were* unusually severe, and that, on average, the Third World has passed its high watermark. They would have been severe even if external conditions had not been especially favourable to city growth up to the mid-1970s. They were especially severe, however, since these conditions *were* especially pro-urban. The 1980s and the 1990s are likely to be different. The endogenous forces of "mobility transition" would have guaranteed that result, but the less pro-urban demographic, technological, and price environment up to the year 2000 is likely to ease city growth problems even more."[25]

The authors predict that "in the absence of any changes in the exogenous economic/demographic environment facing the Third World over the next two decades,...the vast majority of the urban transition will be completed by the year 2000."[26] Their book, they say, "offers little evidence in support of the over-urbanization view adopted by the pessimists."[27] Conditions prior to the 1973–74 OPEC price shocks were unusually favourable to rapid Third World city growth. As for the question whether rural land scarcity has been an important *quantitative* factor in urban growth in the Third World, "the answer is unambiguously 'No'."[28] The impact of foreign capital is small; the growth rates would have been much the same between 1960 and 1973 if there had been no net foreign capital inflow. The "unbalanced character of productivity advance across sectors is far more important than the overall economy wide rate; the terms of trade between primary products and manufactures is far more important than is the relative scarcity of imported fuels and raw materials; and the Malthusian 'bomb' plays a smaller role than conventional wisdom would suggest."[29] Contrary to Todaro's prediction that a rise in urban wage rate increases the urban labour force, "our model makes precisely the opposite prediction: a rise in the wage gap between the urban informal and formal sectors serves to *lower* city in-migration rates, to *lower* city growth rates, and to *lower* the share of the labor force in urban areas."[30]

The book ends on a note of caution: "These conclusions are all conditional upon the assumptions of the dynamic general equilibrium model used throughout this book. That is true of any analytical effort. The conclusions may also be specific to the group of countries underlying our data base. That is true of any empirical effort. So it is that the conclusions of this book must be viewed as working hypotheses only. They must be tested against new data—in particular, tested by the accumulation of country studies. And they must be tested against new models—especially models that introduce more of the institutional realities of the Third World than are present in our simple general equilibrium approach."[31]

This, then, is only the start. It is an impressive start, a veritable *tour de force*, a splendid example of the cliometrician's art. Still, considering all the weaknesses in its basic methodology and its limited data base, it would be dangerous in the extreme to use the model as the sole source of predictions for a particular country, let alone as a basis for policy. This caveat applies with particular forces to countries which are not one of the 40 included in the sample. The model may give some useful predictions on what will happen *on the average* to those 40 countries, and even some guidance for policy. To understand the workings of a particular country, and to prescribe policy for it, it is necessary to take a hard look at the country itself.

Systems of Interactions Through Space

Nearly a decade ago, Benjamin Higgins published an article entitled "From Growth Poles to Systems of Interactions in Space."[32] In it, he made some of the same arguments that are presented in chapter 6 of this volume: it is impossible to construct a concept of growth pole that is logically and empirically correct, and at the same time operational; we need constructs of systems of interactions in space that fit the multi-faceted situation regarding decision making on location, choice of product-mix, and choice of technology of the real world. Much of the recent literature on regional development seems to be endeavouring to produce just such constructs—not, to be sure, because the authors have been influenced by the article, but because they recognize the need for such constructs if we are to understand, and recommend policies for, the world as it is.

The trouble is that regional economics is still dominated by the precepts and concepts of neoclassical economics. Many authors of recent literature therefore still expect to find uniformities of behaviour across time and space. The truth is, however, that when we are confronted with growth-maximizing management *teams* rather than with individual profit-maximizing entrepreneurs, almost anything can happen. The individuals who comprise the teams may be equally intelligent and "rational," and yet have different views of what constitutes the best location for a particular enterprise or activity. Some may prefer large cities, some medium sized cities, some may opt for "factories in the fields." The actual choice of the *enterprise* as a whole is likely to be a matter of conflict-resolution. What happens in a particular country during a certain period—agglomeration or deglomeration, polarization, polarization-reversal, or polarization-reversal-reversal, *in the aggregate*—will depend on the number of enterprises making each choice. There is no reason why the relative numbers should be the same in different countries, or even from one year to the next in a particular country. Location of industry is a gigantic game played by millions of players. Since all players do not abide by the same rules, "economic science" cannot predict the outcome.

John Holmes perceives clearly the difficulties caused by clinging too rigorously to neoclassical ideology and method: "Notwithstanding a number of serious and damaging critiques, the historical models of the market economy and of the firm derived from neoclassical economic theory continued to exercise considerable influence on contemporary industrial location theory throughout the 1970s. In neo-classical economic theory, with its emphasis on the individual firm and household and on the analysis of market exchanges between individual economic actors, it is assumed that firms engage in cost-rational decision making independent of each other. These assumptions, in combination with others, imply that interactions between firms occur through the market place where individual firms meet as equals."[33]

They point out that old firms as well as new ones experiment in location decisions and production organization: "Both old and new industries seem to have embarked on a period of experimentation in locational behaviour and production organization. For example, both the new electronics industry and the old apparel industry have located phases of their production processes in low-wage regions and countries. In addition, revolutionary organizational and spatial strategies are being experimented with on the part of automobile manufacturers. Ford, for example, has created the 'World Car,' which involves international integration of very large scale production units with standardized output, many parallel plants, and the provision of product variety by creating different interchangeable components which are combined with core products to make possible great variety at high levels of output. General Motors is experimenting with precisely the opposite system to Ford's, based on just-in-time parts delivery and flexible automation with a tendency toward locational agglomeration and a focus on corporatist labor relations. Which of the approaches and which spatial pattern will prevail remains to be seen."[34] They think that today the forces of disintegration are more powerful than the forces leading to integration.[35]

Location decisions, Edward J. Malecki argues, are divided into two types, defined by labour force requirements. Production workers, and others who perform standardized and routine operations, are found in a large number of places. Firms using such types of workers can locate in rural areas, where non-union labour is available and wages are relatively low. But enterprises requiring professional and technically skilled workers, especially scientists and engineers, have to locate in centres that are attractive to such people. Typically these will be centres with good educational, cultural and recreational facilities, and other amenities that go to make up a high "quality of life." Thus only metropolitan areas tend to be considered. These two kinds of decisions lead to a spatial division of labour.[36]

David P. Angel seems to agree. The appearance of many low-volume niches, he says, means that "small batch production" can be profitable, using "CADCAM" techniques (Computer Assisted Design, Computer Assisted Manufacturing). Flexible manufacturing of small specialized producers is replacing mass production.[37] Nancy Ettinger makes the same point. Since the

1970s, in both manufacturing and services, there has been a restructuring of activities away from "Fordist" mass production to small batch production, resembling craft production in the late 19th century in the United States. "The small, batch character of non-Fordist production," she maintains "achieves efficiency by externalizing economies of scale and scope. Such externalization, often achieved through subcontracting arrangements, may result in the development of a territorial production complex, where the local network of backward and forward linkages becomes quite dense, and firms benefit from the presence of agglomeration economies."[38]

J.N. Marshall agrees with Scott and Storper with regard to industry but disagrees with respect to the centralization of services. He reports that several "results" do not support the view that organizational changes are promoting the centralization of services. He maintains that in the case of physical distribution services, where the location of goods is important, we are witnessing a decentralization of services to smaller towns with good road access to manufacturing facilities and the growth of retail outlets.[39]

Niles Hansen meanwhile reports on the restructuring of the Provence-Alpes-Côte d'Azur (PACA) and Languedoc-Roussillon (LR) industry: "With increasing vertical disintegration, the economies of PACA and LR have been realizing external economies from the expansion of the entire system of production of goods and services. SMEs, which are especially prevalent in these regions, have contributed significantly to employment expansion, not on an individual basis, but through their growth as an ensemble and through the linkages that they maintain both among themselves and with large enterprises. What has been emerging is a new regional organizational paradigm that combines various forms of expertise in collaborative networks that transcend the older types of industrial strategy based on internal concentration."[40]

Hansen also writes of "Factories in the Fields" in Jutland, Denmark. In the same paper, however, he also sounds a note of caution regarding decentralization: "Most recent studies of possibilities for sustained endogenous development have been made in Western Europe (see, for example, Aydalot 1986; Stöhr 1986; Sweeney 1987; Fischer and Nijkamp 1988; Hansen 1990). However, upon close examination the cases in question in fact typically involve metropolitan areas or areas in proximity to metropolitan areas...It is not surprising, therefore, that Malecki should conclude that 'European experience has suggested that agricultural regions are the least likely to have new firms, largely because entrepreneurial role models are often absent from the local culture.'"[41]

Conclusion

Only one thing emerges clearly from this survey of recent literature in the field of regional development: we are in an era of extreme fluidity and flexibility regarding location of industry, agglomeration and deglomeration, integration and disintegration, polarization and "polarization-reversal." The only principles that seem to prevail are "it depends" and "anything goes." But the discovery that wise men and women can arrive at different decisions as to what is best *for them* in choice of product-mix, scale of production, technology, and location of economic activities—even if they are members of the same management team—means that we *cannot* conclude that whatever managers decide about location of industry is optimal for society. It is not the usual "market failure" that leads to this conclusion; it would hold even if there were no imperfection of competition, indivisibilities, externalities, and the like. We cannot say, without studying each case in minute detail, (and even then the decisions of the managers are likely to be better than our own) whether it is better to choose a product mix and a technology that permits location in a small town where there is a non-unionized, unskilled labour force, with large numbers of docile women and unemployed youth; or a highly skilled labour force, a high level of technology, and a flexible product-mix, which require location in a metropolitan centre, from the standpoint of the enterprise concerned. But the choice being made may generate, on balance, a tendency towards agglomeration or deglomeration, towards reduction or an increase of inflation or unemployment, towards reduction or increase in regional disparities, towards pollution and congestion and a general deterioration in the environment, or towards an improvement of environmental conditions.

It behooves us, therefore, as regional economists, to try to figure out *what* tendencies would be good for society, and then to try to nudge enterprises in that direction. A particular society may have many objectives that are external to the firm. They may be of some importance to the firm as well, in terms of attracting or holding a labour force in a particular place. But in some circumstances they may not be *as* important to the firm as they are to the society. If social scientists can identify trends that are clearly helpful or harmful, and design policies that will influence enterprises towards supporting the helpful and avoiding decisions that strengthen the harmful trends, social welfare would be considerably enhanced.

It is reported in the press that at the last annual meeting of the shareholders, the president of General Motors announced that henceforth, the aim of the management would be to maximize profits, rather than maximizing GM's share of the market.[42] This was a clear confession that the management was maximizing growth, rather than profits, in the recent past. This change in policy will no doubt have implications for the spatial distribution of GM activities. One cannot protest the change in policy as such; maximize profits is what corporations are supposed to do, in the interest of their shareholders. However, the resulting changes in location of economic activity may have both favourable and unfavourable effects on social welfare, both in the United States and in other countries. When the multinational corporation is as large as General Motors, any change in policy may have considerable impact in the countries where it operates.

This case illustrates the difficulties in which those social scientists who study regional development find themselves today. When one assumes that enterprises are run by individual entrepreneurs who are maximizing profit, one can *deduce* what their actions are likely to be in various circumstances. But when one doesn't know what a particular corporation is trying to do, when their decision makers can change their minds as dramatically and suddenly as General Motors did, and when one doesn't even know *who* makes the decisions (the president of GM may have liked the old policy, but was bullied into changing it by his board), the only way to find out how decisions are made, and what their impact is, is to study each case separately and on the spot.

Notes

1. Allen J. Scott and Michael Storper, "High Technology Industry and Regional Development: A Theoretical Critique and Reconstruction," *International Social Science Journal*, May 1987, no. 112, p. 220.
2. Robin Marris, "Equity, Efficiency and the Managerial Paradigm," in Donald J. Savoie and Irving Brecher (eds), *Equity and Efficiency in Economic Development: Essays in Honour of Benjamin Higgins* (Montreal: McGill/Queen's University Press, 1992).
3. Scott and Storper, "High Technology Industry and Regional Development," p. 220.
4. *Ibid.*
5. Fu Chen Lo and Kamal Salih, "Growth Poles and Regional Policy in Open Dualistic Economies: Western Theory and Asian Reality," in Lo and Salih, (eds), *Growth Pole Strategy and Regional Development: Alternative Approaches* (Oxford: Pergamon press, 1978), pp. 243–70.
6. Philippe Aydalot, "La division spatiale du travail," in Jean H.P. Paelink and Alain Sallez (eds), *Espace et localisation* (Paris: Economica, 1983), p. 175.
7. *Ibid.*, pp. 176–79.
8. *Ibid.*, p. 179.
9. *Ibid.*, p. 185.
10. Niles Hansen, "Regional Consequences of Structural Changes in the National and International Division of Labor," *International Regional Science Review*, 1988, vol. 22, no. 2, p. 128.
11. Ray Vernon, "The Product Cycle Hypothesis in a New International Economy," *Economic Bulletin*, 1981, p. 256.
12. Michael Taylor, "The product-Cycle Model: A Critique," *Environment and Planning A*. 1986, vol. 18, pp. 751, 753, 760.
13. Scott and Storper, "High Technology Industry and Regional Development," p. 219.
14. *Ibid.*, p. 220.
15. *Ibid.*

16. *Ibid.*
17. Allen C. Kelley and Jeffrey G. Williamson, *What Drives Third World City Growth: A Dynamic General Equilibrium Approach* (Princeton, Ill.: Princeton University Press, 1984), p. 3.
18. *Ibid.*, p. 75.
19. *Ibid.*, p. 82.
20. *Ibid.*, p. 99.
21. *Ibid.*, p. 101.
22. *Ibid.*, p. 104.
23. *Ibid.*, p. 132.
24. *Ibid.*, p. 140.
25. *Ibid.*, p. 177.
26. *Ibid.*, p. 178.
27. *Ibid.*, p. 179.
28. *Ibid.*, p. 181.
29. *Ibid.*
30. *Ibid.*, p. 185.
31. *Ibid.*, p. 186.
32. Benjamin Higgins, "From Growth Poles to Systems of Interactions in Space," *Growth and Change*, 1983, vol. 14, no. 4.
33. John Holmes, "The Organization and Locational Structure of Production Subcontracting," in Scott and Storper (eds), *Production, Work, Territory: The Geographical Anatomy of Industrial Capitalism* (Boston: Allen & Unwin, 1986), pp. 80–82.
34. Scott and Storper, *Production, Work, Territory*, p. 5.
35. *Ibid.* pp. 11–12.
36. Edward J. Malecki, 1986, "Technological Imperatives and Modern Corporate Strategy," in Scott and Storper (eds.), 67–79.
37. David P. Angel, 1990, "New Firm Formation in the Semiconductor Industry: Elements of a Flexible Manufacturing System," *Regional Studies*, 24(3):211–221.
38. Nancy Ettlinger, "Worker Displacement and Corporate Restructuring: A Policy-Conscious Appraisal," *Economic Geography*, 1990, vol. 66, no. 1, p. 68.
39. J.N. Marshall, 1989, "Corporate Reorganization and the Geography of Services: Evidence from the Motor Vehicle Aftermarket in the West Midlands Region of the UK," *Regional Studies*, 23(2):139–50.
40. Niles Hansen, "Innovative Regional Milieux, Small Firms, and Regional Development: Evidence from Mediterranean France1," *Annals of Regional Science*, 1990, vol. 24, no. 2, p. 121.
41. Niles Hansen, *Factories in the Fields: Innovation, Small Firms and Flexible Production in Rural Denmark* (Austin, Texas, Department of Economics, University of Texas, 1992), p. 4.
42. *The Financial Post*, 5 May 1992, p. 15.

Part II

Policy, Planning, and Programs

Introduction to Part II

We have now covered the major contributions to regional development theory, spanning a century or more, but concentrating on the period since World War II. Some of the theories are derivations from general development theory, utilized to explain regional differences: geography and culture; entrepreneurship; international and interregional trade; bi-modal production and regional dualism; circular and cumulative causation; dependency and uneven development. A few are specifically tied to the explanation of regional phenomena: growth poles and central places; regional science; and almost all the recent theories discussed in Chapter 11. Most of the literature on these theories has been produced in the United States, the United Kingdom, Canada and Australia, although Perroux's preeminence in the field to growth poles and Myrdal's with regard to circular and cumulative causation has resulted in a flood of literature from French and Swedish writers as well. This fact explains why we have chosen these countries to test the theories by seeing how well they worked out in practice; another reason is that in each case at least one of the authors knows the country and its regional development policies very well. Have the countries producing the literature on regional development done better than others in applying it?

The reader will notice a certain asymmetry in the treatment of the various countries. In Great Britain, the European Community and Canada, we discuss the ideological and intellectual underpinnings of the policies undertaken, and then proceeds to outline national policies, legislation, and then proceeds to outline national policies, legislation, and institutions set up to carry out the policies. There are no "case studies" of particular regions. In the case of the United States and Australia, we provide something of the academic and intellectual background of regional policy. For the United States, we proceed to a detailed account of two very different cases; one a large retarded region (Appalachia) and the other a relatively prosperous small region with severe economic and social problems (Austin, Texas). For Australia we look at a series of cases, all at the level of the community or small region.

There are two reasons for adopting this approach. In Great Britain and Canada the regional development effort has involved mainly the attempt to define regional policy at the national level. The result has been a series of government programs designed and implemented by government officials. In the United States and Australia, on the contrary, there has been virtually no regional policy at the national level, but there has been very effective preparation and implementation of regional development plans at the local level. We felt that the application of regional development theories should be tested against a backdrop of both national policy and actual cases. Focusing exclusively on either national policy or specific cases would have left our study incomplete.

12

The United States I: The TVA

The Ideological Background

Economic policy in the United States is the outcome of two rival paradigms. One of these, following conventional wisdom, we may call "laissez-faire"; although few people ever favoured a complete "hands-off" policy on the part of government. The other is more difficult to encompass in a single expression, including as it does fighting inflation and unemployment, regional disparities, and poverty; social security; regulation and public ownership of public utilities; trade unionism; and protectionism. *Faute de mieux*, let us use another french word, often applied to this kind of thought in english: "dirigisme." These two systems of thought have existed side by side for at least a century. Sometimes one, sometimes the other has been predominant. Sometimes, they are more or less evenly balanced. The economic policies that emerge in any period, including regional development policy, are the result of the balance between these two ideological forces.

During the New Deal era of the 1930s, when the National Resources Planning Board was at the height of its influence, a good deal of regional planning took place in the United States. Much of this planning was based on river valleys, with the Tennessee Valley Authority as the prime example. Throughout most of the past century, however, the ideological background has been closer to laissez-faire than to dirigisme. On balance, the American faith in "rugged individualism" and the market as instruments of regional development, in most periods, has been justified. The "log cabin to riches" story has been more than just a legend. Moreover, the United States has been blessed with a "ratchet effect:" Lagging regions become in time leading regions; absolute decline over long periods is virtually unknown, Appalachia being a partial exception. So diversified, and so wide and evenly spread, are the United States resources, that every large region has become urbanized and industrialized. Most of the time there seemed to be little reason for government intervention, at the federal level, in the interests of particular states. True, all states used their two senators to lobby for special attention, and when times were bad the disadvantaged states received more attention than others. But unlike Canada or the United Kingdom, at no time has there been a *commitment* to reducing regional disparities.

Closely associated with this particular mind-set in the United States has been her extraordinary frontier history, and the frontier theories that grew out of it. The boldest and most sweeping of all frontier theories is the one formulated in the late nineteenth and early twentieth centuries by two American historians, Frederick Turner and Walter Prescott Webb.

The Turner-Webb Theory of the Frontier

At the beginning of his classic work *The Great Frontier*, Webb has this to say of Turner: "It was in 1893 that a young and unknown historian appeared before the American Historical Association and read a paper entitled *The Significance of the Frontier in American History*. That paper made him a scholar with honour in his own country, for, brief though his essay is, it is recognized as the most influential single piece of historical writing ever done in the United States..."[1]

On the first page of his famous essay, Turner wrote: "American history has been in a large degree the history of the colonization of the Great West. The existence of an area of free land, its continuous recession, and the advance of American settlement westward, explain American development."[2] For Turner, it was not just that even in the nineteenth century the North American continent was still substantially empty, a vast resource frontier with fertile soil, minerals, and forests waiting to be exploited. The presence of the frontier, its nature, and the relentless way in which it was pushed steadily westward, moulded the American character and shaped American civilization. In politics and social life the frontier—the West—was marked by a certain radicalism, which neatly counterbalanced the conservatism of the East.

Development of the American frontier also brought wave after wave of settlement which ultimately urbanized and industrialized the whole country. Turner describes the process as follows: "Stand at the Cumberland Gap and watch the procession of civilization, marching single file—the buffalo following the trail to the salt springs, the Indian, the fur trader and hunter, the cattleraiser, the pioneer farmer—and the frontier has passed by. Stand at South Pass in the Rockies a century later and see the same procession with wider intervals in between. The unequal rate of advance compels us to distinguish the frontier—into the trader's frontier, the rancher's frontier, or the miner's frontier, and the farmer's frontier. When the mines and cow pens were still near the fall line, the trader's pack trains were tinkling across the Alleghanies, and the French on the Great Lakes were fortifying their posts, alarmed by the

British trader's birch canoe. When the trappers scaled the Rockies, the farmer was still near the mouth of the Missouri."[3]

Walter Prescott Webb's theory was more grandiose, a theory of history on a global scale. The famous British historian Arnold Toynbee, in his Introduction to the 1964 reprinting of *The Great Frontier*, published after Webb's death, expressed his admiration for Webb, whom he obviously regarded as a bird of the same feather as himself: "Being, as he was, a thinker whose mind never stopped producing new thoughts, Walter Prescott Webb became an historian of a kind that is not very common in our time. He managed to combine mastery of a special area of history with a vision of the total history of the world."[4]

To some extent, Webb's analysis is similar to that of Robertson and others who relate the rise of capitalism to the "price revolution" of the sixteenth century. He also had some glimmering of the Keynesian concept of increased banking liquidity leading to lower interest rates and thus encouraging investment. He was by no means clear with respect to either of these arguments, however, and at many points in his argument seemed to imply that gold and silver are themselves productive resources. It is unfortunate that economists and Webb paid so little attention to each other.

The germ of Alvin Hansen's ideas regarding the role of the frontier in economic growth, and of later ideas regarding the impact of the frontier on entrepreneurship and attitudes towards the role of government in economic life, are clearly present in Webb's work: "It was this repetition of the experience for three hundred years as the frontier of America moved slowly and on a broad front from the Atlantic to the Pacific which put the indelible frontier stamp on United States psychology, ideas, and institutions."[5]

Webb also pointed to the relationship between the existence of a moving frontier and faith in laissez-faire. "The theory of laissez-faire is a theory of abundance, of enough to go around, and cannot endure in other circumstances. Therefore, it was a good theory as long as the frontier or some other source which supplied an excess of materials lasted." The frontiers, he says, "were following the principles of laissez-faire for at least a century before Adam Smith formulated the theory. In the midst of abundance they were ready to swallow the theory based on abundance." Far from seeing the development of corporate enterprise as inimical, if not antithetical, to a system of laissez-faire, Webb sees it as part and parcel of the same general picture of a frontier society. "It is important," he says, "for us to see the corporation as the institutionalization of the ideas and practices of individual men at work in a condition of great abundance." Since the frontier was the major source of this dynamism, its disappearance becomes a cause of stagnation. The move towards planning and the acceptance of New Deal social security are in his view manifestations of "the spirit of resignation."[6] He also relates the nostalgia for the past to the passing of the frontier.[7]

Clarence Ayres was Professor of Economics, while Walter Prescott Webb was Professor of History at the University of Texas. They influenced and admired each other. Ayres was a disciple of Veblen, and perhaps the leading institutionalist economist of his day, focus of a whole school of thought at the University of Texas.

Like Veblen, Ayres saw development as a race between technological progress and the inhibiting role of ceremonial patterns and tradition, particularly as embodied in religious institutions. Western Europe's headstart in industrialization is explained by the withdrawal of the Romans, which left western Europe essentially a frontier society, with a technology inherited from an older civilization, but without the social *arteriosis sclerosis* associated with deeply imbedded traditional institutional power.

By the same token, the ever-moving frontier played an important role in the later development of the United States. By definition a "frontier" is a region into which people come from an older centre of civilization, bringing with them the tools and materials of their older life, and while they also bring their traditional values and folkways, these are weakened by a frontier environment. "Existence on the frontier is, as we say, free and easy. Meticulous observance of the Sabbath and the rules of grammar are somehow less important on the frontier than 'back home'."

The Hansen Theory of the Frontier

Alvin Hansen, "the American Keynes," included a "frontier theory" in his general thesis concerning "economic maturity" or "secular stagnation." The peculiar depth and duration of the great depression of the 1930's, Hansen maintained, was to be explained in terms of the weakening of certain long-run forces of economic growth. On the one hand rising income brought swelling personal and corporate savings; on the other, opportunities for equally great increases in investment, particularly at full employment levels of income and savings, were weakened by the declining rate of population growth, the tendency for innovations to become capital-saving rather than capital-absorbing, relative lack of "great new industries," and the disappearance of the geographical frontier and consequent loss of the "frontier spirit."

For Hansen, frontier development meant the opening up of new territories and the discovery of new resources. Included in Hansen's concept of the frontier was a less tangible factor which nonetheless plays an important role: frontier psychology. Cast in plain economic terms this factor might be translated into a relatively low level of liquidity-and-safety preference, and a relatively high marginal efficiency of capital, for any given set of objective conditions. The "frontier spirit" is associated with a willingness to take risks, to migrate from one place to another in accordance with economic opportunities, and to move capital from one place to another whenever significant differences in returns seem possible. It also implies a willingness to undertake innovations, introducing new technologies and new commodities.

According to Hansen, "the disappearance of the frontier" was one of the elements in the peculiar length and depth of the great depression of the 1930s. The depression shook the faith of the American people in "the market" as a mechanism for solving economic problems, including the problem of "uneven development" and regional imbalance. The 1930s brought a surge of regionalism to the United States. This was the era when people talked of a constitutional reform to create a "United Regions of America"; when the National Resources Planning Board was urging upon the American people, with some success, a national programme of regional development planning; when massive regional development projects like the Tennessee Valley Authority were undertaken; when agencies charged with responsibility for reducing unemployment, like the Federal Works Agency, the United States Housing Administration, the Public Works Administration and the Work Projects Administration, thought seriously of reducing regional disparities by providing jobs where unemployment was highest.

Interest in regional policy continued through the Truman years, but largely disappeared with Eisenhower and the postwar boom. It had a rebirth under Kennedy and Johnson, and the Economic Development Administration was created in this period. These swings in federal politics with regard to regional development did not reflect any comparable changes in economic theory. Urban and regional economists went on with their jobs as before; and some neoclassical economists tended to oppose them on grounds of "efficiency" as before.

The United States has produced some distinguished and highly respected regional economists, some of whom have been mentioned in Part I of this volume. Perhaps most influential has been Walter Isard, creator of regional science. Since regional science was born in the United States, it probably has had more impact there than anywhere else. Other names are William Alonzo, Niles Hansen, John Friedmann, Harry Richardson, Lloyd Rodwin, Harvey Perloff, and Karen Polenske. But while economists such as these are highly regarded for work they do, they are regarded as being somewhat apart from the mainstream of economics by the profession as a whole; and as misguided by some of the members of it.

During the 1970s and 1980s, increasingly Americans interested in local and regional planning have turned their attention to the cities. This trend is natural enough, since it is in the cities that the major problems are to be found. Increasingly, too, the tendency is to study, not metropolitan centres as a whole, but particular neighbourhoods within them. It has been found that poverty, unemployment, and conflict among ethnic groups is today less a regional or even an urban affair than it is a neighbourhood affair. The United States developed special programs to deal with localized problems on the spot. The need for new kinds of entrepreneurship is stressed: cooperatives, community-based organizations, workshops, youth enterprises, school-based enterprises. In the United States, the Department of Housing and Urban Development created community development corporations to create new enterprises and retain existing ones in distressed communities.[8]

The Tennessee Valley Authority

The Tennessee Valley Authority is much the most ambitious regional development project ever undertaken by the United States government. In the 1980s it employed nearly 50,000 people (see table 12.1). It encompassed dam construction, flood control, navigation, power generation and distribution, agricultural development, industrial development, resettlement, housing, community development, and indirectly, health and education. It also represented the farthest swing of the pendulum towards dirigisme of all regional development projects. The TVA was the child of the New Deal of the 1930s, and was essentially the brainchild of Franklin Delano Roosevelt himself. Roosevelt regarded the TVA as the first step towards a system of national planning. According to Erwin Hargrove, Franklin Roosevelt had intended TVA to be the first of many regional authorities. Although the Colombia and Missouri Valley authorities were to be decentralized, like TVA, there was an implicit commitment among advocates of authorities to the ideal of national planning through the National Resources Planning Board, with the regional authorities as the implementing agents. The NRPB's death at Congress's hands in 1943 symbolized the demise of an ideal.[9]

Paul Conkin stresses Roosevelt's love of "planning:" "By 1932 Roosevelt loved the word 'planning.' It joined other of his enthusiasms—for preserving scarce resources, for moving as many people as possible back on the land, for making cities as orderly and countrylike as possible, for making farming more profitable and fulfilling. Planning of some sort seemed the means to further these goals, goals embedded in Roosevelt's own sense of identity, in preferences that stretched back to his childhood. By 1931 Roosevelt particularly emphasized 'regional planning.' He had long known and sympathized with the efforts of professional city planners, such as his admired uncle, Frederic Delano."[10]

Roosevelt made no effort to hide the extent of his ambitions for the TVA and planning. On the contrary, in his message to Congress requesting the legislation, he presented TVA as a challenge. The TVA was to be "charged with the broadest duty of planning for the proper use, conservation, and development of natural resources of the Tennessee River drainage basin and its adjoining territory for the general social and economic welfare of the Nation.[11]

The TVA legislation of May 1933 was motivated by a desire to settle the long outstanding question of what to do with two government owned nitrate plants and a dam at Muscle Shoals Alabama. But as the president said in his message to Congress: "It is clear that the Muscle Shoals development is but a small part of the potential public usefulness of the Tennessee River. Such use, if envisaged in its entirety, transcends mere power development; it enters into the wide fields of flood control, soil erosion, afforestation, elimination from agricultural use of marginal lands, and distribution and diversification of industry. In short, this power development of war days leads logically to national planning for a complete watershed involving many States and the future lives and welfare of millions." The president, therefore, recommended "legislation to create a Tennessee Valley Authority—a corporation clothed with the power of government but possessed of the flexibility and initiative of private enterprise."[12] The creation of TVA as an "authority," not attached to any existing federal government department, responsible only to the Executive Office of the President, meant that it was autonomous to a large degree. Its decisions could not be vetoed by the Treasury or the General Accounting Office; it was free of the control of the Civil Service Commission; and it could use current revenues to meet operating expenses, instead of turning them over to the Treasury. It was also independent of agencies with overlapping interests, such as the Department of Commerce, the U.S. Army Corps of Engineers, and the Agriculture Adjustment Agency. Needless to say, such agencies had best mixed feelings about this autonomy, and it gave rise to conflicts with other federal departments. It also resulted in legal battles with private enterprise. In the beginning the very constitutionality of the TVA was challenged by the private power companies.

Difficulties also arose from TVA's administrative structure. It was to be managed by a three-man board. From the outset there was conflict between the first chairman, Arthur Morgan, (president of Antioch College) and one of the two directors, David Lilienthal. As Erwin Hargrove puts it: "Arthur Morgan wished TVA to be a demonstration agency for the nation that would experiment with different modes of regional development. David Lilienthal opposed this vision and sought to strengthen specific statutory responsibilities such as production and role of electric power, the management of the river, and the production of fertilizer for agricultural use. Lilienthal defeated

TABLE 12.1
TVA Personnel by Major Program (estimated for 1982)

Program	Number of Employees
Management and General Services	255
Board of directors	
General manager (budget and planning staff, information, D.C. office, EEOC)	
General counsel	
Management services (union-management relations, property finance, purchasing, personnel, medical, occupational health, safety, and environmental compliance)	
Agricultural and Chemical Development (agricultural and chemical R & D, fertilizer and chemical production)	1,014
Community Development (economic development, community services, regional studies)	255
Engineering Design and Construction (included with Power)	
Natural Resources (land, water, and forest resources, services, and land between the lakes)	1,878
Power and Energy Demonstrations (production, operations, transmission, construction, fuels, utilization, rates, conservation, research)	45,628
	49,000

Source: TVA, *Organization Bulletin* (27 July 1979); *Budget Program* (1982), p. 215. From the beginning TVA, unlike the Corps of Engineers and Bureau of Reclamation, has employed its own construction workers on "force account" rather than spending on private construction.

Morgan because his vision created technological achievements such as cheap power, that won political support and because, unlike Morgan, he understood the need for such support."[13] Roosevelt removed Arthur Morgan as chairman in 1938, and promoted the other director, Harcourt Morgan, to the chairmanship. (Arthur Morgan challenged his dismissal in the courts, unsuccessfully). Harcourt Morgan remained only three years, and was succeeded by David Lilienthal.

But if Lilienthal understood the need for political support, he understood and preached the TVA's official gospel of "grass roots democracy" and "democratic planning" as well. Lilienthal saw a dilemma in the increasing need for centralized power for the federal government to deal with national problems, and the threat to democracy itself involved in such centralization. Selznick says that "For his answer to this dilemma, Lilienthal has turned to (and widely publicized) the formulations of an earlier commentator on American democracy, Alexis de Toqueville. De Toqueville outlined a distinction between centralized government and centralized administration...Lilienthal has endorsed and often quoted the following statement of De Toqueville: 'Indeed, I cannot conceive that a nation can live and prosper without a powerful centralization of government. But I am of the opinion that a centralized administration is fit only to enervate the nations in which it exists...It may ensure a victory in the hour of strife, but it gradually relaxes the sinews of strength.'"[14]

Lilienthal's book, *Democracy on the March*, and numerous articles, speeches, and pamphlets promulgated the themes of "grass roots democracy" and "democratic planning." By and large, the TVA was successful in spreading this image to itself to the general public. On 25 June 1942, the London *Times* published an article on "The Technique of Democratic Planning," in which the author states that while he was impressed by the physical and technological achievements of TVA, what impressed him even more was "the technique which TVA had adopted with the deliberate aim of reconciling over-all planning with the values of democracy."[15]

A Success Story?

Most of the literature on the TVA treats it as a success story. Selznick begins his book on *TVA and the Grass Roots* with the following statement: "The Tennessee Valley Authority has been the subject of widespread comment and study in all parts of the world. In Central Europe, in the Philippines, in Palestine, in China, wherever, indeed, new methods of approach to the problems of resource development and social planning have been discussed, the TVA idea has been in the forefront. TVA has become not merely an administrative model and prototype, but a symbol of the positive, benevolent intervention of government for the general welfare. In America, too, the TVA is unquestionably a rallying point for those who favour a welfare state."[16]

Dewey Grantham, in his review of the TVA experience, states that "The popular response to TVA during these formative years was extraordinary." He quotes Stuart Chase as saying, "There seems to be something about the boldness and vigour of the whole enterprise which fires the imagination and enlists enthusiastic support." He speaks of "an endless stream of visitors," and cites "one chronicler" as exclaiming rapturously "As the great Leviathan rushed its physical works to completion and developed its numerous co-ordinated applications of physical and social science, it became evident that here in the Tennessee Valley, of all places, was emerging one of the marvels of the modern world."[17]

The TVA expanded still further during World War II, as it assumed a role in national defense. In the autumn of 1945 president Truman inaugurated the

Kentucky Dam. This was, according to Grantham, "the last of the main-river dams envisioned by the planners of the 1930s." He continues, "It was hard to deny the technical success of the agency. The massive dams on the Tennessee and its tributaries had harnessed the river, largely solved the problem of the recurring, devastating floods in the Valley, and created a great inland waterway for commercial traffic and recreation. TVA had wrought a physical transformation in the Tennessee Valley. By mid-century the Authority had become the largest producer of electricity in the United States, had developed an integrated power service area, and through its promotional rates had demonstrated how electrical power could improve the lives of people of the Valley. Meanwhile, the agency's internal organization had been perfected, and it had established vital relationships with state and local governments, municipal power boards, rural cooperatives, agricultural colleges, farm organizations, and other federal agencies."[18]

Criticism

But among these paeans of praise, there has been some severe criticism. One of the most savage and dramatic of these came from Donald Davidson, professor of English at Vanderbilt University, who wrote a two-volume history of *The Tennessee*. William Havard characterizes Davidson's attack on the TVA as follows: "In the last part of volume 2 of *The Tennessee* Davidson develops his saga of the Valley's transformation at the hands of TVA. And it is a vastly different story from that told by Lilienthal (in his book *TVA: Democracy on the March*). While fully acknowledging the impressive technical achievements of TVA, and even paying some tribute to the contributions made by the agency to improvements in navigation, agricultural efficiency, and some other aspects of life in the Tennessee Valley. Davidson is concerned with the costs of the transformation, and he finds them high indeed. It was not the reckoning of monetary costs against the returns that bothered him, although he raises serious questions about these...In Davidson's view, the costs were ultimately unaccessible in monetary or any other quantifiable terms because they involved those unmeasurable qualities of man, nature, and society as they exist in symbiotic wholeness. Thus to every claim advanced by Lilienthal, Davidson enters a caveat; conquest of nature was attended by at least as much destruction as reconstruction. Thousands of acres of the best bottom lands were lands were taken out of agricultural production, hasty clearance of reservoir basins denuded rich hardwood forest, and over acquisition of peripheral lands produced greed and exploitation by a few at the expense of the many. The past was so much mortgaged to the future that a proud historical culture was giving way to a dehumanized urban industrial society...The land acquisition program displaced individuals, families, and whole communities in the name of comprehensive regional development..."[19]

Elsewhere, Davidson claimed that, for all its talk of "democracy" and "grass roots," the TVA did not represent the people of the region: "The regional psychology of the TVA conception is not native to the South. The TVA was not created by response to a Southern crusade—although some Southern Congressmen had long agitated for a final disposition of Muscel Shoals. There was no popular outcry in the South for a TVA...The five states concerned had no opportunity to debate the project or to contribute ideas of leading personnel or by any other means to make known their opinion if they had any; the project was superimposed (however benevolently) upon them."[20]

Philip Selznick, Professor of Sociology at the University of California at Berkeley, is almost equally severe, although his main point is that the administrative structure of the TVA was bound to lead to trouble sooner or later, and in fact led to trouble sooner. In his preface to the 1966 edition of his book, *TVA and the Grass Roots*, Selznick quotes *The New York Times* of 4 July 1965: "Long a highly regarded institution, and virtually immune from criticism, TVA is coming under increasing attack from conservationists and residents of coal-producing areas for its major role in encouraging the spread of strip or surface mining for cheaper and cheaper coal." He goes on to quote the governor of Kentucky: "...the people of Kentucky take a dim view of the TVA's returning such a handsome 'profit' to the Federal Treasury at the expense of ruined hillsides, poisoned streams, dead woodlands and devastated farms, a breeding ground of mosquitoes and eradicated wild life. Certainly the TVA which is basically a conservation agency, should insist that good conservation practices should be observed wherever it does business. The conscience of the Authority should not allow the destruction it today is helping to promote."[21]

Selznick argues that through the influence of the agriculturists on its staff the TVA sold out to (was co-opted by, in his terminology) the land grant colleges and the extension service. In their effort to be "democratic," they strengthened local institutions, and thus tended "to reinforce the legitimacy to the existing leadership...In strengthening the land grant colleges in its area the TVA bolstered the position of the existing farm leadership...The traditions and outlook of the established institution will resist goals which appear to be alien, and the initiating agency will tend to avoid difficulties by restricting its own proposals to those which can be feasible carried out by the grass-roots organization."[22] He also feels that TVA's insistence on the advantages of an authority puts it in a dangerous position; "TVA itself may not long maintain its autonomy if a national decision is made against the autonomy of other regional agencies."[23] Already the TVA had a conflict with the National Re-

sources Planning Board over the proposed Arkansas Valley regional organization; the NRPB, in its report, did not recommend the application of the TVA
format to the Arkansas Valley.[24] Selznick also contends that "the TVA has not
significantly affected the overall output of fertilizer."[25] He also itemizes "the
steady retreat from the policy of providing a protective strip of public ownership around the reservoirs."[26] He refers to the "fanaticism" with which the
agriculturalists supported the extension services and local landowners over
land acquisition policy which led to a "sense of underlying disunity."[27]

Selznick concludes his book with the following two paragraphs: "The TVA
has been a particularly good subject for the analysis of these problems. This is
so precisely because it may be said that the Authority has, on the whole, very
effectively achieved some of its major purposes, including the mobilization of
a staff of very high quality. No one is surprised when a weak or corrupt government agency does not fulfil its doctrinal promise. When, however, a mor-
ally strong and fundamentally honest organization is subject to the kind of
process we have described, then the pervasive significance of that process
becomes materially enhanced. In a sense, it is just because TVA is a relatively
good example of democratic administration that the evidences of weakness in
this respect are so important. It is just because the TVA stands as something of
a shining example of incorruptibility in such major matters as noncapitulation
to local political interests in the hiring of personnel or to local utility interests
in public power policy that the evidence of covert cooptation in the agricultural program attains its general significance. For the things which are important in the analysis of democracy are those which bind the hands of good men.
We then learn that something more than virtue is necessary in the realm of
circumstances and power."[28]

TVA and the Environment

In the 1970s, the TVA came under increasing attack on environmental issues. According to Paul Conkin, there were "three large areas of challenge
and controversy. First, the environmental movement came to the Tennessee
Valley to charge TVA with fostering strip mining with its massive coal purchases and polluting the air with its smokestacks. The TVA and the Environmental Protection Agency engaged in a long and bitter fight. The second area
of controversy was about water. The TVA continued to press its mission to
develop water resources, but projects such as the Land between the Lakes and
the Tellico and Normandy dams stimulated fierce disputes within the Valley.
Finally, the cost of electric power increased greatly after the energy shocks of
1973, but TVA continued to project trends of economic growth, thus justify-
ing an extensive program of construction of nuclear power units."[29] William

Havard speaks of "negative images" of TVA produced by "the mounting environmentalist attack on TVA for its dual assault on nature. One charge is directed to the profligate consumption of resources by TVA to meet increasing demands for power to serve unconstrained and imbalanced corporate growth. The critics first launched their attack on the use by TVA of coal (especially strip-mined coal) to fire steam plants, and the assault was later extended to the nuclear part of the program."[30]

The longest legal battle over TVA's environmental impact was fought over the Tellico Dam on the Little Tennessee River. Edwin Hargrove tells the story: "The Tellico Dam controversy was ostensibly about the snail darter, a fish two inches in size which was at that time thought to be able to survive only in the river beneath the dam site and was therefore protected by the Endangered Species Act...Tellico and other episodes of its kind were, in fact, a manifestation of larger controversies over the appropriate uses of land and water. The dam would not generate power but would promote the development of the area around the reservoir through recreation and new settlement, Arcane cost-benefit controversies raged between proponents and opponents within the Valley, inside TVA, and in the Congress."[31]

William Wheeler and Michael McDonald state that at the end of World War II, "by almost any criterion TVA had been one of the great success stories of modern history;" but "the end of World War II marked the beginning of a period of uncertainty, indecision, and drift...Clearly, a `new mission' was necessary to save the Valley and itself."[32] This "new mission" was defined as industrializing the Valley, and the Tellico Dam was an important part of it. That fact explains why the Authority clung so tenaciously to its plans for the dam over two decades. The dam was not completed and closed until June 1978. Wheeler and McDonald comment: "Ultimately, then, the Tellico Dam was built. But the residue of ill feeling had badly damaged TVA's reputation, perhaps irreparably. What began as a showcase project to dramatize the agency's new mission (that of industrial development on the tributaries in "little TVA's") had ended in controversy, and bitterness that many years will not altogether erase. Never malicious nor vicious, TVA wanted only to bring the Tennessee Valley in to the modern age in which a healthy, prosperous, well-educated people could enjoy all the fruits of technology... In the increasingly complex modern age the Tellico project and TVA's new mission stand as an important case study of the dilemma of a society that seeks both technocracy and democracy."[33]

Attitudes of rival federal government departments range from the U.S. Army Corps of Engineers ("While our young men are giving their lives in this fight (against fascism) are we going to let fascism be set up right in this country? Although river authorities are not fascist in name, they are in character") to the more mild statement of Secretary of the Interior Ickes ("It is not too much to say that one of the most important lessons we have learned from the TVA experiment is that time, money and manpower can be saved if future authority legislation incorporates some element of compulsion to insure efficient collaboration between authorities and the rest of the Federal Government."[34])

The last chapter in the volume edited by Hargrove and Conkin is entrusted to William C. Havard, and bears the title "Images of TVA: The Clash of Values." It states: "In sum, the public has seldom seen TVA presented in a favourable light in the media in recent years. One regional magazine referred to 'TVA's Traumatic Mid-Life Crisis,' and presented the crisis (at least by implication) as one related to the image of TVA that arises out of its having been caught in the changed circumstances involving the larger crisis of the modern urban-industrial society. Having had a part in the movement of a substantial subregion of the South from a traditional to a 'modern' society, TVA now finds itself confronted by the values of that traditional society, by values that many now see as badly needed in the 'modern' society, at least in coping with a further transition to a 'post-industrial' society. TVA became established on the basis of perceived societal needs, and it can demonstrate major accomplishments in meeting those needs within the context of a working political tradition. It is solidly established because of those achievements, and because it did not violate the basic expectations embedded in the practice of American politics even when considered from the perspective of its presumed distinctiveness. TVA is unlikely to be dismantled. But excesses of both thought and action were involved in its origin and early development, some of which now constitute serious obstacles to its adaptation to purposes and practices designed to meet changed or changing needs."[35]

In the concluding chapter of their book on *TVA and the Dispossessed*, Michael McDonald and John Muldowny first quote President Franklin Roosevelt speaking to the National Emergency Council on 11 December 1934. The president maintained that the generation and sale of electricity was just a "side function" of TVA. "There is a much bigger situation behind the Tennessee Valley Authority," he said. "If you will read the message on which the legislation was based you will realize that we are conducting a social experiment that is the first of its kind in the world, as far as I know, covering a convenient area—in other words the watershed of a great river."[36] They then comment: "In the short term TVA's 'social experiment' was a failure—a failure brought about by lack of coherent and unified grass roots policy; by conflicting directorial roles and administrative structures; and by highly variant and persistent conceptual views held by people within the TVA of the agency's aims and goals."[37]

In the long run, they argue, the TVA was undermined by its very successes: "In a curiously Hegelian sense, TVA's development guidance, it's success as the Valley's educator, and its water management program and recreational advantages have attracted newcomers who have swelled the Valley's population as "yesterday's people" have left. These technologically skilled outsiders have in many respects formed the nucleus of those who today would halt TVA's continued expansion in the name of environmental and ecological interests. It is ironic that TVA's development has encouraged the process of modernity to the degree that new people have entered the Valley who want to preserve the region as it was, while those who lived in it as it was have either left it or have been unable, in many respects, to secure the advantages which TVA was created to provide."[38]

Whatever its successes and failures, the simple truth is that the Authority was never replicated. How was it that a president so popular and so powerful as Franklin D. Roosevelt was unable to fulfil his dream of a nation covered by a host of River Valley Authorities? This question is often raised in the literature on TVA, but to our knowledge, never satisfactorily answered. We suspect that a major part of the answer was the objection of federal government bodies—including the president's own creature, the National Resources Planning Board—to the very concept of Authorities; the president had other battles to win which were more important and less controversial. A more deepseated reason may have been that TVA was never replicated because it was not replicable: the Tennessee Valley was unique. As Richard Lowitt points out: "At first glance TVA appeared to be a planner's paradise...Here was an agency divorced from the pecuniary considerations of business manager, one in which attention could be devoted to the social goal of improving the welfare of the people in the Valley. For one thing, the area to be served by TVA was located in what was possibly the poorest part of the poorest region in the nation at that time. (It was) the most deprived sections of their respective states and not favoured by the political factions dominating their states. Moreover, the services provided by state, county, and local government throughout the Tennessee Valley were very limited in 1933. In seeking to develop the region, TVA would not be competing against these entities...In short, TVA had unprecedented opportunities for planning and developing one of the most neglected regions in the eastern part of the United States, a region where unemployment was endemic, in which cash incomes per family average less than $100 per year, in which the mountains had been slashed and forests burned, in which a barter economy, even in a city like Knoxville, was becoming widespread, in which spring flooding was taken for granted. In the Tennessee Valley...a technical intelligentsia allied with workers and farmers could create from a devastated region a garden of beauty and well-being, a region in which the capitalist and the financier would be relegated to a marginal role and in which intelligence and good will could prevail."[39] In short, TVA was a special case.

Notes

1. Walter Prescott Webb, *The Great Frontier* (Boston: Houghton Mifflin, 1952), pp. 5-6.
2. Frederick J. Turner, *The Frontier in American History* (New York: Henry Holt, 1920), p. 1.
3. *Ibid.*, p. 12.
4. Arnold Toynbee, "Introduction," in Webb, *The Great Frontier*.
5. Webb, *The Great Frontier*, p. 32.
6. *Ibid.*, p. 113.
7. *Ibid.*, p. 122.
8. United States Department of Housing and Urban Development, *Economic Development: New Roles for City Government* (Washington, D.C., 1979).
9. Erwin C. Hargrove and Paul K. Conkin, *TVA: Fifty Years of Grass-Roots Bureaucracy* (Urbana and Chicago: University of Illinois Press, 1983) p. xiv.
10. Paul K. Conkin, "Intellectual and Political Roots," in Hargrove and Conkin, *TVA*, p. 24.
11. Philip Selznick, *TVA and the Grass Roots: A Study in the Sociology of Formal Organization* (New York: Harper and Row, Torchbooks, 1966), p. 53.
12. *Ibid.*, p. 5.
13. Hargrove, *TVA*, pp. 89-90.
14. *Ibid.*, p. 25.
15. *Ibid.*, p. 3.
16. *Ibid.*
17. Dewey W. Grantham, "TVA and the Ambiguity of American Reform," in Hargrove and Conkin, *TVA*, p. 118.
18. *Ibid.*, p. 318-9.
19. William C. Havard Jr., "Images of TVA: The Clash Over Values," in Hargrove and Conkin, *TVA*, p. 300.
20. Donald Davidson, "Political Regionalism and Administrative Regionalism," *Annals of the American Academy of Political and Social Science* no. 207, January 1940, p. 141.
21. Selznick, *TVA and the Grass Roots*, pp. xii, xiii.
22. *Ibid.*, pp. 72-73.
23. *Ibid.*, p. 75.
24. *Ibid.*, p. 78.
25. *Ibid.*, p. 99.
26. *Ibid.*, p. 202.
27. *Ibid.*, pp. 205-7, 211.
28. *Ibid*, pp. 265-66.
29. Conkin, "Intellectual and Political Roots," pp. xii-xiii.
30. Havard, "Images of TVA," p. 312.
31. Hargrove and Conkin, *TVA*, pp. xiii-xiv.
32. William Bruce Wheeler and Michael J. McDonald, "The 'New Mission' and the Tellico Project, 1945-1970," in Hargrove and Conkin, *TVA*, p. 167.
33. *Ibid.*, p. 189.
34. Craufurd D. Goodwin, "The Valley Authority Idea—The Fading of a National Vision," in Hargrove and Conkin, *TVA*, pp. 274-5.
35. Havard, "Images of TVA," pp. 313-4.

36. Michael J. McDonald and John Muldowny, *TVA and the Dispossessed: The Resettlement of Population in the Norris Dam Area* (Knoxville, University of Tennessee Press, 1982), p. 263.
37. *Ibid.*, p. 264.
38. *Ibid.*, p. 272.
39. Richard Lowitt, "The TVA 1933–1945," in Hargrove and Conkin, *TVA*, pp. 35–65.

13

The United States II: The EDA and the Appalachian Regional Commission

In his chapter on "Regional Economic Development Policies and Programs in the United States" in the volume on *Regional Policy in a Changing World*, Professor Niles Hansen states that "The year 1965 represents a watershed in this regard. In that year Congress established the Economic Development Administration (EDA), the Appalachian Regional Commission, and a number of multi-state regional development commissions as part of President Johnson's Great Society program. In so doing, the federal government assumed an unprecedented degree of responsibility for ameliorating spatial structural problems on a national scale."[1] Other regional commissions, established under Title V of the Public Works and Regional Development Act of 1965, were the Ozarks, Four Corners, Coastal Plains, Upper Great Lakes, Mid-America, Southwest Border, Pacific Northwest, Old West, and New England Regional Commissions. (See Map 13-1) All of these, except the Appalachian Regional Commission, have since disappeared and the EDA has been reduced to a very small scale. Hansen also has this to say: "If the term *regional policy* is understood to mean a consistent and integrated set of programs designed to influence the distribution of population and economic activity, then the United States has never had such a policy at the national level. However, in a looser sense, federal regional development policies have been present since the early years of the nation. Inspired by such concepts as "manifest destiny," vast territories were opened in the nineteenth century and developed with major federal subsidies and guidance."[2]

In this chapter, we shall analyze: the Appalachian Regional Commission, as the oldest surviving institution (apart from TVA) created by the federal government and devoted exclusively to development of one region. In the next chapter, we will deal with the Austin Project, as one of the newest organizations concerned with regional development, in which the federal government—as yet—plays no direct part. Before turning to these cases, however, we shall first say a word about the Economic Development Administration.

MAP 13-1
The Title V Regional Commissions, 1979

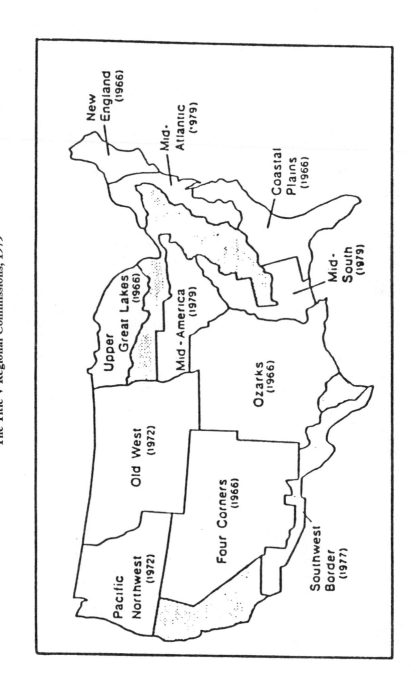

New England (1966)

Mid-Atlantic ('979)

Coastal Plains (1966)

Mid-South (1979)

Upper Great Lakes (1966)

Mid-America (1979)

Ozarks (1966)

Old West (1972)

Four Corners (1966)

Pacific Northwest (1972)

Southwest Border (1977)

The Economic Development Administration

The Economic Development Administration (EDA) survives, although on a much reduced scale, within the Department of Commerce. Its budget for 1991 was $209 million. In its 1991 *Annual Report*, EDA described its functions as follows: "The mission of the Economic Development Administration (EDA) is to promote the long-term recovery of economically distressed areas by assisting states or political subdivisions thereof, Indian tribes or private and public non-profit organizations in generating and retaining jobs and to stimulate commercial and industrial growth in those areas through grants and loan guarantees."[3]

Since in 1980 the Appalachian Regional Commission and the Title V Regional Commission covered the whole country (See Map 13-1), these functions—legally and officially, at least—represent a drastic restriction of federal government activities in the field of regional development.

EDA offers seven types of assistance:

1. Public Works: "EDA provides grants to help distressed areas build and develop essential public facilities under Title I and IV of the Public Works and Economic Development Act of 1965." The bulk of EDA's budget is spent in this manner; in 1991 grants of $140.6 million were made for public works. These are quite small projects. The average grant was a mere $736,000.

2 Business Development: Assistance to private enterprise consists mainly of loans. At the end of 1991 EDA had a portfolio of some $174 million of business loans.

3. Planning: "EDA supports planning efforts that are intended to respond to economic problems and take advantage of opportunities at the state, multicounty, and local levels." These grants are very small, averaging about $6,000 each. In 1991 EDA awarded 377 such grants for a total of $23 million.

4. Technical Assistance: "The Technical Assistance program offers aid nationally, locally, and through university centres program, EDA made 59 grants, totalling $4.8 million "to help colleges and universities mobilize their own and other resources for the economic growth of distressed areas."

5. Research and Evaluation: "EDA awarded 14 research grants for a total of $1.4 million in FY (fiscal year) 1991."

6. Economic Adjustment: "Title IX of the Public Works and Economic Development Act of 1965 authorizes EDA to provide special economic development and adjustment assistance in areas experiencing or threatened by sudden and severe economic dislocation (SSED), as well as areas suffering long-run economic deterioration (LRED)." In fiscal year 1991, EDA made 64 grants of this type, for a total of $23.9 million.

7.   Trade Adjustment Assistance: "The Trade Adjustment Assistance program
     is designed to provide technical assistance to certified firms and indus-
     tries hurt by the impact of increased imports." In FY 1991 the EDC made
     twelve awards, totalling $12 million to Trade Adjustment Assistance Cen-
     tres, which are non-profit, non-government organizations set up to help
     private enterprises qualify for and receive assistance from other govern-
     ment sources. These awards helped over 4,000 firms.[4]

Clearly, operations on this scale have a limited impact on the macroeconomic
level. However, they do achieve two objectives. They maintain a federal presence in the field of regional economic development, which will be a starting
point if and when some future government wants to expand its role in that
field. Second, at the microeconomic level, the EDA grants, small as they are,
may make the difference in determining whether worthwhile projects are carried out or not. For example, the grant of $11,650 to Kent State University to
study regional distribution of defense expenditures may result in a very valuable final product. So might the $100,525 awarded the University of Michi-
gan to do research on the economic significance and probable future changes
in the structure of the U.S. motor vehicle industry. For those who believe that
economic and social problems are most effectively attacked at the regional or
local level, the continued presence of the EDA through the Reagan and Bush
administrations must be counted as a blessing.
    Which of the theories analyzed in Part I of this volume are being applied by
EDA? One might say "all or none." Since EDA disburses its budget in the form
of grants or loans to other institutions, its decision making is limited to choosing
institutions and projects to assist. But in making those decisions almost any of
the theories of Part I might be brought to bear: interregional and international
trade; location theory; bi-modal production and regional dualism. Certainly the
staff of EDA would take entrepreneurship into account. One of their main purposes is to turn cumulative decline into cumulative progress. They are probably
not immune to the growth pole doctrine, even today. They are acquainted with
regional science. They know about dependency, and they certainly know about
uneven development. I suspect, however, that most of these theories are at *the
back of their minds* when they decide how much money to give to this or that
organization or institution to do what, rather than being consciously applied.
Experience, knowledge of the institution and the area where it is located, judgement, and intuition probably play a larger role in their decision-making than
careful application of refined theory.

The Appalachian Regional Commission

The Appalachian Regional Commission (ARC) had its origins in the 1960
presidential election campaign, and in the primary race between John Kennedy

and Hubert Humphrey that preceded it. As the ARC report on *Twenty Years of Progress* puts it, "Exposed to Appalachian poverty day after day in that heated campaign, Kennedy pledged to take action against it if elected to the presidency."[5] Soon after his election, he appointed a task force under senator Paul Douglas (a well-known economist, co-author of the Cobb-Douglas function) to make recommendations for area redevelopment before his inauguration. These recommendations included the creation of a regional commission for Appalachia. Meanwhile, the Conference of Appalachian Governors had been formed, and pressed for federal legislation. In May 1961, the Area Redevelopment Act was passed, the first major piece of legislation of the new administration. However, there was continuing pressure for special legislation for Appalachia. In response, Kennedy announced the formation of a federal and state committee, the President's Appalachian Regional Commission (PARC), to prepare "a comprehensive program for the economic development of the Appalachian Region."[6] The PARC report was submitted to President Johnson in April 1964 (Kennedy having been assassinated). Legislation was drafted on the basis of the report, and was finally passed by both houses of Congress early in 1965, known as the Appalachian Regional Development Act.

The commission as such consists of the governors of the thirteen states and a federal co-chairman, appointed by the president, subject to confirmation by the Senate. The president and the Senate also appoint the executive director as chief of staff. The staff is paid jointly by the federal government and the states, and is instructed to observe the interests of the governors and the federal administration.

The reasons for the Appalachian Regional Development Act are set forth in Section 2 of the Act itself: "The congress hereby finds and declares that the Appalachian region of the United States, while abundant in natural resources and rich in potential, lags behind the rest of the Nation in its economic growth and that its people have not shared properly in the Nation's prosperity. The region's uneven past development, with its historical reliance on a few basic industries and a marginal agriculture, has failed to provide the economic base that is a vital prerequisite for vigorous, self-sustaining growth."[7]

John Cumberland puts the case for government intervention in Appalachia more dramatically: "Economic and social disaster began for the people of Appalachia when the outside world, under pressures of the industrial revolution, discovered the value of natural resources in the region, and began to exploit them as absentee owners. The virgin forests were the first resource to go. Timber rights were acquired over vast tracts by representatives of timber companies at very low prices. Short run profit objectives and competitive pressures led to mining of the timber using destructive practices which stripped away the soil cover on steep slopes. Consequently, not only was the timber lost without regard to reforestation, but the soil from the slopes was left to wash down into the stream. The next wave of destruction was created by strip mining the rich coal reserves of Appalachia. Bulldozing the sides of mountains to get at the coal created spoil banks which slid down upon mountain farms and houses, destroying everything in their path and blocking waterways. The land owners were powerless to protect their land or their homes. Water run off from mined areas was contaminated by sulphur and other elements causing acid drainage into streams which kills fish and wildlife."[8]

Michael Bradshaw, a British human geographer who spent fifteen years studying the region, and whose book *The Appalachian Regional Commission: Twenty-five Years of Government Policy* is one of the most recent and most detailed analysis of the ARC, describes the region more prosaically: "In the minds of most geographers, Appalachia is a physical entity. It is a mountainous region stretching for some 1,200 miles from northeast to southwest, and up to 300 miles from east to west. Although the northern one-third of Appalachia was industrialized from the mid-nineteenth century, it has scarcely experienced the improvements found in the regions that surround it. Those regions have been in the forefront of U.S. economic growth over the last two hundred years. The southern one-third was afflicted by involvement with the southern states in the economic disaster that accompanied and followed the Civil War in the 1860s. The central portion formed part of the 'border states' between North and South; fought over during the Civil War, it was in turn largely isolated and then exploited for its coal deposits. The boom-and-bust economies of coal mining, the decline of farming as a form of employment, the massive outmigration of the younger and better-educated groups, and the environmental pollution caused by mining and industry added to the area's problems in the twentieth century. By 1960 the whole of Appalachia was widely perceived as a region of economic lag, social deprivation, environmental degradation, and political isolation."[9]

The President's Appalachian Regional Commission had been particularly concerned by the region's education lag, its large-scale emigration (especially of its younger and better educated population) and high unemployment. In its *report*, it established four priorities for the region's development program: "*Providing Access* to overcome regional isolation was considered a critical basis for development with Appalachia, and over one-third of the federal investment for 1965–67 should be in the building of highways. Airport services within the region should also be improved, following initial studies of need."

Water Resources Development would require a comprehensive attack on flood incidence, water quality, and the use of water resources. Funds were recommended to accelerate construction of water-management and sewage facilities.

Natural Resources were seen as the key to a more prosperous economy. In particular, the needs of agriculture (acceleration of pasture improvements to expand livestock), the management and marketing of timber through Timber Development Organizations, and the development of coal and other mineral resources were recommended for funding. Studies were also needed of the regional potential for expanding power production (based on coal, gas, oil, and nuclear fuels) and recreational facilities.

Human Resources would require development with linked programs focusing on "food, clothing, medical care, housing, basic education, skills, jobs, hope and dignity." President Johnson's envisaged poverty program would cover many of these, but additional resources should be focused on Appalachia to ensure that the people in the region could profit from other grant aid. In particular, funding was recommended for vocational schools, employment, welfare services, health, nutrition, and housing. This whole area was a major new consideration so far as the U.S. philosophy of public policy and regional development was concerned."[10]

The region is extremely diverse. In the eyes of many Americans living in other regions, Appalachia was a region of "hillbillies" and "poor whites," who engaged in destructive agricultural practices, such as ploughing up and down the slopes instead of contour ploughing. This image was accurate enough; but the northern part of Appalachia was the centre of the world's greatest iron and steel industry. There was also a flourishing textile industry further south. As Bradshaw puts it: "The different parts of Appalachia experienced different trends and had different prospects in 1960, but all suffered from widely recognized economic difficulties. Appalachia contained a range of problems that could be found elsewhere in the United States but were not so concentrated in any other single region: the problems of boom-and-bust resource regions, of marginal hill farmland, of mature industrial regions, and of regions where economic, social, environmental and political factors, some clearly outside the scope and scale of public intervention but others that federal programs could address to an extent. The recognition of these situations led to demands for government action as the only real source of potential assistance."[11]

The Planning Process

Given its structure, with thirteen governors and a federal co-chairman, and its dependence on annual appropriations of the federal and state governments, the planning process of the ARC was bound to be a highly political one. There was no attempt to prepare a "five-year plan," or a plan of any other duration, for the region as a whole. Planning has been in terms of states, or of cities, electoral districts or counties within states. The last sentence of the PARC report wisely stated: "The Commission does not, in fact, foresee the emergence of a single plan for Appalachia at any time in the future. In the years ahead, the Appalachian program will be many programs, unified only by their singleness of focus: the introduction of Appalachia and its people into fully active membership in American society."[12] The planning has been largely "project planning," much of it long term, like the highway system, which was still incomplete after twenty-seven years. The ARC states in its report on *Twenty Years of Progress*: "The early history of ARC is a record of conflict between the realistic need for long-range programs to raise hopes for the children, "the next generation," and political realities requiring fast, visible returns on the Appalachian investment. Nothing brought that conflict into sharper focus than the Appalachian highway program. Obviously, the building of a regional highway system would take many years, and would offer no relief to a child's hunger tonight."[13]

The Growth Centre Approach

The approach was therefore, for the most part, political, pragmatic and *ad hoc*, a realistic response to obvious and pressing needs. Few of the theories discussed in Part I were consciously and rigorously applied, although in a general way such things as location theory and the theory of international and interregional trade entered into decisions regarding the private sector. Coming when it did, however, in the late sixties, the seventies, and eighties, the planning of ARC could not escape some application of the "growth pole" or growth centre approach. The ARC report on *Twenty Years of Progress* puts it this way: "Another unique aspect of the new ARC was the mandate placed on it by law to focus its investments: 'The public investments made in the region under this Act shall be concentrated in areas where there is a significant potential for future growth, and where the expected return on public dollars will be the greatest.' This requirement became the basis for designation of 'growth centers' in which investments would be made and the exclusion of certain rural, isolated areas which would not qualify for investments. The growth centre approach was in direct contrast with 'worst first' approaches of other programs giving priorities to areas of greatest need rather than greater promise."[14]

Since "growth center" was so vaguely defined in the legislation, the selection of them became the subject of heated debate and political pressure, particularly by communities that were passed over. As the ARC report puts it, "I don't know exactly what a growth centre is, said one politically astute public official, but I know there is at least one in every congressional district."[15] The report states that "Ultimately, however, negotiations among the different forces involved in the ARC process brought about pragmatic decisions balancing economic and political factors: while public facility investments would be limited to centres, health and other human resource services should be extended to people where they live."[16]

In any case, whatever the ARC "growth centers" were, it is clear that they were a far cry from Perroux's "pôles de croissance" as discussed in an earlier chapter. They were urban centres, sometimes quite small cities, that could be made to grow through public investment, not dynamic metropolitan centres of innovation that grew through clusters of private enterprise, generating spread effects to spaces defined in global terms.

Patterns of ARC Spending

In its report, *Appalachia: Twenty Years of Progress, 1965–1985*, the ARC said in its foreword: "Twenty years ago, on March 9, 1965, President Lyndon Johnson signed the law that created the Appalachian Regional Commission. It was the culmination of the commitment of two Presidents, of Congress and of Appalachia's governors to reverse a century of neglect and exploitation in this 'Region apart.' And it was the beginning of a unique experiment in partnership—among the federal, state and local levels of government and between the public and private sectors."[17]

The expression "region apart" is a reminder of the extreme isolation, even inaccessibility, of the steep mountains and deep, narrow valleys that comprise most of the region called Appalachia. The region includes all of West Virginia and parts of New York, Pennsylvania, Maryland, Virginia, Ohio, Kentucky, Tennessee, North and South Carolina, Georgia, Alabama and Mississippi. (See Map 13-2) That isolation explains why, from fiscal year 1965–66 to fiscal year 1991–92, nearly two thirds of ARC appropriations went for highways. (See Table 13.1) Of the supplemental grants, however, over two thirds went for community development, mostly infrastructure like water supply, sewers, industrial sites, and airports. (See Table 13.2) As Cumberland puts it, "An issue which has never been in serious doubt in Appalachia has been that of aid to a geographic region versus aid to individuals.... In Appalachia, there was little debate about the necessity to attack broad regional problems of public services and environmental deterioration as a necessary, if not sufficient, condition to helping the people of the region."[18]

There were nonetheless significant, if much smaller, outlays for such things as education, health, and housing.

The picture is somewhat different, however, when state and "other federal" funds are included. As may be seen from Table 13.3, state and local funds financed only 34.8 percent of the costs of highways compared to 42.7 percent of non-highway projects; whereas ARC funds financed 65.3 percent of the highways and only 28.8 percent of the non-highway projects. Altogether, ARC

MAP 13-2
The Appalachian Region

TABLE 13.1
Appropriations for Appalachian Regional Development Programs
(in thousands of dollars)

| Fiscal Year | Highway | Nonhighway | | |
	Total	Area Development	LDD and Technical Assistance	Administration
1965–66	$200,000	$103,450	$2,500	$1,290	$307,240
1967	100,000	54,700	2,750	1,100	158,550
1968	70,000	55,100	1,600	746	127,446
1969	100,000	70,600	3,000	850	174,450
1970	175,000	101,958	5,500	932	283,390
1971	175,000	119,500	7,500	968	302,968
1972	175,000	115,000	7,000	1,113	298,113
1973	205,000	127,000	11,000	1,217	344,217
1974	155,000	107,500	7,500	1,492	271,492
1975	160,000	125,000	8,500	1,747	295,247
1976	162,200	117,500	8,500	1,870	290,070
Transition Quarter	37,500	8,000	4,500	495	50,495
1977	185,000	109,500	8,500	1,925	304,925
1978	211,300	105,000	7,400	2,083	325,783
1979	233,000	137,923	7,700	2,297	380,920
1980	229,000	120,000	7,500	3,105	359,605
1981	214,600	78,400 *	6,300 *	3,192	302,492 *
1982	100,000	44,200	5,800	2,900	152,900
1983	115,133	45,000	5,000	2,900	168,033
1984	109,400	45,000	5,000	2,700	162,100
1985	100,000	44,000	5,000	2,300	151,300
1986	78,980 **	33,053 **	2,807 **	2,105 **	116,945 **
1987	74,961	24,808	3,031	2,200	105,000
1988	63,967	36,433	4,200	2,400	107,000
1989	69,169	34,731	4,200	2,600	110,700
1990	105,090 **	35,403 **	4,197	3,210 **	147,900 **
1991	126,374 **	36,163	4,177	3,284	169,998 **
1992	142,899	38,773	5,044	3,284	190,000
Total	$3,873,573	$2,073,695	$155,706	$56,305	$6,159,279

* After rescission
** After sequestration

TABLE 13.2
Supplemental Grant Projects Approved, by Type of Program
(in thousands of dollars)

	Cumulative Through 1991			1991 Program		
	No.	Amount	Percent	No.	Amount	Percent
Community Development						
Water System	46	$10,749	49.0%	1033	$243,832	27.6%
Water and Sewer	7	1,223	5.6	198	42,895	4.8
Sewage System	24	6,052	27.6	822	150,305	17.0
Recreation and Tourism	—	—	—	190	23,440	2.6
Community Improvement	3	269	1.2	129	25,390	2.9
Industrial Site Development	14	3,204	14.6	301	72,680	8.2
Airports	—	—	—	183	18,903	2.1
Solid Waste	3	180	0.8	63	8,423	0.9
Other	3	253	1.2	48	7,537	0.9
Subtotal	100	$21,929	100.0%	2,967	$593,404	67.1%
Education						
Vocational Education	—	—	—	738	$86,401	9.8%
Higher Education	—	—	—	280	62,207	7.0
Libraries	—	—	—	198	21,322	2.4
ETC and NDEA	—	—	—	108	14,308	1.6
Subtotal	—	—	—	1,324	$184,239	20.8%
Health Facilities	—	—	—	600	$106,902	12.1%
Total	100	$21,929	100.0%	4,891	$884,545	100.0%
Funding						
ARC Supplemental Grants		$21,929	23.4%		$884,545	19.3%
ARC Other Funds		—	—		146,016	3.2
Other Federal Funds		20,876	22.3		1,586,701	34.6
Total Federal		$42,805	45.7%		$2,617,262	57.0%
State and Local Funds		50,925	54.3		1,974,945	43.0
Total		$93,730	100.0%		$4,592,207	100.0%

Note: Totals may not add because of rounding.

appropriations accounted for 44.7 percent of the expenditures, while state and local funds accounted for 39.3 percent and "other federal" funds for 16.4 percent of the total. Total expenditures from all sources are shown in Table 13.4. Expenditures on highways are about 42 percent of the total.

There were, of course, differences in the pattern of spending among states, reflecting differences in geography and social conditions. Alabama, for example, spent less than one third of its total outlays on highways, and more than one third on community development. It also spent substantial amounts on health and education. In 1991, Kentucky also spent more on community development than on highways. Cumulatively through 1991, South Carolina spent less than 10 percent of its total outlays on highways, and spent larger sums on community development, health, and education.

TABLE 13.3
Sources of Funds for Projects, 1991 and Cumulative
(in millions of dollars)

Cumulative	Amount	Percent	Amount	1991 Percent
All Projects				
State and Local Funds	$107.8	36.5%	$5,241.8	39.3%
ARC Funds	161.1	54.5	5,896.3	44.2
Other Federal Funds	26.6	9.0	2,190.8	16.4
Total, All Projects	$295.5	100.0%	$13,328.9	100.0%
Non-highway Projects				
State Funds	$12.5	8.9%	$693.4	9.0%
Local Funds	58.7	42.0	2,582.0	33.6
Total, State and Local Funds	$71.2	50.9%	$3,275.4	42.7%
ARC Funds	42.0	30.0%	$2,209.0	28.8%
Other Federal Funds	26.6	19.0	2,190.8	28.5
Total, Non-highway Projects	$139.8	100.0%	$7,675.2	100.0%
Highway Projects				
State and Local Funds	$36.6	23.5%	$1,966.4	34.8%
ARC Funds	119.1	76.5	3,687.3	65.2
Total, Highway Projects	$155.7	100.0%	$5,653.7	100.0%

Note: Project costs not eligible for federal funding are not included above. Totals may not add because of rounding.

Bradshaw remarks that, despite the extremely cumbersome procedure for getting approval of funding for projects, "the ARC established an early reputation for getting things done through new approaches that circumvented established (delay-inducing) procedures. It had the advantage of not being tied by the long-entrenched bureaucratic practices that are often characteristic of the larger agencies and specific to each one."[19]

TABLE 13.4
Cumulative Project Totals Through Fiscal Year 1991
(in millions of dollars)

Non-highway State and (Projects Approved)	No. of Total Projects	Funds	Percent of Non-highway Funds	ARC Federal Funds	ARC Local Funds	Other Eligible Costs
Health	3,600	$441.1	20.0%	$246.0	$736.5	$1,423.7
Child Development	1,973	170.9	7.7	73.7	87.5	332.2
Education	3,084	533.0	24.1	194.6	761.1	1,488.6
Community Development	3,215	644.7	29.2	1,404.9	1,362.5	3,412.0
Energy and Enterprise Development	674	79.7	3.6	11.0	66.8	157.4
Environment and Natural Resources	262	80.5	3.6	5.9	20.9	107.2
Other Programs and Special Demonstrations	196	21.1	1.0	8.5	17.3	46.9
Housing	317	66.1	3.0	224.7	111.4	402.2
Local Development District Planning and Administration	1,642	94.6	4.3	16.8	62.7	174.2
Research and Technical Assistance	1,845	77.3	3.5	4.8	48.7	130.8
Total	16,808	$2,209.0	100.0%	$2,190.8	$3,275.4	$7,675.2
Highway (Funds Obligated) Appalachian Development Highway System and Access Roads		$3,687.3		n.a.	$1,966.4	$5,653.7
Grand Total		$5,896.3		$2,190.8	$5,241.8	$13,328.9

Note: Totals may not add because of rounding.

The original 1965 legislation for the ARC assumed that by 1971 the commission would have finished its job, and could accordingly be terminated. However, the 1971 authorization not only renewed the ARC financing but expanded its scope. The original executive director, Ralph Widner, resigned, and outlined a three-stage development for the commission in his report for the congressional hearings. The first stage up to 1971, was one of showing visible results and linking the region to the wealthier regions surrounding it, plus outlays for health and education, especially vocational training. After 1971 emphasis shifted from construction of physical infrastructure to its operation, and from vocational training to formal education at three levels and to preschool years. In the future would come the third stage, which would include such things as tax policy and environmental protection.

Bradshaw considers the period 1975–80 the era of "maturity of the ARC." "When a government agency is said to reach 'maturity,' it must have achieved a position where it is functioning at the height of its potential powers and is able to carry out the job for which it was designed. It also involves an element of acceptability by other mature institutions in society and a willingness on their part to work with the agency on equal terms. The ARC was in this position for a relatively short span of six years from 1975 through 1980. During this time it obtained its greatest access to federal grant aid funds and the widest expressions of support."[20]

In 1976, there was talk of an overall plan for the whole of Appalachia; but the thirteen governors were less than enthusiastic about this idea, and all that came of it was a report on *Appalachia: Goals, Objectives, and Development Strategies*, published in December 1977. Jimmy Carter became president in 1977 and organized a series of regional conferences on balanced growth and economic development. In 1979, when the Appalachian Regional Development Act came up for review again, there were plans for joining the ARC with the regional commissions established under Title V of the Public Works and Economic Development Act of 1965 in a nation-wide scheme of regional development. The election of President Reagan put an end to such talk.

The Local Development Districts

Bradshaw maintains that the failure to produce a real plan for the whole of Appalachia was due, not only to the opposition of the governors, but also to the success of the Local Development Districts (LDDs). There were sixty-nine of these, each containing several counties. According to Bradshaw, the "LDD units had become a major focus for the planning and coordination of grant aid within each state. In the period 1975–80 the LDDs became very successful in this function...All the LDDs continued to function through the difficult times of the 1980s, when federal funding for administrative costs was reduced and it became necessary for more local funds to be used to support LDDs."[21] As may be seen from Figure 12.1, relatively small sums were spent directly by the LDDs; but these expenditures went for vital non-highway projects, and for planning and coordination.

As part of his fifteen-year study of the Appalachian Regional Commission, Bradshaw conducted case studies of twelve LDDs. One of the questions he asked concerned the relevance of the growth pole concept to their actual operations. His characterisation of the responses is revealing: "District responses to the question about the relevance of the growth centre concept in the application of the programs to specific local needs revealed how the district staffs viewed their roles. They did not see themselves as either regional or physical planners working from theoretical concepts to determine what they put into practice; instead, they perceived their function as providing a basis of financial and technical assistance that could be used by local jurisdictions within the LDD as a basis for economic development. Thus, they were carrying out an essentially bureaucratic function in response to political decisions, whereas theoretical planning concepts such as growth centres had not been conceived in relation to such priorities. The growth centre concept, enshrined in both ARC and EDA legislation but applied in different ways by the two agencies, was described as 'irrelevant,' 'inappropriate,' or 'inapplicable' by the LDD staff."[22]

He goes on to say that "condemnation of the growth centre concept was general among LDD staff."[23] Growth centres cannot be simply legislated into existence. It is easier to promote growth in existing urban centres. Trying to convert small and medium-sized cities into growth centres overloads the services of such cities, and costs more money than the LDDs had. As for larger urban centres, land acquisition for an industrial park near a highway is very costly. A growth centre policy tends to overemphasize manufacturing employment at a time when we are entering the phase of post-industrial society, and neglects the need for balanced urban and rural development. Bradshaw concludes his discussion of growth centres by saying, "It is no wonder that the growth centre concept had not been of much practical use as a basis for targeting grant aid, especially after the early 1970s."[24]

The Reagan Presidency

When Ronald Reagan assumed the presidency in 1981, he made it clear that regional development programs ran completely counter to his policies of "leave it to the market" and cutting all federal budgets except defence. He got rid of the Title V regional commissions easily enough; they did not have much public support. He tried to terminate the ARC as well. In fact, in every year of his presidency, he submitted to Congress a zero budget for ARC; but he ran into a solid wall of opposition from the Appalachian governors and other supporters of ARC. He did succeed in reducing federal funding for ARC to less than one third of what it had been at its peak. The Economic Development Administration also survived, but suffered even larger budget cuts.

The "Finish-Up Program"

The see-saw battle between the president and the Congress was finally resolved by a compromise: funding would be provided for a greatly reduced "finish-up program," which included completing 620 miles of the remaining 1,303 of the system that were uncompleted; a five-year training and private investment program to create or retain jobs and train people for jobs available in the Appalachian region; a three-year health program; and a development foundation which would strengthen the public-private partnership during the finish-up period and preserve the partnership after the termination of ARC. Eleven years later, the ARC was still "finishing up," on the basis of annual appropriations from the federal and state governments, amounting to $295.5 million in 1991.

Telecommunications

The latest effort of the ARC to overcome the region's isolation is telecommunications, "superhighways of glass," in the words of the ARC's document on *Telecommunications in Appalachia*, prepared for the regional conference on "Telecommunications: Connections for Rural Competitiveness," held in Knoxville, Tennessee in October-November 1991. The document states that "Telecommunications is being transformed from a basic service into a piece of economic development infrastructure as vital as roads and schools."[25] It reports that as late as 1980, when only 7 percent of American households were without telephones, only 71 of the 398 counties in Appalachia reached that standard, and in 186 counties 24 percent or more of the households did not have telephones. The region still has some distance to go to reach the national average. The effort includes cable TV as well as telephones, and in the majority of counties in the region over 75 percent of homes have access to cable TV. The document states that "With the telephone, the facsimile machine, satellites, the computer modems, the business on the other side of the world is as close and convenient as the one down the street. For rural America, the implications are profound: for the first time in history, New York or Tokyo business could operate from an Appalachian hollow."[26]

FIGURE 13.1
The Division of ARC Funds by Category, 1965–90

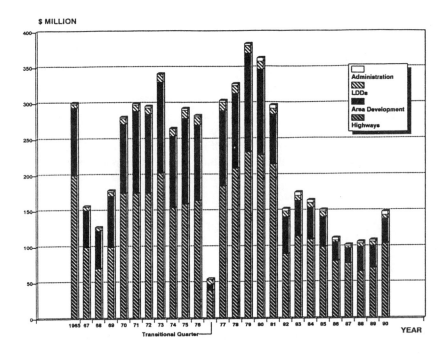

The ARC has provided the bulk of the highway funds, which make up over half of the total, with smaller contributions from the states. ARC area development input has leveraged several times its total from other federal and state sources. It is notable that the administrative funds are such a small proportion and that those designated for local use are so much greater than those for the commission's Washington headquarters.

TABLE 13.5
Progress in Eastern Kentucky

	1965	late 1970s
Income	Fifty percent of U.S. per capita	Sixty-six percent of U.S. per capita; poverty less than half 1960s figure; still only one county above U.S. average income in 1978
Housing	Very poor conditions	Over 10,000 units built under federal programs
Migration	High outmigration	Inmigration replaced outmigration
Infant Mortality	High, with shortage of nurses, doctors, primary-clinics	Reduced to U.S. average; nurse training; nutrition programs; eighteen care clinics
Unemployment	High	Fell until 1979, then rose again during recession
High school	Only twenty-five percent completed (U.S. 52%)	Thirty-six percent completed in 1976 (U.S. 63%). Built forty-six vocational schools, nine child-care centers; new school buildings
Personal involvement	People excluded from political power	Better legal services; medicaid
Public facilities	Decrepit	"Face-lifts" for many town halls
Transportation	Slow internal travel	New highways, airports
Economy	Dependent on coal; few wealthy; little contribution of mining industry to local taxes; many injuries and black lung	Still dependent on coal, but wages higher and jobs different (surface machines); Kentucky severance tax returns money to mining areas

Source: "The Battle for Appalachia," Louisville Courier-Journal, 32 May to 9 June 1981.

The Bush Administration

The Bush administration was slightly more sympathetic to the ARC than Reagan had been. At least the president's budget proposals included modest sums for the commission. It will be interesting to see whether the new president, with his solid majority in both House and Senate, and faced with a serious unemployment problem, will not only keep the Appalachian Regional Commission alive but will reintroduce a nation-wide program of regional development.

Appraisal

There can be no doubt that the ARC brought significant improvements in living standards and productivity to the Appalachian region during its twenty-seven years of operation. Roads were built, health and education standards raised, housing provided, unemployment reduced, and—perhaps most important of all—the population was infused with a new sense of hope and pride, and provided with a new image. The progress from 1965 until 1980 (when the program was hampered by the opposition of the president and severe budget cuts), is illustrated by the case of Eastern Kentucky, shown in Table 13.5.

There were, of course, differences in results from one subregion to another, and still greater differences among states, districts, and counties. The central subregion, which was worst off in 1965 and where most of the ARC expenditures were made, showed the least progress. Bradshaw states, "The great paradox of Appalachian development since 1960 is that although relatively greater sums of money have been invested in central Appalachia, this part of the region has shown the lowest ability to increase its economic and social indicators relative to the rest of the United States...The ARC's role has been made more difficult by the rapid changes and unexpected swings experienced in a country with no national planning goals and no national industrial, transport, land ownership or energy policies. Such policies would be opposed by most Americans, and so the role of a regional development commission in the United States must remain reactive and pragmatic."[27]

Central Appalachia remained dependent on the coal industry, and consequently suffered losses of jobs, net emigration, and low growth in the early 1980s. Over 60 percent of the counties in the subregion had unemployment rates over 50 percent above the national average in May 1986.[28] Northern Appalachia did little better. Southern Appalachia did markedly better and the outlook for 1995 is more promising. (See Table 13.6).

There has been some criticism of the ARC's "overemphasis" on highways. Bradshaw seems to think that, on balance, the highway expenditures were justified. It has, he says, "become clear from studies in the 1980s...that the new highways have assisted greatly in individual mobility, providing access both to a wider range of jobs and also to social services, health care, schooling, and tourist attractions. At the same time they made Appalachian locations more attractive to firms looking for sites."[29]

John D. Rockefeller IV, who has been governor of West Virginia, states' co-chairman of the ARC, and a United States senator, in his foreword to Michael Bradshaw's book, stresses the human resource development aspects of the commission's work: "First, the ARC has helped make West Virginia and Appalachia more economically competitive with the rest of the nation by dramatically improving the quality of life throughout the region. It has helped to

TABLE 13.6
Population and Employment Changes,
1980 to (projected) 1995

Area	Sub-region	Population (000)			Employment (000)				
		1980	1985	% change	1980	1986	% change	1995	% change
United States		226,550	238,739	5.4	98,569	108,233	9.8	122,760	13.4
ARC Region		20,239	20,588	1.7	8,155	8,337	2.2	9,078	8.9
Appalachian	portions of:								
New York	north	1,083	1,072	-1.0	447	436	-2.5	463	6.2
Pennsylvania	north	5,994	5,888	-1.8	2,417	2,342	-3.1	2,479	5.8
Ohio	north	1,262	1,275	1.0	489	483	-1.2	515	6.6
Maryland	north	220	216	-1.8	89	86	-3.4	91	5.8
West Virginia	north and central	1,950	1,936	-0.7	714	653	-8.5	674	3.2
Virginia	central	554	550	-0.7	220	207	-5.9	213	2.9
Kentucky	central	1,077	1,102	2.3	381	354	-7.1	366	1.0
Tennessee	central and south	2,074	2,142	3.3	819	901	10.0	1,018	13.0
North Carolina	south	1,218	1,286	5.6	552	611	10.7	689	12.8
Mississippi	south	483	496	2.7	201	200	-0.5	214	7.0
Alabama	south	2,430	2,511	3.3	960	1,079	12.4	1,230	14.0
Georgia	south	1,104	1,282	16.1	498	593	19.1	695	17.2
South Carolina	south	793	832	4.9	368	392	6.5	431	9.9

Source: Kublawi, 1987

develop a network of clinics to make primary health care available for the first time to many Appalachian residents. It has put in place a network of vocational educational facilities and programs to enable our young people to be better prepared for productive working careers. It has helped to build numerous water and sewer systems to bring modern plumbing to some of the most rural portions of our nation. And it has helped to build a system of highways to bring industry and jobs to our region, with the promise of more to come. Second, it is the only government program that is a true partnership. Everything that happens—from policy changes to program development—is the product of cooperation and consensus between the federal government and the thirteen Appalachian states."[30]

Bradshaw argues that the course of events in Appalachia was more influenced by global forces than by the application of theories of regional development. The role of the federal government, however, cannot be ignored. A "political economy of regional development" is more useful for understanding what actually goes on in a region like Appalachia than a pure economic theory of regional development. Nor does he think that the Appalachian experience makes much of a contribution to economic theory. On the contrary, "One of the main contributions of the ARC experience has been to emphasize the importance of political structures in the functioning and maintenance of such an agency.... It has linked the 'top-down' approach of many federal agencies with the 'bottom-up' involvement of local districts. It has linked federal, state, and local governments and has brought cooperation among a range of federal agencies."[31] He also points out that the ARC accomplished less than it could have done because "For a period during the 1980s the United States chose to be blinded by the political stance that 'more government is bad for you.'"[32] In his final chapter he makes a case for broadening the scope of regional commissions, of the same general nature as the ARC, to cover the whole of the United States.

The ARC is a good illustration of the maxim "In the United States the regional development authority is called the Senate." Since every state in the Union has two senators, every state has equal power in the Senate. This political power in the Senate goes a long way towards an explanation of why the ARC and the EDA have survived, despite the efforts of presidents Reagan and Bush to kill them. With thirteen states represented on the commission, the ARC had a solid bloc of twenty-six senators to fight for retention of such a splendid source of funds; and the Congressmen from electoral districts within Appalachia would fight for the ARC as well. With 21 million people spread over 395 countries, Appalachia packs a good deal of political clout.

Application of Theory in Appalachia

In Appalachia, it is fair to say that theories of the sort discussed in Part I of this volume were applied more to the explanation of regional development problems than to the search for solutions. The commission and its staff would have been well aware of the geographic disadvantages of the Appalachian region, and of the cultural impact of the region's isolation, when the ARC was established. They would have been aware too that one of the region's comparative advantages lay in the mining of its coal seams and its forests, and keenly aware of the disastrous effects of this exploitation of the region's natural resources, mainly by outsiders who spent their profits elsewhere. They could easily have applied the theory of bi-modal production and regional dualism to the region, to explain its relative retardation in comparison to other, more modern, regions. Certainly, they would have been aware of the lack of innovating entrepreneurship in Appalachia, and tried hard to overcome it. They would have observed the effects of circular and cumulative causation, and tried to reverse the flow so that the effects were cumulatively favourable rather than unfavourable. They were confronted with a case of dependency and uneven development, and perhaps applied some of the constructs of regional science. The law under which they operated required them to reject a "worst first" approach, in favour of picking winners, so far as the location of their activities were concerned, and used the expression "growth centers" to designate their choice of "winners."

The truth is, however, that the problems were so many and so varied that what the ARC did was as much a political choice as a matter of economic analysis. They could apply economic analysis to the establishment of priorities for particular projects; but they stopped short of deriving an overall strategy or "grand design" from any general theory of regional development in the author's opinion quite rightly.

In short, the work of the ARC was a matter of good government and good management, informed by good economic theory. The work they are doing is never finished, and never reaches a stage of "finish-up." Even the most prosperous regions have need for such management—as our next case study shows. Appalachia, however, had a good deal of political appeal, as its continued operation after twenty-seven years shows. Appalachia is far from being a homogeneous region, and for serious management or planning must be broken up into smaller regions. But when it comes to getting appropriations from the federal and state governments, the maxim "united we stand, divided we fall" applies well to the Appalachian Regional Commission.

Notes

1. Niles Hansen, "Regional Economic Development Policies and Programs in the United States," Niles Hansen, Benjamin Higgins and Donald J. Savoie (eds), *Regional Policy in a Changing World* (New York: Plenum Press, 1990), p. 119.
2. *Ibid.*, p. 120.
3. Economic Development Administration, *Annual Report*, 1991, p. vii.
4. *Ibid.*, pp. 7–8.
5. The Appalachian Regional Commission, *Twenty Years of Progress, 1965–1985* (Washington, D.C., 1985), p. 19.
6. *Ibid.*, p. 21.
7. The Appalachian Regional Development Act, Section 2, 1965.
8. John Cumberland, *Regional Development: Experience and Prospects 2. United States of America* (Paris and the Hague: Mouton, 1971), p. 91.
9. Michael Bradshaw, *The Appalachian Regional Commission: Twenty-five Years of Government Policy,* (Lexington: University Press of Kentucky, 1991), p. 2.
10. *Ibid.*, p. 38.
11. *Ibid.*, p. 25.

12. The Appalachian Regional Commission, *Twenty Years of Progress*, p. 27.
13. *Ibid.*, p. 28.
14. *Ibid.*
15. *Ibid.*, p. 38.
16. *Ibid.*
17. *Ibid.*, p. 3.
18. Cumberland, *Regional Development*, pp. 92–3.
19. Bradshaw, *The Appalachian Regional Commission*, p. 49.
20. *Ibid.*, p. 67.
21. *Ibid*, p. 70.
22. *Ibid.*, p. 82.
23. *Ibid.*, p. 83.
24. *Ibid.*, p. 85.
25. The Appalachian Regional Commission, *Telecommunications in Appalachia*, 1991, p. 2.
26. *Ibid.*
27. Bradshaw, *The Appalachian Regional Commission*, p. 142.
28. *Ibid.*, p. 117.
29. *Ibid.*, p. 124.
30. John D. Rockefeller IV, "Foreword," in the Appalachian Regional Commission, *Telecommunications in Appalachia*.
31. Bradshaw, *The Appalachian Regional Commission*, p. 140.
32. *Ibid.*

14

The United States III: The Austin Project

In sharp contrast to the Appalachian commission, The Austin Project is brand new, not only in time, but in its conception of urban and regional planning. The concept originated in the mind of a world-renowned economist, Walt W. Rostow, Professor Emeritus of the University of Texas. He is chairman of the task force, a member of the board of directors, and wrote the original memorandum outlining the scheme.

Among the interesting features of the project is that its organization involves practically everyone *but* the federal government. The board of directors includes representatives of the local governments involved (city and county); persons concerned with education, health, welfare and public safety; political leaders or representatives at the local, state and federal levels; representatives of minority groups; representatives of various churches; representatives of the press; and representatives of the private sector. Among these are: the mayor of Austin; two commissioners of Travis County (in which most of the Austin metropolitan area is located); the former lieutenant governor of Texas (now on the staff of the LBJ School of Public Affairs at the University of Texas); a Texas state senator; a Texas member of the U.S. Congress; two judges; the district attorney, and the adjutant general of Texas; a former Texas Congresswoman; a dean and three professors from the University of Texas; the presidents of St. Edwards University and Huston-Tillotson College; a member of the Texas Education Agency; the president of the District School Board; the head of the Hogg Foundation for Public Health; the head of the Department of Public Safety; the publisher of the Austin-American Statesman; the local president of the National Association for the Advancement of Colored People; the chief executive officer of Bank One; the local representative of IBM; and the leading figure in IC^2, an "incubator" company devoted to launching innovative high-tech enterprises, who is also the head of the Institute for Constructive Capitalism.

The task force is a curious mixture, which, nonetheless, judging from one meeting attended by one of the authors, Benjamin Higgins, seems to work. As stated above, Walt Rostow is its chairman. Elspeth Rostow, former Dean of Arts and Sciences at the University of Texas, and also an economic historian, is senior advisor. There are five project leaders: one for each age group (0 to 8, 9 to 16, 17 to 25), and one each for the crime and health issues. There are two statisticians, really econometricians, who are constructing a host of computerized map overlays pertaining to the region. There is an external coordinator and his assistant. One of the statisticians has an assistant who is also a member of the task force. There are representatives of Inter-Faith, City Liaison of Inner City Neighbourhoods, and City of Austin Auditor's Office. There is a wide spread of ages, and about equal representation of the two sexes on the task force. Other interested parties occasionally drop in on task force meetings. At one meeting, there were also present Professor Niles Hansen, regional economist at the University of Texas; a representative of the Association of School-based Nurses; the former coordinator of the Texas Enterprise Zone Program (an organization to attract private enterprises to disadvantaged areas of the city); and the local president of NAACP, a member of the board of directors. Judging from the meeting, the atmosphere of the task force is one of friendly cooperation, combined with a sense of genuine excitement at doing something new and innovative.

The Investment Plan

On 8 September 1992, the task force submitted to the board of directors its first "Plan," entitled *An Investment Plan for the Young: The Austin Project, First Phase.* After a first chapter presenting an executive summary, chapter 2 analyses "the Rationale and Strategy of the Plan." This chapter begins with a paragraph lifted almost *verbatim* from Walt Rostow's memorandum of 20 July 1992, characterising the Plan. "The Austin Project concerns our whole community. A strictly non-partisan effort, it deals with a set of unsolved problems which, in differing degree, are present in every part of the city. They are particularly acute in disadvantaged neighbourhoods stretching unevenly north to south on the eastern side of town. The problems include excessive low weight births and infant mortality; inadequate nurturing and education from birth through grossly underfunded Head Start; alarming levels of child abuse with long-lasting traumatic consequences, including close links to later criminal behaviour; excessive levels of school drop-outs and teen-age pregnancy; imperfect coordination between high school education and requirements for promising jobs in a fast-moving technological era; excessive levels of drug abuse and unchecked expansion of HIV disease; and control expanding levels of serious crime which cast a pall of fear corroding the quality of our communal life and, increasingly, diverts our taxes into the building of prisons as serious crime continues to increase.... On a conservative estimate, these abnormalities cost the Austin community at least $400 million per annum and, unless corrosive forces are checked and reversed, that cost will inevitably rise."[1]

As this citation indicates, The Austin Project (TAP) reverses the usual approach to "regional development." Instead of seeking projects and measures that will raise employment and income through public or private investment, after which maladies such as those described by Rostow will melt away almost automatically, TAP seeks to follow the individual from before his or her birth until he or she enters the work force, dealing with all aspects of his or her growth. In that way, it hopes to maximize the individual's productivity, and to qualify him or her for the highest quality job possible. In so doing, it will maximize income and employment in the region. Instead of maximizing income and employment and hoping that economic and social maladies will then disappear, it tackles these maladies directly, thus maximizing income and employment.

The chapter lays considerable stress on educational problems, especially among Hispanics and African-Americans, or blacks. It makes the startling statement that at the national level over 40 percent of the new entrants into the labour force are Hispanics or African-Americans, and that this ratio "will inevitably rise." This proportion is certainly above the national average in the Austin region. Rostow says in his 20 July 1992 paper that the Austin region "has a larger Hispanic than African-American population; and the flow of Mexican immigrants, legal and illegal, mainly unskilled and poor, is continuing on a substantial scale."[2] Unemployment among both these groups is about twice the national average. Education and training are an obvious solution for this problem but, as Figure 14.1 shows, high school dropout rates are especially high for these particular groups. Assuming that at least a substantial proportion could finish college if their circumstances were better, this high dropout rate entails a substantial income loss for the community, as Figure 14.2 shows.

The chapter proceeds to an analysis of the closely related problem of unemployment. On the national level, unemployment has been roughly twice as high among non-whites as among whites ever since World War II. (See Table 14.1 and Figures 14.3 and 14.3a) Unemployment among teenagers, in turn, is nearly double the national average. Higher dropout rates and lower levels of education go a long way in explaining these differences in unemployment rates. In Austin (Travis County), unemployment in 1980 was at an average level of 3.7 percent. For the relatively poor tracts, which contain a high proportion of the black and Hispanic population, the figure was 7.2 percent. In 1990, the figures stood at 6.3 percent and 14.4 percent, respectively. (See Figure 14.4 and Table 14.2)

The Plan makes the point that various ethnic groups have made their way up the economic and social ladder into the mainstream of American life, without losing their identity, but at different rates: "The Irish came up rather slowly

FIGURE 14.1
High School Dropout Rates

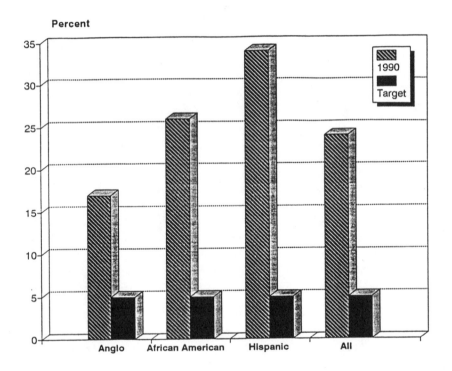

Source: 1990–91 AISD Dropout Report

from extremely difficult beginnings; German Jews came up faster than Eastern European Jews; Cubans faster than Haitians; recent immigrants from Asia
faster than almost other immigrant groups.... African-Americans are, of

FIGURE 14.2
Mean Earnings of U.S. Full-time Male Workers—1987
Dollars

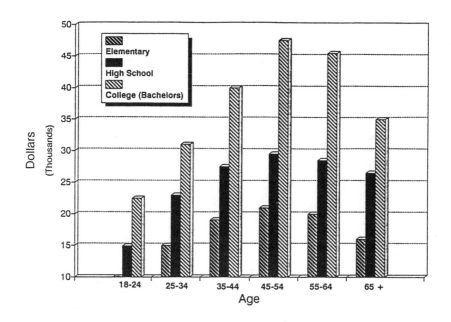

$236,461	Extra income per person over lifetime if graduate high school
$179,710,360	Extra income for AISD students if TAP 5% target is reached (additional 760 students graduate)
Note:	Both figures in current dollars

Source: U.S. Census, 1990

TABLE 14.1
Cyclical Behavior of Black and Other Relative to White Civilian
Unemployment 1948—June 1991

		Average All Workers	White Other	Black & Other/White	**Black &	Males: 16–19		
						White Other	Black & Other	Black & Other/White
P	1948	3.5%	3.5%	5.9%	1.7%	—	—	—
T	1949	5.9	5.6	8.9	1.6	—	—	—
P	1953	3.0	2.7	4.5	1.7	—	—	—
T	1954	5.5	5.0	9.9	2.0	13.4	14.4	1.1
T	1957	4.3	3.8	7.9	2.1	11.5	18.4	1.6
T	1958	6.8	6.1	12.6	2.1	15.7	26.8	1.7
P	1960	5.5	5.0	10.2	2.0	14.0	24.0	1.7
T	1961	6.7	6.0	12.4	2.1	15.7	26.8	1.8
P	1969	3.5	3.1	6.0	2.1	10.0	21.4	2.1
T	1971	5.9	5.4	9.9	1.8	15.1	28.8	1.9
P	1973	4.9	4.3	9.0	2.1	14.2	27.8	2.0
T	1975	8.5	7.8	13.8	1.8	18.3	38.1	2.1
P	1979	5.8	5.1	11.3	2.2	13.9	34.2	2.4
T	1982	9.7	8.6	17.3	2.0	21.7	48.9	2.2
P	1989	5.3	4.5	10.0	2.2	13.7	31.9	2.3
T	1991*	7.0	6.2	11.4	1.8	—	—	—

Note: P = Cyclical Peak; T = Cyclical Trough
* Tentative
** "Black" after 1972

course, a special case. They came to America early and involuntarily. They were for a long time denied access to the ladder by law, by custom and by prejudice (but) a third of the nation's African-Americans had moved into the middle class by 1990, up from ten percent in 1960."[3] The Plan remarks that "the emerging dynamism in Latin America may eventually help with (the problem of Austin's Hispanic population); but The Austin Project and the strategy that informs it aims to make the ladder more accessible and to rule out darker possibilities."[4]

The Plan then raises the question "Why have the large scale public and private efforts made to deal with crucial urban problems since…1965 not achieved their purpose?"[5] It answers this question as follows:

1. Political fragmentation. There has been little common perspective or even coordination among the various public authorities: city, county, school

board, and the criminal justice system, nor was there effective coordination among city, state, and federal authorities.
2. Absence of a strategy. Without an agreed strategy, it was impossible to link efficiently what was done by public authorities with what the business community, the universities, the religious institutions, the foundations, and other agencies in the private sector did or were willing to do.
3. Insufficient emphasis on prevention relative to damage control. Perhaps 60 percent of public and private resources flow to programs designed to limit human and social damage rather than to prevent such damage in the future.
4. Inadequate preventive investment relative to the scale of the problem. There are preventive programmes in the Austin region but the scale of the resources allocated to them is inadequate.
5. Inadequate arrangements for partnership within disadvantaged neighbourhoods for planning and mutual responsibility in executing urban problems.

These are the failings that TAP is designed to overcome. "The Austin Project, in one sense, was set up to unite the political agencies, the private business sector, the universities, the religious community, the disadvantaged neighbourhoods, the military, and all manner of private organizations around a coherent program which does the job without violating the prerogatives of our elected officials."[6] At the same time, TAP "is a communal, not a government project."[7]

The plan of action rests on a number of principles. First, on the "established scientific truth" that by the age of four years human beings have learned a high proportion of all they will ever learn. Between 9 and 16 "they turn good or turn bad."[8] The 17–25 phase "embraces the paths to the work force starting in the last two years of high school."[9] Accordingly, the plan pays special attention to these age groups. The second operational principle is preventive investment. "Its purpose is to strengthen the positive forces which, over time, promise to bring the men, women, and children of the inner city into a life of wider choices and higher income. That is our strategy."[10]

The team regards the Austin region—city and surroundings—as "an interactive system." Rostow states: "The interconnectedness of early childhood capacity to learn, possibilities in the work force, teen-age pregnancies, drop-out and incarceration rates, becomes very vivid indeed in an exercise of this kind. And working together regularly, this Task Force has become a single team, our lines of specialization blurred as we learned of the many sides of each problem."[11]

The chapter closes with a declaration of faith: "When the Austin Project was launched on May 6, 1992, by mayor Bruce Todd, county judge Bill Aleshire and president of the School Board de la Garza, its purpose was defined as

FIGURE 14.3
Unemployment Rates of Whites Compared to Black and Other*

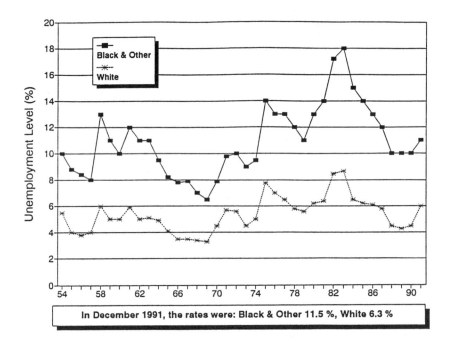

In December 1991, the rates were: Black & Other 11.5 %, White 6.3 %

* Percent of Civilian Labor Force
Data from Citicorp Economic Database, Household Survey, May, 1992
Prepared by Sherwood Bishop, Center for Economic Research, Department of Economics,
University of Texas at Austin

FIGURE 14.3a
Relative Unemployment Rates for Black and White Teen Males

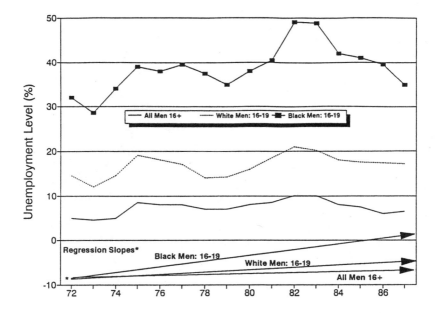

Data from *Labor Force Statistics Derived from the Current Population Survey, 1948–87*, U.S. Department of Labor Bureau of Labor Statistics, August 1988.
* These are linear regressions on the data for each of the three graph lines.
Prepared by Sherwood Bishop, Center for Economic Research, Department of Economics, University of Texas at Austin

FIGURE 14.4
Unemployment Rate—Over 16 (1980 vs. 1990)

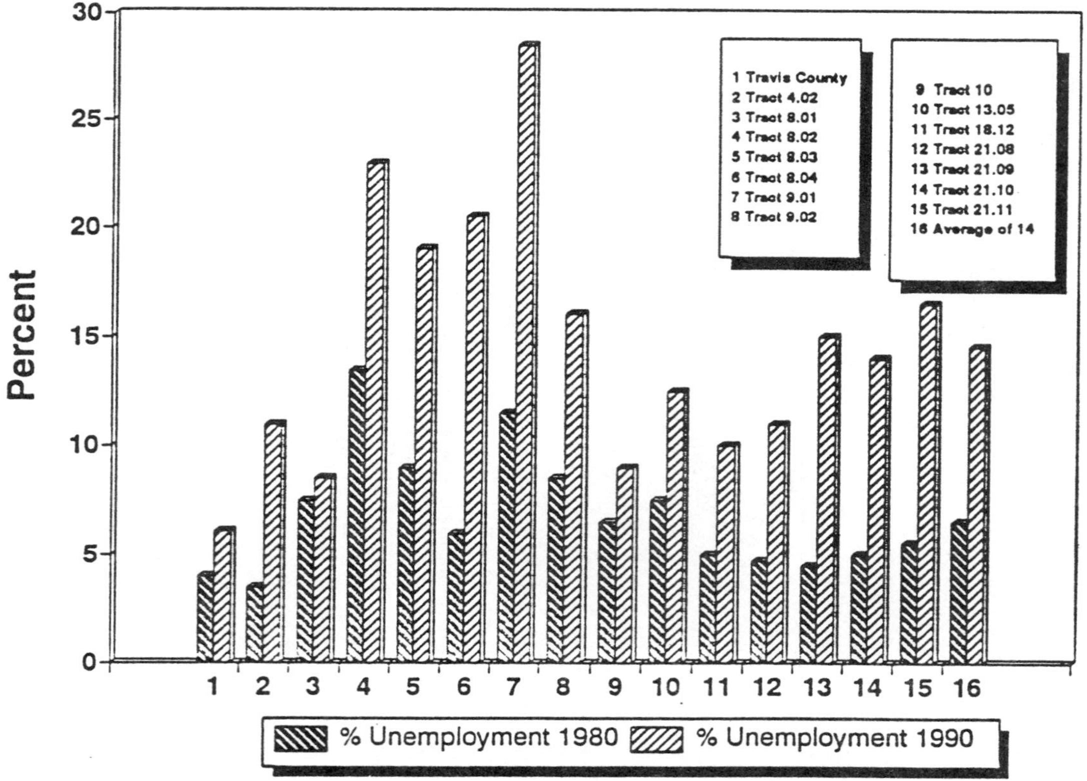

TABLE 14.2
Unemployment by Census Track (1980 and 1990)

	% Unemployment—1980	% Unemployment—1990
Travis County	3.66	6.32
Tract 4.02	3.2	11.12
Tract 8.01	7.55	8.23
Tract 8.02	13.44	22.81
Tract 8.03	9.39	18.75
Tract 8.04	5.83	20.1
Tract 9.01	11.57	27.97
Tract 9.02	8.48	16.98
Tract 10	7.03	8.61
Tract 13.05	7.41	12.22
Tract 18.12	4.59	9.88
Tract 21.08	4.26	11.47
Tract 21.09	3.95	15.71
Tract 21.10	5.28	14.59
Tract 21.11	6.24	17.8
Average of 14	7.24	15.45

* *Note:* These figures represent only 14 of the 21 high priority census Tracts, due to nonconformity of 1980 and 1990 data.

follows: The Austin Project aims to mobilize the public and private sectors of the Austin community for two purposes: To reverse the decline of the disadvantaged inner city neighbourhoods in the next several years; and to set in motion a process which would bring the men, women, and children who live there into the mainstream of American society over the coming generation. Those remain our purposes."[12]

Chapter 3 deals with "Young Children: Austin's Best Investment." It covers the phase of an individual's development from prenatal care to the age of eight. In accordance with the convictions of the authors, it is the longest chapter in the Plan—ninety pages. It starts in dramatic fashion: "Look closely. See that child standing over there in the shadows? It is time for school to begin, but she seems hesitant about going inside. Perhaps she hasn't done her homework. Perhaps she's afraid, ashamed, or depressed. Maybe she is hungry. The bell is ringing and still she hesitates. She seems very much alone. In one sense the child is alone. Her father, an alcoholic, left home in anger one day and never returned. Her mother, trying to keep the family together, is worn out from working two jobs. She herself is burdened with the care of her younger brothers, the baby so tiny and sickly that often she skips school to care for him. As a result she is doing poorly in her classes; she is so young, so tired, and has missed so much. There are temptations beyond the school yard. She doesn't know where to turn. Yet in another sense, this child is not alone. She is just one of the 32,235 Austin children who live in poverty (one out of every five) and one of the 25 percent who live in households headed by a single parent. These factors, with their attendant ramifications, increase her risk of dropping out of school, becoming a teen parent, needing welfare services and in the long run, never reaching her economic potential. Her little brother, a low birth weight baby as a result of inadequate prenatal care, is at high risk of developmental delay, learning disorders and behavior problems. These are her problems, her family's problems. They also are Austin's problems."[13]

The chapter argues that "every baby in Austin deserves a chance for a healthy start in life," but "many Austin infants and young children today lack the essential prerequisites for positive early development and care." Those with low birth weight, neglect of development in the first three years, or subject to family stress will probably fall behind. For every $1 spent on prenatal care an estimated $3.38 are saved on medical care during the infant's first year; for every $1 spent for immunization services, $10 are saved by reducing childhood illness and death from disease; for every $1 spent on quality child care, $6 are saved in social welfare, special education and juvenile justice costs.[14]

Prenatal Health Care and Education

This section of chapter 3 begins with the following observation: "The main development of the brain and other internal organs of the fetus takes place during the first trimester of pregnancy, and it is especially during this period when insults leading to low birth weight and prematurity can occur. Physicians generally agree that to promote good birth outcomes, regular prenatal health care visits must begin as early as possible during the first trimester. This fact is little known and understood by many of our lowest-income and highest-risk pregnant teens and women in Austin."[15]

It is estimated that in Travis County 21 percent of the mothers have inadequate prenatal care. This deficiency is directly related to the fact that infant mortality is high, and also to the fact that infant mortality is twice as high among African-Americans as it is among whites. The rate of low birth rates is also directly related to "the lack of timely and regular prenatal health care and education."[16] The chapter then sets forth targets for prenatal health care, surveys the existing facilities for prenatal health care, estimates the cost of filling the gaps between existing services and targets, and the benefits to be gained. The annual gain is estimated at $1,762,652.

Substance Using Pregnant Teens and Women

The Plan then moves on to the special problems of use of drugs, alcohol, and tobacco by pregnant girls and women. It proposes "A comprehensive residential treatment, shelter and outreach program."[17] Again, the costs and benefits are estimated.

Child Health Care: Birth to Eight

From prenatal care the Plan moves to the first eight years after birth. It states that "Our most vulnerable children, those in poverty, are also most likely to experience health problems. Children who live at or below the poverty level are more susceptible to health related problems are less likely to receive timely medical care."[18] There are services for this age group in Austin but "Given current capacity, the public and non-profit sectors cannot serve all the Medicaid and other indigent clients."[19] Apart from access to medical treatment, "Another critical preventative component of good health is adequate nutrition."[20] Here again, there are good services in Austin, but they are not quite adequate. According to the Children's Defense Fund, 16 percent of low-income children experience growth retardation, and 21 percent of all poor children under the age of two have anaemia. "It is unconscionable that such a large percentage of our children suffer from the effects of malnutrition in this wealthy nation."[21] "Even more disturbing," the Plan says, "is the difference between U.S. and European mortality from intentional injuries; homicide as a cause of children's death is rare in European countries. In Austin, during the past month alone, three infants under age one died of child abuse. Child abuse is the single most destructive behaviour in our society.... Physical, sexual, and psychological abuse are the killer not only of bodies, but also the minds and spirits of our youth."[22]

The Plan stresses the need for educating parents. "Most young parents are ill-prepared for parenting in the modern age.... In addition, many students who drop out of school do so because they are already pregnant or have engendered a child, and need to earn money to support the infant.... In Austin, 70 percent of pregnant and parenting teens drop out of school, and it is believed that 55 percent of them never return to school or alternative educational opportunities."[23]

The Plan lays down targets for the 9 to 8 year old children, lists the services and institutions needed to attain them, and estimates the costs of providing those services and institutions. The cost of providing "the full range of cost-effective early childhood and parenting education services" is estimated at $7,511,500 per year, as compared to $2,847,000 currently available.[24]

At the end of the chapter, the authors return to the problem of child abuse. Research, they say, shows that it is highly correlated with later teenager pregnancy, school drop out, runaway youth, juvenile delinquency, suicide and suicide attempts, mental health problems, need for foster care services, adult criminal behaviour, child molestation, incest and rape, and substance abuse, especially by women.[25] They outline a programme for dealing with it, in considerable detail. The chapter closes with this statement: "The Austin Project proposes to ensure that all of our children and families have the opportunity of receiving services which will enable them to reach their full potential."[26]

Austin's Adolescents

Chapter 4 of the Plan is entitled "Austin's Adolescents: Investing in the Future, 9–16 Year Olds." It begins: "Early adolescence is a turning point. Many young people between the ages of 9 and 26 go through a period of tremendous physical, emotional and cognitive change…According to the Carnegie Council for Adolescent Development, a quarter of American youths—seven million total—are extremely vulnerable to multiple high-risk behaviours and school failures, and another seven million are at least somewhat vulnerable. Indeed, the Austin mayor's Task Force on Gangs, Crime and Drugs estimates that half of Travis County students are at risk, with one-third dropping out before finishing high school."[27]

The Plan then states its principles for dealing with adolescents: "The causes of crime and gang activity, teenage pregnancy, substance abuse, low self-esteem, and unsatisfactory school performance interact with each other;…Since the problems are interactive, so must be the treatment for at-risk youth.… A second theme of this report is 'continuity:' the importance of continual, 'seamless' service delivery for youth, horizontally across the range of an individual's problems, and vertically throughout the young person's life."[28]

A third theme is the central role of the family in dealing with the problems of 9–16 year olds.

Teenage Pregnancy and HIV Disease

Problems arising from the early onset and intensity of sexual activity among Austin's adolescents are pregnancy, AIDS, and other sexually transmitted diseases. The average age at first sexual intercourse in Austin is 14, and sexually active teenagers average three partners during the same period. An estimated 36 percent of sexually active teenagers used no form of contraception. "During last sexual intercourse, an alarming 42 percent did not use condoms, the only contraceptive method recommended for HIV prevention."[29]

A survey of Austin high schools showed 71 percent of the male students and 50 percent of the female students to be sexually active. However, sexual activity was substantially higher amongst Hispanic students than among whites, and substantially higher among blacks than among Hispanics. Among blacks 80 percent of the males and 76.9 percent of the females were sexually active. In all three categories, sexual activity among Austin high school students was significantly higher than the national average. Of those surveyed, 44 percent used no method of contraception or an ineffective method at their most recent sexual intercourse. Family planning education is provided through the school system, but apparently it is inadequate. Prevention of AIDS, says the report, involves similar issues to birth control education and can best achieve its ends by "providing information and skills that enable sexually active adolescents to diminish their risk of contracting HIV and other STD (sexually transmitted diseases)." As for drug abuse, the Austin Rehabilitation Center has capacity for a small number of residents. Most of the youths referred to the centre do so because of adjudication. "There appears to be need for a more comprehensive program for youths re-entering society after in-patient treatment."

Only one percent of the $225,785,418 spent on youth programs and services in Travis County, in fiscal year 1991–92, was allocated to teenage pregnancy services ($2,545,507). The lifetime costs associated with the estimated 5,000 to 10,000 HIV-infected persons in Travis County will be between $510 million and $1,020 billion. Of this amount, the cost of lifetime treatment of those who contracted HIV as teenagers is $25,806,000. In contrast, the cost of providing sex education for all students, and family planning services for all sexually active girls, is $1,078,810. The cost of babies born to teenagers (pre-natal care, hospital delivery, and child health care) in 1990 was $2,884,822. The message, according to the Plan, is "Pay now or pay more later."[30] A list of objectives and strategies for dealing with teenage pregnancies, AIDS, and other sexually transmitted diseases follows.

Chapter 4 then turns to drugs, alcohol, and cigarettes. These do not seem to be a particularly serious problem. Seventeen percent smoke cigarettes, 10 percent are drinking at least once a week, 7 percent are regular users of marijuana, 8.5 percent used other illegal drugs in the past thirty days. However, the Plan aims to improve the situation, and provides a set of objectives and strategies for such improvement. Similarly, the Plan seeks improvement in the incidence of accidents, homicides, and suicides among teenagers.

Public Safety

The task force opens its section on public safety by making it clear that in the United States, crime is Big Business: "The costs of crime are difficult to estimate, but there can be little doubt that they are immense. Economists at the Wharton School of Business found that gross receipts from criminal activity run anywhere from $27 billion to $137 billion per year. Drug abuse costs the nation about $60 billion each year, through reduced productivity of drug users, increased social welfare expenditures, and drug related crimes. Crime control is expensive as well. Federal state and local governments spend about $60 billion a year on police, courts, and corrections, and another $35 billion is spent annually on private security. Nevertheless, crime is only the most dramatic of a long chain of negative outcomes, each of which poses immense costs to the citizens of Austin and the nation. Many more youths die of suicide each year than of murder; the nation's worst problem drugs are not cocaine, but tobacco and alcohol; the economic costs of poor infant health, school dropout, unemployment, and reduced productivity dwarf the worst crime statistics. In large part, the solutions to these problems are the same as the solution to the crime problem..."[31]

Prevention is cheaper than cure. After the age of 18 or 20, it is difficult to redeem habitual offenders. Interventions with 8 or 10 year olds appear to be much more effective.

Many crimes are committed by youths, although it is impossible to say how many, since only about one crime in fifteen results in an arrest, and only data on arrests is available. We do know that 25 percent of felony arrests are persons under the age of 17, nationwide, compared to 26 percent in Austin. A nationwide survey revealed that 30 percent of boys aged 11 to 17 had committed thefts and 15 percent had committed robbery. "By age 18, arrest statistics show that most urban males have had some police or juvenile court contact."[32]

Gangs

Youth crime is a group affair. Nationwide, most crimes committed by youths are carried out by groups. Gangs are an important part of the Texas juvenile crime problem; gangs are prevalent in Texas cities, and Austin is no exception. The risk attached to membership of a gang is not just that crime may become habit forming, or the danger of arrest. "For many youths, increasing involvement with the gang coincides with decreasing involvement with school, jobs, and other aspects of mainstream society."[33]

The chapter ends with an appeal for community policing, following five principles: the criminal justice system cannot do it alone; local systems work best; change the prevailing management style; develop methods for problem-solving; and prepare for the long haul.

The fifth chapter presents "An Investment Program for Youths Age 17-25." It recognizes that many of the problems faced by this age cohort are the same as those of the 9-16 group: drug abuse, delinquency, teen pregnancy, HIV disease. However, there is one difference. "The challenge that is different for the 17-25 year age range is to find a path to the work force that results in a meaningful job with growth potential."[34] Those who leave school before the age of 17 have little hope of finding such a job. About one quarter of Austin high school students drop out before graduation. About the same proportion of students graduate, and enter the work force with no further education. Most of them accept jobs which have little relationship to their high school education. In reply to a question, "Who helped you get your job?" 59 percent of 1990 high school graduates in Austin said "Got it myself," 2 percent said "parents," 5 percent said "college placement agency," 3 percent "high school counsellor," and 2 percent "private employment agency." "The Texas Employment Commission helped no one, in part because the structure of its computerized job machine program does not well serve individuals with little or no job experience."[35]

On the plus side, "Austin already has in place some promising programs for assisting the school-to-work transition for high school students,"[36] and "Some effective programs are in place in Austin for those who need to upgrade their skills."[37] However, much more work is needed before most high school graduates will be able to make a smooth transition from school to work. The Plan proposes a system of small academies, or "schools within schools" with assistance from the private sector, and offering specialized training in various fields. A program of "Action Items" for 1991-92 and 1992-93 is offered. The final words of the chapter are, "Initially, TAP should focus most on the third objective—developing learning and training paths to career opportunities for Austin's high school youth."[38]

Chapter 6 brings an abrupt change of pace, and the economist finds himself on more familiar ground: "The Economics of the Inner City Neighbourhoods." It begins by pointing out that the improvements in social conditions discussed in the earlier chapters will make Austin a more attractive location for industry, and a stronger candidate "for selection under enterprise zone legislation now before congress."[39] The idea of "enterprise zones" appeared in the United Kingdom in the 1970s. It consisted essentially in the creation of employment in the inner cities, by following the example of Hong Kong, Taiwan and other Asian countries. From the U.K., the concept moved to the United States, where legislation was passed in 1982. The Plan cites the dissertation of Dan Dabney, a member of the TAP task force, regarding the disappointing results of these early experiments: "Even though tax incentives are offered to locating firms, in many cases these are offset by higher economic costs such as insurance, transportation, and access to raw materials, therefore negating the tax benefit. Transportation factors have worsened in most urban enterprise zone areas due to deteriorating or inadequate infrastructure, increased distance to suburban and other markets, and lack of proximity to airports...The impact of enterprise incentives on business is marginal except in the case where the value of the enterprise zone incentive is large relative to the amount of investment. Small businesses are most attracted to enterprise zones because of the increased financial importance of the incentives to these firms."[40]

The task force then states that Congress recognizes these limitations, and has accordingly narrowed the number of experimental zones from 50 to 25, thus permitting increased incentives for migration to each zone. But Congress also recognizes that the legislation could not deal fully with problems of labour skill, public safety, infrastructure, etc., thus increasing the chances of designation of cities which are trying to deal with these problems themselves, like Austin. In the view of the task force, however, "it would be unwise to rely on enterprise zones exclusively, or even primarily, to revitalize the neighbourhoods of the inner city."[41] Austin is still a small enough city to permit people to live in the inner city and work in the major plants, perhaps with special transport facilities provided.

The Plan makes six proposals for the inner city: a Development Bank; a Magnet School or Academy for Entrepreneurship; Foundation support for such a school or academy; Mentoring and tutoring by volunteers among the students at the University of Texas School of Business; Apprenticeships in the Austin Incubator; Help from the Service Corps of Retired Executives.

The last few pages of chapter 6 are devoted to the recession and national economic policy. "Historians may well call this the Peace Dividend Recession. Although other forces were at work (notably the extravagance of the previous construction boom) the central fact about the American economy in 1992 has been the inevitable and proper deflation of the military and military industrial complex...The answer is *investment in physical and non-physical infrastructure*. The scale of the infrastructure backlog built up since 1968 is so great (say, $500 billion, 1987) that public investment of this type could hold the American economy close to full employment for the 1990s and beyond...but a lion seems to stand in the path of a policy of radically increasing infrastructure; the enormous federal deficit,...The answer is: Split the federal budget between capital and current expenditures as do more than 40 states and virtually all other advanced industrial countries...The lion in our path is simply a product of bad public bookkeeping in Washington."[42]

The task force justifies this excursion into national policy in the following words: "Without apology, Chapter 6 includes a sustained passage on national economic policy. Here the point is simple and dramatic: protracted unemployment in the inner city is one of the most powerful—perhaps the most powerful—disintegrating social as well as economic forces at work in those neighbourhoods."[43]

To reduce unemployment, the Plan recommends radically increased public investment in long-neglected infrastructure; and as full employment is approached, to contain inflation, equitable tax increases. Finally, "an incomes policy suitable for American institutions should be designed effectively linking the average rates of productivity and money wage increase."[44]

Chapter 7 presents some "Notes on Volunteers: Organization, Training, and Coordination." It includes two brief memoranda by members of the TAP Board: Patricia Hayes, President of St. Edwards University, and Emily Vargas Adams, Director of CEDEN.

The brief final chapter sets forth some "Notes on the Organization of the Inner City Neighbourhoods." It states that "From the beginning of work on The Austin Project, we have taken the view that the process of sharing the burden of development should begin in the planning stage...It is our view that the execution of any such plan as that proposed here will require, if it is successful, a strengthening of organizational structures in the neighbourhoods for a wide variety of purposes." The balance of the chapter makes several suggestions along these lines, such as "sister neighbourhoods" (presumably twinning a poor with a rich neighbourhood) and church-to-church relationships.

The Plan has five appendices. In the first of these Dr. Dan Dabney undertakes a statistical analysis of the gains to be had through fulfilling targets in five fields: household income, savings in public assistance, social security savings, reduction in the incidence of crime, and savings on incarceration. He calculates the net gains at $390,000,000. Appendix B presents a survey of expenditures on youth services in the Travis County area. In Appendix C Dr. Dabney undertakes a cost-benefit analysis of achieving targets of the Plan for prenatal care of teenage mothers and reductions in high school dropout rate. To achieve the 90 percent target for prenatal care of teenage mothers would cost $252,000 and save $851,500. Reducing high school dropouts from 24 percent to 12 percent would cost $6,480,000 and bring future returns of $59,810,000. Appendix D presents a memorandum by D. Sterling Lands, Pastor of the Greater Calvary Baptist Church, on the status of African-American youth. It states: "We are aware that Black youth are being programmed for failure and that the young black male is rapidly becoming an endangered species." Appendix E presents "Integrated Components of Appropriate and Inappropriate Practices in the Primary Grades. For example, appropriate practice requires that "Each child is viewed as a unique person with an individual pattern and timing of growth." The inappropriate (actual) practice is that children are evaluated against a standardized group norm; all are expected to achieve the same narrowly defined, easily measured performance.

ASCEND

On 15 March 1994, the Austin Project published a progress report entitled *Austin's Strategy for Collaborative Economic and Neighbourhood Develop-*

ment (ASCEND). It relates that in May 1993, a year after the formal launching of TAP, financial support was sought from three foundations to undertake an intensive planning effort. When each of these foundations awarded TAP a twelve-month grant, TAP hired a full-time executive director and assembled a full-time staff of six professionals. By mid-summer 1993, ASCEND continues, "it became clear that in order to design and implement the type of comprehensive economic and social transformation which was envisioned, a serious, multi-year commitment of the expertise, talents, experience, and energies had to be made by three major constituencies:

— Residents of Austin's low-income neighbourhoods and the variety of advocacy, social and religious organizations that represent them;
— Business enterprises, public and private agencies and professionals who work within these same neighbourhoods on a daily basis; and
— The principal political, economic, religious, and educational institutions of the Austin community."[45]

Under TAP auspices and "orchestration," these three groups came together in December 1993 to create ASCEND, which is essentially a twenty-year plan for the Austin region, divided into two phases: a seven-year period during which "a comprehensive model-prototype" is implemented in three of Austin's economically most disadvantaged neighbourhoods; and a thirteen-year period during which "the comprehensive model-prototype will be brought to scale throughout Austin."[46] To finance this ambitious plan, the city of Austin is applying for federal funds from the President's Community Enterprise Board.

The overall objective of ASCEND is said to be to: "Marshall the resources of the entire Austin community to ensure that all of its members are able to participate fully in the social and economic mainstream." Its *individual* outcome goals are: 1) physical and emotional security and health; 2) the ability to exercise freely one's autonomy, creativity, and spirituality; 3) effective choice of relative independence, interdependence, and social participation; 4) the extent to which caring and loving relationships with others are formed and maintained and; 5) the realistic opportunities to live a productive and economically self-sufficient life."[47] Its *community* goals are: 1) personal safety and social stability within the community; 2) a healthy and nourishing physical environment; 3) cultural, religious, racial, ethnic, and linguistic diversity ("pluralism"); 4) improved family formation and functioning; 5) increased neighbourhood self-sufficiency; 6) social integration and harmony and the levels of social participation and contribution of citizens ("citizenship") and; 7) economic growth, prosperity, and the level of economic participation and contribution of citizens ("productivity"). ASCEND also identifies four "SYS-

TEMS-CHANGE OUTCOME GOALS," such as "public resources are shifted from income support to prevention." Finally, it specifies three "operational goals": healthier children, stronger neighbourhoods, and full employment. The "conceptual model" is depicted in chart 1.

Next, the ASCEND report specifies measures for each of its operational goals (chart 2) and a series of outcome measures for its other targets for the three "pilot neighbourhoods." It then identifies the barriers to attainment of its operational goals. For example, the barriers to full employment are identified as follows: 1) the mismatch between available jobs and the education and skill levels of unemployed and underemployed residents; 2) the absence of comprehensive school-to-higher education strategy; 3) the fragmentation of post-secondary education and training efforts; 4) the fear of loss of fringe benefits (e.g. health care, subsidized rent); 5) the absence of affordable child care and personal savings; 6) the lack of experienced community-based entrepreneurs; 7) the lack of capital for new business formation and development and; 8) poor transportation links between low-income neighbourhoods and job-training and employment sites. The next step is to specify the "principal service approaches" to be undertaken to overcome the barriers. For attaining the objective of "strong neighbourhoods" (which has much the shortest list of services, but will serve to illustrate the principle involved) the services to overcome, the barriers to attainment of this goal are: active support of neighbourhood improvement initiatives; establishment of public housing rent ceilings; resident cooperative purchasing and management of rental housing; and housing improvement and construction training of neighbourhood youth... Finally, costs of these services are determined and a budget set.

Particularly interesting are the "services" to be undertaken to achieve full employment. The major effort will be in education and training designed to fit the supply of skills to the demand for them. An individualized study plan, endorsed by a parent or guardian, will be developed for each high school student. Each high school will establish and operate at least one "career academy," such as finance, health care, or electronic manufacturing. High school students going directly into the work force will be supported by job counselling and placement assistance, in a fashion similar to that of the existing High Expectations program which, in turn, is modelled after the Boston Compact, designed to ease the transition from school-to-work. The city of Austin will establish an Austin Training Foundation, which will operate through affiliated steering committees in each of Austin's major industry sectors.

A distinction is made among school-to-work and unemployment-to-work; a different treatment is prescribed in each case. In order to permit deserving children of poor families to attend college, a Post-secondary Education Fund will be established. ASCEND recognizes that the most difficult problems arise in the case of unemployment-to-work: "The problem of chronic unemployment in Austin is a particularly vexing one because new jobs are being created on a country-wide basis at an excellent pace. The central problem is the mismatch between the education, skills, and experience of the residents of Austin's low-income neighbourhoods and the jobs that are being created."[48] ASCEND plans to create 2,000 new jobs over the first seven-year period for residents of Austin's low-income neighbourhoods.

Appraisal

The two TAP reports certainly make for unfamiliar reading for an economist. Even if we insist on an interdisciplinary approach to regional development, on teams studying regions on-the-spot, small enough to be seen steadily and seen whole, and on participation of the target population in the planning and execution of projects, it seems strange to plan in terms of prenatal care, reducing dropout rates, reducing the number of teenage pregnancies and the incidence of AIDS, juvenile crime rates and the prevalence of gangs. Does this kind of exercise deserve classification as "regional development planning" at all?

I think the answer is "yes." It may even be the wave of the future so far as regional development planning is concerned. Similar exercises are being undertaken in a host of American cities: Atlanta, Baltimore, Chicago, Columbus Ohio, and Los Angeles. Although the planning is centred on one city, it is not small-scale. The greater Austin region has close to one million people, more than the province of New Brunswick and many times more than Cape Breton or Prince Edward Island. After all, the overwhelming majority of Americans live in cities, and the cities are where the problems are. Take care of the cities and you take care of most of the nation. The ultimate objectives of TAP, as already noted, are the same as those of the Appalachian Regional Commission: improved income and employment, health and education, better housing, enhanced social welfare generally. But the Appalachian Commission goes about its task primarily by spending federal funds on infrastructure, especially roads. TAP goes about it primarily through investment in human resources.

One similarity of ARC and TAP is an assumption of continuity. Neither is a matter of bringing in an outside team of "experts" who will prepare a 5-year plan or a 20-year plan and then go away (like the Greater Moncton plan). The process is a continuous one, and should go on forever. In this respect, it is like "corporate planning" of a successful private enterprise, and should perhaps be called "management" rather than planning.

It is worth noting that the process is at once more interventionist and less interventionist than traditional regional development planning. It is more interventionist in wanting to take care of individuals from before the cradle to the grave. But it is less interventionist in that it does not attempt to allocate all the land or all the capital or all the manpower of the region. As already noted, where either the public or the private sector is operating satisfactorily—or both together—it leaves them alone. TAP attacks only the deficiencies, the gaps, the maladies left by the operation of public and private sector combined.

The plan has one deficiency: it is too exclusively long term. "Take care of the long run and the short run will take care of itself" is one attitude, but "take care of the short run first or you may never see the long run" is another. This statement applies particularly to employment and unemployment. It is all very well to assure that the Austin region has a healthy and well trained labour force, so that it is able to fill the kind of jobs that are offered to it. But it is equally important that jobs are there for the kind of labour force that exists at the moment, and particularly jobs for school leavers. With the kind of information that is being gathered and translated into computerized map overlays, the task force should know in intimate detail what are the characteristics of its labour force. It can then endeavour to create jobs, in the private or public sector, to fit that labour force. This effort may bring some surprises. With today's technology, it is not true that high-tech industries require only highly skilled workers. Some technologies are so advanced that they are virtually automatic, and require only unskilled labour. And if all the workers cannot be absorbed in the private sector, there must be plenty of useful public work projects to be done. These may require state or federal funds. With the cuts in defense expenditures, however, the attitude of the administration toward regional development and public works may be about to change. Austin should be able to cash in on any change of the federal government in this direction.

We have learned that today's unemployment is not really a macro-economic problem. Certainly inappropriate monetary, fiscal, or foreign trade policy can make unemployment worse. But the unemployment today is concentrated in certain sectors, age groups, and *places*; lowering the federal reserve discount rate by 1 percent will not take care of high school dropouts in Austin Texas. The only way to reduce unemployment and inflation together is to create jobs in places where unemployment is high and reduce inflationary pressure where it is generated. While it may need state and federal funds to implement its programs, an organization like TAP is well designed to discover just who the unemployed are, what are their characteristics, and craft a tailor-made employment program to provide them with jobs they can do, whether in the private or the public sector.

Notes

1. Walt Rostow, "Memorandum of 20 July 1992, (Austin, University of Texas), p. 1.
2. *Ibid.*, p. 3.

3. *An Investment Plan for the Young: The Austin Project, First Phase*, (Austin, Texas), 8 September 1992, p. 47.
4. *Ibid.*, p. 48.
5. *Ibid.*
6. *Ibid.*, pp. 52–3.
7. *Ibid.*, p. 53.
8. *Ibid.*, pp. 53–4.
9. *Ibid.*, p. 55.
10. *Ibid.*, p. 56.
11. *Ibid.*, p. 57.
12. *Ibid.*, pp. 59–60.
13. *An Investment Plan for the Young*, chapter 3.
14. *Ibid.*, p. 64–66.
15. *Ibid.*, p. 66.
16. *Ibid.*, p. 68.
17. *Ibid.*, p. 78.
18. *Ibid.*, p. 80.
19. *Ibid.*, p. 81.
20. *Ibid.*, p. 83.
21. *Ibid.*, p. 88.
22. *Ibid.*
23. *Ibid.*, p. 93.
24. *Ibid.*, p. 121.
25. *Ibid.*, pp. 141–2.
26. *Ibid.*, p. 149.
27. *An Investment Plan for the Young*, chapter 4, p. 151.
28. *Ibid.*, p. 152.
29. *Ibid.*, p. 163.
30. *Ibid.*, p. 167.
31. *Ibid.*, p. 181.
32. *Ibid.*, p. 184.
33. *Ibid.*, p. 188.
34. *An Investment Plan for the Young*, chapter 5, p. 206.
35. *Ibid.*, p. 208.
36. *Ibid.*, p. 211.
37. *Ibid.*, p. 213.
38. *Ibid.*, p. 215.
39. *An Investment Plan for the Young*, chapter 6, p. 233.
40. *Ibid.*, pp. 233–34.
41. *Ibid*, p. 235.
42. *Ibid.*, pp. 239–40.
43. *Ibid.*, p. 242.
44. *Ibid.*, p. 243.
45. *Austin's Strategy for Collaborative Economic and Neighbourhood Development*, report published by the Austin Project, 15 March 1994, pp. 1–2.
46. *Ibid.*, p. 2.
47. *Ibid.*, p. 5.
48. *Ibid.*, p. 54.

15

Great Britain and the European Community

The "regional problem" in the Great Britain is in many ways more complex than in other countries. This is true despite the fact that Great Britain is not a federation. Without state governors or provincial premiers to give voice to regional grievances, one can assume that regional tensions will not be as great in Britain as they are in the United States, Australia or Canada. Yet in Britain the "regional problem" goes beyond a concern for underdeveloped areas. It speaks to issues of urban decay, congestion and town and land use planning.[1]

Britain has also seen dramatic shifts in policy in the regional development field. G.C. Cameron has compared the history of regional policy in Britain to that of "a man with a grumbling appendix."[2] The pain comes and goes and so do various policy prescriptions. The various forms of the perceived regional problem and important differences in the two political parties that have held power in Britain ever since regional policy has been in fashion explain the varying degrees of enthusiasm the government has had for regional policy prescriptions.

The Intellectual Underpinnings

Great Britain has been the home of many of the well known economists and theorists of economic development presented in the first part of this book. Britain was the dominant economic power, particularly in the nineteenth century, and economics became an "overwhelmingly British subject."[3] Adam Smith, the apostle of economic liberalism, wrote persuasively about the need to do away with restrictions on the market and the supply of labour.[4] Few economists in Britain or elsewhere, for that matter, challenged Smith's economic liberalism. Indeed for over one hundred years after Smith's death, economists would seek to "amend and sharpen its conclusions, struggle to resolve his ambiguities and seek otherwise to complete his system."[5]

To be sure, classical orthodoxy was challenged by Karl Marx and others.[6] But it was the depression of the 1930s that pointed in a dramatic fashion to its shortcomings. Classical orthodoxy had no policy prescriptions to respond to the crisis, to year after year of high unemployment and no or negative growth. John M. Keynes, the Cambridge economist, made the case in his classic *General Theories of Employment Interest and Money* that the modern economy does not always or necessarily find its equilibrium at full employment.[7] He insisted that it can find equilibrium with unemployment and that there can be a shortage of demand. Keynes' call was for government spending and intervention in the economy. Keynesianism soon became conventional wisdom, not least because of the depression years and the inability of the classical economies to deal with the crisis.

The depression years also revealed, in a very harsh fashion, the regional imbalance in the British economy. The effects of the depression were not uniform. Whereas the unemployment rate in London and the southeast rose to 15 percent by the early 1930s, elsewhere, it was even more alarming, rising to more than 30 percent in Wales, for example, and in some areas and towns as high as 70, 80, and even 90 percent. By 1934, unemployment in the traditionally more prosperous regions began to fall to relatively acceptable levels. However, in Wales, the north, and Scotland it remained high.[8]

The government responded by setting up a Royal Commission on the Distribution of Industry and Population (the Barlow Commission). In its final report in 1940, the commission concluded that there was, indeed, cause for concern. It recommended "national action" to deal with the situation and identified several measures to be taken, ranging from the establishment of a new central authority to specific initiatives to decentralize both industry and population. But as D.W. Parsons writes, the commission did not present its report at the "most propitious time." By 1940, he explains, the commission's "*raison d'être* was...seemingly as redundant as the promises extracted by Chamberlain from Herr Hitler."[9] Clearly, the problem of unemployment that was in any event being temporarily resolved through rearmament, was being shunted aside for a more urgent task. But the report was to have a strong influence in shaping regional development efforts for some time to come; some of its recommendations were only introduced in the 1960s. Indeed, the Barlow report, together with another government-sponsored report, the Beveridge Report on Employment Policy, combined with the espousal of Keynesian economic principles, were to form the basis for Britain's postwar policy on full employment and the regional dispersion of industry and population.

Policies and Programs

Britain wanted to avoid a return to the prewar situation of depressed areas and the political will to prevent this from happening was strong. The immediate postwar British Labour government did place considerable emphasis on regional policy. Expenditure levels under the Distribution of Industry Act, if nothing else, confirm this. Over £30 million were spent by the Labour government under the program between 1946 and 1949, compared with £11.6 million spent between 1956 and 1959 by its Conservative successor.[10]

The Labour government also made extensive use of its power to control industrial location in the immediate postwar years through a building license system. The government kept a strict control on permits granted for new buildings in undesignated areas, and this attempt to redirect investment did meet with some success. The development areas, representing only 20 percent of the population, obtained over 50 percent of all new industrial buildings between 1945 and 1947.[11]

A committee of public servants from various departments was established to decide on the merits of allowing firms to develop or expand new facilities in nondesignated areas, thus depoliticizing the process. But the procedure to obtain a licence was lengthy. Industrialists complained, time and again, not only about the policy but also about the process. The government, however, stood firm against this criticism. It even pressed ahead with still stronger control measures. The Town and Country Act of 1947 introduced a requirement to obtain industrial development certificates from the Board of Trade for all firms wishing to launch new industrial development of more than 5,000 square feet before planning permission was granted.[12] This provision raised criticism in the private sector, but this time mostly about the delay in obtaining a certificate. However, in some ways, "delay was the policy," in that investors would decide to locate in designated regions simply to avoid the slow process.[13] As well, it was also clear that the committee was quite prepared to take "tough" positions on applications to locate in the more prosperous regions.

The government provided loans and grants to build new factories in the designated areas and redirected some of its own purchases to firms in these regions. It made new provisions for public services and for industrial and local infrastructure, as well as putting in place a policy of urban development. New towns were built, albeit designed to deal more with urban congestion than with regional development. Still, the government did turn to the Town and Country Act to create new towns in designated development areas, the earliest being Aycliffe and Peterlee in the northeast, Chombran in Wales, and Clenrothes in central Scotland.

All in all, the postwar Labour government had set itself ambitious regional development goals and demonstrated a political will to put in place measures to work towards these goals. The chancellor of the exchequer made this clear in his 1946 budget speech when he declared that "the battle for the Development Areas is not yet won, but we mean to win it." He added, "I have told my colleagues that I will find, and find with a song in my heart, whatever money is necessary."[14]

The Conservative party, elected to power in 1951, was anxious to limit government intervention in the economy. Consequently, measures to promote regional development now became subject to close review and scrutiny. There was, of course, an ideological basis for this review.

Building licences were abolished in 1954. Although the requirement for industrial development certificates continued, the process was considerably relaxed—so much so that it became fairly easy to obtain a certificate for new development even in the southeast. Consequently, very little in the way of new economic activity was "diverted" to designated areas and, although the "carrot-and-stick" policy instruments of the first postwar Labour government remained on the statute books, they were rarely employed. The government had made it clear that it sought to promote general industrial development and would intervene only to "attract a few industries to those areas hardest hit."[15] Direct government spending for regional development also dropped significantly during the early 1950s. This was true for all government programs for regional development, including grants to firms locating in the designated development areas.

It was not long, however, before the government was jolted out of its complacency. By 1958, areas dependent on traditional industries were experiencing economic decline. The 1958–1959 recession was felt particularly hard in the slow-growth areas and to sterm the worsening economic conditions (and with an eye on the electorate), the Conservative government began to reconsider its position on regional development. For one thing, it started to exercise greater control over industrial development certificates. The government also passed the Distribution of Industry Act (Industrial Finance) in 1958. The act added some areas of high unemployment previously not designated under the Development Areas Act. New funds were earmarked for regional development in designated areas, and new areas were designated on the basis of unemployment levels. This approach prompted many observers to argue that British regional policy was now viewed in the context of social, rather than economic, policy, in that the focus was on the problem of unemployment rather than on the strengths and development opportunities of slow-growth regions.

The opposition Labour party meanwhile called for a return to the approach it had introduced in the immediate postwar years. In an argument replayed several times since, Labour spokesmen insisted that the government had turned Britain into two nations—the haves and the have-nots. The Conservatives countered that the unemployment problem was only local in nature and concentrated in certain pockets. They insisted that the problem could be resolved with appropriate government measures and, once returned to power for a second term in 1959, they quickly identified regional development to be of top priority.

Up until the 1960s, the elements, if not their application, of British regional policy had been relatively stable. It is true that some adjustments were made to the policy from time to time and, in the immediate postwar years, some ambitious initiatives had been launched. But changes were not frequent and with the exception of the negative location powers that had been forcefully exercised by the postwar Labour government, they were also not far reaching.

All that changed in the early 1960s. From then until the present, important changes to regional policy would occur every 3 to 4 years, reflecting changing economic or political circumstances, a change in government or simply because things were not working as well as expected.

Certainly in 1960, regional policy took a dramatic turn. The Distribution of Industry Act, which had underpinned British regional development efforts since the war was repealed and replaced by the Local Employment Act (1960). Like its predecessor, the employment act provided for grants and loans to be made for new economic activity in designated regions. But it went further in other ways. The business community could now obtain financial assistance for building factories. In addition, the development areas were abolished and replaced by smaller *development districts*. The term is somewhat of a misnomer in that the areas designated did not so much show prospects for development as an existing or potential high rate of unemployment.

The new area designation process served to deschedule many areas, at least, initially. Under the new scheme, some 14 percent of the total population was initially covered, as compared to 19 percent under the development areas.

The new legislation, however, provided for considerable flexibility in designating development districts. Areas could be designated or dedesignated by the Board of Trade without having to obtain parliamentary approval. The board established a benchmark of 4 to 5 percent unemployment as the trigger that would designate new areas. Still, the areas designated included many of the old problem areas, including part of central Scotland, South Wales, West Cumberland, Merseyside, and the northeast. But changes to area designations were frequent, given the fairly automatic criteria employed, ranging from a coverage of 7.2 percent of the total population in late 1962 to 16.8 percent in 1966.

The 1960 Local Employment Act made assistance much easier to obtain and as a result expenditure levels under regional development increased substantially in that decade. Firms were no longer required to show their inability to raise funding from other sources. And, as noted earlier, grants were now offered for the construction of new buildings. Initially, firms were allowed to claim 85 percent of the difference between the cost of a new building and its actual market value once finished. Thus, slow-growth regions were favoured under the scheme because new buildings in economically depressed regions would have a substantially lower market value than those in the more prosperous areas. Later, the program was revised, and a standard grant of 25 percent of construction costs was made available.

In 1963, assuming that new industries locating in development areas would require labour with new or updated skills, the government began to make available funds for a new retraining program. That same year, still other new measures were introduced or existing ones made more generous. Grants, for example, were made available to local authorities to assist with the reclamation of derelict areas. In some instances, the government assumed up to 90 percent of the cost. Added to this was a series of specific initiatives, such as new public works projects in designated areas and special government procurement from firms or shipyards located in the areas.

But the more important commitments to regional development were not in the form of ongoing regional programs of grants and loans to local authorities or private firms. The most far-reaching intervention was the government's renewed determination to influence and even direct the location of new industry. The control over industrial development certificates was considerably tightened to something like was seen during the immediate postwar years.

In selected sectors, the government went further and initiated discussions with industry to encourage firms to locate in designated regions. An excellent case in point was the automotive industry. The then president of the Board of Trade served notice in 1960 that he would seek to direct new investment to areas of high unemployment.[16] The government entered into negotiations with individual firms; its position was to oppose all expansion in the south or allow it only if the firm agreed to further expansion in areas of unemployment. The government was successful in this regard and set the stage for the investment pattern of the automotive industry for the next several years. The government later explained that its objective was not simply to encourage growth in slow-growth areas but also to limit inflationary pressure in the Midlands and the South. Once again, this coincided with the emergence of town-planning concerns and several commissions examining the problems of growth and congestion.

The government instituted still other important measures. The prime minister appointed a minister, Lord Hailsham, to be responsible for the northeast. It is hardly possible to overemphasize the importance of this development. It signalled that regional development was now a top political priority and that regional concerns would be brought directly to the Cabinet table. Giving a minister responsibility for a specific region also signified that future regional development efforts for the area would be a highly political and open process.

No special ministers were appointed for Scotland or Wales because the secretary of state for Scotland and the Minister for Local Government for Wales would play a similar role. However, a new Scottish Development Department was set up in June 1962.

But it was Lord Hailsham who took the lead both inside government and in public to develop the government's regional policy. Geography and spatial considerations now became far more central to economic policy planning, and a process was put in place that provided an opportunity to question orthodox thinking on economic policy.

Lord Hailsham came to espouse the "growth center" approach to regional planning. As elsewhere, the approach was heralded as a panacea for slow-growth or stagnant regions. Hailsham issued a report in November 1963 that identified various growth centres as the way ahead for regional development policy in Britain.[17] His report called for massive investment in "growth points" in road-building, housing, and other public service infrastructure. At about the same time, a similar study was also released for Scotland.

The growth centre approach had obvious political appeal. On the one hand, it sent a signal to economically depressed areas that the government was truly concerned about regional unemployment. On the other hand, it sent out a positive economic message that the approach would serve to build up the regions by focusing on the economic strengths of the designated areas. But as happened in virtually all countries where the approach was adopted, the growth centre concept in Britain was pushed and pulled to cover an extremely wide area. It would apply to most of the northeast and to areas of Scotland.

The growth centre approach was not given much time to prove itself. One of the first things the new Labour government did on assuming power was to do away with the approach, stating instead that it would rely on comprehensive economic planning both at the national and regional levels to a far greater extent than the previous government had done. No more, the new government boasted, would there be a piecemeal approach to regional development.[18]

Shortly after coming to office, the government launched an ambitious series of planning exercises. In addition to Scotland and Wales, which were treated as separate regions for planning purposes, England was divided into eight planning regions. Surveys and development strategies were prepared. Regional development was seen in a highly positive light in that it was considered as supportive to national growth. J. Jones suggests that the decade from the early 1960s to the early 1970s represented "a unique period in which there were thought to be no real conflicts between the regional equity and national efficiency objectives of regional policy. During this period the argument was formulated in such a way that the two objectives were thought to be mutually compatible."[19]

Early in its mandate, the government also introduced new organizations for regional development that were to be, as it turned out, only the beginning of ongoing attempts to find a solution to the problem. The search is still continuing. This, as is apparent elsewhere, is not an experience by any means limited to Great Britain.

Underpinning the government's planning efforts was a new government structure. The Department of Economic Affairs would provide the necessary support and infrastructure for planning the national economy. Regional planning councils were established to assist the exercise at the regional level. These councils were representative institutions, bringing together individuals from local government, trade unions, the universities, and business. Although the councils were advisory bodies only and had no executive power, they were nevertheless assisted by a planning board of permanent government officials. The intention was that the regional councils and their plans would shape the national economic plan.[20]

The failure to integrate the nation's regional and national economic planning, however, did not prevent the government from introducing a host of new measures to cope with the issue. In 1966, Labour overhauled its regional development programming. It introduced the Industrial Development Act and extended the assisted areas to cover most of the traditional areas of high unemployment, in particular, large parts of Scotland and Wales. These were the largest areas ever designated and included over 40 percent of the land and 20 percent of the population.

The act provided cash grants to firms willing to locate in designated areas. Investment grants of 40 percent for development areas and 20 percent elsewhere were made available. For new buildings in designated areas, firms were eligible for a cash grant of 25 percent. Other measures introduced under the Employment Act were retained, most notably, loans, reduced rents, and assistance for worker training. Moreover, local authorities in designated areas could obtain grants to cover up to 85 percent of the cost of improving the environment. The government also renewed its commitment to tighten the industrial development certificate process.

Still new measures were introduced later on. In 1967, a new program was designed to subsidize employment in designated areas.[21] Under the regional employment premium program, a direct subsidy was made available to employers for each new employee hired in the manufacturing sector. The premium represented a subsidy of about 7 percent of the average earnings of employees. Employers were also granted a tax rebate for providing employment in the designated areas. The program was highly controversial and was abolished in 1974 by the Conservative government—only to be reintroduced shortly after by the next Labour government.

D.W. Parsons maintains that regional employment premiums "proved to be the straw that broke the camel's back—the cat amongst the regional pigeons."[22] The nondesignated areas or the "gray areas," which were also experiencing economic decline, began to direct strong criticism at the government's regional policy. Assistance to designated areas was much too generous, they insisted, and it invariably drew development away from their communities. The same year that the program came into force, the government responded to this criticism by appointing Sir Joseph Hunt to lead an inquiry. This is not to suggest that the government's regional development efforts were considered to be successful even in the designated areas. The movement of people from the north to the south continued. From 1961 to 1966, over 2 million people changed residence, and the south registered important net gains in the population flow.

Thus, the promise of integrated regional and national economic planning and the ambitious measures announced by the Labour government since coming to power in 1964 began to turn sour. The government's regional policy was being assailed from all sides—the designated, intermediate, and the prosperous areas were all critical, though for various and often conflicting reasons. The designated areas were largely of the view that the policy was not working well; the intermediate areas felt strongly that their potential for growth was being systematically sapped by overly generous assistance to the designated areas; and the most prosperous areas contended that regional development efforts were playing havoc with national growth and national economic efficiency. Added to this was a strong resurgence in regionalism in Britain. The Scottish Nationalist party, for example, made impressive gains in local elections during this period. The government responded by appointing royal commissions on local government and on the Constitution.

Meanwhile, representations before the Hunt inquiry were largely critical of the government's regional policy. Few voices in support of the current approach were heard. When Hunt did report, he called for a new commitment to regional planning, including an extension of assistance to the intermediate areas. He also recommended the dedesignation of Merseyside. Such recommendations were obviously politically explosive, and coming as they did shortly before a general election was to be called, the government rejected the recommendation on Merseyside but agreed to that which would assist the intermediate areas. Seven new areas were designated, and new funding was made available for the construction of new buildings, for advance factories and for worker training. In addition, new funds were made available to local governments.[23]

While in opposition, during most of the 1960s, the Conservatives were highly critical of Labour's approach to regional development, claiming that the government should not have abandoned the growth centre concept, and maintaining that it had adopted an uncoordinated, helter-skelter policy that amounted to little more than an increase of spending on a host of initiatives. They argued, time and again, for greater selection and more focus in terms of policy instruments and areas. The Conservatives insisted that the emphasis should be on areas with strong potential for growth rather than on unemployment.

When returned to power, under Edward Heath, the Conservatives quickly announced their intentions to phase out the regional employment program, cut back on the industrial development certificate controls, move away from investment grants, and introduce investment tax allowances.[24] Moreover, the government reported its intention to return to the growth centre concept and declared that its regional development policy would not be employed to prop up "losers." Rather, regional policy would now focus on the strengths of the regions instead of on their weaknesses.

But this policy was short lived. D.W. Parsons explains the reversal in policy in this fashion: "Overnight lame ducks became sacred cows...Regional policy under the Conservatives was looking more and more like Labour's approach. Confronted with rising unemployment levels, particularly in traditionally depressed regions, the Heath government responded with all the political sensitivity of a Macmillan or Wilson government."[25] As early as January and February 1971, the government designated Glasgow, Tyneside, and Wearside as special development areas. Shortly after, £100 million was allocated to new public works projects for designated areas. And that was only the beginning.

In 1972 the government passed a new Industry Act. This act, which introduced an elaborate structure of regional industrial incentives, demonstrates more than any other initiative, the virtual complete reversal of the government's position on regional policy. An automatic regional development grant (RDG) was also established.[26] The grant was adjusted to correspond to the different area designations. For special development areas, assistance of 22 percent of the building cost and machinery was made available. In the case of development areas, 20 percent was made available, also for both building and machinery. For the intermediate areas, assistance was only available for building cost, and the level was set at 20 percent.

The act introduced a discretionary, project-related assistance in the form of soft loans, equity finance, loan guarantees, or capital grants. The latter was by far the most popular. Assistance was calculated on a cost per job basis, and the amount provided was considered the maximum required for the project to go ahead.

A scheme to encourage office and service industries to locate in disadvantaged areas was also introduced. The assistance was discretionary and project related. Grants were made available to all such firms willing to move to or establish offices in the three kinds of designated areas. Assistance varied, with the offer being more generous for special development areas and least generous for the intermediate ones.

The government also used its own expenditure budget to assist designated areas and continued with programs that funded the construction of roads, industrial estates, ports, and so on. It also sought to tilt its own purchasing policy to favour the designated areas. It continued a policy, first introduced in the immediate postwar years, to decentralize government offices—in particular, out of central London to the designated areas. This was in addition to a deliberate policy to locate new government positions outside of London.

1973 saw an important event that would have a strong and lasting impact on British regional policy. In that year, Great Britain became a full member of the European Economic Community (EEC). New comparisons of regional economic well-being were now being made both between nations and regions.

It is well known in its early years that the EEC had a rather uncoordinated approach to regional development. Several agencies had their own instruments—the European Investment Bank and the European Social Fund, to name just two. Some attempts had been made to bring coherence to the various regional programs but they had met with limited success. However, in 1972, the community confirmed that regional policy would in future enjoy priority status. Britain attached considerable importance to the community's regional policy and held discussions with it before becoming a full member. The Thomson report, released in 1973, argued that a major funding instrument was necessary to reduce regional disparities within the community.

Britain saw yet another change of government in 1973. While in opposition, the Labour party had reassessed its regional development policy, concluding that a fundamental revamp of the government's role in the economy, particularly at the regional level, was required. A much tighter control of the firms, especially the large multinationals, was thought to be essential. Once back in power, the party, however, began to backtrack and to look once again to the traditional approaches.

The new Labour government did, as it had promised, establish new planning agencies at both the national and regional levels. A National Enterprise Board was set up. At the regional level, development agencies were put in place for Scotland and Wales. The government tightened once again the industrial development certificates and sought to disperse offices away from London. It reintroduced regional employment premiums which the previous Conservative government had phased out. But by 1977 Labour, too, abolished the scheme.[27]

Hand in hand with its emphasis on sectoral planning, the government turned its attention more and more to urban problems, particularly urban decay. 1977, it has been observed, "was the year when the inner city finally arrived as a political problem."[28] They were now the new economically depressed areas, and the press gave the issue a high profile. The *Sunday Times*, for example, initiated a campaign to save the cities and attempted to do for the inner cities "what its sister paper had done for the depressed areas in 1934."[29] Shortly after the campaign, the government passed the Inner Urban Areas Act and established the Inner Area Program. By the late 1970s, whatever new resources were available were destined for sectoral planning and the inner cities. Regional development policies and programs of the kind Britain had known in the 1960s and 1970s were less and less in vogue.

The stage was set for the coming of a Conservative government under Margaret Thatcher. J.D. McCallum summed up the situation by arguing that the future of British regional policy was at best uncertain: "A consensus nearly fifty years in the making," he wrote, "is probably collapsing: it is unclear what will take its place."[30]

On coming to power, the volte-face made on regional policy in the early 1970s by Conservative Prime Minister Edward Heath was not forgotten by Margaret Thatcher. She made it clear that her government would be different and that she "was not for turning."[31] She became firmly convinced that the Keynesian-Beveridge consensus had failed and had "brought Britain low."[32] The new conservatism was to be more rigid in its views. Early in her mandate, Mrs. Thatcher and her senior ministers explained that they intended to disentangle the government from the web of industrial incentives and planning. They also rejected out of hand the notion that jobs should go to the regions. People, they insisted, must be encouraged and willing to move to find work.

To be sure, the Thatcher government made important cuts in regional programming. But on regional policy, the lady did turn at least somewhat from her position while in opposition. Contact with political reality saw to this.

The Thatcher government did move quickly after coming to office to end office development permits and industrial development certificates. The government also abolished regional economic planning councils. Regional development grants were continued, but cuts were made both in eligibility and spatial coverage. Access to the grants was withdrawn for research and development training activities and for maintenance expenditures. The grant-approval process was also tightened up, with grants given only to those projects that could demonstrate need and only when the jobs created were considered new. With respect to geography, the coverage of special development, development and intermediate areas was reduced from over 43 percent to about 25 percent of the British working population. The areas dropped then and subsequently were the predominantly rural, agricultural districts, rather than the declining urban areas. Regarding size coverage, minimum value requirements for assets were raised from £100 to £500 for plant and machinery and from £1,000 to £5,000 for building and works. On 1 August 1980, a decision was also taken to eliminate assistance for intermediate areas. One of Thatcher's most influential advisors, Sir Alan Walters, reports that one of Thatcher's greatest accomplishments was "to bring regional development in Britain to an end and to stop all the nonsense."[33]

Later, in 1983, the government tabled in the Commons a paper on regional industrial development. The paper argued that "although an economic case for regional industrial policy may still be made, it is not self-evident."[34] But the paper went on to point out that "the government believes that the case for continuing the policy is now principally a social one with the aim of reducing, on a stable long term basis, regional imbalances in employment opportunities."[35]

Later, in 1984, the government announced that it would abolish regional assistance for replacement equipment. Thus, only new equipment would now qualify. In addition, the government placed a ceiling on its regional programming so that grants could not be provided if they represented more than £10,000 per job created. The government declared that it intended to save some £200 million per year by 1987–1988 in regional programming and it did this by abolishing special development areas and downgrading the development areas to intermediate status. Accordingly, the regions would not be eligible for automatic regional development grants but only for selective assistance.

The minister of State for Industry, Norman Lamont, explained in a major policy statement that in future, British regional policy would place greater emphasis on job creation, while at the same time, attempt to improve its cost-effectiveness. He expressed the hope that, after a transitional period, regional policy would cost £300 million less per annum.[36]

To achieve greater cost-effectiveness, the minister announced that the map for designated areas would have two tiers instead of three and that the "inner tier, which will qualify for automatic grants as well as regional selective assistance, will be restricted to 15 percent of the working population."[37]

The basis for designating areas was employment patterns. The minister went on to explain that "it is only right that any policy as expensive as regional policy should be tied more closely to jobs." He concluded by arguing that: "The most important feature of our policy is that money will now be spent in the areas with the worst problems and that, in terms of new jobs per pound of expenditure, the new policy will be far more effective than the old."[38] The government, thus, essentially retained the position that regional industrial incentives should continue to play an important role in attempts to influence the location of economic activity. In addition, it sought to establish a closer link between regional policy and urban development, by attracting private investment into the inner cities. In the end, the government was to continue with its regional industrial incentives scheme. D.W. Parsons put it in this fashion: "By and large, it chose to reduce financial resources rather than rid itself of the institutional morass of regional subsidies."[39]

The government also sought to redraw the designated areas map by moving away from growth centres and concentrating more on "black spots." But, as was the case with previous governments, political pressure played havoc with this attempt to redraw the map. Norman Lamont explained that the government "tiptoed through a minefield."[40] Tiptoe it did, for designated areas went from 27 percent of the working population in 1983 to 35 percent in 1985.

The Thatcher government also introduced a new program to establish "enterprise zones." In the budget speech, the chancellor of the Exchequer explained that enterprise zones constituted an experiment in reducing government intervention in the economy and allowing private sector firms greater freedom to develop. The central purpose of the legislation, he explained, was to tackle problems associated with regional, inner city, and derelict land policy. The zones were to be designated for a period of 10 years, subject to renewal. Both new and existing private sector firms were eligible to take advantage of the program. Measures within the designated zones included exemption from development land tax, 100 percent capital allowance on industrial and commercial property for income tax and corporation tax purposes, abolition of general rates on industrial and commercial property, exemption from industrial training levy, a minimum of government requests for statistical information, and priority status in dealing with customs.[41]

Notwithstanding Sir Walters' contention, regional policy under the Thatcher government did not undergo a complete overhaul. The *Times* argues that regional policy under Thatcher underwent some changes, some updating, but not a "fundamental rethink."[42] One can also speculate whether at least some of the Thatcher changes to regional policy would not have also occurred under another government. It will be recalled, for example, that even the previous Labour government had initiated cuts in regional programming toward the end of its mandate.

Britain in the early 1980s, like other Western industrialized nations, faced the twin problem of high unemployment and inflation. Regional development had few friends in Britain, as elsewhere. In Britain, the problem of the 1980s was not one of regional disparities but of generalized industrial decline. The search for solutions would take place at both the national and international levels. Unemployment was now a problem in the traditionally prosperous areas. If there were still a spatial economic problem in Britain, it was not so much regional, as urban. There was, it will be recalled, widespread rioting in British cities in 1985, principally in protest at the lack of employment prospects for the young. This led to further reviews of what should be done to improve conditions in the inner cities.

Regionalism, as we knew it, was in a headlong retreat politically. Devolution for Scotland and Wales no longer dominated either the media or the political agenda as it once had. D.W. Parsons explains: "One paradigm—the region—has been lost; another paradigm—the inner city—has been found."[43] In addition, new urgent questions were now being asked about Britain's ability to compete internationally, about "national" unemployment, about national recovery, about youth unemployment, and about urban decay.

Given this shift, one may well ask why did British policy and programs also not go in a complete headlong retreat? Why, in other words, did the lady decide to turn on regional policy? The fundamental rethink of British regional policy, as promised, has yet to take place. Why?

There is, of course, the politics of regional policy that invariably influences policy. In the case of Britain, it has dogged both Labour and Conservative governments since the war. They all revised their regional policies or at least those they had adopted while in opposition or on first coming to power. The Thatcher government is no different. It has simply "tiptoed through the minefield" like all governments before it. In Britain, as elsewhere, regional policy has been employed to check regional discontent.

Thatcher's free market ideology and supply side economics also come face to face with the EEC Regional Development Funds. The funds make available significant resources annually for regional programming. Standing to one's ideological gun would have meant foregoing EEC funding. It also could have meant seeing EEC funds earmarked for some regions in Britain going to other regions in other countries. Ideological purity has its limits. A loose confederate arrangement like the EEC has the ability, provided it has money, to hold in check as determined an ideologue as Margaret Thatcher. The EEC with its emphasis on forging partnership with national governments in the regional development field is making it exceedingly difficult, if not impossible, for member countries to stop regional development programming. The Thatcher government admitted as much in a policy paper on regional development. It reported that it took the "contributions [of EEC funding] fully into account in determining expenditure on regional policy." It then added that it "strongly support[ed] the development of community regional policy."[44]

The European Community now has three funds from which member countries can draw resources to promote regional development. In addition, the community can give loans for regional purposes through the European Investment Bank and the European Coal and Steel Community. The three funds include the European Regional Development Fund (ERDF) set up in 1975 to reduce regional imbalances, the European Social Fund (ESF) set up in 1958 to support training, and the Guidance Section of the European Agricultural Guidance and Guarantee Fund (EAGGF) established in 1964 to promote agricultural production and marketing. The community sought to strengthen its commitment to regional and rural development in February 1988 by increasing substantially the level of resources of the three funds. In 1987, the three funds represented about 19 percent of the community's budget. It is envisaged that the funds will account for one-quarter of the budget by 1993.[45]

The European Community reports that it has made every effort to limit the areas qualifying for funding under the three funds to avoid "spreading our resources too thinly." Recent reforms have resulted in about 40 percent of the community's population being eligible for assistance from "all" the funds. The bulk of the funding, however, is made available to "less-developed regions and countries" or for "objective 1" funding. "Gross domestic product" and "gross domestic product per capita" measured against the community average determine whether a region is eligible for funding. Objective 2 funding is geared to selected areas hard hit by industrial decline, and the criteria for qualifying include unemployment rates and shares of industrial employment. Objective 3 funding seeks to address the problems of long-term unemployment, objective 4 is designed to help young people enter the labour market, and objective 5 funding is for modernizing agriculture. Fully 80 percent of the ERDF is earmarked for objective 1 activities and the "region" qualifying for funding consists of the entire countries of Greece, Ireland, Portugal, and Northern Ireland, parts of Spain and Italy, and the French overseas departments. The fund supports a variety of measures and projects mostly for infrastructure and industrial development initiatives. Projects are agreed to only after member countries have formally submitted multi-year plans. The European Commission then approves "national aid and schemes and individual aid proposals." The commission reports that it now seeks to forge "partnership" in regional development between the commission itself and national, regional, and local governments.[46]

What the above suggests is that the EEC regional development policy is posing new challenges to the ability of nation states in Europe to manage their "national" economy. If the policy could stop someone as ideologically committed as Margaret Thatcher dead in her tracks, imagine what impact it is having on national governments that are not strongly committed to their policy agenda.

The road to European economic union, it has been observed, "will be paid with regional money."[47] But, as nation states line up to get their shares of the EEC regional development money, they will lose the ability to plan and implement in relative isolation regional development programs and even specific projects. Regional targets are set, priority areas are established and administrative processes are designed to guide the spending of EEC funds. Regional groups will be guide to argue—as many already have—that there is too much insensitive and remote bureaucracies from Brussels and London involved—

in the case of Britain—for regional development measures to have any chance of success. Commission officials are now reporting that regional strategies must be formulated locally "where people know the problem best" to have greater chances of success.[48] The question that comes to mind is—if Brussels has the funds and plans are to be developed locally where does the nation state and its national government fit in the schemes of things?

Notes

1. See Niles Hansen, Benjamin Higgins and Donald J. Savoie, *Regional Policy in a Changing World* (New York: Plenum Press, 1990).
2. G.C. Cameron, "Regional Policy in the United Kingdom," in Niles M. Hansen (ed.), *Public Policy and Regional Economic Development: The Experience of Nine Western Countries* (Cambridge, Mass.: Ballinger Publishing Company, 1974), p. 65.
3. John K. Galbraith, *Economics in Perspective: A Critical History* (Boston: Houghton Mifflin Co., 1987), p. 89.
4. See, for example, Eric Roll, *A History of Economic Thought* (New York: Prentice-Hall, 1942), p. 156.
5. Galbraith, *Economics in Perspective*, p. 73.
6. *Ibid.*, chapters IX–XVI.
7. John Maynard Keynes, *The General Theory of Employment Interest and Money* (New York: Harcourt, Bruce, 1936).
8. Cameron, "Regional Policy in the United Kingdom," p. 91–4.
9. D.W. Parsons, *The Political Economy of British Regional Policy* (London: Croom Helm, 1986), p. 51.
10. Gavin McCrone, *Regional Policy in Britain* (London: Georges Allen & Unwin, 1969), p. 114.
11. *Ibid.*, p. 113.
12. The Committee of Enquiry Under the Chairmanship of Sir J. Hunt, "The Intermediate Areas," Cmmd 3995, HMSO, 1969.
13. Parsons, *Political Economy of British Regional Policy*, p. 101.
14. Quoted in ibid., p. 99.
15. See House of Commons Debates, *Hansard*, 30 October 1952, col. 1090.
16. See, among others, Parsons, *Political Economy of British Regional Policy*, p. 146.
17. *The North-East: A Programme for Regional Development and Growth*, CMBD 2206, HMSO, 1963.
18. See H. Wilson, *The New Britain: Labour's Plan Outlined by Harold Wilson* (Penguin: Harmondsworth, 1964).
19. J. Jones, "An Examination of the Thinking Behind Government Regional Policy in the UK Since 1945," *Regional Studies*, vol. 20, no. 3, p. 263.
20. See, among others, J. Levrez, *Economic Planning and Politics in Britain* (London: Martin Robertson, 1975).
21. See *The Development Areas: A Proposal for a Regional Premium* (London: D.E.A., April, 1967).
22. Parsons, *Political Economy of British Regional Policy*, p. 217.
23. House of Commons Debates, *Hansard* (14 April 1969, cols. 548–553).
24. See, for example, *Investment Incentives* CMBD 4516, HMSO, 1970.

25. Parsons, *Political Economy of British Regional Policy*, p. 241.
26. For a detailed review of regional incentives in Britain, see Douglas Yuill and Kevin Allen (eds.), *European Regional Incentives: 1980* (Glasgow: Centre for the Study of Public Policy, University of Strathclyde, 1980), pp. 329-67.
27. See Stuart Holland, *Capital versus the Regions* (London: Macmillan, 1976), pp. 249-54. See also Parsons, *Political Economy of British Regional Policy*, p. 244.
28. Parsons, *Political Economy of British Regional Policy*. p. 250.
29. *Ibid.*, p. 246.
30. J.D. McCallum, "The Development of British Regional Policy," in D.M. MacLennon and J.B. Parr (eds.), *Regional Policy Past Experience and New Directions* (Oxford: Martin Robertson, 1979), p. 38.
31. See, among others, L. Pliatzky, *Getting and Spending* (Oxford: Basil Blackwell, 1982), passim.
32. See, Peter Hennessy, *Whitehall* (London: Fontana Press, 1989), p. 592.
33. Consultations with Sir Alan Walters in Brasilia, Brazil, 10-12 June 1992.
34. *Regional Industrial Development*, Cmmd 9111, HMSO, 1983, p. 4.
35. *Ibid.*, p. 3.
36. Regional Industrial Policy, *Press Notice*, Department of Trade and Industry, reference 681, 28 November 1984, p. 2.
37. *Ibid.*
38. *Ibid.*, p. 3
39. Parsons, *Political Economy of British Regional Policy*, p. 254. It should be noted, however, that the government did announce a $300 million cut in regional programming.
40. House of Commons Debates, *Hansard*, (28 November 1984, col. 947).
41. See *Invest in Britain Bureau* (Kingsgate House, London, Investment Brief no. 21/80, August 1980).
42. *The Times* (London), 28 November 1984, p. 13.
43. Parsons, *Political Economy of British Regional Policy*, p. 261.
44. *Regional Industrial Development*, Cmmd 9111, HMSO, 1983, p. 6.
45. *The New Structural Policies of the European Community*, Commission of the European Community (Brussels, June-July 1990), p. 3.
46. "Regional Policy in Europe of the 1990s," opening address by Bruce Milan to the International Congress on Regional Policy (Madrid, 30-31 May 1989), p. 11.
47. Geoffrey Edwards of London's Royal Institute of International Affairs quoted in *International Management—The Voice of European Business*, vol. 46, no. 7 (September 1991) an issue on "Sustaining Europe's poorer regions," p. 44.
48. *Ibid.* In addition consultations between Donald J. Savoie and senior officials with the British government, May 1992, London.

16

Canada

Among the countries currently classified by the United Nations as "industrialized market economies," Canada is surely one of the most highly regionalized and its economy is accordingly one of the most badly fragmented. Toronto is one of the world's leading economic hot spots. Some 1,000 kilometres to the east, however, there are communities that suffer from extremely high unemployment, low earned per capita income and low productivity. A number of communities in Canada's North are underdeveloped by any standards, with their economies resembling those of less developed countries (LDCs). Canadian politicians have realized this fact intuitively for some time and national economic policy has been to some extent regionalized.[1] The Canadian government has over the past forty years introduced a wide array of regional development measures. Some of these include revenue sharing schemes with the provinces, regional industrial incentives programs and efforts to tailor national policies and programs to meet regional economic circumstances and conditions.

Canadians have imported both regional development theories and policy prescriptions from abroad. The Canadian public policy literature, for example, frequently refers to the growth pole theory, regional science and regional comparative advantages. Canadians have also contributed to regional development theories either by adopting international theories or by bringing forward original thinking on regional and economic development problems.[2]

Theories of Regional Development: Canadian and Imported

Well known Canadian economic historian, Harold Innis, rejected any thinking that suggested universal applicability. He argued that any theory could only be formulated on the basis of a thorough analysis of a given situation. He maintained that theories developed in, say, Europe could hardly apply very well in Canada given its distinct historical, political and economic development.[3]

Yet Innis developed a staples theory of economic development which his associates subsequently refined. He argued that Canada's development was shaped by the export of "staples" to the heartlands of Europe and the United States, insisting that: "Concentration on the production of staples for exports to more highly industrialised areas in Europe and later in the United States has broad implications for the Canadian economic, political, and social structure. Each staple in its turn left its stamp, and the shift to new staples invariably produced periods of crisis in which adjustments in the old structures were painfully made and a new pattern created in relation to a new staple.[4]

The staples theory applied very well to the Canadian setting. Indeed, the premise of this theory is that Canada's poorer regions were at one time prosperous, which, in fact, explains why they were populated in the first place. The staple that gave rise to this prosperity began to decline in importance, either because it was exploited, because of changes in world demand, or because of competition from lower-cost producers elsewhere. This in turn led the way to a decline in the region's fortunes. This theory has a strong appeal, if only because it appears to be a succinct explanation of Canada's economic history. New Brunswick's forest industry, for example, accounted for that province's prosperity at the turn of the twentieth century. With the decline of the forest sector, New Brunswick's economic prosperity also took a downward turn. More recently, Alberta's economic strength, which became evident in the 1970s, was due in large measure to its oil and gas reserves. In short, once marketable resources are discovered, an inflow of capital and firms will follow. This in turn brings higher incomes and a growing labour demand. Once the resources are depleted or no longer marketable, however, capital leaves the area. As a result, income falls, and the more mobile sector of the labour force also leaves. Labour out-migration is excluded as a cure, stimulating production of other marketable products through subsidization becomes a viable alternative. Alternatively, transport costs may be subsidized. The important point is that if growth is to be sustained after staple exports decline, a shift in resources into more diversified economic activities will be required.

In short then, the economic fortunes of a region, according to the staples theory, depend on the availability and marketability of its natural resources. On the face of it, the theory seems to explain the changing economic fate of the Atlantic provinces. But it does not appear to explain the high unemployment rate in British Columbia, an area richly endowed with marketable resources.

By the 1940s and 50s, several scholars looked to the work of Innis and began to study Canada's resource-dependent economy from different perspectives. One looked at resource development and its impact on provincial economies, another on foreign investments and yet another on government planning for economic development.[5] Yet by the 1960s the theory was being challenged on a number of fronts. For one thing, the sweeping historical generalizations were being subjected to empirical scrutiny. The Economic Council of Canada, for instance, argued that "the absence of resources in Switzerland does not prevent economic access, and their presence in Argentina does not guarantee it."[6] For another, the theory itself was being undermined by new approaches and methodologies in social sciences, including behavioral and systems approaches.[7] In any event, Perroux's growth pole concept became the new fad in the economic development literature in Canada as it did elsewhere.

Indeed, several students of economic development tried to apply Perroux's growth pole concept to Canada not long after it appeared. The HMR study, for example, sought to define a new economic development strategy for the Quebec region by looking to the growth pole concept.[8] The report attracted a good deal of attention not only in Quebec but also in the rest of Canada and in Europe. The authors wrote the report when interest in growth poles was at its height internationally. They sought to identify cities in Quebec other than Montreal to act as "development poles." They concluded, however, that rather than try to identify new cities to develop as growth poles, further efforts to promote economic development in Montreal were required. Montreal, it was argued, was the key growth pole for Quebec and yet its economic strength was waning. It made little sense, the authors argued, to go looking for new growth poles when the province's key economic engine was ailing.

Students and increasingly practitioners of economic development in other provinces also began a search for growth poles for their own regions.[9] During the late 60s, few students or practitioners were questioning the wisdom of the growth pole approach. Conferences and seminars on the approach were held in many Canadian universities and regions within provinces were busy identifying communities to serve as their growth poles.

Under the title *Living Together*, the Economic Council of Canada produced an ambitious study on regional disparities in Canada. The study reviews theories of regional disparities, including the staples approach, the development approach, the neoclassical approach, the Keynesian approach, and the regional science approach. The authors find none of these approaches totally satisfactory. One senses, however, an underlying faith in neoclassical economics. One also senses that the authors regard the persistence of regional disparities as an affront to economic science. Thus Chapter 4, on "The Anatomy of the Problem," begins with a side heading, "Do regional disparities exists?" The team tried very hard to make the problem go away. For one thing, they offer several alternative measures of regional income disparities; if one looks at average family disposable income, for example, the range was only from 9 percent above the national average for Ontario to 26 percent below the national average in Newfoundland. Quebec's average family disposable income was only

2 percent below the national average.[10] If these figures were the measure of the problem of regional disparities, one might ask, "What is all the fuss about"?

The council argued that the main explanation of differences in per capita output and income among Canadian regions lies in differences in productivity in given occupations. Differences in structure of output and employment were accorded a relatively minor role. The council added that aggregate demand and urban structure also explain the existence of regional disparities in Canada.

Turning to policy, the authors express their preference for non-discriminatory monetary and fiscal policies, with some degree of regionalization of these policies, to any kind of federal policy that would deliberately discriminate in favour of people in some regions and against people in others. They find that fiscal policy does have a differential impact by region. Ontario, the country's richest region, benefits most during periods of fiscal ease, but is also most affected by a tightening of fiscal policy. The poorest region—Atlantic Canada— neither benefits greatly during a period of fiscal ease nor suffers much during periods of fiscal tightness. Quebec and the Prairies fall somewhere between Ontario and the Atlantic region, while British Columbia "exhibits the most erratic behaviour."[11]

The authors offer some mild criticism of neoclassical theory: the criticism is limited to pointing out that the neoclassical theory does not deal effectively with distance and geographical dispersion, that international trade theory offers but limited help, that location theory has remained highly formal, and that "while it is useful to know that properly functioning relative prices and free mobility of factors may be helpful in curing a region's problems, it is more useful to know why some regions' problems persist so long, despite equilibrating market forces."[12] They also note that for residents of a region, outmigration is regarded more as a problem than as a solution. Nonetheless, there is throughout the study an underlying theme that market forces and mobility of factors of production *ought* to be able to eliminate regional disparities.

Notwithstanding the council's criticism, the neoclassical theory came in fashion in the early 1980s to explain Canada's regional disparities. One of its main proponents, Thomas Courchene, argued that Canada approached regional policy with "a concept of gap closing rather than a policy of adjustment accommodation. We see disparity out there...and we rush to remove it with one set of funds or another rather than letting it adjust itself on its own."[13] Courchene's argument has been vigorously debated among Canadian academics and policy makers over the past ten years. Increasingly, one hears the view that a strong reliance on government transfer payments makes a region dependent on these to support current levels of consumption and services, which are much higher than can be sustained by the economic output of the region. It is this dependence that in the end serves to blunt or sterilize the required long-term adjustment that would bring production and consumption back into line.

The notion of dependency in regional development goes beyond what the neoclassical approach labels "transfer dependency." As we saw in Part I, others talk of a theory that attributes dependency "to the systematic draining of capital and resources from one region by other regions."[14] Ralph Matthews, a Canadian sociologist, contends that "dependency theorists can legitimately argue that the eastern regions of Canada would not need today's transfer payments if they had not earlier been drained of their wealth."[15]

Clearly, though both the proponents of the neoclassical approach and the dependency theorists talk about dependency, they do not share the same perspective. The neoclassicists would like to see "natural" economic adjustments come into play to solve regional disparities. These adjustments would include a lowering of the minimum wage in slow-growth regions, a gradual reduction in federal transfer payments, and outmigration of workers or surplus labour so that the region can return to its natural balance. The dependency theorists argue the opposite. They contend, for example, that outmigration is simply a continuation of the "systematic draining" of resources from one region by other regions.[16]

Dependency theorists also argue that governments and international economic forces, notably the multinationals, have made local communities and small entrepreneurs dependent on forces that they cannot control. Rather than providing a setting in which local initiatives can be defined and carried out, the "system" does the opposite. Major economic decisions are taken in Washington, New York, and Detroit, and new economic plans and possible initiatives are defined in far-away Ottawa, in provincial capitals, or worse still, in countless federal-provincial committees of officials that are often hardly visible to those outside government. Regional economic plans are formulated by officials, it is suggested, and local communities are expected to comply with what they come up with, on the assumption that it is obviously in their best economic interests to do so.

One of Canada's leading economist, Richard Lipsey argues that "for all the concern about regional area development and regional problems in Canada, we don't really have an underlying theory. We don't know what we would have to do, what are the conditions under which this would be regional equality, however we define equality."[17] With very few exceptions, even the staunchest supporters of any one theory will readily admit that the theory only explains part of the situation and that it needs to be complemented by another theory or that more work is required on the theory itself. Several approaches are not completely different or even opposing theories. They often have complementary perspectives. Staples theory for example, is a Canadian variant of export base theory, which is coherent with neoclassical reasoning and even growth pole theory.

In an uncharacteristic fashion, the Economic Council of Canada summed up the situation this way: "Doctors used to try to cure syphilis with mercury and emetics. We now know that mercury works but emetics do not and, moreover, that penicillin is best of all. We suspect that the regional disparity disease is presently being treated with both mercury- and emetic-type remedies, but we do not know which is which. Perhaps one day an economic penicillin will be found."[18] The Economic Council did not discover such an economic penicillin, nor has one been discovered to date.

Regional Development Policies and Programs: The Canadian Experience

During the period from Confederation (1867) to the mid-1950s, the federal government had no explicit policy of regional development. It directed its economic policy essentially toward the development of the national economy. The prevailing belief was that a strong national economy, based on east-west trade, would benefit all regions.

Still problems in the fiscal capacities of some provinces started to manifest themselves shortly after Confederation. Ottawa made a number of special and even supposedly final federal subsidies and grants to the provinces. In the 1920s it established a royal commission to look into the financial difficulties of the Maritime provinces. The commission recommended special grants to assist the Maritime provincial governments with their budget deficits and based this proposal on the need for greater equality among the provinces.[19] But, here again, the federal government's concern was not so much with the pace of regional activity as it was with a specific problem— government deficits in the Maritime provinces. In short, the principal motivation behind national economic policy remained growth, not regional balance in the country's economic growth.

Only after the Second World War did the federal government show greater concern for a regional balance in economic activity. Shortly after the war, the Federal Department of Reconstruction called a Dominion-Provincial Conference of Reconstruction. The federal government's submission revealed a total faith in Keynesian public works planning and in the need for federal control over fiscal policy.[20] The federal government offered generous subsidies to provincial governments for planning and implementing public works, provided that the provinces agreed to place fully planned projects into a reserve or "shelf" to be implemented at a time to be designated by the federal government. For a variety of reasons, including continuing prosperity, little came of Ottawa's plan.

What brought the federal government to recognize regional economic imbalances was the fiscal weakness of the poorer provinces. In a very harsh manner, the depression years had revealed this weakness. The Rowell-Sirois Commission had been established in 1937 to re-examine "the economic and financial basis of Confederation and the distribution of legislative powers in the light of the economic and social developments of the last seventy years." Essentially pessimistic about the capacity of governments to work together efficiently in joint activities, the commission had favoured a clear delimitation of power. It had concluded that the Canadian fiscal system should enable every province to provide an acceptable standard of services, without having to impose a heavier-than-average tax burden. It had recommended a strengthening of the federal government's economic powers and a series of national grants to the poorer provinces so that they could offer public services broadly equivalent to those in the richer provinces.[21]

Two decades later, in 1957, the federal government set up the fiscal equalization program. It was intended to reduce disparities between regions, to achieve a national standard in public services, and at the same time to equalize provincial-government revenues. Ottawa thus undertook to ensure that all provinces would have revenues sufficient to offer an acceptable level of public services. Payments under the equalization schemes were and are unconditional, and eligible provinces need not spend the resources on economic development.[22] The payments help poorer provinces provide services, but do not necessarily assist them in integrating their economies more successfully into the national economy and in supporting regional growth from within.

Another royal commission was to come forward with suggestions about establishing special development plans. The Royal Commission on Canada's Economic Prospects (the Gordon Commission) reported in 1957 that "a bold and comprehensive and coordinated approach" was needed to resolve the underlying problems of the Atlantic region, which required special measures to improve its economic framework. Those measures included a federally sponsored capital-project commission to provide needed infrastructure facilities to encourage economic growth. The commission called also for measures to increase the rate of capital investment in the region. In many ways the commission was breaking new ground in advocating special measures to involve the private sector in promoting development in slow-growth regions. Perhaps for this reason the commission remained cautious in its recommendations. It argued: "Special assistance put into effect to assist these areas might well adversely affect the welfare of industries already functioning in most established areas of Canada."[23]

The 1960 budget speech unveiled the first of many measures Ottawa has developed to combat regional disparities. The budget permitted firms to obtain double the normal rate of capital-cost allowances on most of the assets they acquired to produce new products—if they located in designated regions (with high unemployment and slow economic growth).[24] Shortly after this measure was introduced, Parliament passed the Agriculture Rehabilitation and Development Act (ARDA). It was an attempt to rebuild the depressed rural economy and represented Ottawa's first "regional" development program. Later, in 1966, the program was renamed the Agricultural and Rural Development Act, and its objectives were adjusted. ARDA was expanded to include non-agricultural programs in rural areas, designed to absorb surplus labour from farming. Thus, reducing rural poverty became ARDA's overriding objective.[25]

The federal government introduced the Fund for Rural Economic Development (FRED) in 1966, another program designed to assist rural areas.[26] The program could be applied only in designated regions, with widespread low incomes and major problems of economic adjustment. In the end, five regions were identified under FRED: the Interlake region of Manitoba, the Gaspé peninsula in Quebec, the Mactaquac and northeastern regions of New Brunswick, and all of Prince Edward Island. Separate "comprehensive development plans" were then formulated for those five regions to develop infrastructure and industry.

The federal government introduced in 1962 yet another development initiative—the Atlantic Development Board (ADB).[27] Unlike other regional development programs, this board would be active only in the four Atlantic provinces, as its name implied. Largely inspired by the Gordon Commission, the ADB was initially asked to define measures and initiatives for promoting economic growth and development in the Atlantic region. A planning staff was put together, mainly from within the federal public service. Considerable research was undertaken on the various sectors of the regional economy, and some consultations were held with planners at the provincial level.

Shortly after its creation, the board was given an Atlantic Development Fund to administer. By and large, the fund was employed to assist in the provision or improvement of the region's basic economic infrastructure. Over half of the fund, which totalled $186 million, was spent on highway construction and water and sewerage systems. Some money was spent on electrical generating and transmission facilities and in servicing new industrial parks at various locations throughout the region. The fund did not provide direct assistance of any kind to private industry to locate new firms in the region.

The federal government did, however, introduce in 1963, measures such as the Area Development Incentives Act (ADIA) and the Area Development Agency (ADA), designed to encourage the private sector to stimulate growth in economically depressed regions. This was to be done by enriching existing tax incentives and by introducing capital grants in designated areas.[28]

Regions of high unemployment and slow growth were the target of these measures. Only regions reporting unemployment rates above a specified threshold level would become eligible. Manufacturing and processing firms were then invited to locate or expand operations in these regions. Three kinds of incentives were applied sequentially: accelerated capital-cost allowances, a three-year income-tax exemption, and higher capital-cost allowances. In 1965, a program of cash grants was introduced over and above the capital-cost allowances. Assistance was provided automatically on a formula basis.

With the election of the Pierre Trudeau government in 1968, Canada would see a much stronger emphasis on regional development policy. Throughout the 1968 election campaign, Trudeau himself stressed time and again the importance of regional development to national unity. He went so far as to suggest that the problem of regional development was as threatening to national unity as the language issue and English-French relations.[29] In fact, he saw the two as somewhat interwoven, in that regions which were predominantly francophone were also economically underdeveloped.

Once elected, he moved quickly to establish a new department with specific responsibilities for regional development—the Department of Regional Economic Expansion (DREE). Because of its high priority status, funding for regional development initiatives "was never a problem in DREE's early years."[30] DREE integrated the various regional development programs administered by several departments and agencies and introduced two new major ones.

Underpinning the very purpose of these two new programs was the "growth pole" concept. Senior DREE officials publicly embraced the concept and came forward with a "special areas" program and one for "regional industrial incentives." The two programs shared the same objective—to encourage manufacturing and processing industries in selected communities within slow-growth regions having growth potential.[31]

Specifically, the following would take place. Industrial centres with the potential for attracting manufacturing and processing firms would be identified. A special area agreement with the relevant provincial government would then be signed. This would provide for the construction of the required infrastructure, such as roads, water and sewer systems, and schools, thus laying the framework within which industrial growth could occur. The thinking here was that the industrial framework and the physical infrastructure in slow-growth regions were as unresponsive and stagnant as the state of industrial activity.

The second program, one that remained important throughout the life of DREE, was a regional incentives program. This provided grants to companies calculated on the basis of new jobs created in a designated region and on capital cost of the new or expanded plant. Later, a loan guarantee program was added to the regional incentives scheme.

Only a few years after the two programs were introduced, however, DREE came under persistent attack on at least one program—the special areas program. Provincial governments in particular argued that the program was highly discriminatory in that it favoured certain communities over others. More important, the provinces were highly critical of DREE's approach to federal-provincial relations. Ottawa, provincial governments insisted, had adopted a "take-it-or-leave it" approach to federal-provincial relations in the area of regional development that made close federal-provincial cooperation impossible.[32]

A major policy review of regional development policy was launched. Concluded in late 1972, the review argued that the special areas program had too narrow a focus and did not lend itself to new and imaginative ways of pursuing development opportunities; and second, that federal regional development programming had to be pursued in close harmony with provincial governments.[33]

The review gave rise to the General Development Agreement (GDA) and to the decentralization of DREE. GDAs were broad enabling documents that permitted the federal government and individual provincial governments to sponsor a variety of projects under individually negotiated subsidiary agreements.[34] These subsidiary agreements could be province wide in scope, concentrate solely on a specific subprovincial area, an economic sector, or even a single industry.

Provincial governments grew particularly fond of the GDAs. They applauded their flexibility and the kind of cooperation that they promoted. They had strong reasons to do so. An opportunity presented itself in Halifax with the possible development of a world-class dry dock facility. DREE and the province simply got together and signed an agreement, and the project went ahead. No program limits existed to restrict activities. Criticism of GDA approach, however, was frequently heard in Ottawa. From an Ottawa perspective, not one of the GDAs pointed to an overall development strategy. Senior public servants felt that provincial governments employed the GDA to secure federal government funds for whatever project they wanted.

At the political level in Ottawa, it was fast becoming obvious that cabinet ministers and government members of Parliament were less than enthusiastic about the GDA approach. Essentially, they regarded it as an instrument substantially financed with federal funds but clearly favouring the political profile of provincial governments. Even Pierre DeBané, the new minister of DREE appointed in 1980, suggested publicly that: [he] would be surprised if 10 percent of Canadians are aware that DREE grants to business account for only 20 percent of the department's budget, the rest going to the provinces.[35]

These forces led the federal government to launch a second major review of its regional development policy. This review revealed that the regional balance in the national economy was changing and that now both problems and opportunities existed in all regions. To deal with this development, the review recommended that regional economic development concerns should be central to public policy planning at the federal level. A key element of the review was federal-provincial relations. On this point, the review stressed the importance of close federal cooperation but stated that "joint implementation of economic development programming [i.e., DREE's GDA approach] may not always be desirable."[36] Direct federal delivery of regional development initiatives should be preferred in a number of situations.

Shortly after the policy review was completed in early 1982, the then prime minister, Pierre Trudeau, unveiled a major reorganization of the federal government. DREE would be disbanded, the GDAs would be replaced by a new and simpler set of federal-provincial agreements that would enable the federal government to deliver projects directly rather than having to go through the provinces, a new central agency charged with the responsibility of ensuring that regional development concerns would be central to decision making in Ottawa was to be established, and a regional fund would be set up. DREE, the prime minister explained, had not been able to launch a sustained effort at promoting regional development. As a simple line department, it had been incapable of directing the departments to contribute to Ottawa's overall regional development policy. A new central agency, the Ministry of State for Economic and Regional Development (MSERD), would now be able to ensure a "governmentwide" focus on regional development, thus strengthening Ottawa's commitment to regional development, and a new line department, the Department of Regional Industrial Expansion (DRIE), would deliver regional and industrial development programs.[37]

During the 1984 election campaign, Brian Mulroney pledged to strengthen Canada's regional policy. Shortly after he came to office, his government adjusted regional development programs. By 1986, however, the government concluded that new adjustments would not suffice and sweeping changes were required. Provincial governments, in particular those in slow-growth regions, had become highly critical of Ottawa's approach.

In response to the criticism, Mulroney announced the establishment of new regional development agencies—one for Atlantic Canada, one for Western Canada and another for Northern Ontario. Quebec was also given a substantial regional development budget through the Department of Industry, Science and Technology.

The agencies have federal-provincial agreements modelled somewhat on the GDA approach. These agreements can be tailored to sponsor a variety of measures. The most important emphasis, however, is on entrepreneurship which constitutes the central feature of the Mulroney government's approach to regional development. New programs, and the bulk of the resources available in the three agencies, depend primarily on the private sector and on promoting entrepreneurial development.

The Mulroney government unveiled the three agencies a little over a year before it called its first general election. There was strong pressure on all three agencies to get new programs in place quickly. All three looked at adapting existing government programs rather than launch new ones. The Atlantic Canada Opportunities Agency (ACOA) turned to the Atlantic Enterprise Program (AEP) and introduced a number of changes to make it more flexible. It also relabelled the program—the Action program. The changes enabled ACOA to provide contributions for a broad range of manufacturing, processing and repair and maintenance facilities. They also raised the maximum level of government support to 75% for commercial operations and 100% for non-commercial ones and to make cash assistance available toward eligible costs for business establishment, new product expansion, modernization and expansion, for marketing and the development of business plans, feasibility studies, venture capital search and the hiring of qualified personnel to implement a marketing plan.[38]

The basic tests applied by ACOA in reviewing applications under its Action program are fairly straightforward. It first assesses a project's commercial viability to determine whether it has a reasonable chance of success. It then looks to see whether the project will result in economic benefit for Atlantic Canada and, finally, it reviews the need for assistance for the project to proceed.[39]

The program's ability to support virtually any kind of initiative no doubt explains its success with the region's business community. The agency reported after only a little more than a year that the Action program had generated more applications than any previous regional development programs over an eighteen month period. The agency had processed 6,800 applications and approved 2,700 projects under the Action program.[40]

The agency also sought to "update" federal-provincial agreements for regional development. The GDA approach had been updated, it will be recalled, in the early 1980s to provide for direct federal government delivery of some projects if only to strengthen the visibility of the federal government in the field. ACOA would leave the format unchanged but would seek to "focus" new agreements to strengthen the private sector and to improve the ability of entrepreneurs to develop, adapt and commercially exploit new technologies.[41]

The Western Development Department (WD) also turned to an existing program to prepare its policy and program structure. The federal government had introduced in 1983 a Western Transportation Industrial Development (WTID) program to diversify the region's economy. The new agency concluded that the program had been effective and recommended it be amended to launch the new Western initiative. The government agreed to a number of changes all of which were designed to give the agency "maximum flexibility."[42] Maximum levels of government assistance went up from 50 to 75 percent of eligible costs of projects and virtually every sector, including the service sector, became eligible for assistance. In turn, the agency insisted that its assistance to the private sector be in the form of repayable contribution and that a number of guidelines overseeing the program's approval process. It established a list of ineligible activities, including projects whose purpose is to sustain an existing business (e.g., bail out), projects that were eligible for another government programs and projects to assist the commercial operations of financial institutions.[43] WD, like ACOA, reported early on that its programs—the Western Diversification Program—was having considerable success. By the end of June 1990, the department had approved a total of 1,827 projects involving nearly $800 million of government funding.[44]

WD proved much less enthusiastic about continuing federal-provincial agreements for regional development than ACOA. By the summer of 1990, WD had yet to sign one new agreement with any of the four Western provinces. WD officials argued that the Western provinces were sufficiently wealthy to put in place their own regional development programs without federal assistance and that other federal government departments should also turn to their own programs to promote development in the region. The federal government rejected this argument, with ministers from Western Canada pointing out that if the federal government was going to sign agreements with the Atlantic and the two large central provinces, then it should also do so with Western provinces.[45]

FEDNOR (Federal Economic Development Northern Ontario) launched two new programs designed to assist small business and entrepreneurs. The agency borrowed from earlier federal and provincial incentives programs to develop the two programs. The programs provide assistance for new buildings, machinery, research and development, feasibility studies and market research.[46] Parts of the assistance are also non repayable.

The Department of Industry, Science and Technology (DIST), established by the Mulroney government at the same time the agencies, was made responsible for regional development in Ontario and Quebec. Part of DRIE's legislative mandate gives the department the kind of authority for regional development in Ontario and Quebec that ACOA and WD have for the Atlantic provinces and the West. It gives DIST the authority to "promote economic development in areas of Ontario and Quebec where low incomes and slow economic growth are prevalent or where opportunities for productive employment are inadequate" and to "formulate and implement policies, plans and integrated federal approaches to regional economic development in Ontario and Quebec."[47] Much as it did in the case of ACOA and WD, Parliament also gave DIST full authority to "coordinate the policies and programs of the government of Canada in relation to opportunities for regional economic development in Ontario and Quebec; and to lead and coordinate the activities of the government of Canada in the establishment of cooperative relationships with Ontario and Quebec and with business, labour and other public and private bodies in relation to regional economic development in Ontario and Quebec.[48] The legislation also points to developing "entrepreneurship...(and) promoting small- and medium-sized enterprises" as the proper vehicle to promote regional development.

DIST also has in place incentives programs for the private sector to launch new economic activities or to expand and modernize existing ones. In addition, the department has signed federal-provincial agreements to promote regional development. In the case of Quebec, the agreement represents by far the most important programs. The federal government signed a five-year $820 million agreement with the Quebec government in 1988 to develop the province's regions. Ottawa agreed to contribute $440 million and Quebec $380 million. The funding was increased by an additional $283 million in 1989. The agreement divides Quebec's regions into two broad categories; the central regions and the peripheral or resource regions. The central regions were awarded a larger share of the funds—$486 million. The resource regions consist of eastern Quebec (e.g., Bas-St-Laurent, Gaspésie), the North-Shore, the North-Centre (e.g., Lac St-Jean), the western region (e.g., Rouyn-Noranda), and the northern region (e.g., Abitibi). The central regions cover the rest of Quebec so that all of the province is covered.[49] The programs under the agreement are all-encompassing. Indeed, it is difficult to imagine many types of economic activities that would not qualify. Assistance is provided for business development; productivity improvement; an agri-food strategy; studies, including feasibility studies; tourism development; research and technological development; aquaculture development; more efficient resource-management operations; infrastructure development; services for industrial and tourism development; and human-resources development.[50]

Looking Back

Keynesian economics, probably more than anything else, gave rise to regional development programs in Canada. As it did in many countries, Keynesian economics captured the Canadian treasury. Canadian policy makers came out of the depression and the war years determined to attenuate the lows in economic cycles and to soften the sting of economic misfortune. Keynesian logic provided a solid rationale for government to intervene in the economy. But if the national economy was to be healthy, not only was there a need to avoid dramatic swings of inflation and unemployment in the economy, it was also important to strike a national balance so that some regions would not have continuing high levels of unemployment while others had to deal continually with overheated economics. Such thinking began to surface in academic circles in the late 1930s, later in one royal commission or another and still later in government circles. One can easily trace the evaluation of Canadian regional development to these developments.

From modest beginnings, Canadian regional development efforts became more and more ambitious over the years. The early Trudeau years, in particular, saw a strong priority given to regional development policy. There was also some theoretical underpinnings at play here with Canada seeking to apply the growth pole concept to its regional development planning. The federal government limited the number of communities designated as special areas which it considered vital to the success of the approach. Substantial amounts of public funds were quickly committed by the federal government and the provinces to spur economic development in selected urban areas. Yet only a few years after its introduction, the growth-pole approach was rejected outright. This rather sudden rejection was based not so much on empirical evidence as on an intuitive belief that something else, a new approach, would be much better. The growth-pole concept was "too narrow" and "too restricted" for Canada. In any event, politicians from economically-depressed rural areas came to challenge Ottawa's approach arguing that regional development funds were being allocated to relatively healthy urban areas and not to the more economically deserving ones.

The growth pole strategy gave way to the "comprehensive" GDA approach, which in turn gave way to other equally comprehensive federal-provincial agreements. Putting aside the issue of political visibility, the various agreements have offered little that is new in terms of regional development programs. Like the GDAs, subsequent federal-provincial agreements in the regional development field are essentially enabling instruments for governments to "cost-share" projects or put in place special measures under the broad label of regional development. Governments in Canada have described this process as a "pursuit of development opportunities."

It is difficult to discern the theoretical framework behind past and present GDA, ERDA (Economic and Regional Development Agreement), and Cooperation programs. The variety of projects sponsored is so wide that no conceivable theory could possibly cover all initiatives. Indeed, the various federal-provincial agreements for regional development do not even provide a proper checklist against which new proposals can be tested.

What now drives Canadian regional development policy is more a profound sense of regional grievance tied to a "discourse of entitlement" than a solid theoretical foundation.[51] Public opinion surveys reveal that "Sixty-four per cent of Canadians feel their province gets back less in federal spending than the taxes sent to Ottawa. Nearly three quarters of Canadians feel that the federal government favours one region of Canada over the others, and very few feel that their region is the one favoured."[52] This constant regional competition for federal dollars has given rise to "the Canadian disease"—the politics of regional envy. Canadian regional development policy has been over time "pushed and pulled" to cover virtually every area and community of the country. Trudeau's first regional development minister, Jean Marchand, could argue that if at least 80 percent of federal government spending for regional development was not spent east of Trois-Rivières, then Ottawa's regional development efforts would fail. One no longer hears this line of argument. Indeed, during the 1980s, the rest of Canada has caught up to Atlantic Canada in the level of business assistance the federal government provided. Outside the Atlantic region, business assistance per capita more than doubled to $252 between 1980 and 1987, while it fell to $133 in Atlantic Canada.

The situation is now such that one of ACOA's main concerns in early 1991 was that its Action program was "uncompetitive" with federal assistance offered to the private sector in other regions. The Action program has to compete with attractive federally-funded "regional development" incentive programs available in Quebec, parts of Ontario, and western Canada.

But this only tells part of the story. ERDA agreements, WD in the West, FEDNOR in northern Ontario, DIST in Ontario and Quebec, ACOA in Atlantic Canada, and tax incentives now make billions of dollars available annually everywhere in the country to an array of projects in the name of regional development. Indeed, few projects anywhere are ineligible for funding. If nothing else, this has given regional development a "bad reputation" and many would argue that it has become the main impetus to the "Canadian disease"— regional envy. Economic development theories, particularly prescriptive ones, have little chance of being relevant in this scheme of things.

Notes

1. See Donald J. Savoie, *Regional Economic Development: Canada's Search for Solutions* (Toronto: University of Toronto Press, 1992).
2. Clyde Weaver and Thomas I. Gunton, "From Drought Assistance to Megaprojects: Fifty Years of Regional Theory and Policy in Canada," *The Canadian Journal of Regional Science*, vol. 1, no. 1 (Spring 1982).
3. Harold A. Innis, *For Trade in Canada: An Introduction to Canadian Economic History* (Toronto: University of Toronto Press, 1956), p. 358.
4. *Ibid.*

5. See, among others, W.T. Easterbrook, "Recent Contributions to Economic History: Canada," *Journal of Economic History*, vol. 19, 1959, pp. 76-102; and John H. Dales, *Hydro Electricity and Industrial Development in Quebec, 1898-1940* (Cambridge, Mass.: Harvard University Press, 1957).
6. *Living Together* (Ottawa: Economic Council of Canada, 1977), pp. 24-5.
7. See, for example, David Easton, *A Systems Analysis of Political Life* (New York: Wiley, 1965).
8. Benjamin Higgins, Fernand Martin, and André Raynauld, Les orientations du développement économique régional de la province du Québec (Ottawa, DREE, 1970).
9. See, for example, Savoie, *Regional Economic Development*.
10. *Living Together*, Chapter 4.
11. *Ibid.*, p. 103.
12. *Ibid.*, p. 27.
13. Thomas J. Courchene, "A Market Perspective on Regional Disparities," *Canadian Public Policy*, vol. 7, no. 4 (Fall 1981), p. 515.
14. Ralph Matthews, *The Creation of Regional Dependency* (Toronto: University of Toronto Press, 1983), p. 75.
15. *Ibid.*
16. *Ibid.* Matthews also suggests that "dependency theory sees migrants as the victims of an exploitative economic system," p. 76.
17. Quoted in André Raynauld, ed., Seminar on Regional Development in Canada: Transcript of the Proceedings (Montreal: Le Centre de recherche en développement économique de l'Université de Montréal, 24 October 1980), p. 105.
18. *Living Together*, pp. 215-16.
19. Canada, *Report of the Royal Commission on Maritime Claims*, 1926.
20. Based on a presentation by Benjamin Higgins at the Canadian Institute for Research on Regional Development, Moncton, New Brunswick, in November 1984. Professor Higgins was employed by the federal government to work on the reconstruction conference.
21. Canada, *Report of the Royal Commission on Dominion-Provincial Relations*, 1940, pp. 269-76.
22. There are numerous studies on Ottawa's equalization program. See Canada, *Fiscal Federalism in Canada*, pp. 157-76. See also Douglas H. Clark, "Federal-Provincial Fiscal Arrangements for the 1972-76 Fiscal Period," pp. 206-14.
23. Canada, *Report of the Royal Commission on Canada's Economic Prospects*, 1957, p. 404.
24. Frank Walton, "Canada's Atlantic Region: Recent Policy for Economic Development," in *The Canadian Journal of Regional Science*, vol. 1, no. 2 (Autumn 1978), p. 44.
25. See, among others, Anthony Careless, *Initiative and Response: The Adaptation of Canadian Federalism to Regional Economic Development* (Montreal: McGill-Queen's University Press, 1981), pp. 71-99.
26. See, among others, Thomas N. Brewis, "Regional Development in Canada in Historical Perspective," in N.J. Lithwick, ed. *Regional Economic Policy: The Canadian Experience* (Toronto: McGraw-Hill Ryerson, 1978) p. 220.
27. Walton, "Canada's Atlantic Region," p. 44.
28. See Careless, *Initiative and Response*, pp. 91-108.
29. Walton, "Canada's Atlantic Region," p. 44.
30. See Savoie, *Regional Economic Development*.

31. See, among many others, J.P. Francis and M.G. Pillai, "Regional Economic Disparities, Regional Development Policies in Canada," in *Regional Poverty and Change* (Ottawa: Canadian Council on Rural Development, 1973), pp. 136-7.

32. Careless, *Initiative and Response.*

33. Donald J. Savoie, *Federal-Provincial Collaboration: The Canada-New Brunswick General Development Agreement* (Montreal: McGill-Queen's University Press, 1981), pp. 25-44.

34. *Ibid.*

35. "Provinces Must Fit Programmes to Ottawa's—DeBané says," *Globe and Mail* (Toronto), 13 August 1981, p. 1.

36. See Canada, Department of Finance, *Economic Development for Canada in the 1980s* (Ottawa: Department of Finance, 1981), p. 11.

37. Canada, Office of the Prime Minister, *Release—Reorganization for Economic Development,* 12 January 1982.

38. Canada, *The Atlantic Canada Opportunities Agency Action Program* (Moncton: Atlantic Canada Opportunities Agency, n.d.).

39. Canada, *Report of the Minister for the Fiscal Year 1988-89* (Moncton: Atlantic Canada Opportunities Agency, 31 August 1989).

40. *Ibid.,* p. 31.

41. Donald J. Savoie, *Regional Economic Development: Canada's Search for Solutions,* 2d. ed. (Toronto: University of Toronto Press, 1992,), p. 133.

42. *Ibid.,* pp. 147-49.

43. Canada, *Annual Report 1987-89,* Department of Western Economic Diversification.

44. Savoie, *Regional Economic Development,* 2d. ed., p. 150.

45. *Ibid.,* see Chapter 10.

46. Canada, *The FEDNOR Review,* Department of Industry, Science and Technology, 1989, p. 6.

47. Canada, An act to establish the Department of Industry, Science and Technology to reveal the Department of Regional Industrial Expansion Act and to make consequential amendments to other Acts; second session, thirty-fourth Parliament, 36 Eliz. 2, 1989, p. 8.

48. *Ibid.*

49. See Canada, *Canada-Quebec Subsidiary Agreement on the Economic Development of the Regions of Quebec,* Department of Industry, Science and Technology, 9 June 1988, schedules B, C, and D.

50. *Ibid.*

51. See Richard D. French, "The Future of Federal-Provincial Relations ... if Any," paper presented to the Institute of Public Administration of Canada, National Capital Region, 14 June 1990, p. 2.

52. *Ibid.*

17

Regional Development in Australia

It is fair to say that in Australia at least until 1993 there has never been a federal policy of regional development, and still less a policy of reducing regional disparities. There is a mechanism for a modest degree of revenue sharing, with the objective of making it *possible* for all six states to achieve comparable levels of public service; but as Russell Mathews, former Director of the Australian National University's Centre for Research on Federal Financial Relations, and a member of the Commonwealth Grants Commission, makes clear, that is *all* the commission is supposed to do. When the commission was established in 1933, and ever since, it has *not* been charged with reducing gaps in household incomes among states, nor with promoting general economic development.[1] In Australia regional policy has never been directed towards reducing disparities in income and unemployment among the states. The objective has been to assist disadvantaged social groups, wherever they are, and to deal with economic and social problems of relatively small communities, rather than to aid disadvantaged states.

A second objective, sporadically, has been decentralization. Sydney and Melbourne, especially, have every so often been regarded as "too big," and efforts have been made to pull population and economic activity to smaller centres—anywhere, no matter what state. Finally, since World War II there has been a minerals boom, most of it in the thinly settled North. Consequently, Australia has had, at last, a "moving frontier;" not, however, a westward movement into the interior, as in the United States and Canada, but a movement from the more densely populated South towards the northern rim. This movement required provision of infrastructure of all kinds, and "resource frontier development" became a major objective of regional development policy.

Since the great depression of the 1930s, another objective of the federal government illustrated has been integrated fiscal policy. The chief instrument for this aim is the Commonwealth Loans Council, consisting of the treasurers of the Commonwealth and of the six state governments, which determines the amounts and terms of borrowing by all governments. Decisions of the council certainly affect economic development at the State level, but its objective is stabilization at the national level, not regional development. Although the states have considerable power over land use, even the state governments can hardly be said to have made efforts to reduce regional disparities. They have all tried to lure new enterprises to locate within their borders; but since all are rich in natural resources, all have comparable fiscal capacities, and all are currently at about the same level of development, these efforts tend to cancel each other out, and have limited impact on either regional development or regional disparities.

Intellectual Underpinnings

The economics profession as a whole has shown even less interest in regional development in Australia than it has in the United States, Canada or Britain. More work has been done on regional analysis by sociologists and geographers than by economists. One could count on the fingers of one hand the number of economists with a solid reputation in the profession who have specialized in regional development. *The Economic Record*, official organ of the Australian Economic Society, almost never publishes an article on regional economics, nor is there an Australian economic journal specializing in the field. This lack of interest does not, however, reflect a widespread faith in the market as a device for solving regional problems, or any other economic problems. On the contrary, Australians have long looked to government to manage the economy in such a way as to make it perform better, particularly in terms of social justice and the creation of "the Workers' Paradise," and have never been reluctant to "repeal the law of supply and demand" in order to achieve social goals.

The first generation of Australian economists to capture international attention were active during the great depression of the 1930s and the war and reconstruction. They included L.F. Giblin, Colin Clark, Frederic Benham, Douglas Copland, Francis Walker, Edward Shann. They were all highly policy-oriented, and their works aroused interest because of their proposals for dealing with unemployment, wartime and postwar inflation, and the transition from a wartime to a peacetime economy. Giblin, the first Ritchie Professor of Economics at the University of Melbourne anticipated the Kahn-Keynes theory of the multiplier, but used his status as a Labor Party supporter to persuade the Australian Confederation of Trade Unions to accept a wage cut in 1931 to reduce unemployment. Their interest in policy, however, did not extend to regional development. In the whole history of Australian economic thought, regional development has never played as significant a role as it has in Canada, or even in the United Kingdom, or the European Economic Community.

One reason for the lack of interest is that Australia never really had a frontier. Among large countries of recent settlement, Australia provides the most striking contrast to the United States with regard to history of the frontier. The opening up of the Australian center did not lead to urbanization in the interior, but rather to population growth in the handful of cities on the coast, particularly in the two great metropolitan centres of Melbourne and Sydney. Moreover, the Australian frontier, such as it was, was always a "rich man's frontier." The Gold Rush, for example, lasted barely a decade as a small man's operation; after that, it was a matter of corporate enterprise crushing quartz. In any case, the mineral discoveries in Australia were almost in the backyards of the great cities. The center itself is dead, consisting of unattractive desert. Frontier development in Australia took the form of "rich-squatters" acquiring huge tracts of land, hiring a very small labour force, and running large numbers of animals. This sort of development created employment opportunities in the suburbs of Melbourne and Sydney but not in the center of the country.

This pattern of development engendered no American-style frontier spirit. It requires a different sort of attitude to set up a grocery shop in a suburb of Sydney than to move hundreds of miles to the westward and launch a new enterprise in a strange new territory, menaced by Indians and blizzards. Moreover, the opportunity to start a small business, and watch it grow into a large one as the city grew around you, was confined to a few coastal centres. The "log-cabin-to-riches" legend had much less meaning in Australia than in the United States. As Professor Fred Alexander put it, "use of the term 'frontier' to cover gold rushes to such places as Ballarat and Bendigo, not far distant from the established center of Melbourne and considerably within the outer rim of existing pastoral settlement, is unduly stretching the definition given in the opening paragraph of this essay."[2] The Australian frontier, like the Brazilian, is "hollow."

Contrast the following passage from the Australian historian Hancock with our earlier one from Turner: (chapter 11) "There is a famous gap in the range of the Blue Mountains, that wall of rock and scrub which for a quarter of century hemmed in this colony of New South Wales within the coastal plain. Stand at this gap and watch the frontiers following each other westward—the squatters' frontier which filled the western plains with sheep and laid the foundations of Australia's economy, the miners' frontier which brought Australia population and made her a radical democracy, the farmer's frontier which gradually and painfully tested and proved the controls of Australian soil and climate. Stand a few hundred miles further west on the Darling river and see what these controls have done to the frontier. The farmers have dropped out of the westward movement procession, beaten by aridity. Only the pastoralists and prospectors pass by. In the west-center of the continent, aridity has beaten even the pastoralists. On the fringe of a dynamic society there are left only a few straggling prospectors and curious anthropologists, infrequent invaders of the aboriginal reserves."[3]

When the white man arrived in Australia, there were no urban settlements and no stable agriculture. Moreover, there was very little settlement or development before 1820. In that year, Sydney and Hobart were still essentially small convict settlements. Brisbane was established in 1824, the Swan River settlement (Perth) in 1829, Melbourne in 1835, and Adelaide in 1836. Thus, the settlements that were to become the state capitals were essentially established within one generation. Moreover, they were all settled by essentially the same kind of people. In all of the colonies, most people lived in the capital city from the beginning, whereas the extensive farming and grazing and the mining drew few people into the interior. The cities did not grow much by rural-urban migration because there were practically no rural people to migrate; the cities grew by migration from the United Kingdom. Another very important feature of all of these societies is that from the beginning, the average incomes in the countryside were much the same as in the urban centres; poverty was not primarily a rural phenomenon.

Another feature of the six primate cities worth noting is that they are all ports, and that there are no major ports apart from the six cities (although Darwin, Geelong, and Broome are increasing in importance). For two centuries, virtually all overseas trade and all immigration have gone through them. Consequently, the domestic transport system—rail, road, and air—focuses on them, the more so because transport is essentially a state responsibility. Consequently, industries and services wishing to serve the domestic market, as well as those linked to world markets, have tended to locate in the capital cities. The communications system also centres on them.

In sum, then, each state economy consists of a large capital city with a set of manufacturing activities and a wide range of services, and of a prosperous hinterland engaged in extensive agriculture and mining, with much the same product mix and occupational structure in all of them. With so high a degree of similarity in the structure of the state economies and so much homogeneity in the societies that developed in each of the six spaces, when "regions" are defined as states, as they usually are, large regional disparities do not appear. Nor are there sharp differences in race, religion, or language to bring interregional conflict of the sort that has plagued other large, regionalized countries.

Absence of Regional Disparities

Why has reduction of regional disparities played no role in Australian regional development policy? Because when "regions" are defined as states, which are the only really significant political units apart from the federal government, there never have been serious regional gaps. Regional disparities arise when different regions of a country develop at different times and at different rates, on the basis of different resource endowments, and so with different product-mixes and occupational structures, as in Canada. In Australia the six states developed almost simultaneously, with similar resource endowments, and much the same occupational structures and product mixes. From the beginning most of the population of each state lived in the capital cities, and these cities were all settled by essentially the same kind of people. The rest worked on farms and in mines, where they earned incomes about the same as those earned by the urban populations.

All states had mineral resources, all States produced sheep and cattle, (and beer and wine) and most states produced wheat. These products were major exports, sold in the same world market. For the "rich-squatters" producing them, holding vast tracts of land and hiring very few people, their activity was highly profitable most of the time. Agricultural development of this kind, rather than pulling population into the interior, created industrial and service jobs in the capital cities, all of which were on the seashore, and major ports. The one third of the country, at its centre, which was desert, remained empty. The further one third of the country which was semi-desert remained nearly so. Moreover, most of the early mineral discoveries, when they came, were virtually in the back yards of the existing cities; so they didn't move the population either. Indeed, nothing did. Population growth took place mainly in the existing capital cities, on the seashore in the southern part of the country, so that about two thirds of the population lived in them. Each state consisted of a primate city and a hinterland devoted to extensive agriculture and mining, largely of the same sort. With such similarity of economic structure, and similarity of timing of development, large regional gaps never appeared. There were other uniformities as well. Until about 1950, 98 percent of the Australian population was of British origin. Thus there were no great differences in the ethnic, linguistic, or cultural backgrounds of people in different regions. There were tensions between Irish Catholics and various Protestant sects, but these did not take a regional form. Since most people lived in seaside cities, in every state, and since incomes were much the same, patterns of living were much the same too.

This happy State of affairs (or affairs of State) is not the result of a long period of convergence from an initial condition of extremely large regional disparities, as in the United States, nor the result of effective regional policy in the past. In Australia there never were any large gaps.

More recently, however, as the statistics have improved, it has been found that there *are* significant regional disparities among smaller units, such as the

Department of Statistics' 60 regions or the Department of Industry, Technolgy and Regional Development's 94. But these units have no political identity of their own, and little political power. They do not influence federal policy, nor even state policy, to any significant degree.

Ideological Background

The unique pattern of European settlement in Australia, starting out with prisoners (mostly petty working class criminals) and guards, then social protestors like the Chartists, with scarcely any voluntary immigration before the gold rushes of the 1850s and 1860s, has left its mark on the social philosophy and ideology of the country. It is not surprising that most early settlers were not enthusiastic about capitalism and the "free market," and that the "workers' paradise" became the goal. The ideal of the "workers' paradise" was realistic enough. Some years ago, a group of distinguished economists and philosophers met in Sydney to define for Yale philosopher Professor Northrop the economic philosophy on which Australia's peculiar society and economic institutions were based. After some days of rather hesitant discussion, the best the group could come up with was "Protection and the Fair Go;" protection of all Australians from all foreigners, and protection of all individuals, social groups and classes within Australia from all other individuals, social groups and classes within Australia; plus a basic egalitarianism, cast in terms of equality of opportunity for all and an almost feudal sense of responsibility of the richer and more powerful for the welfare of the poorer and weaker. Vague and unwritten though it was, this ideology resulted in an effective social contract. To' use the power of any group—trade unions, bosses, bankers, or farmers—in a matter and to a degree that did real harm to any other group, was something that was just "not done." (Some Australians old enough to remember may raise questions about the coalminers and the "wharfies" in the years after World War II, who certainly caused considerable inconvenience to their employers, and to the general public at times, but by and large the statement stands.) Institutionally, this economic philosophy was reflected by such legislation as the Immigration Restriction Act, the Commonwealth Arbitration Court (Commission), the Loans Council, and the Commonwealth Grants Commission. It is not reflected in any federal or state legislation regarding regional development.

The compulsory arbitration system, implemented by the Commonwealth Arbitration Court (later Commonwealth Arbitration Commission and later still the Industrial Relation Commission), was established by the very first session of Parliament after Confederation. The commission established the basic wage and the number of hours worked per week for the entire country, and State

Industrial Commissions determine the margins for skill for each specific occupation. These tend to be much the same in each state: the principal is that people doing a particular job should receive the same income *wherever they are*, regardless of differences in productivity from one region to another. Obviously, if everyone is paid the same for a particular job, no matter where they are, and if the occupational structure is more or less the same in every major region, there is no need for a program designed to eliminate *regional* disparities, with regions defined as states. Attention has tended to focus instead on small regions with special problems or special potential.

One by-product of this pattern of development is that there are virtually no poor farmers, and that farm incomes on the whole are high and much the same everywhere. In Canada many relatively poor regions have been areas of unproductive agriculture. The "rich-squatters" (large-scale landholders) are still at the top of the economic, social, and political scale in Australia. The fact that relative poverty is not associated with agriculture obviously influences the pattern of regional development policy in Australia. It has been concentrated almost entirely on urban centres. Since municipalities are the responsibility of the states, and the states are jealous of their powers, it means that the role of the states, relative to that of the federal government, has been more important that the relative role of the provinces in Canada. Moreover, since regional development is not translated into efforts to develop states as a whole, but is more concentrated on particular communities, it means that the role of municipalities in regional development is considerably greater in Australia than in Canada.

With the increasing Americanization of Australian society, this social contract is breaking down. So far, however, the breakdown has not generated any loud calls from individuals and groups injured by the breakdown for new forms of protection at the *regional* level.

Even at the level of the Bureau of Statistics' 60 regions, the disparities, while significant, are not so dramatic as the disparities that have appeared in the past in Canada, let alone as dramatic as the 400 percent gap in per capita incomes between richest and poorest of the eight major regions in the United States in 1860. The 1981 census revealed a spread in per capita incomes from $7,600 in the richest of the 60 to $4,500 in the poorest. Unemployment, however, ranged from 2.7 to 10.6 percent. There are also significant differences in structure of the six states, which appear as a by-product of disparities among small region. For example, Western Australia has no low-income region within it, and no high unemployment region. Next-door Southern Australia has no high-income region but only one low-income region. Tasmania has no region with low unemployment, no high-income region except its capital city, and all the other regions in the state have low incomes. Queensland has no region with low unemployment. The Northern Territory has low incomes in every region except its capital city, but low unemployment throughout.

These figures call for more detailed inquiry into *causes* of disparities among small regions in Australia. It is clear enough, however, that they lie basically in differences in occupational structure and product-mix from one small region to another. Put in a slightly different way, Australia's economic and social problems lie in the intensity and nature of *specific needs for structural change and "adjustment" in small regions*. For more than a century Australia has had one of the most strongly protected economies in the world, with the result that a majority of the labour force is now engaged in activities where they have a comparative *disadvantage*. Further economic progress in Australia is dependent on particular forms of structural change; not shrinking the relative size of the primary sector, and growth of the industrial and services sector; that has already taken place in much the same degree as in other industrialized capitalist countries. What is needed now is replacement of inefficient enterprises and activities by efficient ones in particular *places*. And the activities that need replacing in one small region are not the same as those that need replacing in other small regions. In one it may be textiles, in another it may be automobiles. But there are industries that need replacing in all *states*. Indeed, many of the activities requiring adjustment are to be found in every state.

It follows that the need for adjustment is not concentrated in one or two particular states, does not lead to marked disparities among states, and cannot be met by programmes aimed at particular states. Australia has, and has had, no real retarded regions like Atlantic Canada and Quebec. The nature of Australia's development problem has been understood, at least intuitively, by the succession of governments since World War II; and this understanding is one of the reasons why there has never been any effort to solve development problems by any sort of programme for development assistance from the federal government to the states. But while this understanding has prevented governments from undertaking programmes that would be inappropriate, it has not prompted them to undertake programmes that would be appropriate. The former Hawke and Keating governments, and the succession of coalition governments, have relied on macro-economic policies, mainly monetary policy, plus "the market," to bring the needed sectoral change and "adjustment." There have been sporadic efforts to assist particular sectors or industries (such as the wool industry) to adjust to changing market conditions, but these have been largely ineffective. Their understanding has not penetrated deeply enough to lead governments to policies designed to assist troubled sectors, industries and enterprises in particular small regions. For all governments such policies would run contrary to the Australian ideology or treating individuals and definable social groups in the same manner, wherever they are, and of seeking a maximal degree of equality among them. For the Hawke, Keating, and coalition governments, such policies would also smack too much of "planning."

In sum, then, the problem of regional development in Australia is not one of reducing disparities among large regions, but of facilitating structural change and "adjustment" in small regions. This is a problem which cannot be resolved within the nexus of federal-state relations. Nor is it merely a problem of regions with low incomes and high unemployment; it is equally a problem of prosperous small regions that want to stay that way. "Adjustment" is not just a matter of making necessary changes to deal with harmful events in the past. It is also a matter of anticipating events in the future which will necessitate changes if enterprises in the small region are to remain competitive. At the local level, there has been a good deal of comprehension of this state of affairs. The almost total neglect of the real problems of structural change and adjustment by the federal and state governments has at least kept attempts to solve them out of the morass of federal-state financial relations, and left the door open to ingenuity and innovation at the local level.

Whitlam and DURD

It is important for the purpose of this study to review the efforts of the Whitlam government of 1972-75 in the regional development field, especially the Department of Urban and Regional Development (DURD). The traumatic experience of the Whitlam government with regional development still had an inhibiting influence on the Keating government in 1993; and current attitudes of the federal government towards regional development cannot be completely understood without some knowledge of that experience.

When in 1972 the Labor Party came to power after 23 years in the wilderness, few Labor MP's or Cabinet ministers had any experience with actual government, and their revolutionary zeal was not matched by their political skills and know-how. Moreover, most of the senior civil servants had been appointed by and served conservative governments, and regarded any proposal for radical change with distaste and apprehension. Instead of enthusiastic support from the bureaucracy, that might ease the government through its youthful growing pains, it encountered, instead, stubborn resistance to its program of reforms. The one major effort to construct a national policy of regional development, integrated with state and local policy, came during the Whitlam regime. It was imaginative, bold, innovative, and essentially on the right track, but it is generally regarded as a dismal failure. The resistance to the program from top bureaucrats was only one reason for the failure. Opposition from state governments was another. Inexperience was a third. Finally, the Whitlam government was never given the opportunity to learn by doing. It was dismissed by the Governor-General after less than three years in office, because the death of a Labor senator left it one seat short of a majority in the Senate, and it could not carry its supply bills. Whitlam's fundamental ideology was similar to that which is associated in the United States with "liberals," like John Kenneth Galbraith and John F. Kennedy. He *wanted* to increase the role of government in the economy and in the society, as distinct from reluctantly accepting large budgets as unfortunate but inevitable, in the manner of Mulroney, Reagan, Bush and Thatcher. He wanted to bring both the state and local governments into the development act as full partners, even offering local governments direct access to the Loan Council. Since local governments were creatures of the states, the state governments regarded this policy as an invasion of their territory. They also resented Whitlam's eagerness to enlarge the role of the federal government in such fields as urban and regional development, housing, health and education, fields which they regarded as their own.

In the field of urban and regional development, Whitlam had a unique approach. Far from showing concern for disparities among states, his main concern was for the urban poor, particularly in the two major metropolitan centres of Sydney and Melbourne, and above all in the working class suburbs of those cities. One can imagine the fate of a Canadian prime minister who insisted that the regional development effort be concentrated in Toronto and Montreal. In his major Policy Speech of 1972, Whitlam maintained that "in modern Australia inequality is fixed upon families by the place in which they are forced to live even more than by what they are able to earn." In accordance with this philosophy, the government's program for upgrading urban infrastructure began in the western (working class) suburbs of Melbourne and Sydney. However, decentralization of economic activity and population was also part of government policy, so 14 small country towns were also designated as growth centres. None of these was a success.

The Department of Urban and Regional Development was the main vehicle for the government's policies and programs in that field. Its mandate was broad in the extreme. Like DREE in Canada some three years earlier, it was conceived by the government as a superministry, with responsibilities for housing, urban transport, sewage systems, overcrowding in city centres, conservation, the environment, land use and land prices. And like DREE, it never became a superministry, partly because it lacked the technical competence to do so, and partly because of opposition from within the government itself. The Labor caucus elected 27 Cabinet ministers, and each had to have a department to run; and many of the departments were responsible for the very fields that DURD wanted to control. Consequently, DURD was not able to play an integrative role to the full.

Another problem was that as a new department DURD brought to Canberra a flock of young do-gooders with experience limited to such things as community development programs in small towns. As Dr. Leonie Sandercock puts it, "Missionary zeal, moral outrage, and shorts and thongs, were not styles of negotiation that got far in the dour, pseudo-neutral, quiet-suited world of the Canberra bureaucracy."[4] Benjamin Higgins' appraisal of DURD is summed up as follows: "In retrospect, despite the lofty underlying idealism, breadth of vision, and brilliance of conception, there does seem to have been something inchoate and half baked about the Whitlam program on urban and regional development.... The Labor party lacked the experience and the skills to implement smoothly and quickly a program of major reforms. The bureaucracy lacked them too because no such program had been under way for over two decades, and many of the top people in the civil service were highly suspicious of the whole venture."[5]

The Fraser coalition government which succeeded Whitlam quickly scrapped Labor party's urban and regional development program. More important, when Labor came back to power in 1983, and ever since, it has taken great care to distance itself from the Whitlam regime—perhaps even more care than to distance itself from the Fraser government, with which it has many similarities. Certainly nothing resembling Whitlam's program of urban and regional development has been reintroduced by the Hawke or Keating administration. In Canberra, "DURD IS STILL A DIRTY WORD."

The Industrial Policy Statement, March 1991

On the thirteenth of March 1991, former Prime Minister Hawke delivered a major economic policy speech to Parliament, which became known as the industrial policy statement. Mr. Hawke began his statement by saying, "early this year I determined that I should deliver a major statement about what we must do together to meet the economic challenges facing this country." The statement is primarily concerned with the need for structural change that will permit the Australian economy to adjust to "this tough, increasingly competitive world of five and a half billion people.... The days of our being able to hitch a free ride in a world clamouring for our rural and mineral products are behind us." These products will still be important, but the challenge is to "export more manufactured goods and services and substitute more quality Australian production for imports."

In Canada, such a major economic policy statement by the prime minister could scarcely have avoided references to the regional aspects of the problem and the manner in which regional policy must be adapted to meeting it. Mr. Hawke's approach, however, was highly macro-economic; and when any desegregation of his policy proposals was mentioned, it was in terms of particular industries or sectors, rather than in terms of particular regions. In his one specific reference to *states* as regions, he seemed to regard them as a nuisance, and to plead for more centralisation of economic powers to cope with Australia's need for modernisation. Speaking of the Trade Practices Act, he complained that too many enterprises are beyond the reach of federal legislation, and added: "This patchwork coverage reflects historical and constitutional factors, not economic efficiencies; it is another important instance of the way we operate as six economies, rather than one."

In terms of macro-economic policy, combatting inflation remained the priority objective, although unemployment was even then heading for two-digit numbers. Monetary policy remained the principal instrument for fighting inflation; the statement even offered businesses some tax cuts.

However, as unemployment continued to rise, and to be heavily concentrated in certain sectors, industries, social and age groups, and regions, the government came under heavy pressure from the trade unions, from employers, the opposition, social welfare groups and the media to do something about it. Nonetheless, in his economic policy statement of 14 November 1992, not only did Prime Minister Hawke make no suggestions for fighting unemployment on a regional basis, he made no suggestions for fighting unemployment at all. He reiterated his view that the best thing the government could do to strengthen the Australian economy was to continue its fight against inflation, predicted that unemployment would continue to increase for some months, but that recovery would set in during 1993. He specifically rejected any kind of "pump-priming" or "artificial" make-work projects. He did, however, promise more funds for retraining workers so as to facilitate their movement into higher-productivity, more competitive industries. There was no hint of any modification of his extremely low-profile regional policy, and he categorically refused any income tax sharing with the states.

The Country Centres Program

Until 1993, the series of Labor Party governments under Robert Hawke and Paul Keating have maintained a low profile with respect to regional policy, but that does not mean that nothing was done. A Regional Development Division (RDD) has been established, first in the Department of Local Government and Administrative Services, and then in the Department of Immigration, Local Government and Ethnic Affairs (DILGEA), which replaced it in 1987, as part of a general administrative shake-up designed to reduce the total number of departments in the government. RDD first divided the entire country into 75 regions for purposes of analysis and planning. Fundamentally, these regions were the hinterlands of 75 urban centres; the analysis and planning is urban-based in large degree. Later, the six state capitals, all of them metropolitan centres, were split into 24 regions, making a total of 94 regions in all. (See Map 17-1)

The next step was to assemble a data bank with respect to economic and social conditions in each of these regions, designed to measure disparities at the local level. This task has been carried out with exemplary patience and thoroughness; until today there are some 500 statistical series for each of the 94 regions. Indeed, Australia may well have the richest data bank for regional analysis in the world.

One of the first applications of RDD's analysis to policy was the Country Centres Program. A survey was conducted in 1986 "in eleven rural centres suffering the cumulative pressures of the downturn in rural industry and changes in a range of mining, manufacturing and service industries."[6] DILGEA's justification for this undertaking is highly perspicacious, indicating how governments committed to privatization, deregulation, and the creation of a free market economy can nonetheless find means for effective intervention at the local level:[7] (See Map 17-2)

The Country Centres Project (CCP) was a pilot initiative of the Commonwealth Government's 1986 Rural Economic Package. The project was con-

MAP 17-1
DILGEA Regions

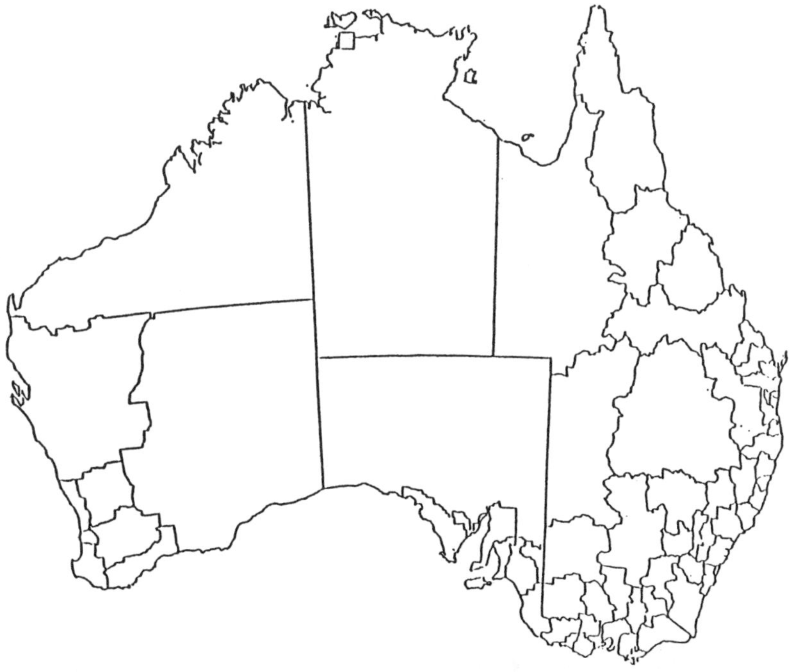

MAP 17-2
Country Centres

ducted by the Regional Development Branch of the former Department of Local Government and Administrative Services, in eleven rural centres suffering the cumulative pressures of the downturn in the rural industry and changes in a range of mining, manufacturing and service industries.

— Within a framework of minimal government intervention and expenditure, the CCP sought to test whether:
— there is scope for local communities to adopt self-help strategies and management systems to identify and facilitate feasible options, including economic and social opportunities, with maximum private sector involvement; and
— local processes can assist government in cost-effectively targeting and tailoring appropriate programs to local needs and circumstances to facilitate positive adjustment.

The original idea of the CCP was to extend the program to all regions experiencing difficulties of one sort or another and eleven regions were initially selected. The main concern expressed in the accompanying policy statements was the deteriorating state of the rural economy, in both agriculture and mining, and its negative impact on services and industry in the rural urban centres. A major aspect of the deterioration was declining terms of trade for the rural sector, with rising costs and falling prices of commodities produced. In other words, the analytical framework of the CCP treated the urban centres as "central places" rather than as "growth poles;" the idea was to save the cities by improving conditions in their peripheries, rather than to save the countryside by measures that would generate growth in the urban centres. At the same time, it was recognized that a large proportion of crippled industries, such as food and beverages; textiles, clothing and footwear; and wood and wood products, is concentrated in small towns. Given this situation, plus the fact that the long run prospects for these industries are not bright in Australia, a major objective of CCP was "enabling local communities in rural areas to adjust positively to the cumulative impacts of economic and social change."[8]

Financially, the program was on a small scale: a package of support measures costing $210 million for 1986-87. The emphasis was on finding things that members of the troubled communities could undertake themselves to improve their situation, rather than on pushing or pulling economic activities from one region to another, nor was there any element of subsidization of inefficient industries to keep them going in the government's rationale for the project. On these matters the government was quite explicit: "In this new economic climate past regional and decentralization policies have been perceived as inappropriate and too expensive. No longer can government undertake spending to compensate for short-run income loss, or to encourage economic and employment growth through expensive job creation infrastructure and growth centre strategies. Many of the earlier regional programs, as a result, have been progressively abandoned."[9]

These considerations, said DILGEA, led to a rethinking of regional policy, with more emphasis on economic regeneration and restructuring, and less emphasis on redistribution. Within this new framework, more attention was paid to differences in structure and potential of regions across the nation, with the aim of increasing the cost-effectiveness and efficiency of regional development policy, by tailoring programs to the specific conditions of each region, and designing them so as to realize potential in each area. The social aspects of regional policy are aimed at increasing long-run economic viability of each region, restructuring its economic base in accordance with changing conditions, rather than compensating for income losses in the short run.[10]

All the state governments approved the project in principle, but their roles varied according to their own policies and administrative structures for regional development. According to DILGEA, "The Commonwealth's major role in the project, apart from coordination, was to provide information, technical support and funding to liaison committees. The information provided to each region by the Commonwealth included a regional profile mainly derived from census data. The Regional Development Branch undertook an in-house evaluation of statements, and provided each Centre a brief written appraisal of its regional economic strengths and weaknesses in relation to those of other regional areas (regional comparative advantage)."[11]

Achievements of the Country Centres Project

Just how much did the CCP achieve by way of regional development in Australia? As of 1987, the claims of DILGEA for the project were rather modest.[12] The eleven centres identified 58 business opportunities, but by DILGEA's own admission, not much came of them. "The CCP emphasized a self-help approach by local communities to the ultimate commercial realization of opportunities, with maximum private sector involvement. The Commonwealth provided no guarantee of financial support to assist with implementation. However, it became apparent through the CCP that there was virtually no spontaneity demonstrated by local communities to progress their identified opportunities to commercialization."[13]

Accordingly, DILGEA commissioned the Chisholm Institute of Technology, through its Centre for Development of Entrepreneurs (CDE), to undertake pre-feasibility studies of the 58 opportunities. CDE found that 19 of these were worth carrying to the feasibility study phase, but their budget allowed them to make only seven such studies. These seven did not seem particularly exciting, nor calculated to bring dramatic "structural adjustment" to their regions: export of hay; lucerne cubing; aquaculture; table grapes; marketing fruit and vegetables; production of honey, bees, and pollen; tanning cattle hides.

The regional development branch of DILGEA came to the not very startling conclusion that structural change and "adjustment" of lagging small regions, through "self-help" alone, is hampered by a lack of entrepreneurship, technical skills, information, and professional advice. They thought that "regional networks of entrepreneurs" might be the answer but did not explain how "networks" of regions, all of them lacking entrepreneurs, could solve the problem of entrepreneurship.[14] They did, however, point to the success of the South Coast Development Project in New South Wales, which was jointly managed by the NSW government, private enterprise, and the trade unions, and "brought local engineering subcontractors together in a consortium to design, develop, and manufacture sophisticated products; established an innovative work skills training scheme; and built an industry and labour market indicative planning facility for the region."[15] They did not, unfortunately, go on to draw the obvious lesson from this contrasting experience: success in development programs for stagnating or declining regions, or for regions with unutilized potential, requires the assembly of teams of professionals with the requisite skills from *outside* the region (including entrepreneurial skills) as well as "grass roots community involvement." Since virtually all regional development programs in less developed countries are organized in this manner, this lesson is more likely to be learned by people who have been involved in these programs, as well as regional development efforts in industrialized countries. We have made this point before, in an earlier publication,[16] and will return to it below.

DILGEA concluded that the CCP experiment was worthwhile: "The CCP has shown, however, that a cost-effective, flexible and more coordinated positive adjustment approach is possible by integrating the various efforts of government, industry and the community at the local level. It has demonstrated that communities are not only prepared to recognize the seriousness of the economic climate in their local areas but are also willing to do something positive about it."[17]

In order to improve the preparation of proposals for new business ventures in the regions, the Office of Local Government (OLG) of DILGEA prepared in 1988 a detailed and sophisticated manual entitled *COUNTRY CENTRES PROJECT FEASIBILITY STUDY GUIDE,* in which they measure and rank what they call the "resilience and vulnerability, economic and population change," for each of their 94 regions, utilizing the whole of their rich data bank. This is probably the most exhaustive regional analysis ever produced by any government in the world, exceeding in completeness of coverage even the studies undertaken by the Malaysian Economic Planning Unit in 1973. The survey includes hundreds of tables and dozens of maps.

The Australian government therefore has available to it a wealth of information for carrying out regional development policy at the local or community level. The CCP was a step in that direction. Unfortunately, perhaps because of the Hawke Labor government's supreme faith in private enterprise and "the market" and their ability to solve any economic or social problem, perhaps because of the sombre shadow still cast by the memory of DURD, this project shunned everything that might be construed as "regional development planning." It consequently left out of the local level development process one key ingredient: the requisite expertise. As a consequence, the program had only a limited impact.

Regional Cooperation: Regional Organizations of Councils

DILGEA's Office of Local Government supported one other form of "bottom up" planning of regional development: Regional Organizations of Councils (ROCs). The basic idea behind this movement was that local governments, such as town councils, can be strengthened and made more efficient in their development efforts by bringing together several councils in the same region for various kinds of cooperative effort. The idea was not new. At the state level it goes back at least to the New South Wales State Development and Country Assistance Act of 1966. Under this legislation the NSW Department of Decentralization and its successors undertook a variety of regional development programs. However, at the present time the idea of regional cooperation among councils is enjoying considerable vogue, and there are over 40 Regional Organizations of Councils operating throughout Australia. (See Map 17-3)

In 1990 the Office of Local Government organized a major two-day conference in Canberra devoted to regional cooperation. It was attended by 100 delegates from all over Australia, including representatives of 24 ROCs, together with representatives of state and Commonwealth government departments and various organizations concerned with local governments and community development. The conference was opened by the minister for local government, and a keynote address was given by Gordon Craig, OBE, summarizing the report that he prepared for OLG, on the experience with ROCs.

In the course of his study, Mr. Craig visited fourteen ROCs, and his findings on these visits were presented in his report. In general, he found that the ROCs were a symptom of a changing role of local government in response to increasing demands on it, such as promotion of industrial development, job creation, human services, and meeting problems of youth, housing, the environment and recreation facilities. These demands, Mr. Craig says, "call for a completely different perspective on local financing and intergovernmental relationship."[18] Local governments are continually being called upon to implement programs launched by the Commonwealth or state governments, in such

MAP 17-3
Location of Regional Organizations of Councils

Cairns GLADA

Mt Isa NWQROC

Sydney
Adelaide   SSROC
MCRO   WSROC
EMRO   NSROC
WRC   MACROC
NMRO   Toowoomba   Brisbane
SROC   EDROC   PCG
                                MRO
        Inverell NAROC Byron Bay NOROC
           Barmera   Coffs Harbour
 Cannington Peterborough RLGA NCROC
 SEMLACDG   NLGA   Maitland HRAC
Kwinana
SWMLAM   Wodonga
                        NEVRC.   Kiama
                                  IROC

Melbourne   Yarrum
AIEC   Natemuk   GMA
IMRA   NWMA
MWRC   Horsham   Flinders Is
NEROC   WDA   NTRO
NRC   Drysdale   Ulverstone
OEMA   GMF   NWTMR
          Kyneton   Glenorchy
          CVAC   HMCA
                       Huonville
                       HMA

fields as job creation, retraining for different jobs, social development and welfare; but usually the finance for such programs is provided only for limited periods, and local government is left holding the bag. There is a communication gap among federal, state, and local governments.

The ROCs derive most of their funds from annual grants, and spend most of their money on projects or research. Some projects yield income; Craig mentions as an example the regional tip (dump) operated by the Southern Regional Organization of Councils, each of the member councils paying a fee to the regional organization for the service. All ROCs are autonomous bodies, but some support services may be provided by one or more of the councils. No bureaucracies or permanent organizations of any size have been established. The typical secretariat consists of an executive officer with perhaps a research officer or an assistant and a secretary, appointed annually, making for a lack of continuity, stability, and accumulation of experience. Craig also finds that there is at the local government level "a continuing tendency...to allocate resources to the alleviation of problems rather than correcting the cause of the problem."[19]

But what do the ROCs actually do? The best way to answer this question is to give some examples.

Outer Eastern Municipalities Association (OEMA)

The OEMA consists of five cities and four shires in the rapidly growing eastern sector of Melbourne. It was established in 1978 and has an annual budget of about $110,000. Since 1981 it has had one full-time executive officer and one full-time secretary. It meets once every six weeks, each council sending one delegate officially, usually the councillor. The chief executive officer of each council normally attends the meetings as well. The OEMA has set up a management group of CEOs and three working groups: a Community Services Reference Group, a Town Planning Officers Group, and a Technical Services Managers Group. Major programs developed through OEMA include: a roads arterial network; a study for Meals on Wheels; a regional study as the basis for a proposal to establish an institution of tertiary education in the region; a group training scheme; a regional waste management group. Craig says of it, "The body has developed from a grant application group to one that carries out many regional tasks."[20]

Inner Metropolitan Regional Association (IMRA)

IMRA comprises eight traditionally working class municipalities in central Melbourne. Population is moving away from the inner city, and working

class areas are being "gentrified," creating a shortage of working class housing. Traditional manufacturing is moving away from the inner city and there
is pressure to redevelop the area in a different pattern. These changes create
social problems. IMRA was formed in 1986 as a voluntary grouping. The
population is about 235,000, the budget about $175,000 from council contri-
butions, plus grants for specific projects and programs from the federal and
state governments. Projects undertaken by IMRA include: urban consolidation case studies; power sharing; an industrial land use study; study of a regional waste recycling system.

Hunter Regional Association of Councils (HRAC)

HRAC was organized in 1984, but the Hunter region has a long history of
regional cooperation in various forms. The present association includes three
cities and 11 shires to the north and northwest of Sydney plus the cities of
Newcastle and Lake Macquarie as provisional members. The total population of this aggregation of municipalities is around 650,000. The association
consists of three representatives each from Newcastle and Lake Macquarie
and two each from the other municipalities. The budget is small for an aggregation that large, about $60,000. HRAC operates through a number of
committees; administrative, made up of the municipal clerk and nominees
of the engineers, town planners and health surveyors from each council; and
a roads committee, with six members nominated by the engineering representatives. There are also project committees for decentralization, ports administration, and development controls. HRAC has representatives in a
number of other regional organizations, such as the Hunter Planning Committee, the Hunter Regional Enterprise Agency, and the Hunter Industry and
Technical Education Council. HRAC defines its own role as "leadership in
regional cohesion."[21] It has presented views and proposals regarding various issues before the state government, such as: decentralization and regional development in New South Wales; efficiency of planning control;
waste disposal; port management; raising the tax on automobile fuels in
NSW; control of noxious weeds in the Hunter region. HRAC has established
a computer data base relevant to local government and organized training
programs for local government staff and councillors.

Western Sydney Regional Organization of Councils (WSROC)

With over one million people in its region, WSROC has much the biggest
population of all the ROCs studied. Indeed, Western Sydney has 31 percent of
Sydney's total population, and considered as a separate city would be Australia's

fourth largest, after Sydney, Melbourne, and Brisbane. It contains nine municipalities, which together contribute about $176,000 to the budget. With various grants, the total operating budget is about $215,000. WSROC has been operating since 1973, and now has a director, an assistant director and two full-time administrative assistants as well as temporary staff when needed. It has four committees; administrative, technical, town planners, and community services and children's services. Except for the technical committee, made up of the chief engineers of the municipalities, which meets as required, all committees meet bimonthly. The WSROC is also represented on several committees of other organizations, such as the Western Sydney Planning and Development Committee.

Some of the major achievements of WSROC are as follows: reclassification of roads; improved management of human services; establishment of the Western Sydney Information and Technology Centre; the Western Sydney Information and Research Service. WSROC's persistent lobbying over the years led to the decision by the Commonwealth and state governments to establish the University of Western Sydney.

Regional Commissions

As indicated above, the absence of comprehensive regional development programs at both the federal and state government levels during the last decade, has opened the door for exercise of initiative at the local level, with encouraging results. By way of illustration, we shall present here brief analysis of the operations of two of these initiatives, the Geelong Regional Commission and the Latrobe Regional Commission.

The Geelong Regional Commission (GRC)

The Geelong Regional Commission was established in August 1977. Its authority extended over the city of Geelong and eight other municipalities. Geelong itself is on the southern coast, just 72 kilometres southwest of Melbourne. (See Maps 17-4 and 17-5) The commission was a creature of the Victoria government, and consisted of five commissioners appointed by the Victoria Governor-in-Council, and one for each municipality, appointed by the municipal governments, fourteen in all. The region thus defined has a population of about 200,000 and an area of 2,500 square kilometres. In the mid-nineteenth century, Geelong was primarily a wool centre, and wool is still a major factor in the city's economy. Today, however, 25 percent of Geelong's labour force is in manufacturing, the rest in various services. It is an important port, sixth in Australia, and second in grain handling. The region is on the whole a prosperous one, but it is one of the small regions badly in need of structural change and adjustment. Many of its manufactures are traditional ones threatened by foreign competition, such as textiles, food and beverages, base metal products, tobacco products, coal products, chemicals and automobiles. It has essentially reduced dependence on products such as these that the commission is trying to achieve, but it recognizes the necessity of keeping some of them alive until the transition is accomplished.

Considering the relatively small scale of the region's area and population, the commission's full-time secretariat was sizeable, consisting of the chairman (appointed for five years, renewable) and 34 other professional people. (See Table 17.1). The secretariat had four divisions: Economic Development, Planning and Design, Administration, and Development and Construction, in order or size. The biggest of these, Economic Development, was directed by an economist and had also a regional economist and nine other professionals. In 1990 the commission had revenues of $8.3 million, the major sources being the state government grant and interest on investments. (See Table 17.2).

While the secretariat did some planning, both long-term and short-term, it was not a "planning commission" in the usual sense of the term. It worked continuously with the private sector, and its function was more entrepreneurial than planning. For example, one of its major functions was to buy plant from enterprises that were in trouble and to find a way of using it so as to provide continuous employment. The biggest such venture was the purchase of the International Harvester plant. This company had been one of Geelong's biggest employers, but its work force had been cut from 2,300 to 600, and the company was talking of closing down altogether. The GRC bought the plant and then leased it to small manufacturers producing a variety of products. The biggest of these produces agricultural machinery and was organized by the commission itself. In another case, it bought a failing company producing transmission components, paid cash, then sold it back on the basis of a long term loan, so that the company could keep on going. A manufacturer or surf boards and related equipment (the Rip Curl Company) could not find space for expansion at Torquay, the region's major seaside resort, and planned to move to Queensland. The commission managed to negotiate the purchase of 5.7 hectares at Torquay. Rip Curl stayed and other companies moved in. On the basis of this success the commission embarked on a multi-million-dollar venture named Surf Coast Plaza, a tourism, sports, and retail centre on the coast. In 1989–90 they managed to stage an inaugural Australia/United States Surfing Challenge, as part of the official international surfing titles season. A Surfworld Museum and an Australian Surfing Hall of Fame are being built next to the Torquay Community Hall.

In their 1989/90 fiscal year, the commission directly assisted 21 companies to establish new operations or to expand existing ones in the region. One of these was the first overseas operation to be established by the major British textile manufacturer, the Basford Textile Group. The refurbished National Wool Centre won the title of top Heritage and Cultural Attraction for Victoria, and Geelong has become once again one of Australia's leading centres for wool sales. Altogether GRC has assisted 170 new firms to come to Geelong, and 109 to expand, in 13 years, creating 5,014 additional jobs.

One of the GRC's most ambitious plans was designed to refurbish and revitalize the old central core of the city, on the waterfront. It was labelled "The City by the Bay" and was expected to cost $30 million. The National Wool Centre is one of the old waterfront buildings that have been restored as part of this project. A plan called the Bay Front Strategy was released in 1981 and approved by the Victoria government in the following year. Stage 1 of the plan included two retail complexes, Market Square and Bay City Plaza, and the Foreshore Precinct. The first of these was opened in 1985, the second in 1988. The Foreshore Precinct project ran into opposition from the Geelong City Council and the Port of Geelong Authority, and the commission mounted a major publicity campaign explaining and defending its plan. In 1990 the GRC made some concessions to their opposition, dropping from their plan a drygoods supermarket and a fruit and vegetable market, against which objections had been raised. At the time their 1989-1990 *Annual Report* was published, however, the stalemate had not been broken.

Industrial parks played a significant role in GRC's development strategy. At their City Side Estate all available lots have been sold, and their six unit factories leased. In their Breakwater Industrial Estates 38 businesses employing 600 people are located. In more recently completed estates, such as Ocean Grove Industrial Park and Corio Bay Industrial Park, the available lots are sold or leased as they are completed.

The commission took full advantage of the presence within the region of Deakin University, a youthful and dynamic institution eager to share the results of its research with the private enterprise community. An effective partnership was worked out for the commercialization of promising results of research undertaken at the university. The commission also benefited from the presence in Geelong of the famous Geelong Grammar School, where Prince Philip of England received his secondary school education. The GRC established a computerized data bank providing information about research skills and other specialized skills available in the region. The bank also includes high-technology plant and equipment in the region. It covers 300 identified types of specialized equipment and 600 specialized skills available from 56 research centres in the region. As of 30 June 1990, 36 subscribers were utilizing this information.

MAP 17-4
Location of Geelong in Australia

LOCATION OF GEELONG IN AUSTRALIA

 GEELONG REGION

—··— STATE BOUNDARIES

N

MAP 17-5
The Geelong Region—Municipal Boundaries

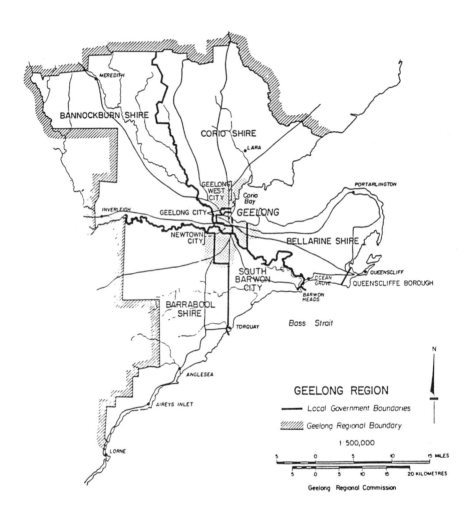

Geelong Regional Commission

TABLE 17.1
Organizational Structure

Geelong Regional Commission (as at 30 June 1988)
The Commission—Full-time (Chairman) (1)—Part-time Appointees—Councils
(9)—Governor-in-Council (4)
Chairman and Chief Executive—C.K. Atkins

Development and Construction	Planning and Design	Economic Development	Administration
R.J. Patterson, Director	D.P. Matthews, Director	G.A. McLean, Director	G.R. Cowling, Director
- Engineering Support	- Statutory Planning	- Economic Development	- Administrative
- Architecture	- Strategic Planning	- Department of Industry	- Finance & Accounting
- Drafting	- Research Development	- Technology & Resources	- Insurance
- Project Management	Implementation &	Agent for Regional	- Government Liaison
- Development Projects	Monitoring of Planning	Industry Policy Delivery	- Legal
- Maintenance of Commission Archives	- Planning Policies for Conservation & Pre-servation	- Property Acquisition and Sales	- Commission Secretary
- Records and Research	Property	- Economic and Market	- Computing and Word Processing
- Identification of the Need for, and Encouragement of the Educational, Cultural & Recreational Facilities	- Convention Bureau	- Public Relations and Provision of, Social	- Corporate Planning Publication Production
- Urban Design	Strategy Co-ordination	- Geelong Region Development	

Source: Geelong Regional Commission, *Annual Report 1987–88*, p. 4.

On the planning front, the commission's major product was their development strategy, published in August 1988, under the title "Directions: The Geelong Region Development Strategy," by the Victoria minister for Industry, Technology and Resources. It consisted of a 5-year plan and a 10-year "vision," plus a rolling one-year action plan. It was four years in the making, and involved a special study team and the local governments of the region, as well as the commission and its staff. Apart from this document there were

TABLE 17.2
Geelong Regional Commission Revenue and
Expense Statement for Year Ended 30 June 1990

	Note	1990	1989
Operating Revenue			
– Providing Fund Inflows			
State government grant	15.1	2,187,270	2,063,000
Municipal contributions	15.1	366,566	334,150
Proceeds from sale	—	—	—
Development properties	13	1,781,550	3,243,200
Rents from development properties	15.2	1,066,662	855,060
Interest on investments	15.2	2,168,664	1,971,080
Proceeds from sale of fixed assets	15.1	10,195	331,455
Other revenue	—	693,264	234,440
Total Operating Revenue			
– Providing Fund Inflows		**8,274,171**	**9,032,385**
Less Operating Expenses			
– Requiring Fund Outflows			
Operation and promotion costs	15.1/2	3,092,256	2,336,249
Interest on loans	15.2	2,000,022	2,245,381
Maintenance of development and			
community properties	15.1/2/3	437,987	681,297
Bad debts written off/recovered	7	4,643	(2,045)
Audit fees payable			
– Auditor general	15.1	8,000	8,000
Commissioners' emoluments	15.1	19,859	18,610
Book value of assets disposed of		793,065	2,278,045
Total Operating Expenses			
– Requiring Fund Outflows		**6,355,832**	**7,565,537**

many individual studies. It has already been noted that "The thoroughness, care, and professional competence with which these background studies were carried out is apparent from the documents themselves. Equally evident is the prudence with which the people who are interested in the results of implementing the strategy were brought into the planning process itself."[22]

In 1993, as part of the Victoria's strategy for simplifying and rationalizing local government in the State, the various municipalities in the Geelong Region were amalgamated into one city, Greater Geelong. The functions and responsibilities of the former Geelong Regional Commission were transferred to the town planning board of the new city.

TABLE 17.2 (Con'd)
Geelong Regional Commission Revenue and
Expense Statement for Year Ended 30 June 1990

	Note	1990	1989
Operating Surplus **– Providing Fund Inflows**		1,918,339	1,466,848
Operating Expenses **– Not Requiring Fund Outflows**			
Depreciation			
– Development properties		433,482	270,293
– Fixed assets		74,753	43,260
Provision			
– Long service leave		40,056	65,287
Total Operating Expenses **– Not Requiring Fund Outflows**	14	548,291	378,840
Less Operating Revenue **– Not Providing Fund Inflows**		—	—
Operating Surplus/Deficit **– Not Providing Fund Outflows**		(548,291)	(378,840)
Operating Surplus/Deficit for Year	15.4	1,370,048	1,088,008
Retained Surplus at 1 July 1989		2,439,970	2,185,593
		3,810,018	3,273,601
Available for appropriation			
Transfer to:			
– Capital profits reserve	3	106,641	833,631
Retained Surplus at 30 June 1990		3,703,377	2,439,970

The accompanying notes form part of these financial statements
Source: Geelong Regional Commission, *Annual Report 1989–90*, pp. 20–21.

The Latrobe Regional Commission

The Latrobe Regional Commission was established by the Victoria government (Ministry of Industry, Commerce and Technology) in December 1983, by the Latrobe Regional Commission Act. The region contains 9,382 square kilometres and has a population of about 120,000 people. It is located in the southeast corner of the state, about two hours drive from Melbourne. (See Map 17-6). There are 18 commissioners; 1 each for the 10 municipalities of the region; 1 each to represent the trade unions, the employers, and the water and sewage board; 2 representing community and welfare organizations; and 3 nominated by the minister. The staff is much the same size as the GRC staff:

the chairman; 14 administrative officers, including 1 economist, 1 accountant, a director of social development, a social research officer, and a development specialist; 5 town planners; 2 senior executives, 1 for economic development and 1 for social development; 1 landscape architect; 1 project engineer; 1 arts consultant; 1 marketing consultant; 1 scientist (environment officer); 2 drafting officers; 3 clerical officers; 2 word processors; and 2 secretaries; 40 in all.[23]

The objectives of the commission are said to be:[24]

a)   to co-ordinate the planning of the economic, physical, environmental, and social development of the Latrobe region;
b)   to improve the co-ordination of and to facilitate the development of major projects in the region;
c)   to assist in the implementation of state policies in relation to the region;
d)   to assist in the economic development of the region;
e)   to involve the regional community in decision-making in relation to the region.

The economic and social problems confronting the Latrobe region seem to be more serious, or at any rate more visible, than in the Geelong region. Employment is heavily concentrated in three resource-based activities: electricity generation (SECV); forestry, pulp and paper product (APM); and oil and gas production (ESSO-BHP). These three enterprises employ almost one-third of the labour force and produce more than half the gross regional product. SECV alone generates more than one third of the region's total employment. Thus the region is uncomfortably dependent on these three enterprises, which are not expanding. Indeed, SECV has recently reduced its work force by 25 percent, and plans further cuts. APM has also made major cuts, and ESSO-BHP is moving its administrative staff to Melbourne. With its major employers shrinking, the region becomes heavily dependent on unstable fields of activity, like construction. Consequently, the regional economy is subject to severe fluctuations. As the commission puts it in their strategy document, *Steps Ahead*: "The development of the Latrobe Region has been characterized by peaks and troughs of activity associated with the development of brown coal and other natural resources. The cyclic pattern of accelerated development followed by periods of slow growth or decline has paralleled the development of power stations and is a characteristic of resource-based communities."[25]

The nature of the region's base industries has demographic repercussions. The work force is young and male-dominated, with few employment opportunities for females. There is a relatively high demand for technical and trade skills, with a corresponding lack of professional and managerial positions. This situation leads to a net inflow of single males or males with young fami-

MAP 17-6

The Latrobe Region

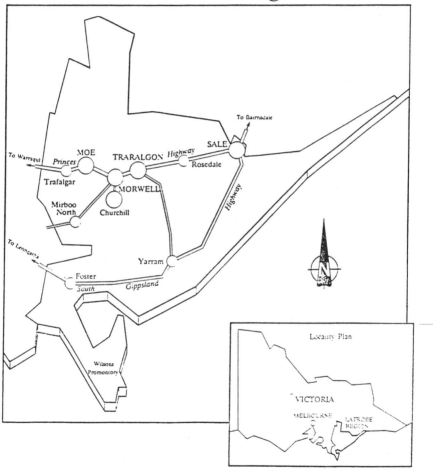

lies, resulting in a high proportion of population in the 25–40 group and net outflows of population in the 15–19 and 45 and over age groups. This situation must lead either to a rapid increase in the demand for jobs in the next few years or a net outflow of residents of the region who are in a particularly productive age group.

According to the commission's *Annual Report* for 1989/90, the region produces 85 percent if the state's electricity, has 87 percent of Australia's crude oil reserves, 53 percent of its natural gas liquids, and 36 percent of its natural gas reserves. Aren't these substantial blessings? Perhaps, but as stated above, if the region is to grow and prosper, it must generate employment in high-tech, high-productivity, and high-income enterprises. When it comes to attracting such industries, and the kind of people they need to be successful, the commission worries about the "image" created by the region's "blessings." "The old images of power stations, holes in the ground, pollution and so on still linger on."[26] The commission has therefore launched an "Image Project," which includes promotion of arts and cultural projects within the region, and publicity of various kinds to present "a more diversified and vital image which reflects (the region's) various strengths and lifestyle advantages."

The kind of activities which the commission undertakes in its efforts to diversify and strengthen its economic base can be illustrated by a few examples from its most recent *Annual Report* (1989/90). A major triumph in 1990 was attracting to Morwell the Data Processing Centre of the Australian Securities Commission. "This Centre will employ over 300 people and is one of the most advanced data processing and retrieval centres in the world."[27] This success should certainly contribute a good deal to improving the region's "image." The commission considers it "a landmark in diversifying the region's economy, and hopefully, created a precedent for future action."[28] (p. 4). The commission also launched a major marketing promotion for its plastics industry; opened a new horticulture venture with hydroponics techniques and warm water from the Hazelwood Power Station cooling tower; launched the Regional Strategy Plan, the Regional Land Use Policy, and the Regional Environment Policy as outlined in its document *Steps Ahead*; continued its arts and crafts promotion through its Arts Marketing Association and a 5-day concert series by the Melbourne Symphony Orchestra; established a Gippsland Regional Chamber Orchestra; provided funding to help in opening a fast ferry service from Gippsland to Tasmania; assisted over 500 businesses; assisted the regional tourism industry; organized a campaign to have the proposed very fast train from Sydney to Melbourne, routed through Gippsland; provided over a quarter of a million dollars for landscaping and tree planting; completed arrangements for two new TV stations in the region; continued assistance to enterprises attracted to the region in the recent past, and its campaign to attract new ones.

At the end of the fiscal year 1990 the commission had assets of $7.9 million. During the year it received revenues of $4.6 million, $2.8 million from the government of Victoria and about $900,000 from rentals, leases, and interest. It spent $3.3 million, earning a surplus of $1.3 million. (See Table 17.3).

Steps Ahead

The commission's "Regional Strategy Plan" is a document of 54 pages, with supporting studies. It was published by the Victoria Ministry of Planning and Urban Growth in April 1990. It has three major parts: I. The Regional Strategy; II. The Regional Land Use Policy; and III. The Regional Environment Policy. Part I presents an analysis of the physical and environmental, economic, and social features of the region. It points out that there is no one dominant town in the region; instead of concentrating on one growth pole for the region, the plan encourages the towns "to develop their own distinctive range of specialist functions."[29] In addition to the problems outlined above, it notes that the housing sector is on the decline because of the stagnation in the principal sectors; the increased numbers of residents of the region who are living on government transfer payments of one sort or another; and the broken families and distorted age and sex structures resulting from emigration of "breadwinners" following delays in starting construction of two proposed new power plants. The commission estimates that 18.6 percent of the region's families are living below the poverty line, as compared to 18 percent for the state as a whole. From this point of view, therefore, Latrobe is not a particularly distressed region. However, the commission concludes its "Community Profile" by stating, "At present, socio-economic indicators of community well-being and buoyant economic conditions are declining and those reflecting social distress are increasing."[30]

Turning to the future, the commission is not highly optimistic. The region will be "largely influenced by developments in the principal sector;" and even if all new base load power stations in Victoria are built in the region, "a period of rapid regional growth cannot be expected." To create the target number of jobs each year (400), the strategy must be capable of developing regionally-based industries, revitalizing established industries, and attracting investors from outside. Among other things, the strategy must ensure that education and vocational training are oriented towards establishing a wider skills base. In luring industry from outside, the strategy will concentrate on "those industries where the Region has a demonstrated competitive advantage," and which need the kind of technical and professional skills the region has to offer.[31] The target for established industry is essentially a holding action, but even that will require heavy investment. The strategy envisages the expenditure of more than $1 billion over 5 years by SECV alone. It also envisages a good deal of expenditure on infrastructure.

The Land Use Planning discussed in Part II operates under the Planning and Environment Act of 1987, which defines the LRC as a Regional Planning Authority. The general goal of the planning is defined as "to ensure a high quality of life for the people of the region and the responsible use and management of the Region's resources." This part contains maps showing actual and proposed land use.

The LRC is empowered to deal with environmental issues under the Latrobe Regional Commission Act, and required to do so under the Planning and Environment Act of 1987. Given its geography and the nature of its economic base, the region confronts severe environmental problems. One of these that gives the commission and the population of the region much concern is the greenhouse effect. Part III of *Steps Ahead* states bluntly, "The Region's brown coal-fired power stations are, however, a very large contributor to the production of Greenhouse gases and thus it could be expected that measures to reduce Greenhouse gas emissions would particularly affect this Region."[32] A related problem is the coal overburden dumps. The mines are open cut, and overburden has to be removed and dumped, leaving a badly scarred landscape. Under public pressure the SECV is undertaking a rehabilitation policy for open cuts and overburden dumps. A third major problem is air pollution, especially the smoke from SECV's chimneys and the offensive odours from APM's mills. Both of these are being substantially reduced. There is also concern regarding the region's coastline, some of which is threatened by erosion and rising sea levels. Apart from these major issues, there are the usual problems of forest management, tree planting, landscaping, waste disposal, streams and catchments, water quality and Heritage sites. All of these are addressed in Part III of *Steps Ahead*.

Application of Theory in Australian Regional Development

We have seen that the Australian states do not differ much from each other, and that, accordingly, redistribution from more prosperous to poorer states has never played a significant role in Australian regional policy. We have seen too that the early history of Australia as a penal colony, with settlers as prisoners and their guards, made Australia into a land of social protest: "The Workers' Paradise" was the goal, rather than operation of "the market." The goal was expressed as an unwritten social contract, consisting of "Protection and the Fair Go." Protection took many forms, but one of them, when Australia began to industrialize in the late nineteenth century, was tariffs and quantitative controls. Since most of the population lived in the capital cities, and there was not much difference between them, the spatial pattern of industrialization was somewhat haphazard. Now, however, the government is realizing that after more than a century of this kind of development, Australia has become a highly inefficient country. The present (Keating) government is committed to a policy of reducing protection, although the country is still in recession, with unemployment above 10 percent, and youth unemployment reaching 50 percent in some areas.

Given all this, and the difficulties the rural sector is currently facing, after decades of prosperity, regional policy is increasingly defining itself as helping areas with particularly pressing adjustment problems. These are scattered all over the country. Nor are particular industries in difficulties because they are in the wrong *place*; textiles, clothing, boots and shoes, base metal products, furniture, even automobiles, would be in difficulties wherever they were, and indeed are found in all states. Moreover, the Australian attitude is that people should not be disadvantaged because of the *place* where they live; and with some justice, because the places where they live are not basically all that different.

The Country Centres Program was on a very small scale. As we have seen, only 11 centres were established. Fifty-eight business opportunities were identified, of which 19 were deemed to be worth carrying to the feasibility study stage, and only 7 were actually studied. There was a lack of management, entrepreneurship, and skills, which is not surprising in small country towns in need of "adjustment." The Regional Organizations of Councils were also too small to be effective. Even the Western Sydney Regional Organization of Councils, whose nine cities taken together would constitute the fourth biggest urban centre in the country, has a budget of only $215,000 and a full-time staff of four. If the ROCs are given the task of coordinating the work of the Regional Economic Development Organizations, as recommended by the task force, their importance will be considerably enhanced.

The regional commissions are another matter. The Geelong Regional Commission had a staff of 35 full-time professionals, the Latrobe Commission 40. They were capable of having a significant impact, and have done so. What theories, then, lay behind their work?

Both the theory of international and interregional trade, and location theory, has been "applied" in the first sense, of explaining how these regions got where they are today. They have also been used in the second and third senses, of interpreting and explaining what is happening now, and predicting what is likely to happen in the future. They have even been "applied" in a pragmatic way to the selection of activities for the future. Both regions have tried to

TABLE 17.3
Revenue and Expense Statement
for the Year Ended 30 June 1990

	Note	1990($)	1989($)
Revenue-Providing Fund Inflows			
Funds From Government and			
Municipalities			
Victorian government grants			
Recurrent	13	1,753,398	1,419,093
Special development fund		1,114,000	904,000
ASC project	6	414,181	—
Municipal council contributions	14	491,149	446,887
Funds From Corporation			
Rental and lease interest	15	350,231	352,253
Mortgage interest	11	148,140	82,278
Interest on short term deposits		293,424	197,022
Other	12	65,187	108,757
Total Revenue—Requiring Fund Inflows		**4,629,710**	**3,510,290**
Less Operating Expenses—Requiring			
Fund Outflows			
Salaries and associated expenses	16	1,454,254	1,281,085
Special development fund	17	517,810	520,465
Office accommodation and services		174,931	173,421
Regional promotion		72,365	111,181
Gippsland Region Information Bank			
Contribution		88,450	78,750
Commissioner's allowances and expenses	18	36,043	34,514
Consultants' fees		136,354	75,252
Administration expenses	20	402,359	315,847
ASC project	6	414,181	—
Total Operating Expenses—			
Requiring Fund Outflows		**3,296,747**	**2,590,515**
Operating Surplus Requiring			
Fund Outflows/Inflows			
Before Finance Charges		**1,332,963**	**919,775**
Less Finance charges			
Interest charges on government loan		274,996	274,956
Operating Surplus Requiring			
Fund Outflows/Inflows		**1,057,967**	**644,819**

TABLE 17.3 (Con't)
Revenue and Expense Statement
for the Year Ended 30 June 1990

	Note	1990($)	1989($)
Operating Expenses Not Requiring Fund Outflows			
Depreciation non-current assets	10 & 1/1/2	122,783	74,889
Amortisation leasehold improvements	10 & 19	12,255	9,145
Net increase in provision for long service leave		30,140	39,000
Increase in provision for annual leave		14,120	16,300
Operating Deficit Not Requiring Funds Outflows		**179,298**	**139,334**
Operating Surplus Before Extraordinary Items		**878,669**	**505,485**
Extraordinary Items			
Net recovery from insurance claims	21	41,250	736,916
Solatium on exchange of land with roads corporation			
Profit on sale of industrial property	21	30,000	71,250
		115,000	851,916
Surplus for Year		**949,919**	**1,357,401**
Retained Surplus/Deficit at beginning of year		**945,531**	**(28,335)**
Available for appropriation		1,895,450	1,329,066
Transfer to reserve: – Special development fund		596,189	383,535
Retained Surplus/Deficit at end of year		**1,299,261**	**945,531**

Source: Latrobe Regional Commission, *Annual Report 1989–90*, p. 41.

build on their comparative advantage and the strong features of their location, in attracting new enterprises to the region. Both have tried to overcome disadvantages, particularly Latrobe.

In the same way, both regions have applied the theory of regional dualism. Both are within the sphere of influence of the city of Melbourne, and both are keenly aware of the need to offset the attraction of that centre if they are to establish enterprises in their region. The planners in both commissions know very well that Melbourne is *the* "pôle de croissance" in their region, and look for ways of offsetting that fact. They recognize that they are "central places" rather than growth poles; which does not mean that they cannot grow.

When it comes to entrepreneurship, rather than just theorizing about it, the regional commissions have provided it themselves, and created conditions which have attracted it from outside the region. That has been their great achievement. Canada, by way of contrast, has relied too much on entrepreneurship being available within the community, and providing it with loans, grants, and infrastructure. Sometimes, as in the case of Moncton, this system works, because the entrepreneurship is there. But in other circumstances, as in Cape Breton or Northeast New Brunswick, the entrepreneurship available is limited to the traditional industries of the region, and merely throwing money at it does not bring "adjustment" or expansion.

Australian Regional Development Policy 1993–1994

During the campaign leading up to the elections of March 1993, the Labor Party announced its new economic strategy, entitled "One Nation," as a response to the Liberal-National Coalition's strategy statement "Fightback." The prime minister followed this statement with two other economic policy speeches, in February 1993, on "Investing in the Nation" and "Building on Strength." All three statements included measures which would make Australia more competitive in the global economy. These included government investment in infrastructure, education and training, microeconomic reform of government business undertakings, industrial relations and workplace reform, improvements in management and productivity, substantial reductions in tariffs, reduced company taxation, incentives for research and development, and incentives to investment more generally.

As part of the package, the government outlined a new commitment to regional development in Australia. It announced that it would set up a new Department of Industry, Technology and Regional Development and, within in, an Office of Regional Development and a Task Force for Regional Development. In his first major speech after his victory at the polls, in June 1993, the prime minister elaborated his new regional development policy. In effect, he recognized that a strategy of national economic development, involving a good deal of restructuring and adjustment, and a commitment to full employment, would require analysis, planning, and implementation at the regional level, and cooperation of private enterprise, labor, and federal, state and local governments. "Regional" in this context, means essentially *all* of Australia outside the major metropolitan centers. The objective is not to redistribute income and employment from rich to poor regions, but to raise productivity, employment, and incomes in *all* of the ninety-four regions distinguished by the Office of Regional Development, by studying them, in collaboration with the private sector, in relation to their problems and potential, so that each region can move towards the activities for which they are best suited. Thus, regional development is seen as an integral and major aspect of national economic policy. Regional disparities may be reduced as a byproduct of measures taken to realize to the full the potential of all regions, but reduction of regional disparities is not the major objective.

In this speech, the commitment to full employment was quite explicit. The prime minister said: "It seems to me that to say that we are not committed to full employment would be to say that we are not committed to Australia. Of course, we are committed to full employment, but we have to do more than say so."[33]

He also made it clear that the program of regional development was essential to the achievement of full employment, as well as other objectives outlined in "Investing in the Nation" and "Building on Strength." The proposed investments in various infrastructure projects "are essential to allow Australia to reach its full potential. But it must also be understood that they will allow *regions* to reach their full potential. Regional development is a matter of high priority. The process of structural adjustment has had geographic dimensions which we cannot ignore. The dimensions are unemployment, hardship, and disaffection.... There is a lot to be gained by success in (regional development): the stimulation of industry and employment in regional Australia; the maximum use of our natural and human resources;...very often regional industries have specialized character that sells abroad;...Regional development means national development on a regional basis.... The role of the Commonwealth will not be to deliver money by the drayload, but to assist the regions to take advantage of their potential."[34]

In a paper delivered to the 13th Meeting of the Pacific Regional Science Conference Organization in July 1993, Steve Garlick, General Manager of the Office of Regional Development, characterized Australia's new regional development policy as follows: "For the Australian Government, regional development is about generating the best economic and social return to outlay for the nation as a whole, across the private, public and household sectors. Only by better matching the diverse economic, physical and human resource potential of our regions to existing and emerging market opportunities will the full economic flow-on benefits from broad macroeconomic and microeconomic measures and concurrent growth international and domestic demand occur."[35]

The promised Regional Development Task Force was inaugurated in July 1993. Support of organized labor is virtually assured by the nomination of

Bill Kelty, Secretary of the Australian Council of Trade Unions, as chairman. The Secretary of the Department of Industry, Technology, and Regional Department is a member, more or less *ex officio*. The other nine members are prominent representatives of private enterprise and local government. Its terms of reference are to: 1) identify key economic and industry development issues from a regional perspective; 2) examine factors affecting private sector investment in regional development; 3) examine whether any adjustments should be made to Commonwealth policies and programs are required to enhance the adjustment process and regional development in Australia.

The terms of reference also state: "The Task Force will be complementary to the current industry Commission Inquiry on Regional Industry Adjustment and will report to the Minister for Industry, Technology and Regional Development by 10 December 1993." The general manager of the Office of Regional Development also serves as senior manager of the Regional Task Force Secretariat.

The Task Force Report

The report of the Task Force on Regional Development was published just before Christmas 1993. Its title indicates its approach: *Developing Australia: A Regional Perspective*. Its main concerns are to reduce unemployment at the *national* level, by concentrating the attack on unemployment in the regions where it is highest and to make the *national* economy more internationally competitive. It covers a wide range of policies, including many that are not usually considered part of "regional" policy. The report is in two volumes. The first presents a statement of objectives, and makes 129 recommendations, on financing regional development, transport, the labor market, education, industrial policy, communications, agriculture, water, the environment, aboriginal and Torres Strait Islanders, culture and heritage, tourism, energy, business support, and empowering the regions. The second volume presents profiles of 66 regions, defined by the task force on the basis of public meetings organized by them in the regions. In the course of their three months of investigations, the team "visited nearly every region in Australia" and received over 300 submissions from regional authorities, private enterprises, educational institutions, mayors, town councils, government departments and private individuals. In his Foreword to Volume Two, Bill Kelty writes: "I am delighted to present this landmark document. It is a report from the Regional Development Taskforce, but more importantly it represents the views of men and women working in the regions which make up Australia. It is a vision, region by region, of what Australia could, and should be an expression of the plans and hopes of Australians for Australia."[36]

The most original sections of Volume One are those concerned with Financing Regional Development and Empowering the Regions. With regard to the first of these, after a brief summary of the concerns of people from "the regions," the report states: "The report outlines a regional development plan on a national scale and is, in effect, a plan for national development. The Taskforce believes that wherever possible the private sector should be encouraged to play a major role in financing development through the regions. However, there is an argument for greater public investment in infrastructure and increases in taxes and charges to pay for it. The argument is based on the link between efficient infrastructure and economic development—the link between good roads, ports and railways for example and the ability of companies which use them to compete in global markets."[37]

It should be noted first of all that the recommendations of the task force do not involve net increases in federal government expenditures, deficits, or transfer payments to lower levels of government. The projects to be financed by the federal government are all within existing programs. The "regional" aspect of these programs consists in deciding, on the basis of careful analysis of the problems and potential of *all* regions, *where* to put *what* projects and *when*. It is hoped that, even in infrastructure, much of the investment will be private. The "One Nation" program allowed private enterprises to issue "infrastructure bonds" to finance public road or rail transport, port facilities, and electricity generation, on public land, and allowed more generous depreciation for tax purposes. The task force urges government to encourage the development of an infrastructure bond market.

Under the heading of Empowering the Regions, the main recommendation is the establishment of regional economic development organizations: "The Taskforce believes that the Federal Government should establish a program to provide financial assistance to Regional Economic Development Organisations (REDOs)."[38] Cooperation among REDOs could be attained through the Regional Organizations of Councils. The form of financing the REDOs should be determined in consultation with the states, but the funding should come from within existing programs.

The Committee on Employment Opportunities

The Committee on Employment Opportunities was commissioned on 28 May 1993, and its report was also published towards the end of December 1993, entitled *Restoring Full Employment: A Discussion Paper*. The two reports are complementary to each other, as *Restoring Full Employment* makes clear: "Ultimately, the success of the CES (Commonwealth Employment Service) in placing people in jobs will depend upon whether the labour market programs and services it manages are relevant to local and regional employment conditions. Programs need to equip jobseekers with the skills required by local employers. Recent employment growth has been concentrated in the small and medium business sector (Chapter One). Much of this business has a regional or local focus. It is, therefore, increasingly important that assistance be targeted at this level (p. 155)....the capacity and potential of regional communities to respond to the problem of unemployment is relatively untapped."[39]

Thus, we see that today in Australia, restoring full employment and regional development policy are closely linked.

In a manner reminiscent of the early days of DREE in Canada, the Commonwealth government is trying to harmonize the approach of the various departments in the federal government to regional development, and also to harmonize the approaches of the Commonwealth and the State and Territory governments. A Ministerial Council of Industry, Technology and Regional Development has been established as a forum for discussion of regional policy issues. One of the council's first tasks will be to examine the reports of the task force and the industries commission, to assure greater harmonization of regional policies and programs. Within the Commonwealth government, officials will review programs that have an impact on regional development so as to improve their coordination. A government caucus committee has been established to provide political advice on regional development issues. This committee will consider the draft reports of the task force and industries commission, examine Commonwealth programs in terms of their effectiveness for regional development, and visit a number of regions to identify their problems and potential. All proposals coming before Cabinet from Commonwealth departments and agencies will be required to include an assessment of their regional impact. A contract has been let to a competent private consulting firm to prepare a major study of the factors influencing decisions of private enterprise concerning location of industry, especially in the "regions" (outside major metropolitan centres). On the basis of all of these initiatives, a policy statement will be issued early in 1994, and policy recommendations for regional development will be included in the Commonwealth budget for 1994-95.

The States

Supplementing these initiatives at the Commonwealth level are various measures by the states. Early in 1993, the government of Victoria established its own Office of Regional Development (ORD) in the Department of Business and Employment. To the Victoria government, "regional" has much the same meaning as to the Commonwealth government: "outside the main metropolitan centres." The main function of the Victoria ORD is to coordinate all government efforts concerned with development of rural and small-town areas of the state. There are twenty-one regional economic development organizations, including the three statutory corporations of Geelong, Latrobe and Albury-Wodonga. They make financial grants to firms, study industries in certain sectors, establish regional teams to coordinate state and local government development efforts, and work with business and community groups.

In 1993, Western Australia introduced a Regional Development Administration bill dealing with all aspects of regional development. It established nine regional development commissions, administered by ten-person boards, with three representatives each from local government, the community, and the government of the state, and the director *ex officio*. Each commission has a small (7–12) full-time staff.

Queenland's regional development policy was stated in an announcement by the premier in April 1992, entitled: "Leading State: State Economic Development Policy." The two main themes were that the government's strategy for regional development must take account of the needs and potential of all regions in the state, and that economic development must take account of the needs and potential of all regions in the state, and that economic development should be commercially viable, rather than depending on government support in the long run, regional development is the responsibility of the Department of Business, Industry and Regional Development (DBIRD), which now has twelve regional offices with twenty-nine percent of DBIRD's total staff of 130, compared to six regional offices with six percent of the total staff four years ago.

South Australia has an Economic Development Authority (EDA), which funds ten regional development boards, which are expected to grow to thirteen in the near future. The EDA prepared a state economic plan that was announced late in 1993, incorporating proposals for regional development based on South Australia's submission to the Regional Development Task Force.

Tasmania's government feels that it is too small, too insular, with sixty percent of its widely dispersed population living outside the capital city, Hobart, to be divided into subregions for development purposes, and accordingly advocates a "One Region" approach. The Tasmania Development Authority, established in 1985, operates on an industrial and sectoral basis for its development planning and implementation rather than a regional basis.

New South Wales has a Department of Business and Regional Development, which was established in July 1993. Its policy was also announced late in 1993, following consultation through regional forums. Eleven country regions have been defined, each with its regional development board.

The DBIRD has an Office for Regional Development with thirteen offices throughout the state.

The Northern Territory is preparing a "strategy for the top end" which will be released late in 1994. The territory is divided into five regions for planning purposes, including the capital city, Darwin.

Thus the same forces which led to an absence of federal legislation and budgets to encourage development of disadvantaged states, also led to provisions for development of small regions, no matter what state they are in. The objective is not to redistribute income from richer to poorer small regions. The gap between the richest and poorest small region in the country is not insignificant; but the aim of the development programs for small regions is to raise productivity, create jobs, raise incomes, improve levels of social services, and protect the environment of any, and ultimately every, small region, no matter where it stands at the moment on scales of prosperity or social welfare. The instruments made available for achieving this end are: the injection of the requisite professional skills and entrepreneurship in the decision-making process; thorough knowledge of the region, its people, its problems, and its potential; working continuously with the target population, the entrepreneurs who will implement the program, and governments at all three levels; and, of course, judicious allocation of modest amounts of money, to launch new enterprises and to expand and improve existing ones. None of these instruments involves *replacing* private enterprise and private decision making with public enterprise and decision making by politicians and bureaucrats.

At time of writing, it seemed probable that the Commonwealth government would adopt most of the recommendations of the task force, leading in effect to a regionalization of national economic policy. An article in *The Australian*, one of Australia's three or four leading national dailies, (February 16th, page 2) had this to say: "The Government is expected to adopt an important plank of the Kelty Taskforce on Regional Development—a network of regional economic development organizations to deliver a range of government services. Rather than adopting a raft of new programs, ministers plan an overhaul and expansion of existing schemes to provide enough places to meet the "job compact" guarantees of jobs or training places for the long term unemployed.... An important aspect of the plan for regional development organization will be "shopfronts" that provide a range of social security, employment, and business services under one roof.... It is expected the Prime Minister, Mr. Keating, will combine the main elements of these policy initiatives in a White Paper policy statement, which will be supported by separate policy statements on employment, regional development, and industry."

The section of the report of the task force entitled "Issues for Regional Development" is highly pragmatic, dealing with such mundane matters as the nation's need for better and safer roads; the importance of harmonizing the gauges of the state railway systems; the necessity of tackling the unemployment problem, which differs enormously in intensity from region to region; the importance of access to higher education and improving the international competitiveness of Australian industry; the need for access to telecommunications outside the major metropolitan centers; improving the quality and quantity of the nation's water supply; protecting the environment; and creation of a national electricity grid. These are primarily technical and engineering problems rather than economic problems; they are "economic" problems only to the extent that the measures taken to solve them must be financed without aggravating inflation; and this problem, according to the present Australian government, is a matter of national monetary and fiscal policy, not of regional policy. There are very few clues in the report as to what general theories of regional development underlay the recommendations of the task force.

There were no professional regional economists on the task force, although there are some in the Office of Regional Development. This fact, together with the very small role of regional economics in the academic profession of economics in Australia, and the absence of lively debate on regional development issues in Australian books and journals on economics, would account for the "lack of clues" to underlying theories in the report. Perhaps, as the regionalization of national economic policy takes effect, all this will change. It will be interesting to watch and see. It seems that Australia now has the apparatus for undertaking national planning at the regional level. It is a highly decentralized system, both in the planning and the implementation phases. Private enterprise and labor organization will play a major role in both phases. Federal, state and local governments will be involved, as well as various organizations and groups, from the community level to the Commonwealth Cabinet. In principle, it is capable of providing the "grass roots democracy" and "democratic planning" that the Tennessee Valley Authority was established to achieve in the United States, but never quite delivered.

Notes

1. Russell Mathews, "Regional Disparities and Fiscal Equalization in Australia," in Russell Mathews, (ed), *Regional Disparities and Economic Development* (Canberra, Australian National University, 1981), pp. 1-20.
2. Fred Alexander, *Moving Frontiers* (Melbourne: Melbourne University Press, 1947), p. 28.
3. H.K. Hancock, *Australia* (Melbourne: Penguin, 1945), p. 405.
4. Leonie Sandercock, "Urban Policy," in Allan Patience and Brian Head (eds), *From Whitlam to Fraser* (Melbourne and Oxford: Oxford University Press, 1979), p. 170-71.

5. Benjamin Higgins, "Regional Development Policy: The Australian Case," in ed. Niles Hansen, Benjamin Higgens, and Donald J. Savoie, *Regional Policy in a Chaning World* (New York: Plenum Press, 1990), p. 172.

6. DILGEA, Canberra, *Australian Regional Development: 8-1 Country Centres Project 1986*, 1987, p. 2.

7. *Ibid.*

8. *Ibid.*, p. 11.

9. *Ibid.*, p. 12.

10. *Ibid.*, p. 13.

11. *Ibid.*, p. 18.

12. *Ibid.*, pp. 20–22.

13. *Ibid.*, pp. 21–22.

14. *Ibid.*, p. 24.

15. *Ibid.*, p. 25.

16. Benjamin Higgins and Donald J. Savoie, *Canadians and Regional Development at Home and in the Third World* (Moncton: The Canadian Institute for Research on Regional Development, 1988).

17. DILGEA, 1987, p. 30.

18. Gordon Craig, *Regional Organizations of Council*, (Canberra: DILGEA, 1990), p. 11.

19. *Ibid.*, p. 19.

23. Latrobe Regional Commission, *Annual Report, 1989–90*, p. 39.

24. Latrobe Regional Commission, *Annual Report, 1986*, p. 8.

25. Latrobe Regional Commission, *Steps Ahead* (Australia, 1989), p. 6.

26. Latrobe Regional Commission, *Annual Report, 1989–90*, p. 31.

27. *Ibid.*, p. 4.

28. *Ibid.*

29. *Ibid.*, p. 5.

30. *Ibid.*, p. 9.

31. *Ibid.*, p. 16.

32. *Ibid.*, p. 8.

33. The Honorable Paul J. Keating, *Speech to the New South Wales Labor Party State Conference*, 13 June 1993, p. 9.

34. *Ibid.*, pp. 10–11.

35. Steve Garlick, "Competitive Regional Development: New Policy Initiatives of the Australian Government," Speech to the 13th meeting of the Pacific Regional Science Organization, Whistler, B.C., July 11–14, 1993, p. 8.

36. *Developing Australia: A Rgional Perspective*, report of the Task Force on Regional Development, Canberra, Ministry of Industry, Technology and Regional Development, December 1993, vol. 2, foreword.

37. *Ibid.*, vol. 1, p. 18.

38. *Ibid.*, p. 69.

39. *Restoring Full Employment: A Discussion Paper*, report of the Committee on Employment Opportunities, Canberra, December 1993, pp. 155–56.

18

Regional Development in Developing Countries

In its annual report on *World Development*, the World Bank lists 101 less developed countries (LDCs). These range in per capita income (1990) from $80 to $7,050; in rates of growth (1965-1990) from -3.3 to + 8.3 percent; in rates of inflation (1980-1990) from -2.7 to + 432.3 percent; in population (1990) from 1.1 million to more than 1,000 million; in area from 2,000 square kilometres to more than 20,000,000; in proportion of urban population from 5 to 77 percent; in proportion of gross domestic product produced in agriculture, industry and services, respectively, (1990) from 67, 7, and 26 percent to 3, 80, and 18 percent. Obviously, any generalization about a group of countries as diverse as these risks concealing more truth than it reveals. Nevertheless, for the majority of LDCs that are not in some way "exceptional," it is possible to say something about their application of regional development theory, and their regional policy and planning.

In the first place, nearly all of the LDCs are engaged in national development planning—partly, curiously enough, at the insistence of the multilateral and unilateral donors who would never dream of recommending national planning for their own countries. Most of the LDCs have a Ministry of Planning, a Planning Commission, or some similar body which is preparing regularly plans for the development of the country. These bodies are frequently among the most powerful and most competent in the country's bureaucracy. This fact changes entirely the atmosphere of regional planning in the LDCs. When regional plans are seen as components of a national plan, which has legal status, the role of regional planning is much greater than in countries where nothing like a national plan exists. Moreover, in recent years several LDCs have understood that the best way to prepare a national plan is through aggregation of regional plans; the national economy is simply an aggregation of regional economies, more or less loosely or tightly integrated. Among the countries that have proceeded in this fashion are countries as diverse as Brazil, Malaysia, Thailand, Sri Lanka and Haiti.

Regional development has become a favourite aspect of national development for foreign aid donors to support. There has been a tendency for countries preparing both national and regional development plans to carve up the national economy into regions, and offer them, as though on a platter, to various aid donors. Foreign aid is thus obtained for both the preparation and implementation of regional plans. A country or international agency which has provided a team of experts to prepare a regional development plan is quite likely to provide capital assistance for implementation as well.

The use of teams provided by technical assistance programs of the United Nations and various countries—Australia, Canada, France, Holland, Israel, Norway, Sweden, the United Kingdom, the United States—in different regions of the same LDCs inevitably led to some difficulty when it came to integrating the various regional plans into a national plan. The teams used different techniques and methodologies, stressed different aspects of regional development, began and ended their work at different times. On the other hand, it led to a great deal of cross-fertilization and innovation. When the regional planners of one LDC work together with regional planners of several different industrialized nations, new ideas are bound to emerge. When teams from various nations were in the field at the same time, they usually made contact with each other and compared notes, thus learning from each other.

The United Nations itself made two major contributions to thought about regional development. The United Nations Research Institute for Social Development mounted a research program on regional development under the direction of Antoni Kuklinski. Between 1971 and 1992 this program produced the 12 volumes of the UNRISD-Mouton Regional Planning Series, and 8 other volumes directly and indirectly related to this series. The authorship of these volumes was widely international, and included scholars and planners from Australasia, North America, Europe (both East and West) Africa, Asia and Latin America.

At about the same time, the United Nations Centre for Regional Development was established in Nagoya, Japan. There were to have been ten such centres in various parts of the world, but finance was forthcoming for only one. The UNCRD is both a training institution and a research centre. In its publications can be found many of the same names as on the UNRISD series. At its various conferences, seminars, and training programs as well, the same names turn up over and over again. Indeed, the chief contribution of UNCRD may be the building up of a world-wide network of scholars and practitioners of regional development, and the provision of a Centre where the same people could meet at frequent intervals for discussion. In this way the UNCRD probably made the biggest contribution to *theory* based on *practice* of all such institutions in the world. As time went by, UNCRD developed the atmosphere of a private club, whose members all knew and respected each other. Antoni Kuklinski, director of the UNRISD project was a member of the UNCRD "Club," and a frequent visitor to Nagoya. The two UN programs were thus closely integrated. The 1970s, when the two programs were running parallel and there were active programs in Australia, Canada, France, the U.K. and the U.S., was probably a peak period for regional development theory and its application.

The "Third World" provided regional planners from Australasia, Europe, and North America with a rich and highly varied laboratory in which to conduct experiments in regional development. Comparative analysis of experience in different LDCs became inevitable, and proved highly rewarding. They learned that a strategy and tactics that worked well in one region of one LDC might not work at all in another region in another—or even the same—country. They became keenly aware of the importance of cultural factors, which might have escaped their notice if they had worked only in their own or similar countries. They also learned about the impact of the political framework within which regional policy was formulated and implemented. They became doubtful of the universality of the laws of regional science in countries with such vast differences in natural resource endowment, soil, climate, hydrology, and topography. All in all, working in LDCs, as well as in their own countries, was a tremendous learning experience, and the literature on regional development has been greatly enriched as a result.

Many of the regional planners from Australasia, Europe, and North America actually spent more time during the 1970s and 1980s working on regional plans in Third World countries than in their own countries—including the present writer. Much of the new regional development theory was produced as a reaction to the efforts to develop LDCs. The applications of theory that we made was mainly in LDCs, and the lessons we learned were learned mainly in LDCs. However, we did not make a sharp distinction between what we learned in LDCs as group and in industrialized countries as a group. The learning process was a continuous one, and included experience in both less developed and industrialized countries.

Brazil

Brazil provides us with an example of a large, resource-rich, highly regionalized, country of recent settlement. For the last thirty-five years regional development has been a high priority objective of national economic policy. With an area of 8,512 million square kilometres, it is larger than Australia or conterminous United States. With a population of 150.4 million, it is much the most highly populated country in Latin America (the "Colossus of the South") but it still has resource frontiers and, on the whole, is not densely populated. It has a per capita income of $2,689 (1990) and a growth rate of 3.3 percent, putting it in the upper-income, high-growth bracket among developing countries. It has a very high rate of inflation (284.3 percent in 1990), but has had chronic inflation ever since the "price revolution" of the sixteenth century, following the discoveries of gold and silver by the Portuguese. By now it is well adjusted to inflation. Most incomes are indexed in some fashion or other, and the people have learned to live with it. The ratios of investment and savings to gross domestic product are high: 22 and 23 percent, compared to 16 and 15 percent in the United States. In 1990 Brazil was less dependent on exports of goods and services than any other country on the World Bank list, less developed or industrialized: 7 percent compared to 10 percent for the United States.

The history of the economic development of Brazil, from the sixteenth century to the mid-twentieth, has been one of repeated boom-and-bust. The first region to be settled and prosperous is precisely the one that gives most trouble today, the Northeast, especially the coastal areas. Sugar brought early prosperity to this region, with per capita incomes well above those prevailing in Europe at the time. In the early eighteenth century the boom was in gold, and Brazil became for a time the world's leading gold producer. It did not hold this position long. The peak in gold production was reached in 1760, and by the end of the century the boom was over. Coffee was planted early in the nineteenth century, but did not become the principal export until the last quarter of that century. With coffee, population and economic activity moved still further south. Brazil still exports coffee, but it has lost its importance as an export. Next came wild rubber, but that boom collapsed when it was found that plantations in Malaysia and Indonesia, using Brazilian clones, were more productive and more profitable. Since 1950 Brazil has turned increasingly to manufacturing, some of it quite high-tech.

Regional Disparities

Brazil suffers very large regional disparities, owing to the concentration of the modern sector in the South Central, and to a lesser extent the Southern region, and the concentration of the traditional sector in the Northeast and the North (Amazonia). Through the centuries the centre of population has moved from north to south, never very far from the Atlantic coast. The interior remains to this day largely unsettled, although in recent decades there has been an effort to open up the Amazon valley. Until 1959, when SUDENE (The Superintendency for the Development of the Northeast) was established, regional development was largely a matter of opening up new resource frontiers. The government's role was limited to providing transport and communications, rather inadequately. About the same time that SUDENE began operations the capital was moved to Brazilia, in a totally empty region. The construction of Brazilia, and of a road connecting it to Belem in the North, did succeed in pulling some population to the empty centre for the first time. At the time about one-third of the total population still lived in the Northeast, another 6 percent in the North. The per capita income of the richest region, the South Central, was four times that of the Northeast. The richest state, Guanabara (formerly the Federal Capital District) had a per capita income ten times as high, and the next richest state, São Paulo, six times as high as the poorest state, Piaui.

Yet when SUDENE was first set up, it was not the reduction of regional disparities that was its principal objective. Rather it was to offset the regular alternation of drought and floods, so that the peasants of the region would not inundate the South Central region, seeking food and employment, whenever disaster struck their own region. But by the time SUDENE published its First Master Plan, for the years 1961-63, it was thinking in terms of integrated regional development, and not just disaster relief. By the mid 1960s SUDENE's staff had grown to some 3,000 people, supported by about 150 American (USAID) experts and about 120 UN experts. A sister institution, the Banco do Nordeste, had also been established to deal with the problems of financing the implementation of the plans. The Third Plan for 1966-68 stated explicitly that its objective was to "diminish the inequality of income between the man in the drought polygon and his counterpart in the Center-South," and aimed at a target rate of growth of regional domestic product of 7 percent. It also stated that it aimed to promote the spatial and sectoral integration of the Northeastern economy, linking it more tightly to the national economy.

Amazonia

In 1963, the Banco de Credito da Amazonia, originally created to finance the rubber industry, was converted into a regional development bank, similar to the Banco do Nordeste. Together with SPVEA, the "Superintendency for the Economic Improvement (Valorization) of Amazonia" it promoted agriculture, livestock, mining and manufacturing in the North. They also built the Brazilia-Belem road, other roads, electricity plants, municipal water supply, and subsidized private enterprises in such fields as petroleum products, shipping lines, and air lines. In 1966, the names of the two authorities were changed to Banco do Amazonia S.A. (BASA) and Superintendencia do Desinvolvimento do Amazonia (SUDAM), but their policies remained much the same. They have concentrated mainly on badly needed infrastructure, especially roads. They undertook a modestly successful experiment with rubber plantations. Another interesting venture was POLAMAZONIA, designed to create rural growth poles with mixtures of agriculture and grazing, and of agriculture and mining.

The first official and formal expression of concern for regional development was the provision in the 1946 constitution that "in the Economic Valorization Plan of Amazonia, the Union will apply, during at least twenty years, a specified quantity of not less than 3 percent of its tax revenue" (Article 199). It adds, "The States and Territories of the region (Amazonia) along with their respective *municipios*, will reserve for the same goal, annually, 3 percent of their respective tax revenues. The resources which this paragraph concerns will be applied through the Federal Government."

Amazonia is the most vast of all Brazilian frontiers, with 59 percent of the country's total area and only 4 percent of its population. It is pierced by the mighty Amazon system and is still largely jungle. It has always captured the imagination of the Brazilian people. Yet for several years, Article 199 was more honoured in the breach than in the observance. Little was done in Amazonia, partly because of sheer technical difficulties of operating there and partly because the government in far-away Rio de Janeiro was more concerned with other matters. It was not until 1953 that the Superentendencia para Valorizacõ Economico do Amazonia (SPVEA), the regional development authority *(Superendencia)* for Amazonia was set up and a plan prepared. This first Five Year Plan was not yet implemented in 1966 because the Congress had not yet ratified it.

Thus it happened that the first "big push" in regional development took place, not in the mysterious and romantic north, but in the more mundane and calamity-ridden northeast.

All the richer states in the south and south central regions have their own development planning authorities. The State Planning Commission of São Paulo is among the most competent development authorities in the country. There is also the Conselho de Desenvolvimento do Extremo Sul (CODESUL), which prepares and implements development plans for the three prosperous states of the extreme southern region of the country: Parana, Santa Catarina, and Rio Grande do Sul. The organization of this council is of interest to people concerned with federal-provincial (or federal-state) relations in other countries. It consists of the governors of the three states, three representatives of the Union appointed by the president and the director-president of the Banco Regional de Desinvolvimento do Extreme Sul (the regional development bank established to supplement CODESUL) and an executive secretary. Thus both federal and state interests are protected in the administration of the regional authority.

In Brazil there is general recognition that even the more prosperous states need planned development. The planning, however, is designed to aid and abet decision-making and investment in the private sector, not to replace it. Concern for the welfare of people in lagging regions does not mean neglecting the interests of people in the more prosperous regions. The attitude is that there is more scope for raising productivity in the lagging regions than in those regions that are already dynamic, where technology is already advanced, and resources are already efficiently allocated. It is in this manner that regional disparities are to be narrowed, not by encouraging more rapid growth in the lagging regions *at the expense of growth* in the leading regions.

Regional development in Brazil has been a cooperative effort of the states, the regional authorities, and the national government. Because national development is regarded as an aggregation of regional development programs, it could not be otherwise, especially in a federal state. But by the same token, the national government has not hesitated to intervene when it felt that a state or regional authority was on the wrong track, or off the track altogether. Thus in 1970 SUDENE found itself unprepared for the renewed drought that struck the northeast in that year. The federal government then embarked on a new development strategy for the northeast, with increased emphasis on agricultural development, that largely sidetracked SUDENE's own program. They also prepared a special program for the São Francisco Valley. Two years later the national government prepared a 3-year plan for the northeast that replaced SUDENE's 5-year plan. This plan was followed by a national five-year plan (1975–1979) in which 37.7 percent of the budget allocated to the northeast was for social development, only 15.7 percent for infrastructure, and 14.1 percent for industry, a sharp shift from the strategies reflected in the series of plans prepared by SUDENE.

In fact regional policies in Brazil since World War II have not reduced regional disparities. What they have done is to prevent the gaps from getting worse in percentage terms. Growth rates in the poorer regions have been about the same as in the richer ones. More important, during most of the period the growth rates in all regions have been high, especially between 1965 and 1980. Given the obstacles that had to be overcome, that was no mean achievement.

It is an objective of national policy also to reduce regional gaps. However, there is no wish to achieve this goal by weakening the strong states. São Paulo is less clearly "the locomotive that pulls the other 20 States along" than when the Paulistas coined the phrase 20 years ago, but it is still the most dynamic state, and it is no part of regional policy to reduce that dynamism. Regional gaps are to be diminished, not by *redistribution* of income as a matter of social justice and political stability, but by eliminating excess capacity and unemployment and improving resource allocation in the lagging regions. Nor is there opposition to migration as a solution to poverty and unemployment. The Brazilians are a highly mobile people, and internal migration has played a major role in the country's development. There is objection only to the poor and unemployed flooding the plantation and mining areas, and the great cities, in search of jobs that are not there and that cannot be provided there.

In Brazil, attacking regional gaps by decentralizing urbanization and industrialization makes good sense. All the industrial and urban growth cannot take place in São Paulo and Rio de Janeiro. These are already huge cities, with population growth too rapid to handle. São Paulo may well be the most modern city in the world; it makes Manhattan look like a village. Rio is not far behind, but both now suffers from congestion and pollution. Rio is squeezed between mountains and sea, can grow only along the coast, and is eating up its beautiful bay to reclaim land for freeways. São Paulo sits in a bowl, a recipe for smog.

Meanwhile, here are these gracious, vital capital cities in the lagging states. Why not use them? Petrobras can function efficiently in Salvador. Electronics firms can operate efficiently in Recife or Belem.

The scale of regional policy—planning and implementation—may well be larger in Brazil than in any country in the world. We have noted the size of staffs and budgets of the regional development authorities. There are, in addition, the state planning authorities and the city planning authorities. Within the Ministries of Planning and Finance, and within the Central Bank, there are also large numbers of high-level people concerned with regional policy. Indeed regional policy and planning are a major part of national policy and planning. One could justify replacing the term *regional policy* or *regional planning* by *decentralized policymaking* or *decentralized planning*.

One of the great advantages of the Brazilian approach to regional policy is that the regional authorities are involved in implementation as well as planning. Consequently, the planning itself is highly pragmatic and project and problem oriented. There is in the authorities a good deal of concern for technical problems, and engineers, architects, agronomists, hydrologists, and so forth outnumber the economists and econometricians.

Regional policy since World War II has been concerned with getting things done, with identifying good projects and assembling good programs, with encouraging and supporting private enterprise while being prepared to take into government hands things that need doing but private enterprise will not do. Hence regional policy has been less subject to whims and fads in Brazil than in some other countries. Brazilian regional planners may not have discovered brilliant new techniques for doing the professional planner's job. They have seen their task rather as year-by-year, month-by-month, day-by-day management of their regions, and thus, in the aggregate, of the national economy as a whole. From 1965 to 1980, at least, they managed it rather well.

Theories

Brazilian economists are well-trained, and the economists responsible for regional planning could be expected to be acquainted with all the theories discussed in Part I. The most obvious application of growth pole theory was the creation of the new capital of Brazilia, at the precise geographic centre of the country, in a totally unsettled area. It was designed to open up the centre, and together with the construction of the Brazilia-Belem road, it seems to have done so. Otherwise all the state capitals have been regarded as "growth poles" for their own state, and the growth of all of them has been encouraged. The one major effort to redistribute economic activity was the removal of the government-owned petroleum company, Petrobras, from Rio de Janeiro to Salvador; but the objective was as much decongestion in Rio as economic expansion in Salvador. In general, the federal government has tended to favour locations outside of Rio and São Paulo for its projects or enterprises, whenever it is feasible; but it has also recognized that the forces favouring a particular centre for a particular activity are too strong to interfere with them. As in the United States, interregional trade is much more important than international trade, and regional policy has been rather sparingly used to promote exports, except perhaps for coffee, which is grown in a particular region. The efforts of SUDENE and SUDAM might be regarded as attempts to combat bimodal production and regional dualism. On the whole, however, regional development planning in Brazil has been highly pragmatic, and aimed at the selection, design, and implementation of particular investment projects, in either the public or the private sector, rather than conscious and conscientious application of precisely formulated theories.

Malaysia

Malaysia is in the same income bracket as Brazil; per capita GNP in 1990 was $2,320 compared to Brazil's $2,680. Malaysia is also a rapidly growing country: from 1965 to 1990 annual growth of PNB per capita averaged 4.0 percent. Both countries have had rapid structural change in recent years. Both countries have a high ratio of investment and savings to GNP, but Malaysia's figures are substantially higher than Brazil's: 34 and 33 percent. Both still have frontiers.

There, however, the similarities end. Malaysia is a Southeast Asian country, a member of ASEAN (Association of South East Asian Nations), with a predominantly Moslem religion and vestiges of a Hindu-Bhuddist culture. It is a small country measured by either population or area: 18 million people in 330 million square kilometres. Whereas Brazil is one of the most closed economies in the world, Malaysia is one of the most open, exporting a staggering 79 percent of its GNP. Brazil has one of the highest rates of inflation in the world, Malaysia one of the lowest, only 1.6 percent from 1980 to 1990.

Malaysia is one of the success stories in the field of economic development. Its rapid growth has been combined with a high degree of stability. There has been some success in improving income distribution among ethnic and occupational groups, and among regions—which is almost the same thing, since the East is relatively poor, relatively rural, and 80 percent Malay. The rapid structural change has been of the right sort; much of the new industry is high-tech. The Malaysian "trade-off curve" is one of the lowest in the world. The government has recently estimated unemployment at 3.9 percent. With inflation at 1.6 percent, this is a remarkable achievement. Malaysia may be currently the fastest growing country in the world, with Gross National Product increasing at an annual rate approaching 10 percent. Moreover, Malaysia, not having built up inefficient "smokestack" industries by a century or more of protection, does not face the horrendous problem of "adjustment" faced by Argentina, Australia, Canada, New Zealand, Uruguay, and to some extent even the United Kingdom and the United States. At the present moment the Malaysian economy is one of the best-behaving—perhaps even *the* best behaved—economy in the world.

A frequently expressed view is that the Malaysian success story can be explained as by application of the neo-classical paradigm. This may seem to be a simple enough sort of statement, but in fact it is very complicated. Does it mean *laissez-faire*, a complete hands-off strategy on the part of the government? Malaysia is certainly not an example of that sort of approach. But proponents of a neo-classical approach could argue that a truly neo-classical strategy could involve a good deal of government intervention, to offset, counter-balance or remove sources of market failure: monopoly power of all kinds; imperfect knowledge; unequal access to information and slow and unequal spread of new information; uncertainty and imperfect foresight; externalities and indivisibilities. Is that what Malaysian governments have been doing, or even thought they were doing? I think not. Enthusiasts for the neo-classical paradigm can also find room for public enterprise, provided it conforms to the rules of efficient performance laid down for private enterprise: minimize average cost and set prices equal to marginal cost. It would appear that some Malaysian public enterprises have been very efficient on private enterprise standards, some have been subsidized, and some made monopoly profits. I doubt if the most ardent supporters of the neo-classical system would argue that Malaysia's success is to be explained by the strict conformity of her *public* enterprises to the rules for efficient performance of a market economy.

There are however three types of criteria that might be applied to judge the success of an economy and of the system under which it operates. The first relates to growth and the incentive system which promotes it. The second refers to efficiency of resource allocation and utilization. The third is concerned with equity and distribution of the fruits of progress. A strictly neo-classical system is (or would be if it ever existed) rather deficient on the first criterion. A system which never allows more than a normal profit does not provide much incentive to undertake the risks attached to innovation. Technological progress and growth could be slow under such a system, and in fact it *was* slow during the period when the world economy most closely approximated such a system, in the latter half of the nineteenth century. But the system adopted by Malaysia was not as strictly neo-classical as this. It came closer to the Schumpeter-Perroux paradigm, providing succulent monopolies as bait for innovation, and expecting growth to be concentrated in certain industries, sectors, and regions at any one time, rather than being spread evenly throughout the economy in such a manner as to preserve "equilibrium."

Malaysian governments have violated neo-classical principles in at least two important respects. The New Economic Policy (NEP), following the race riots of May 1969, set out, very consciously and deliberately, to change the allocation of labour, capital, and management, so as to give Malays better access to skilled, technical, and professional jobs, and to ownership and management of industrial and financial enterprises, as well as to redistribute income. It was, in fact, a deliberate effort to make resource allocation more *inefficient* in the short run, in the hope that the loss of efficiency could be redressed in the long run. A solid neo-classical economist would be obliged to oppose the NEP, unless convinced that it was necessary to assure enough social and political stability for development to be possible, which may well have been the case.

The other violation of neo-classical principles was the program of regional development. A strictly neo-classical solution to regional disparities would accelerate migration of labour to the richer and more dynamic regions and encourage migration of capital to the poorer and more stagnant regions. Malaysian policy was quite different. The effort was to *decelerate* migration of labour into prosperous Selangor, and to encourage migration of both labour and capital into middle-income, moderately prosperous and moderately dynamic regions like Johore and Pahang. No serious effort was made to lure private capital into the really poor States of Trengganu and Kelantan, perhaps because the governments knew that such an effort would probably fail. Rather the strategy was to count upon spread effects from growth poles at Kuantan

and Penang to solve the problems of the country's northeast. Also, considerations of equity were not predominant in the minds of the decision-makers;
the aim was not to redistribute income from west coast to east. The aim was to
strengthen the entire national economy, including booming Selangor and
Penang, by turning relatively poor and stagnant States into relatively rich and
dynamic ones. The means to this end was exploiting existing resource potential, opening up new land, building infrastructure, and providing incentives.
Certainly the governments had in mind that the regions for which development plans were prepared were or could become predominantly settled by
Malays. But there was no thought of killing off geese that were already laying
golden eggs, and during the whole period that the regional development policies were being executed there were parallel policies which encouraged industrial expansion in the Kelang Valley and Penang. The *theory* behind the
regional development policy was much closer to Myrdal's or Schumpeter's
theories of cumulative causation, or Perroux's theory of growth poles, than to
a strict neo-classical theory.

When Malaysia became independent in 1947 it made a clear-cut choice for
the private enterprise system, for economic and diplomatic ties with the West,
for an open economy, and for British-style parliamentary democracy. One
might even say that it opted for a nineteenth century liberal philosophy, involving individual freedom and rule by law within a constitutional monarchy.
The communist insurgency after World War II, was fought and ultimately sup-
pressed. Moreover, there has been a high degree of continuity in basic ideology and resulting economic policy from government to government. It is not
just that this ideological and policy framework encouraged both foreign and
domestic investment. One of the major conclusions that emerges from study
of the development problem is that for any society to develop rapidly it must
have an articulated ideology, which most people in the society accept, and
which simultaneously provides a basis for unifying the society and a framework within which development can take place. Western Europe, North America
and Australasia had such an ideology in the eighteenth and nineteenth centuries. The Soviet Bloc had one for part of the twentieth.

While Malaysian governments have intervened in market processes to further social and political objectives such as the NEP, private enterprise has
nonetheless been given its head and left free to make a profit where it can.
Public enterprise has played an important role, but much if not most of it has
been managed along the lines of efficient enterprise (FELDA for example).
Gross inefficiencies, and the operation of public enterprises as welfare agencies have not been typical of the Malaysian public sector.

International trade and international capital movements have been left com-
paratively free. Moreover, the stress in foreign trade policy has been on export

promotion rather than import replacement. Not that import replacement is always bad policy; as Albert Hirschman says, countries tend to develop a comparative advantage in commodities they *import*. A country with the vast domestic market and technological capacities of Brazil can do, and has done, very well by import replacement, turning former imports into strong, competitive exports within a few years: automobiles, aircraft, electrical equipment, and now computers. But there can be little doubt that more waste and inefficiency has been introduced into national economies by import replacement than by efforts to promote exports, especially in economies of limited size, and that by and large Malaysia has not been prone to this disease.

These three elements of the neoclassical paradigm have served Malaysia well. Beyond that, there has been a good deal of common sense and *ad hocery* at top political levels which has steered Malaysia's ship of state around the parlous reefs of extremism of all kinds. Finally, the country has made good use of expertise in many forms, much of it indigenous, some of it provided by the World Bank, the Ford Foundation, the United Nations and its Specialized Agencies, and various bilateral aid programs. And the interjection of the requisite expertise into the process of policy formation is what development planning is all about.

Behind Malaysia's success is certainly a little bit of luck; discoveries of petroleum and the rise in oil prices, for example. More important has been a great deal of good management. Among the forms that the good management has taken is the use of regional and urban plans as building blocks for construction of national economic development plans, from The Third Malaysia Plan on. Malaysia may have the most completely integrated regional and national plans in the world.

After the race riots of May 1969, the government realized that henceforth the problem of regional disparities, with all its related polarities, would have to be tackled directly and head on, rather than counting on mere growth of national income to solve it. These joint realizations crystallized in the New Economic Policy (NEP), which was incorporated into The Second Malaysia Plan for 1971–1975 as Chapter 1. With the introduction of the NEP, the concept of regional development changed. It was no longer merely a matter of contributing to growth of national income by opening up and settling resource frontiers, wherever the potential appeared to be good. There were still frontiers to develop, certainly; but henceforth regional development was to be designed to contribute to the objectives of the NEP: to reduce regional disparities and thus reduce disparities among ethnic groups; to raise incomes of Malays, wherever they might be; to draw Malays into urban centers while retarding migration to Kuala Lumpur and other major centers—that is, to create or expand urban centers in retarded regions; to draw Malays into industry, commerce, and finance, not just as employees but as owners and managers as well; and to improve levels of health and education of the Malay population. As work on the Third Malaysia Plan got under way, the EPU was ready to experiment with the idea of aggregating the various regional plans into the national plan. Behind the effort to integrate regional and national planning was certainly a kind of growth pole strategy, but it was less naive than the notions that underlay plans for individual regions, in Malaysia and elsewhere in the world, at that time. It was recognized that in order to achieve a certain, defined pattern of regional development, as distinct from a policy of merely encouraging growth in one individual region after another, it is necessary to plan the growth of the entire urban structure. Accordingly, the EPU launched a massive study of Malaysia's urban structure and of all kinds of flows among cities. From these studies emerged a strategy. Policy would be directed toward slowing down the growth in the Kuala Lumpur-Port Kelang area to a pace some 30 percent lower than that which was expected in the absence of such policies. That would still be a high rate of growth. Penang would be left to its own dynamic devices; its growth would be neither encouraged nor discouraged. An effort would be made to resuscitate the economy of Malacca. Johore Bahru would be stimulated to grow faster through investment in infrastructure and incentives to private enterprise. The Big Push, however, would be in the east coast cities, and especially in Kuantan. In addition, small and medium-sized towns in the poorer regions of the west, north, and south, which were smaller and weaker than they would be in a "normal" (rank-size rule) hierarchy, would be stimulated to more rapid development. Thus all regions were to be encouraged to grow, but some would receive more encouragement than others. Note too that there was no effort to redistribute economic activity, industry, or income *from* rich regions to poor ones, as there has been in much of Canadian regional policy.

Things did not work out in quite the way that the regional planners would have liked. The experiment was new. There was little in the experience of Malaysia, or indeed of other countries, to guide them. They soon found out that in order to integrate regional plans into a national plan it is better to have that idea before the regional planning itself begins. As it was, the various regional plans were prepared by different consulting firms, from different countries, under different foreign aid programs, at different times, with different scopes and methodologies, even with somewhat different objectives in mind. It was almost impossible to add them up.

In some ways that were worse, the *theory* was not very rigorous or refined, let alone tested. It was not the rigorous and refined theory of François Perroux that was being applied. The planners were trying to formulate regional policies to alter the spatial distribution of economic activity in accordance with stated goals of national policy. In other words, they were not content to leave the location of spread effects to the market and let them fall where they might, even outside the country. They wanted spread effects to end up in certain spaces, to benefit particular societies. They did not really know how to do that, and there was no very convincing and generally accepted literature, no received doctrine, to guide them.

The "experts," advisors, consultants, and planners who formulated regional policy, both Malaysian and foreign, were in constant touch with the ebb and flow of world thought in the field. Moreover, Malaysians have made major contributions to that thought and to the international literature. Malaysians have played a major role in the conferences, seminars, and workshops of the United Nations Centre for Regional Development in Nagoya and have made substantial contributions to its publications. Thus in saying that Malaysia reacted to ideas from abroad, we are far from saying that Malaysians had no original ideas of their own; we are saying rather that in contributing original ideas they started from the same *international* corpus of literature, theory, doctrine, ideas, and debate as people in other countries who were concerned with regional policy. It was not a matter of foreigners pushing alien ideas down their throats; Malaysians and foreigners were members of the same international community of professionally trained people concerned with regional policy.

It is worthy of note that the expansion of manufacturing was accompanied by an upgrading of quality. Malaysian manufacturing is becoming increasingly high-tech. Not only is Malaysia one of the 20 leading exporters of manufactures in the world, it has become the world's largest single exporter of electronic components. Over half the new manufacturing jobs created during the 1970s were in electronics. Malaysia is the biggest supplier of integrated circuits to the United States, produces 14 percent of the world supply of semiconductors, 40 to 70 percent of the world's supply of 64K chips. The city of Penang alone is the world's leading exporter of these chips.

Malaysia has also made progress in the specific goals of the NEP. The former urban-rural-Chinese-Malay polarization has been considerably diluted. Even more striking is the change in occupational structure among Malays. The proportion of Malays in the manufacturing labour force rose from 19.6 percent in 1957 to 28.9 percent in 1970 and 53.5 percent in 1980. Conversely the share of Chinese in manufacturing employment fell from 72 to 65.2 percent and then to 45.5 percent in 1980. The proportion of primary employment accounted for by Malays and Chinese respectively scarcely changed between 1970 and 1980, but in the secondary and tertiary sectors, the proportion of Malays rose, and the proportion of Chinese fell. More important, the role of the primary sector in the employment of Malays declined, and the importance of the secondary and tertiary sectors increased. Thus the polarization of occupational structures of Malays and Chinese has also become less sharp. Meanwhile, substantial structural change has taken place in the economy as a whole. There is also some evidence of regional convergence.

Less progress had been made in terms of Malay ownership and management of industrial enterprises, but even there the situation had improved. By the end of 1985, the share of Malay ownership in commercial and industrial corporate enterprises has risen to 17.8 percent, as compared to 4.3 percent in 1971. Very important is the fact that the succession of governments since then have been *seen* by all major ethnic and social groups as making a sincere effort to resolve the tensions. There has been no renewed outbreak of racial violence.

The Pahang Tenggara Program

Much the biggest of the various regional development programs in Malaysia is the one for Pahang Tenggara (the southeast part of the state of Pahang), for which the present writer served as Senior Economist. A CIDA project, it took a team of 50 professionals two years to prepare a plan and would require investment, public and private, of approximately $1 billion to implement. Implementation is in the hands of a regional development authority, known as DARA. My most recent visit to the DARA region was in November 1991, when I was in Malaysia on a CIDA mission. The drive to Muazdam Shah, where DARA had established its headquarters, from Kuantan, was a revelation. Twelve years before there had been only a narrow and dusty dirt road through the jungle. Little land had been cleared and less planted. This time we drove on an excellent surfaced highway, through lush, immaculately tended rubber, oil palm, and tea plantations, past cattle farms and attractive villages. We arrived at the impressively large and handsome office building of DARA, where we were greeted by various staff members and had a preliminary round of conversation. I was impressed by the obvious sense of consecration, even of excitement, among the staff, some of whom had been with DARA from the very beginning. As I got to know them better, I was also impressed by their competence; the senior officers nearly all had higher degrees from the United States, the United Kingdom, Canada or Australia. We were taken to lunch at the attractive and comfortable DARA resthouse, where we stayed for two nights. After lunch we had a meeting with several senior staff members in the elegant "operations room" of the office building, surrounded by maps and charts, and were given a thorough briefing.

Land development is on schedule, in accordance with the Masterplan. However, instead of 500,000 people being settled in the region, as foreseen by the plan, there were only 200,000. How was that possible? Part of the answer is that the pace of Malaysian industrialization and urbanization has been so rapid that the country faces labour shortages, in construction, on plantations, and in certain industries and services requiring special skills. DARA too has faced labour shortages, especially in construction and on the private plantations. As a consequence, it has been necessary to bring in workers from abroad; of the 200,000 settlers, 50,000 are Indonesian immigrants, who come in as single men, leaving any families they may have in Indonesia. The team had estimated that the average size of family among the Malay settlers we expected in the region would be at least five. Multiply the 50,000 Indonesians by 5 and the total population of the region would not be far below the figure we estimated. The average size of holdings per household had been somewhat increased as well.

Obviously, with so many fewer people in the region, the degree of urbanization is much less than planned. The number of urban centers has been reduced and the size of individual centers as well. The plan envisaged all plantation workers living in urban centres and commuting to work by motorized transport. A good many of the Indonesians are in the country illegally, and do not have work permits. They dare not live in the towns, and live instead on the private plantations, in somewhat poor conditions. The plan envisaged Muazdam Shah as the principal centre, and it was expected to have about 150,000 people by 1990. In fact it has about 11,000. The town plans and housing schemes designed for 150,000 people are useless for 11,000. Bandar Tun Razak, which was supposed to be the region's second town in 1990, with around 50,000, has about 20,000 people. It looks a bit more urbane that Muazdam Shah, but not much. One of the main objectives of the original plan, in accordance with the NEP, was to provide urban jobs for second-generation Malays in the region. It doesn't look as though that objective is going to be attained, at least for the present "second-generation." On the other hand, there are signs of entrepreneurial endeavour in the two towns, some of it successful. Some settlers have managed to set up business enterprises while operating their farms, perhaps turning over the management of the farm to their wives, and are making money selling used cars, operating a brick kiln, building houses, and various commercial activities. Some of the houses built privately are both large and handsome, almost mansions.

DARA itself has built houses, schools, clinics, and shopping centres. The DARA officials said that the transport system is adequate for the time being. The venture into cattle has apparently been successful, and is being privatized. The road through Muazdam Shah is the main artery between Kuantan and Johore Bahru, and there are also surfaced roads to the coast at Rompin and westwards to Kuala Lumpur and Port Klang. DARA has entered into several joint ventures, but the number of such companies has been reduced from 18 to

10. Some 5,000 hectares have been held as a nature reserve and tourist resort at Tjini Lake with elephants and tigers.

On the whole, DARA gives the impression of an ambitious, well-managed, and dynamic scheme. There are, however, some disappointments, largely the result of shortcomings in the original plan. The extent of industrialization and urbanization is much less than we envisaged. The prefabricated housing enterprise on the coast, which looked promising ten years ago, has gone bankrupt. The two forest product factories, based on permanent-yield forestry, were supposed to be using high technology and producing sophisticated products like plywood, laminated wood and veneers. They have reverted to traditional techniques even in their forestry operations, and are producing only sawn lumber. These are of course private (and foreign) enterprises, and are guided by market and profit considerations. It may be that the failure to achieve population and urbanization targets made their original plans unattractive. It may also be that the general shortage of skilled labour made it unprofitable to conduct sophisticated operations in such a remote region. They may have preferred to conduct such operations in the Klang Valley, Penang or Johore Bahru. In any case, it is clear that our rosy visions of urbanized patterns of settlement and secondary industry and tertiary services in the region were sadly misplaced.

A second disappointment, that is clearly the result of inadequacies in the original plan, is that our idea of resettling the river-people in the plantation towns didn't work, and had to be abandoned in 1984. We should have studied the river villages and their people more thoroughly, and then we might have been able to predict that the idea of resettlement wouldn't appeal to the river people, and proposed instead a pattern of village development that would raise the standards of living of the river people where they are, as DARA is now doing.

A third disappointment is that the problem of the Orang Asli has not been satisfactorily solved. That problem is another one that we didn't study thoroughly enough. We didn't go much further than setting aside some jungle as a reserve, where the Orang Asli could pursue their traditional way of life. But of course they could not be expected to be forever satisfied with this life, side by side with a highly visible process of modernization. DARA has resettled them in 9 regions, where they can become modernized small farmers. Their material standard of living will certainly be raised; but we found the one Orang Asli settlement that we visited a bit depressing, with small houses crowded together (instead of widely spaced as in their settlements) and untended orchards. Of course the problem of "Orang Asli" (original people) remains unsolved in many countries—witness the Indians in both North and South America, the aborigines in Australia, and the Maoris in New Zealand. Finding ways of permitting such peoples to preserve their traditional culture and at the same time enjoy the standard of living of a modern industrialized society is no simple task. Still, we could have done a better job of it in Pahang Tenggara.

In various publications on the Pahang Tenggara project I have stressed three major shortcomings of the plan prepared by the Canadian team: our naivete in thinking that development of the region could make Kuantan a growth pole that would generate "spread effects" to the impoverished northeast; our failure to take enough account of the effect of other regional development projects on the availability of resources to DARA; and our failure to anticipate the industrialization and urbanization that made resettlement schemes less attractive. But if these feelings had been all, the development of Pahang Tenggara could still have proceeded in *something like* the pattern envisaged in the plan. What has transformed the picture completely is the emergence of a *labour shortage* in Malaysia, something we never dreamed of. For the labour shortage and the resort to immigrant labour in the DARA region means that the highly urbanized settlement patterns that we envisaged, with the related creation of manufacturing and services jobs within the region, cannot happen in this generation. The inevitable consequence is that a good many of the second generation will leave the region, especially if they are provided with the kind and level of education to which they are entitled. And, of course, the population of the region will then continue to grow more slowly than originally intended, making it all the more difficult to create within the region the high-level jobs that might hold educated young people. The time has come for a whole new study, on the same scale as the original one undertaken by the Canadian team, leading to a brand new perspective plan, and hopefully one that will contain fewer errors of foresight than the original.

Conclusions

What does Malaysian experience tell us about the applicability of the theories discussed in Part I of this volume?

The regional development schemes were mainly export oriented, not just towards exports from the region, but exports from the country. The theory of interregional and international trade was therefore present in the backs of the minds of the planners. The existence of a world market was taken as given. The planners did have to try to estimate prices over the next 20 to 30 years, for such products as rubber and oil palm, always a risky business. But any private enterprise would, and did, do the same. Rubber trees, once mature, bear for 25 to 30 years, oil palm 15 to 20. Estimating the internal rate of return or net present value per acre requires guesstimating the prices over the life of the trees. Other things, like cattle or sago, are easier. Since the forestry complexes required heavy investment in plant and equipment, as well as in trees, they too required estimating prices over long periods. The theory of international and interregional trade was not much help here; it told the planners only that if prices were favourable over a long period, income and employment would expand.

The theory of location was applied in an inverse manner. The planners did not ask, "What explains the economic activities that are present in each region?;" that was easy. The planners asked instead, "What activities can be attracted to each region?," and applied location theory to get an answer.

Little use was made of the theory of bi-modal production and regional dualism. Most of the planned products were in the modern sector. Regional cycles and trends would depend on what was put into the plans, rather than the other way around; although cycles and trends were considered when estimating the long run prices. Geography entered into the deliberations mainly through such things as soil analysis, hydrological surveys, rainfall, slopes, forest inventories and the like. Account was taken of the cultural differences between the *Orang Asli* and potential settlers, and forested land was set aside where the *Orang Asli* could preserve their traditional way of life. As for circular and cumulative causation, the planners thought they were breaking an existing vicious circle, by giving poor peasants a chance to live cumulatively better lives. As for entrepreneurship, that was the least of our worries. The entrepreneurs were already there, in the private and public sectors, and taking a helpful hand with the actual planning. In the newly settled regions like DARA, when the land was cleared and the roads built, they were ready to move in.

Two related theories, however, predominated in the work of the Pahang Tenggara team: the theory of development poles, growth centres and central places; and the Lasuen variant of the rank-size rule. Lasuen had found that in many countries city-size approximated ever more closely the rank-size rule, and that the urban structures were becoming more rigid, in the sense that individual cities did not change their rank. Malaysia seemed to obey both elements of "Lasuen's Law." That worried us, since we were creating an urban structure of our own, and our small towns and cities would have to fit into the urban hierarchy somehow. Once the land had been allocated to particular uses, we had a fairly good idea of the future population of each area of the region—or thought we had. Our physical planners could then prepare town plans and the transportation network for the whole region. But what if the existing towns would not relinquish their places in the urban hierarchy? All this was a bit vague; but in the end, as we have seen, we were right to worry about it.

The other theory led to our attempt at "spatial engineering." We were not so foolish as to think that Kuantan would already be a development pole by 1990; but we thought that it would be *on its way* to becoming a true development pole by that time. We were also convinced that Kuantan was the only city in the east with a chance of becoming a development pole by that time; and there, we were right. To maximize its chances, we wanted to link it to the development of the region as quickly as possible, and to avoid the region being linked to the existing west coast axis from Penang through Kuala Lumpur to Johore. We also thought that by 1990 Kuantan would be generating significant spread effects to Trengganu and Kelantan. In the event, we failed on both counts. If the deepwater harbour at Kuantan had been quickly finished, and if the Malaysian government had stuck to the plan of developing the north first, would we have been proven right? We will never know for sure, but I tend to think not. The basic flaws in the Boudeville version of the development pole theory, which predominated at the time, expecting "spread effects" in the form of increases in income and employment in the peripheral region of the urban centre chosen as the "development pole," would still have appeared; and the basic labour shortage which undermined our plan for Pahang Tenggara would have appeared too.

19

Regional Development in
Least Developed Countries

Some years ago, the United Nations, recognizing that the expressions "The Third World" or "Less Developed Countries" hid from view the enormous diversity of the countries they included, carved out separate category of "Least Developed Countries," or "The Fourth World." These are countries which are not only poor, but which show little sign of being anything else for the next decades. They are, in other words, countries with a particularly recalcitrant development problem. They include such countries as Bangladesh, Haiti, the countries of the African Sahel and Sri Lanka. In these countries, the scale and nature of the regional development problem, as well as the overall problem of development, is so different from those of the countries discussed in the previous chapter, as to warrant separate treatment. In this chapter, we shall use one Latin American country (Haiti), one country in the African Sahel (Mauritania) and one South Asian country (Sri Lanka) to illustrate the special nature of the regional development problem in these countries.

In general, the per capita GNP of the Least Developed Countries is low (from $80 to $500 in 1990); the rate of growth is typically low as well. In some of them it is even negative (Niger –2.4 percent from 1965 to 1990). Sri Lanka is an exception; per capita GNP rose at an average of 2.9 percent from 1965 to 1990, but has fallen since. Typically, about one third of GNP is produced in agriculture, but because of low agricultural productivity, the proportion of total employment in agriculture is much higher. The share of industry and services in GNP also averages about one third each, but there is considerable variation from country to country. The same is true of savings and investment; Haiti, for example, saved 1 percent and invested 11 percent of GNP in 1990, but the group as a whole saved an astonishing 28 percent of its gross domestic product, and invested 31 percent, compared to the United States' 15 and 16 percent.

Haiti

Haiti shares a small island with the Dominican Republic, and is a very small country indeed, 6.5 million people in 28 thousand square kilometres. Its GNP per capita in 1990 was $370, its growth rate from 1965 to 1990 just 0.2 percent. Most of its population consists of peasants using the most primitive techniques, and living slightly above, or slightly below subsistence level. Its forests are mostly gone, cut for firewood, and it suffers badly from erosion. Only 12 percent of its GNP was exported. Yet at the time it gained its independence from France, in 1804, it was known as "La Perle des Antilles," and had a per capita income higher than France.

The Basic Needs Approach: DRIPP in Haiti

Between 1974 and early 1979, I was intermittently engaged in a large-scale regional development program in Haiti, "Développement Régional Intégré Petit Goave-Petit Trou de Nippes," or "le DRIPP," as it came to be known. The DRIPP region was a least developed region in a least developed country, a far cry from Pahang Tenggara. It required a totally different approach. In Pahang Tenggara we had tried to apply a unified approach, but we gave little heed to direct satisfaction of basic needs; we concentrated on the modern sector. The approach in DRIPP was also "unified," but the major emphasis was on direct satisfaction of basic needs, although the ILO's "enthronement of basic needs," had not yet taken place when the project began.

Haiti is one of the countries that opted for regionalization of its national development planning in the early 1970s. The regime under Jean-Claude Duvallier had been liberalized enough, in comparison to his father's harsh rule, for the various donors to decide that Haiti, which was the one "least developed country" in the western hemisphere, needed and deserved help. There were in fact over 300 donor agencies operating in the country, most of them Non-Governmental Organizations (NGOs), including church organizations. The country was carved up into regions, which were offered to donors as a sort of menu, so the first phase of our project was to go to Haiti and look more closely at the menu, in order to select a region from it. The region chosen extended from Petit Goave to Petit Trou de Nippes, on the north coast, and about two-thirds of the way through the mountains towards the south coast, making a region much the same size as Pahang Tenggara. There were three reasons for choosing this region: nobody else wanted it; it was a least developed region in a least developed country, and so offered real challenge; and the Inter-American Development Bank was financing the construction of a highway, being built by a Canadian engineering firm, from Port-au-Prince to

Les Cayes. Most of it was in the region, and it seemed to offer possibilities of doing something new there.

Petit Goave had once been the coffee capital of Haiti, and contained some beautiful old houses, badly run down, and a splendid lycée with a campus that would grace most universities, but virtually no trained teachers. The municipal water supply had long since broken down, the electric power plant operated only about two hours a day, and—most troublesome in terms of operating the project—there were no telephone or telegraph connections with Port-au-Prince. It was less than 100 kilometres by road from Port-au-Prince to Petit Goave, but when the project began the state of the road was such that one was lucky to make the trip in five hours. This lack of communications was one of the major difficulties that confronted the project. We had to be in touch with the government in Port-au-Prince, and particularly with the Ministry of Agriculture to whom we were attached, and we had to be in our region.

The project was set up with two parallel teams, one Canadian and one Haitian. There was an Haitian Director-General and a Deputy Director-General to match the Canadians with the same titles, and so on down the line. The Haitians were high ranking civil servants seconded to the project, and CIDA supplemented their salaries so as to diminish the income gap between the Canadians and the Haitians on the team. This form of organization, which looked sensible enough on paper, was to be the major source of trouble in the project.

At the outset the region was divided in two, Sub-region A from Petit Goave to Miragoane, site of the Reynolds Minings Company's offices, about half way along the coast to Petit Trou de Nippes; and Sub-region B from Miragoane to Petit Trou de Nippes. There was no road at all between Miragoane and Petit Trou de Nippes, only a trail said to be *faisable* by jeep, which sometimes disappeared altogether in the long grass and involved much climbing up and down rocky crags. One hoped to average 10 kilometers an hour. Finally the project bought a battered open fishing boat in order to be able to get to Sub-region B. Our Director-General found all these logistical problems a bit daunting, and decided that in the first couple of years we would concentrate on Sub-region A, postponing any effort to do serious planning for "B."

There were difficulties enough in Sub-region A. There were virtually no statistics, and we soon began to suspect those that did exist. For example, there seemed to be many more people around than was stated in the Census. The Census was based on a sample of a sample; only certain areas of each region were covered, and only a sample of households in each area. We made friends with the Army Commandant in Petit Goave, and he organized his men to make a house-to-house count in Sub-region A. There turned out to be just twice as many people in the region as the Census estimated. When it came to such things as production, yields, livestock numbers and the like, we simply had no idea. Covering that mountainous terrain on foot in order to make our own counts was an arduous, time-consuming task. It took us too long to discover the usefulness of aerial photography. We did finally get aerial photos of the entire region, from which the experts were able to give us detailed maps of land use, livestock numbers, number of houses per village, and the like.

The lack of data led us to cut down again on the areas selected for detailed study. We chose some areas in Sub-region A as "Zones d'Intervention Concentrée," or ZICs. To study the ZICs we reverted to an essentially anthropological method. We had on our team a number of graduates of the MA course in *"animation sociale"* at Laval University in Quebec City, to my knowledge the only university outside France to give such a course. This group of young men and women trained a still larger group of young Haitian men and women. Then mixed teams of Haitians and Canadians would go out to the villages in the ZICs and stay there for three to six months, observing the people, their way of life and manner of earning a living, and gathering data. This way of acquiring information has many advantages; but it is, of course, slow.

Meanwhile, back in Ottawa, CIDA was getting impatient. They wanted to spend money in Haiti, and to spend money they had to have projects. They thus ordered us to find some good projects and submit them to the Haitian government and themselves even though "our studies were not nearly finished." Also, they said, it would be our responsibility to see that the projects were implemented. We would find Canadian or Haitian entities capable of execution, and then monitor them. We were very nervous. How could we select projects on the basis of such imperfect knowledge? And we were not used to remaining in a country while the plans we had formulated were being implemented, let alone being responsible for implementation. But we had no choice.

We instituted a system of "minimization of risk"—that is, of minimizing the risk of making serious mistakes in our selection of projects and making fools of ourselves. Every quarter we submitted a list of recommended projects to CIDA and the Haitian government, while continuing to make studies of other projects and other areas. We picked projects where we felt confident that nothing we might learn later could prove them to be a mistake. As time went by and projects began to be implemented, our knowledge was greatly improved by the experience with implementation. I now think that this manner of running a development program—research, analysis, planning and implementation all proceeding concurrently, with feedback relationships amongst them all—is the most efficient that can be designed. It is, after all, the manner in which any efficient, large-scale private enterprise operates.

Early in the project we began to worry about our relationship with the Haitian team. In a country like Haiti the word "corruption" has almost no meaning. Civil servants and others on salaries scarcely above the poverty line look for any opportunity of improving their financial condition. We soon learned, for example, that construction equipment provided to the project was being used to build roads into the beach estates of the multi-millionaires. The Deputy Director was collecting kickbacks from the younger Haitians on the staff; if they wanted the higher paid jobs that the project offered, they had to pay. He then tried to do the same with the younger Canadians, saying that he could have them fired if they refused. The state of the project accounting was deplorable. No one really knew where all the money was going. When we reported our fears to the Haiti desk officer in Ottawa she said, "We must do what the Haitians want to do." We replied, "Which Haitians? The President For Life? His mother, his sister? The Cabinet? The Parliament? The millionaires? The People? They all want different things, and we are trying to serve the people." Eventually, however, even CIDA could not ignore the "anomalies" and the misallocation of resources, and closed the project down.

The DRIPP project accomplished a good deal. In retrospect, its innovations in the planning-implementation process were of major importance. The on-the-spot approach to project analysis resulted in many good projects that might otherwise have been ignored. For example, we were taken one day by Haitian colleagues down "highway no. 2," marked on the map with a thick red line. It turned out to be a stream bed, with water up to the hubcaps, but even so the stony bottom was smoother than Highway no. 1. We turned a corner and found ourselves confronted with 200 hectares of irrigated fields. The irrigation system was not working, because the iron sluice gate that diverted water from the stream to the irrigation channels had rusted solid in the "up" position, and the little barrage had been washed out. The NGO that provided the gate had not provided oil to lubricate it, and the peasants could not afford it. An outlay of about $3,000 by CIDA created 200 hectares of irrigated land, providing a living for 200 households. There are many such examples in the DRIPP story.

There were many successful projects. The Petit Goave water supply was restored, the power plant put into condition to run twenty-four hours a day. The market was rebuilt and enlarged. The port was improved. Hundreds of demonstration plots were developed, and the successful technologies and product-mixes from the DRIPP experimental farms applied to them. Roads, irrigation systems, hospitals, clinics, schools were built. Anti-erosion projects were instituted. Net yields were doubled by getting rid of the rats. Simple storage devices were installed to protect crops from other marauders. The pharmacy of the Petit Goave hospital was rebuilt after a fire—a hospital with two doctors and six nurses to serve a region with 600,000 people. All these projects were based on exhaustive studies of the socio-cultural and economic framework, marketing and transport problems, soil analysis, hydrology, topography, and the like. As in Pahang Tenggara, the team was large, competent, covered a wide range of disciplines, and spent a long period in the field. Our *animation sociale* team learned a good deal about the aspirations of the peasants, our scientists and technicians even more about the potential for raising productivity in various fields and in various ways. The two sets of information together enabled us to conduct sophisticated cost: benefit analyses, and the constraints imposed by both the human and the physical environment narrowed the range of choice to a degree that was close to being cruel. It was not so hard after all to come up with virtually risk-free projects.

Yet there were failures too. Pavel Turcan, in his excellent article on DRIPP in the *Special Issue* of the UNCRD journal entitled *Small Island Nations* (Fall 1982) shows that projects were more likely to succeed the more capital-intensive they were, the more they depended on the foreign experts, the more isolated they were in space and time, and the less they depended on direct participation of the target population and interaction with other projects. For example, the demonstration projects worked well so long as they were managed directly by the foreign technicians; but as they were turned over to peasant associations they bogged down. The project spent many millions of dollars, but could not launch a simple system of agricultural credit. The "bicephalic" administration made the direction of the program formalistic and bureaucratic.

Turcan does not believe that regional development programs in countries like Haiti can be truly "integrated." It is impossible to do everything at once. It is better to design an optimal *sequence* in time and in space, sector by sector and region by region, with full cognizance of the feedback relationships amongst sectors and regions, and of spread effects to other sectors and regions. Regions can still be the building blocks of national development schemes, but only limited areas should be planned at any one time.

Feeder Roads

In 1978 it became clear, partly through the work of the DRIPP team, that the Port-au-Prince/Les Cayes highway, financed by the Inter-American Development Bank (IADB) and built by a Canadian firm, was having little impact on the development of the region through which it passed. Such agricultural surpluses as there were had been getting to the local markets anyway, on the backs of donkeys or, more frequently, on the heads of the peasant women. From there they went to the cities by bus or truck on the old road, mostly in the company of the "Madame Sarahs" (intermediaries between local and urban markets) on the bus. The trip from village to city was slow, uncomfortable and dangerous; but the produce got through. With the new highway the Madame Sarahs had rides that were quicker, more comfortable and safer, but most of them were well designed to sustain the roughness of the old road and they had time to burn anyway. The owners of the buses and trucks spent less on repairs and made more profits. Fewer people were killed by overcrowded buses overturning in metre-deep potholes, but more were killed by speeding weekenders from Port-au-Prince showing off their sports cars. Experts attached to DRIPP could commute between Port-au-Prince and Petite Goave more rapidly, more pleasantly, and more often; but whether efficiency was enhanced thereby was doubtful. Madame "X" attracted more clients to her resort hotel at Taino and doubled its capacity, but by and large the expected spread effects on output, income and employment had not taken place, and the impact on Haiti's rate of growth was minor.

Therefore IADB and the Haitian government decided that, to make the new road effective, it should be connected with small towns and villages by feeder roads. The question was where these roads should be built. IADB agreed to finance a study to answer this question. They favoured labour-intensive techniques, using the target population of the region, for construction of the roads (except for blasting and compacting). It was more for this reason, rather than the fact that the highway had been built by a Canadian firm, that IADB turned to a large Canadian engineering firm, with experience in planning and building such roads in Africa, to make the study. They appointed me as Senior Economist on the team, mainly, I suppose, because of my experience with DRIPP. The study was in many ways an expansion of DRIPP, although it covered a bigger region, extending all the way from Port-au-Prince to the western tip of the island.

The first step was to assemble an agenda, or "menu," of possible feeder roads linking various towns and villages with the highway. We ended up with some three dozen of these. We then proceeded to a cost:benefit analysis of each of them, to measure their social rate of return, exclude the roads on which the rate of return was too low, and rank the others in order of priority.

We soon ran into serious obstacles. The same problem arose with the feeder roads as had arisen with the highway itself. Except for the coffee-growing areas in the mountains west of Les Cayes, where improved transport would permit more specialization and an expansion of the area under coffee, there was no assurance that the feeder roads would increase agricultural production. Every square metre of arable land was already under cultivation. Indeed a good deal of land was being cultivated that should have been left under forest or lying fallow. Deforestation and erosion were major problems in the region. The technology in use, though primitive, was suitable to the factor endowment, the scale of operation, the pattern of land holding and the product-mix. Changing these would involve social upheaval, and the roads by themselves would not bring major social change in that highly traditional society.

The returns to the roads in terms of increased output would depend a good deal on the success of the DRIPP in bringing about consolidation of land holdings, adaptation of the product mix to the physical conditions, and a higher degree of specialization. Of course the roads could permit trucks to come to the farmgate, releasing women from the need to go to the market; but they had no other employment opportunities, and missing the market would spoil their fun for the week.

It was clear that the people in the villages wanted the feeder roads, mainly to get to the clinics or hospitals in the case of injury or illness, and for children to attend school more easily. For the girls, an important consideration was easier access to water. It was their responsibility to fetch the household water supply each day, and many of them spent so much time clambering up and down mountain trails that they were unable to attend school. If the trace of a feeder road went by the streams and springs, much less time could be spent in gathering water and more in school, a good illustration of the Unified Approach. All these benefits were real enough, but hard to quantify, especially in money terms.

On the cost side we were on firmer ground. Our capable engineers could choose the best trace, in consultation with the villagers to determine their interests in access to things other than the highway, and estimate the cost of any necessary blasting, and of mechanized compaction. The labour would be provided by the target population of each road, in periods when they would otherwise be idle (outside planting and harvesting seasons) and so labour costs would be essentially zero, except for any additional food requirements. The company had found, however, that it did not pay to remove large boulders or cut through mountain walls, nor to do the compacting, by labour-intensive methods.

Being in a position to measure costs with a high degree of precision, but benefits only approximately, we turned the usual procedure on its head. Instead of trying to measure cost:benefit ratios and ranking projects accordingly, we asked, "With the discount rate of 10 percent favoured by the IADB, what must the returns be to each road, given its cost, to justify its construction?" With costs as low as they were, the result of this exercise was that *all* of the roads were justified. However, we did rank roads in order of priority, in case there was not sufficient finance for all of them. The IADB, however, was happy with our methodology, and with our results. They were quite willing, if not indeed eager, to finance all the roads. This story illustrates once again the importance of conducting development planning at the regional and community level, on the spot, and in touch with the target population. Only in this way could we have arrived at reasonably accurate estimates of benefits. It also illustrates once again the usefulness of the Unified Approach, with a multidisciplinary team considering all the objectives to be served by the project in question, and all the feedback relations among them. Finally, it underlines the need for inventiveness and flexibility in field operations, the importance of not being slaves to the methods and techniques taught in the "manuals." This need is much less apparent if one is never "in the field."

Mauritania

Mauritania is on the Western "bulge" of Africa. The northern part of it consists of the Sahara desert, the southern part consists of the African Sahel, semi-desert with some scrub growth. The population of the desert is mainly Moorish, the population of the Sahel mostly black. It is a much bigger country than Haiti, over one million square kilometres, but the harshness of its geographic conditions permits a population of only 2 million. Its per capita GDP was $500 in 1990, its growth rate between 1965 and 1990 -0.6 percent. Its GDP is fairly equally divided between agriculture, industry, and services: 26, 29 and 44 percent. Its exports are 47 percent of its GDP, mainly minerals and fish. Because of the importance of foreign investment in these export industries, there is a gross inequality between savings and investment: 3 percent of GDP versus 15 percent. Its inflation rate averaged 9 percent between 1980 and 1990.

Early in the 1970, the Department of Economics at the Université de Montréal set up a Centre de recherche en développement économique. One of the earliest, and one of the biggest, longest, and most important of its projects was a mission of assistance to the Ministry of Planning in Mauritania. It was initially funded by the United Nations, who came to us with a proposal for general support to the Ministry of Planning. The team had to be francophone, but the Mauritanians did not want a team mounted by an institution in a former imperial power such as France or Belgium. Thus the Université de Montreal and CRDE were selected through a simple process of elimination.

When we first arrived in Nouakchott, Mauritania's capital city, we quickly discovered why the government had asked the United Nations for help. The Ministry of Planning had three divisions: Planning, Foreign Aid and Information. The Planning Division was relatively well off. Both the Minister himself and the Deputy Minister had done postgraduate work in economics in Paris. There was also a Chief of Division with French university training. Apart from that there was a secretary and no one else: and the Deputy Minister was also Deputy Minister of Fisheries, and had to spend some time in Nouadibou where the fish processing plant was. The Foreign Aid Division consisted of the Chief, a secretary, and no one else. The Chief had studied in Moscow under the Russian technical assistance program, and returned to

Mauritania with a deep hatred for the Soviet socialist system but with a good background in administration and foreign aid. The Information Division had a Chief and a secretary, but the Chief had never gone beyond high school and came to the Ministry from the protocol section of the Ministry of Foreign Affairs. The Canadian team substantially outnumbered the total personnel of the Ministry, and the entire staff of the two together could meet in a good sized seminar room.

Nouakchott is an artificially created capital city, like Brasilia or Canberra. It sits on the margin of the Sahara to the north and the Sahel to the south. It was at the time a town of about 70,000 people. Its uncertain water supply came from a pipeline to an oasis in the interior, provided by the Chinese, and a desalination plant on the coast, provided by the French. It had no port and no railway, only a long wharf out into the sea where shallow-draft ships could pull up and unload. There was no university in the country. The streets were unpaved and could become impassable after a sandstorm.

Mauritania's main development problem was that it really had no *national* economy or national society. Mauritania as then defined had never before existed as a unified nation-state. Its economy consisted of a handful of distinct sectors, overlapping with as many distinct regions, with very little interaction among them. Nouakchott was a sector and region unto itself. Apart from government, the modern sector consisted of the copper mine at Akjoust, some 60 kilometers to the north, the iron mine at Zouerate in the northeast corner, the fish processing plant at Nouadibou on the north coast, and the abattoir at Kaedi on the Senegal River. Except for the government, the modern sector was tied almost entirely to the outside world. It bought little from and sold less to Mauritanians, and employed virtually no Mauritanian people. The essentially self-sufficient camel economy, "les grands nomades," wandered from oasis to oasis in a crescent-shaped region in the northwest. The raisers of livestock (mostly cattle and goats) followed a regular migratory route in search of water and pasture, in the southern part of the country, ending up in the markets of Senegal. Settled agriculture was limited to a rather narrow band just north of the Senegal River, in the Sahel, always threatened with drought and starvation. The settled farmers were blacks, the rest of the population Moors.

The task was to find a way to tie together these disparate sectors, societies and regions into a more integrated economy and society. There was little hope in the existing modern economy. The British mining company at Akjoust was exporting high-grade ores while using the small Mauritanian mine to experiment with their patent process for utilizing low-grade ores, for application to their much more important holdings in Zambia and Zaire, charging the costs for tax purposes against their profits from the high-grade ore. It was clear that the mine would not remain long in operation anyhow. The iron mine was also approaching the exhaustion of its high-grade ores. If it closed down, the fate of the one railway line in the country, linking the mine with the port at Nouadibou, was uncertain at best, as was the future of the country's lone international airport, also at Nouadibou. The fishing in Mauritania's fabulously rich waters was done by Norwegians, Japanese and Greeks with modern trawlers. They took most of their catch home with them, bringing into the plant at Nouadibou only the amount required by their contracts with the Mauritanian government.

One possibility occurred to us. Mauritanian cattle, by the time they reached the end of the migratory route and arrived in a market in Senegal, were skin and bones, and fetched a very poor price. If installation of irrigation channels, using the water of the Senegal system, could produce grain surpluses, these could be used to fatten cattle in the feedlots near Kaedi. Then they could be slaughtered and processed at the abattoir, and flown to European markets where meat would bring high prices. The abattoir would need to enlarged and the runway at Kaedi's airport lengthened; but no doubt foreign aid would take care of that. At any rate, this was the kind of project that Mauritania needed, linking together the livestock sector, the stable agriculture sector, and the abattoir and transport in the modern sector. If enough such linkages could be created we would have the beginnings of a national economy.

How much could be achieved through irrigation? A Chinese technical assistance team was experimenting with the growing of rice in the Senegal River valley. They had brought from China not only experts but also workers, equipment, seed—and cooks. The rice fields were beautiful; but all we knew in the Ministry of Planning was that Chinese farmers directed by Chinese experts using Chinese seed and Chinese tools and equipment—and eating Chinese food prepared by Chinese cooks—could produce rice in Mauritania and get apparently high yields. We knew nothing about costs, and even if the Chinese were prepared to release their figures to us—which they were not—it would be hard to translate them into Mauritanian terms. Still more uncertain was whether or not Mauritanian farmers left to their own devices could get comparable yields.

There is a branch of the Senegal—the Gogol—that flows through Mauritania. An FAO team was experimenting with various crops on irrigated experimental plots. The results looked promising. When the Yogoslav director of the FAO team handed us a draft of his report, it was enthusiastic. Accordingly, we planned to include the Gogol project in the Second Plan. But then we got the revised report from FAO headquarters. The top level experts in Rome warned us that we should on no account proceed with the project; it was bound to be a failure. The Yugoslav director was furious, and offered to resign from FAO and direct the implementation of the project himself if we put it in the Plan. What to do? In Saint Louis, at the mouth of the Senegal, was the headquarters of the Organisation des Pays Riverains du Sénégal (OPRS). Together with a couple of my colleagues I set off for Saint Louis. The Secretary-General said that OPRS had 10,000 reports on irrigation in the Senegal system, some enthusiastic about the possibilities and others warning of silting and salination and other environmental disasters. He said that a team was arriving shortly to go through the 10,000 volumes and arrive at some sort of conclusions.

This story illustrates the kind of uncertainties and limitations of knowledge with which any regional development planning team must contend. There is no way of avoiding such problems. The decisions must be made, and the decisions are not marginal. They involve large-scale, long-term commitments.

Another puzzle concerned millet flour. Millet was the staple food of the Sahel. It grew virtually wild, and was gathered rather than cultivated. The women derived much of their status in Sahel societies from the fact that it was they who gathered the millet, ground it into flour with a mortar and pestle, and cooked it into gruel. The flour was highly unstable, and had to be cooked soon after grinding. Then a scientist attached to the FAO mission in Niger discovered a method of stabilizing millet flour, so that it could be stored, and made into bread, biscuits and pasta. These activities would provide a basis for commercialization of millet cultivation, opening the door to high-yield varieties of millet, irrigation, fertilizer, pesticides, and all the elements of a Green Revolution for millet of the sort that had already taken place for maize, rice and wheat in other countries. Our anthropologist warned that such a revolution would change the whole fabric of Sahel society, particularly the status of women, and God alone knew what the result would be. In any case, a meeting with the scientist concerned, and other meetings with the FAO and the Niger government, disclosed total confusion regarding the legal status of the invention. The scientist maintained that the patent was his. The FAO argued that since he was an FAO employee the patent belonged to the FAO. The Niger government insisted that, since the process emerged from a government project merely assisted by FAO, the patent was theirs. The millet flour story provides another example of the roadblocks that bestrew the path of development, and of the wide range of inter-related knowledge, constituting a complex feedback system, that is necessary for effective decision making.

Starvation is always around the corner in countries of the Sahel, and nutrition can never be far from a planner's mind. In the Senegal River valley, where hope for increased output of foodstuffs through stable, irrigated agriculture is highest, about half the people suffer from malaria, about the same proportion suffer from bilharzia (river blindness) and intestinal parasites. Hence many people are debilitated by all three at once. No one does much work who has all three of these maladies together, especially when undernourished as well. Yet a successful Green Revolution in Mauritania, associated with the extension of irrigation, not only requires that the work connected with planting, irrigation, weed control, fertilizer and pesticides be done, but that all of it be done at the right time. The farmer cannot wait until tomorrow or next week when he may be feeling better. Moreover, all three of these maladies are water-related. Enlarging the irrigated area without a frontal attack on the related health problems could reduce productivity, not raise it.

Are countries like those of the African Sahel simply nohopers? Certainly there was no basis for considering them simply as countries at an earlier stage of development than the industrialized ones, ready to follow the same path if only proper policies were adopted. Putting Mauritania or Niger, and Argentina or Chile, into the same category, labelled less developed or developing or Third World is little short of absurd. Both the causes and the cures of their respective maladies are totally different.

Sri Lanka

Sri Lanka is a marginal case of a Least Developed Country. Had it not been for the armed conflict between the Tamils and the Senhalese during the past decade, it may well have graduated from the ranks of the LLDSs by now. Its levels of education and health are high; For example, in 1989 107 percent of the age group attended primary school (some children were still in primary school who should have graduated) 74 percent of the age group were in secondary school, and 4 percent in tertiary education. Adult literacy in 1990 included 88 percent of the population. The life expectancy in that year was 71. Nutrition was adequate: daily caloric intake was 2,277 calories per capita. Per capita GDP in 1990 was $470, its growth rate from 1965 to 1990 (as already noted) 2.9 percent. Exports accounted for 30 percent of GDP, savings 15 percent, and investment 22 percent. Its structure of production was quite modern: 26 percent in agriculture, 26 percent in industry, 48 percent in services. Between 1980 and 1990 its inflation rate was high enough to cause problems, and to cause the International Monetary Fund and the World Bank to look anxiously over the shoulders of the Department of Finance and the Central Bank: 11.1 percent.

When the Lower Uva project began in 1980, Sri Lanka was in a transitional state. President Jayawardene had only recently come to power, replacing Madame Banderanaike and her "socialist" or "welfare state" government. He and his colleagues were determined to accelerate growth of the economy through a program of deregulation, liberalization, industrialization and encouragement of private enterprise. Needless to say, the Sri Lankan population was divided in its reactions to this programme; many of the poorer people were hurt by it, while many of the intellectuals and higher income groups were exhilarated by it. Like Haiti and Malaysia, great importance was attached to regional development as a fundamental aspect of national development; the country had been divided up into regions, and foreign aid donors given the opportunity to "bid" for the region that appealed to them most, in the planning and in the implementation stages. Lower Uva, in the Southeast corner of the country, fell to Canada, and CIDA awarded the contract to Development Planning Associates of Ottawa. The team faced an extremely complex situation, economically, socially, and politically.

Sri Lanka at the time had a population of 14.9 million people (March 1981). With its area of 66,000 square kilometers, it is one of the world's most densely population countries. In 1980, GNP per capita at current prices was about US $250. On the other hand, standards of health, nutrition and education in Sri Lanka were already high in comparison to average levels of income and compared favourably with the standards achieved by many middle income countries. These high standards, combined with a relatively equitable income distribution, mitigated to some extent the low average incomes. The structure of the Sri Lankan economy, in terms of broad economic sectors had changed very little over two decades. In 1960, 56 percent of the employed labour force was employed in agriculture, and in 1978 this figure was still 52 percent.

Sri Lanka's dependence on tea, rubber and coconut for export earnings decreased very little over this period. Despite the large size of its agricultural sector, Sri Lanka was dependent on food imports. Sri Lanka imported all of its wheat, over 75 percent of its refined sugar, and over 8 percent of its rice. The pricing policies in place prior to 1978 offered insufficient incentives to farmers to adopt more modern farming practices. Between 1960 and 1980, the proportion of the population living in urban centres experienced only a small increase, from 18 to 27 percent, while Colombo's share of the urban population actually declined between 1970 and 1980; reflecting the slow pace of industrialization.

Sri Lanka's growth performance improved at the end of the 1970s, as GNP rose by 8.2 percent in 1978, 6.2 percent in 1979 and 5.5 percent in 1980. Over this three year period, the average growth rate of GNP per capita was 4.7 percent per year, and in 1979 and 1980 over 300,000 new jobs were added to the country's employed labour force, to reach nearly five million in 1980. These increases in output reflected the large scale investment program implemented in 1978, in particular the three "lead" projects of the government: the Accelerated Mahaweli Program; the Housing and Urban Development Program; and the Greater Colombo Economic Commission, designed to encourage export-led industrial growth. As a consequence, investment as a proportion of gross domestic product increased sharply to 20.0 percent in 1978 and 33.5 percent in 1980. Other factors underlying the improved growth performance included the economic liberalization policies of the new government, apparent sharp increases in crop yields and production of paddy and most subsidiary food crops, and the strong growth in earnings from tourism.

Sri Lanka, in comparison to many other ex-colonial countries, was well endowed with human resources. Consequently absorptive capacity for capital assistance was relatively high. A favourable factor in the Sri Lankan economic position was the soundness of its monetary, fiscal and foreign exchange policies. The expansion of the money supply had not been excessive, and reflected a cautious monetary and fiscal policy. The foreign exchange rate had been relatively stable.

Underlying all other aspects of the basic economic problem in Sri Lanka, however, was the population explosion, which came late to Sri Lanka. It was largely a phenomenon of the post World War II era. Dramatic and rapid reductions in death rates through eradication of malaria brought to Sri Lanka one of the highest rates of population growth in the world, and abnormally high ratios of children and aged people in the population, resulting in a very high ratio of unproductive to productive members of the population. Combined with the "welfare state" penchant current in Sri Lanka before the Jayawardene government replaced Madame Banderanaike, the rapid growth of population created enormous requirements in the fields of health, education and housing, which threatened all other parts of the economic development budgets.

This, then, was the economic situation and socio-political atmosphere in which the Lower Uva project was launched. The motivation behind "regional planning" and "regional development" in Sri Lanka was more the outcome of a commitment to national socioeconomic development rather than of a deep seated commitment to development of "regions" having political, socio-cultural, and economic significance of their own. "Regions" in Sri Lanka were regarded essentially as spatial subdivisions of the country for purposes of national planning and development, based essentially on Districts, but modified where needed, so as to define "regions" more convenient as planning units.

The Team's Perception of the Region

One of the first things the management of the Lower Uva project did to launch the planning exercise was to hire a small plane to give key members of the team a general overview of the region. I shall never forget that flight. We flew only a few hundred feet above the surface, and as we flew, no matter where within the region we were, the air below us was filled with smoke, with hundreds of fires glowing within it as far as the eye could see. The whole region looked like one big forest fire; which, in fact, was about what it was, except that all these fires were deliberately set as part of the chena cultivation. As we travelled by surface, especially in the northern part of the region, we got a closer look at the destruction, desolation, and erosion caused by centuries of shifting, slash-and-burn agriculture. Reluctantly, but rather quickly, we abandoned our Steering Committee's vision of Lower Uva as a resource frontier and "land bank" capable of providing substantial relief to population pressure in other parts of the island. As I pointed out in an earlier publication:

> It was rather a region which had been over-cut, over-planted, and over-irrigated for centuries. Its ecology was precarious, emphasis had to be placed on saving what was left, and much of the program consisted of planting trees of one kind or another for various purposes. It did not take much longer to convince the steering committee that these were the hard facts of Lower Uva life.

The Plan

As finally completed, the plan consisted of five volumes, plus a considerably greater number of individual studies. The five volumes were: Volume I: Summary; Volume II: Regional Analysis; Volume 3A: Proposed Projects; Volume 3B: Proposed Projects; and Volume 4: Impacts and Assessment. The plan was heavily project oriented, and centered around nine projects, which among them allocated every hectare in the region to a particular land use—much of them, of course, the same use they were in before the planning exercise began, but the possibility of changing their use was considered for all of them.

The goal of the Lower Uva Regional Development Plan was to maximize the employment and income benefits generated by the region's resource base in a manner which is sustainable and which is consistent with the region's current stage of socioeconomic and institutional development. The Plan would alter the use of 109,000 ha of land (13 percent of the region) which were mainly active or inactive chena lands. The new uses for this land consist of:

- 29,000 ha rainfed agriculture settlements
- 26,000 ha for forestry development
- 10,000 ha for new irrigated paddy settlements
- 5,000 ha for fruit growing
- 3,000 ha for some gardens
- 25,000 ha for wildlife parks
- 5,000 ha for pasture
- 6,000 ha for reservoirs

The Plan would support the construction of 27,500 homes for 165,000 people and 3,000 classrooms for 75,000 children. Safe drinking water would be provided to approximately 90 percent of the current residents and all of the population on plan projects. Construction employment would reach a peak of 16,000 man years in year 6, while operating employment created directly by the Plan would be over 96,000 from year 15 on. Total employment resulting directly and indirectly from the Plan would be 134,000 full-time jobs, a 100 percent increase over the current level. With the Plan, the total population of the region by the year 2000 would be about 980,000; 370,000 more than expected without the Plan.

Internal rates of return and net present values were calculated for all of these projects. For the program as a whole the internal rate of return was calculated at 22 percent. It was not, in other words, a program that would need incentives or subsidies in order to be effective.

Some of these projects deserve comment. First, the emphasis on housing resulted from the team's finding that housing was the number one requirement for improving the levels of health, education, family planning, agricultural extension services, and the like. Highly trained people like doctors, nurses, and extension workers would not come to the region for lack of housing. Here is a good example of the "Unified Approach;" the solution to problems in some sectors were to be found in other sectors. Second, the approach to irrigation was wherever possible to restore the ancient tanks rather than launching large-scale, capital intensive projects to use the rivers. Third, a good deal of stress was laid on conservation and preservation of the environment. This emphasis led to the inclusion of an elephant walk to connect Yala National Park with forest reserves so that the elephants could follow their customary migratory routes without crossing peasant holdings and destroying crops (See Map 19-1). The Sri Lankans love their remaining elephants dearly, but no so much that peasants will stand by and see their source of livelihood destroyed rather than reaching for a rifle. (The peasants whose land was taken for elephant walks were given better, irrigated land nearby, taken from the national park. The swap left everyone better off, especially the elephants).

The approach used to evaluate the economic viability of the LURD Plan is based on the Squire-van der Tak methodology developed for the appraisal of projects considered for funding by the World Bank. The main elements of this methodology include the valuation of all goods and services at border prices, the use of the "present value of uncommitted public income measured in foreign exchange" as the numeraire and the application of conversion factors to convert non-traded goods from domestic prices to border values.

To facilitate Plan evaluation, a "most likely" or benchmark scenario was prepared as a point of reference in all sensitivity tests. This scenario represents a rigorous test of Plan viability, for it includes as benefits only the direct effects of the Plan, but incorporates all Plan expenditures, including the costs

MAP 19-1

Source: Lower Uva Regional Development Plan. Prepared for: Sri Lanka Ministry of Lands and Land Development and Canadian International Development Agency. Prepared by: DPA Consulting Ltd., Canada.

of non-revenue generating projects. The results of the benchmark scenario are summarized in Table 19.1, together with the findings from the "standard package" of sensitivity tests employed in all project evaluations.

The internal rate of return of the total LURD Plan after 25 years is 22.2 percent. The package of sensitivity tests showed that the Plan's rate of return is sensitive to major changes in benefits and costs.

The Role of Theory in Regional Development Policy and Planning in Lower Uva

As in other regions, the regional development theories analyzed in Part I of this volume were helpful in explaining the past and present of Lower Uva. It must be admitted, however, that even there, their usefulness was limited. The overwhelmingly important factor in Lower Uva's past and present has been the centuries long process of destruction of the region's natural resources: forests, soil, rainfall, rivers. Consequently the region lags behind the national average in per capita income, health, education, housing and transport. True, in the decade before the project began the population, Gross Regional Product, and per capita income grew *faster* than the national average; but this seemingly promising performance was the result of immigration and expansion of chena cultivation, much of it on crown land and illegal. Slash-and-burn agriculture is a means of combining a lot of land with relatively little labour, and can yield quite high returns *per manhour*, so long as there is some land and some forest still to exploit. But it is equivalent to "mining the forest and the soil," and in Lower Uva it was reaching its limit. Meanwhile in paddy (irrigated rice), cultivation, acreage, yields, and production were all falling.

Two thirds of the labour force of the region was still engaged in agriculture; fishing and forestry absorbed another ten percent. Much of this activity was self-sufficient. Thus the "base-industry-export-multiplier" theory, and indeed theories of interregional and international trade in general, played a minor role. Location theory helped to explain the lack of industrialization and urbanization: new industries, and enterprises already established in Colombo, Kandy, and elsewhere in the wet zone, had good reasons for *not* going to Lower Uva. These considerations of course influenced the team in their search for some means of turning things around.

On the whole, however, regional development theory had relatively little to do with the formulation of policy and the preparation of plans for the development of the Lower Uva region. Perhaps our most conscious application of theory was our *rejection* of growth pole doctrine—not Perroux' grand general theory, but Boudeville's revisionist concept of an urban centre capable of generating spread effects to its own peripheral region. There was in fact no city in

TABLE 19.1
Economic Appraisal of LURD Plan

Time Span	IRR (%)	Net Present Values (Rs million)		
		10 %	15 %	20 %
15 yrs	16.1	898	118	(298)
25 yrs	22.2	3,776	1,368	273
45 yrs	23.0	6,260	1,978	440

Sensitivity Analysis for 25 Years
Internal Rate of Return

		Benefits changed by (%)					Benefits Delayed by (%)	
		−20	−10	0	10	20	1 yr	2 yr
Costs	0	14.6	18.6	22.2	25.5	28.7	16.5	12.7
Increased	10	11.4	15.4	18.9	22.2	25.2	13.9	10.5
By	20	8.4	12.5	16.0	19.2	22.2	11.5	8.3

the region big enough and dynamic enough to serve as a growth pole in this sense. Our urban policy was directed rather at making the existing towns more attractive as central places.

There was no marked dualism *within* the region, except perhaps for Moneragala's position, small as it was, as its "primate city." Much of the region's modern sector was concentrated in and around its capital city. Of course Sri Lanka as a whole had a marked dualism between Colombo, Kandy, the plantations, and the wet zone in general, and the dry zone of which Lower Uva was a part. Much of its relative poverty could be explained in those terms; but the income gaps between the "modern" and "traditional" regions was much less than in most developing countries at the time.

Being so heavily concentrated on agriculture, and so open to the vagaries of climate, the region had its own pattern of economic fluctuations, as well as being influenced by cycles in the national economy, and by related shifts in monetary, fiscal, foreign trade and wage-price policies.

The pattern of development (and underdevelopment) of the region was obviously greatly influenced by its geography; but the team, although it conducted a sociological survey, found no cultural differences between the people of Lower Uva and those of other regions that could explain the relative retar-

FIGURE 19.1
Distribution of Employment and GRP—Lower UVA Region

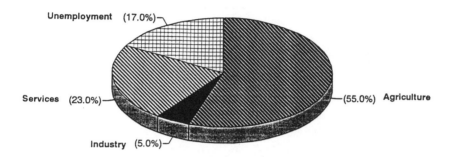

Employment

Unemployment (17.0%)

Services (23.0%)

Industry (5.0%)

(55.0%) Agriculture

Total Labour Force = 150,000

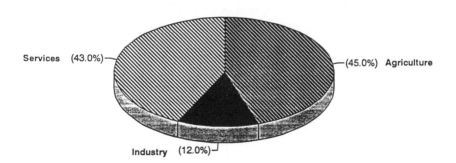

Gross Regional Product

Services (43.0%)

(45.0%) Agriculture

Industry (12.0%)

GRP = Rs 1,400 million

dation of Lower Uva. Similarly, while there was an obvious shortage of entrepreneurial activity in the region, that seemed to be the result of the physical characteristics of the region and the educational lag rather than of the fundamental nature of the people.

There is no reason to suppose that circular and cumulative causation would not operate in the region if any dramatic economic event took place; but there has been so little innovation or structural change, and the non-monetary sector is so large, that circular or cumulative forces have been weak. By the same token, the region will need some kind of Big Push, which the Plan is supposed to provide, if a cumulative and progressive movement is to be launched.

On the whole, Lower Uva has been less dependent on colonial and neo-colonial powers than other regions in Sri Lanka. Apart from law and order, the British were not much interested in Lower Uva, leading to a policy of benign neglect rather than active exploitation. There was very little foreign enterprise or foreign investment in the region.

Finally, the constructs of regional science were not of much use in formulating policy and preparing plans to develop Lower Uva. It was not that the principles were wrong, but that the scale and structure of the economy made regional science a less powerful toolkit than it can be in larger and more complex and highly developed economies.

But if regional development theory did not lead to the choice of projects and the allocation of resources recommended in the Plan, what did? Essentially, it was the physical characteristics of the region. The Plan was essentially a land-use plan; the allocation of labour and capital was determined by the allocation of land amongst various uses. The most useful tool in the planning process was the computerized map overlays. By the time such factors as population growth, ground water supplies, rainfall in wet and dry seasons, soils, slopes, temperatures, evaporation, transport facilities and the like had been mapped for each of the very small subdivisions of the whole region, the map overlays virtually dictated the use of every hectare.

Were the economists useless, then? Not quite. They still had to calculate cost; benefit ratios, internal rates of return and the like. They had to make marketing surveys and forecasts. They had to calculate the impact of probable government policies on the development of the region, and also the impact of developments taking place in other regions. But most important, they had to serve as watchdogs, or goal keepers, to make sure that major mistakes were not made. The economist, more than any other professional, is trained to think in terms of "a multiplicity of ends and a scarcity of resources that have alternative uses," to consider all alternatives at once, and the opportunity costs among them. He is therefore less inclined than other specialists to pursue single objectives or single means of attaining them, with excessive enthusiasm, because of the nature of his or her training. It is good to have some economists on the team to keep an eye on their colleagues. And whatever other use the regional development theories may have, at least some of them are complicated and hard to understand, so that it is good mental discipline to study them.

Part III

Looking Back—Looking Ahead

20

Lessons Learned

The preceding chapters may have led the reader to conclude that both theorists and practitioners of regional development are in disarray. We reviewed a wide variety of theories, sometimes apparently, in direct conflict with one another, explaining the existence of regional disparities, or pointing to measures to promote regional economic development. In many ways, government officials have been left on their own to pick and choose specific items from the menu prepared by the theorists. Yet, to many practitioners in government, theories of regional development have been of limited value. Neo-Marxist and neoclassical models and recent literature on regional dependency, exude an aura of other-worldliness to many of the bureaucrats in government departments planning regional development initiatives. There is no manual for dependency theory planning, nor can there ever be one.[1]

But what does it mean to "apply" theories of regional development to government policies and programs? "Application" of theory can take at least four different forms. First, theory can be used to *explain* what has happened in the past, like the "big bang" theory of the creation of the universe. Second, it can be applied to *interpret and explain* what is happening now, as when a geologist analyses an earth quake or eruption of a volcano while it is taking place. Third, if the theory is sufficiently precise, it can be applied to *predict* what will happen in the future, as when an astronomer predicts the date of an eclipse. None of these types of application implies any degree of *control* whatsoever. However, in some kinds of theory there is a suggestion that through its "application," future performance of the system being analyzed can be *improved*, in terms of some specified objective or objectives. Most economic theory, including regional development theory, carries with it the implication that it can be "applied" in all four ways. Note that there is a progression in the four types of application. It is unlikely that the second form of application would be possible without the first, and the third requires both of the first two. The fourth, however, clearly requires all of the three others.

Thus one could "apply" the theories outlined in Part I to sharpen analysis of economic history, explaining why and how some regions have developed faster or slower, or in different patterns, from others. Having done that, one would obviously be in a better position for, let us say, prescribing policies to reduce regional disparities, than one would be without it; but one would not necessarily come out with good policy recommendations on that basis alone. Even with the capacity to undertake the second and third types of application, additional knowledge, plus skill and perhaps luck, is needed to complete the fourth kind of application successfully.

When economists speak of applying theory, they are usually thinking of designing strategies, making plans, and formulating policies. It is this fourth kind of application that is our primary concern. However, to evaluate the theories in a comprehensive fashion, we shall examine them in terms of the other three criteria as well.

Our review of regional development theories in Part I discovered none that is just plain *wrong*, in the sense of being internally inconsistent, disobeying the rules of logic, flagrantly in conflict with the known facts, or definitively disproved by standard empirical tests. For example, we argued that the "base industry + export multiplier" (b.i.e.m.) theory could not be accepted as a *general* theory of regional development; somewhere, sometime, expansion must take place in a region where its growth cannot be traced to an increase of imports into another region. Once that happens, but only if that happens, a chain reaction may set in which affects many regions. However, if we combine b.i.e.m. with a theory of development through innovations, of the Schumpeter or Perroux type, and apply both types of theory at the regional level, we can certainly *explain* the development of some regions in some periods in that fashion. Expansion of the steel industry in response to growth of the automobile industry, bolstered by proximity to coal, iron, and industrial water, certainly goes a long way towards *explaining* the development of the Pittsburgh region in the first half of the twentieth century. The b.i.e.m. theory could also show how growth of the automobile industry in Detroit and Flint brought development to northern Sumatra, through expansion of rubber plantations, and innovations in rubber planting and processing.

Similarly, we pointed out the elements of indeterminacy in location theory, and the difficulties inherent in its use as a regional development planning tool. At the same time, however, location theory goes a long way in *explaining* what has happened with regard to location of industry, and thus in explaining why some regions have grown rapidly while others have grown slowly, stagnated, or declined.

It follows that all the theories presented are to some degree applicable, at least to the first degree. Ultimately, however, as noted earlier, we are interested in theories that can be applied to the fourth degree: that is, which help the regional policy makers and the regional development planners to improve the outcome of measures taken to encourage the development of particular regions. For that reason, the second part of our book looks to countries where there has been, in recent decades, a formal, official, integrated attempt to improve the prospects for development; and where this attempt involved, explicitly or implicitly, efforts to apply some theory or theories in order to achieve this objective. More simply put, they are regions where some development planning exercise has been carried out. They are also regions in which at least one of the authors, in some way or another, has been involved in this planning exercise.

We wish to make it clear that we are *not* evaluating regional development projects, plans, or programmes *as such*. Our approach is not that of a funding agency, a government, or an international organization. We are not appraising the degree of competence with which either the planning or the implementation was performed. We are not even comparing one planning exercise with another, as we did in our *Canadians and Regional Development at Home and in the Third World*.[2] We are appraising the comparative usefulness of the *theories* applied; asking why some theories were applied and others were not, case by case; and then asking whether the ones that were applied have more intrinsic merit than those that were rejected or ignored. Of course, in order to do that kind of appraisal of *theory*, we must say something about the regions themselves, the nature of their problems, the task that confronted the planners, and the processes by which the application of theory led to particular projects, plans, policies, and programmes. But the end result sought by this analysis is not statements of the order "that was a good (bad) plan," but rather of the order "those were good (bad) theories that were applied in that case."

In the various cases of regional development policy and planning that we have considered, very few of them carried any particular theory through to the fourth stage—except, perhaps, a somewhat bastardized version of the "growth pole" or "growth centre" doctrine. Does that mean that the theories are useless, or even wrong? Not at all. In the first place, the guiding principle behind all scientific investigation is pushing back the frontiers of knowledge, or contributing to the *understanding* of observed phenomena in the universe. When Einstein pieced together his theory of relativity, he was not thinking of the atom bomb or nuclear power plants. All the theories presented in Part I contribute to our understanding of the functioning of a market economy. They also indicate how powerful are the forces at work which determine the distribution of economic activity in space. The policy maker who would utilize these forces (if he considers them benign), or offset or alter them (if he considers them malign), must first understand them. Most of our cases indicate some dissatisfaction with the operation of the market—whether due to "market failure" or "government failure"—and constitute efforts to bring about better results through intervention, of one sort or another.

The builders of neoclassical micro-theory, for the most part, were not really interested in application. They were devoted to the analysis and exposition of the manner in which the market functions. Many of them stopped there. Those who went on to consideration of policy split into two groups: those who thought that the market works very well, in the absence of misguided government intervention; and those who thought that the market works rather badly in the absence of astute management and good policy. In his 1978 presidential address to the American Economics Association, Robert Solow commented on this fundamental split among more or less mainstream economists. The policy recommendation of the first group was laissez-faire, and as Joan Robinson explained: "Logical structures of this kind have a certain charm. They allow those without mathematics to catch a hint of what intellectual beauty means…(but) apart from the advocacy of Free Trade there was not much to say on practical questions. The policy recommended was laissez faire, and there was no need to describe in any detail how to do nothing."[3] The other group proposed various kinds of intervention to deal with unemployment, inflation, economic fluctuations, inequalities, health, education, housing, etc.

Since much of regional development theory produced particularly in recent years is derived from neoclassical theory, we should not be surprised that the same dichotomy should appear in regional theory as in general economics. The "laissez-faire" school argues that the market, left to itself, will bring about a kind of "Pareto Optimum" in the distribution of economic activity in space, and so has no recommendation beyond "leave the market alone." For them, "do nothing" is the application of theory to regional policy. Since none of our cases are examples of "doing nothing," we have left out a wide range of "application." Indeed, in recent years, in such countries as the United States, Australia, and the United Kingdom, where so little has been done by way of effective policy to deal with unemployment, inflation, and regional disparities, we may well have neglected the most prevalent form of "application" of regional theory.

Theories and Their Policy Impact

Putting aside Perroux's growth pole concept for a moment, one could easily conclude that too many theorists and practitioners of regional development have been working in isolation from one another. One could also conclude that many theorists, particularly since the late 1970s, have thrown up their hands and given up. The wave of neo-conservative thinking, the election of right of centre politicians, the disenchantment with the performance of public bureaucracies and the difficult fiscal positions of most governments in Anglo-American democracies, explain why a good number of theorists have given up and turned to the market to bring about the "Pareto Optimum." A leading economist, it will be recalled, has observed that for all the political concern about regional disparities and regional development, we do not have an underlying theory.[4] Another argued that "if we have learned anything about the development process during the past thirty years, it is surely that there are *no* panaceas for development."[5] Recently, Albert Breton went further and argued that every government in the world pursues regional development policies even when most economists say that they should not and should instead be encouraging mobility of people.[6] Quite a few theorists now appear to be asking, "Why can't governments do like us and give up?"

It was not always so. Perroux's growth pole concept became fashionable not only in academic circles but also in government departments. Government planners everywhere embraced the concept as the answer for alleviating regional disparities. It was applied in one form or another in the countries surveyed in this book and in many others.

For a few years at least, it was a panacea. It was simple to explain or, at least, it sounded easy to understand. It held promise that at least one or two centres in an economically-depressed region could prosper. Best to have people move to a larger community one hundred miles away than leave the region or even the country altogether. Government planners applauded the concept. Initially at least, it held the promise of being a neat and tidy approach, arbitrarily laying down which communities and, at times, which sectors were in and which ones were out. To the policy planner, the growth pole concept would also force politicians to focus their efforts and to concentrate limited resources on communities that held the most promise for development. Once politicians had designated the growth centres, planners would then be free to plan and implement appropriate measures.

Politicians, at least for a while, also applauded the concept. Politicians representing designated centres could claim credit for seeing communities designated as growth poles, and they did. Politicians not representing designated communities could press the government to designate them, and they too did, often publicly, thereby raising expectations in certain communities that they would be next. In Canada, for example, politicians on both the government and opposition benches gave their demands for designating communities they represented a high public profile. The demands invariably placed the Canadian government on the defensive. It continually had to explain why any number of communities could not be designated. It was a public debate that the government simply could not win. It responded by designating communities such as Hawke's Bay, Come-by-Chance and Goose Bay as growth centres, communities as far away from what Perroux had in mind when he wrote about clusters of propulsive industries, as one could possibly imagine. The Canadian government eventually gave up and scrapped the growth pole concept as the centrepiece of its regional development policy. In the United States, an official summed up the application of the growth pole concept well by reporting that he did not know exactly what a growth centre was but that he knew that there was "at least one in every congressional district."[7]

Still, in the period since 1960, which includes all of the cases of regional policy covered in this volume, the one policy most widely carried through to application at stage 4 has been some version of the growth pole, development pole, or growth centre doctrine. Again, what was "applied" was a far cry from the elegant, sophisticated, but complex and non-operational theory of François Perroux. In the United States, the doctrine was translated into the practice of putting public investment into centres with some hope of growing. In Canada and other countries, it became a matter of luring private enterprise to urban centres through cash grants of one kind or another in hopes of generating spread effects to the peripheral region, usually a retarded one. In no case was it construed to mean recognizing that there is a strong pull towards clustering of innovating enterprises in metropolitan centres, generating spread effects to global spaces defined as "fields of force," as Perroux would have it. Perroux's disciples hit upon the idea of using government intervention to create *other* centres as "pôles d'équilibre;" Perroux would have said that the idea was a good one, but such a program would be very difficult to implement and very expensive.

Let us consider again very briefly the other theories outlined in Part I, and see to what extent they have been applied in the various cases discussed in Part II. Geography—soil, climate, topology, natural resources—is by and large taken as given. In a frontier region new resources may be discovered, and even in a settled area technological discoveries (nuclear power) may bring into use new resources that were not considered before (uranium). "Improving" the environment, such as building dams for hydro-electric power, raises environmental questions which the policy maker or planner must take into account. Such factors are handled in a routine way, almost unconsciously, in all the cases we considered. Only when dramatic environmental changes are involved—the Aswan Dam in Egypt, the St. James Bay hydro-electric project in Quebec, the TVA in the United States, the Snowy River project in Australia—does geography play a major role in the actual planning or policy-making process.

To the degree that education and training enter into the planning process, "culture" may be said to play a role. In some of our case studies—the Austin Project, Appalachia, the Latrobe and Geelong Regional Commissions—upgrading the quality of the labour force was a major objective. Providing or generating entrepreneurship where it is absent or inadequate also may be regarded as a "cultural" factor and was a major component in planning for Appalachia, Austin, Geelong, and Latrobe and more recently in Atlantic Canada. In industrialized countries, however, cultural revolutions are usually not contemplated in regional development plans and policies, even where it may be needed, as in Quebec in 1965 or the Rest of Canada (ROC) in 1992.

In a general sort of way, interregional and international trade have been considerations in all of our case studies. The theory of international and interregional trade has, however, moved a long way from Ricardo's concept of comparative advantage, illustrated by exchange of "tuns of wine" from Portugal and "bolts of cloth" from England. With today's technology the tendency is to think in terms of "competitive advantage," in terms of complex and subtle human factors, rather than the more obvious "comparative advantage" based on geographic factors. Today almost any country can consider producing and exporting almost anything, whether or not the required natural resources are found within its borders, as the cases of Japan, Hong Kong, Singapore, Taiwan, Malaysia, and South Korea demonstrate.

Similarly, in any location decision, the policy maker or planner would have to ask: "Could such-and-such an industry operate successfully in this region?" The answer, however, would not come easily, and would not come at all without some discussion with representatives of the private sector. Today, the range of choice of location is infinitely more wide than it was a generation ago. The president of a high-tech enterprise may choose to locate his plant in New Mexico or Arizona because he wants to build a mansion there, to live in after his imminent retirement, and his product-mix and his technology are such that costs of production will be much the same wherever he locates it. One of Hotelling's ice cream vendors may set up an attractive stand on the highway leading to the beach, and capture all the business. Location theory today is much more complex and more than ever indeterminate. But nonetheless, the policy maker must endeavour to find out what the factors are that determine what activities might succeed in his region, and take them into account. We have seen, in the case of the two Australian regional commissions, that such organizations can actually *provide* entrepreneurship, not merely attract it, or train others to provide it.

For reasons given in Chapter 10, regional science now needs an overhaul, to see whether any of its "immutable laws" still stand up in the face of the more flexible decision-making that accompanies the new technologies of today. The concept of "cumulative causation" was certainly in the minds of the planners and policy makers in Appalachia. Indeed, the whole effort might be described as an attempt to replace cumulative decay by cumulative progress;

and on the whole, the commission and its staff succeeded in their efforts. In other words, the theories are there, almost unconscious, in the minds of policy makers and planners, and are sometimes consciously applied, when the concrete problems of a particular region demand application of a particular theory.

Theories in Search of a Theory

Underpinning all theories outlined in Part I was the view that it is possible to separate governments and the market and to some extent even separating the role of politicians and defining optimal policy prescriptions. Theorists did not begin with the premise that politicians and politics matter or that the challenge at hand was not one of economics but rather political economy.

Perroux's concern was to explain patterns of economic development and what could be done to influence these patterns. The regional science literature, which embodies so well mid-twentieth century techniques of economic analysis, seeks to explain why economic development takes place in certain areas at a given pace. The same is true for other theories, including the international and interregional trade theory.

It only takes a moment's reflection to appreciate that it was hopelessly naive to construct theories, particularly prescriptive ones, in isolation from how the public sector broadly defined would respond in implementing them. Keynes, Perroux and others of like mind may well have been right in thinking that the operation of market forces did not guarantee a harmonious "equilibrium" in space. To define a new theory to correct this without taking into account the "behaviour" of the public sector in implementing them was simply a non starter. The study makes clear that the failure of the growth pole concept has as much to do with this factor as it had with any conceptual shortcomings.

Proponents of the neo-conservative approach are "equally" naive in thinking that governments would stand idly by and let the unfettered market call the adjustment tune.[8] One can hardly imagine a more ideological or committed leader to neo-conservatism than was Margaret Thatcher. Yet, as we saw in Part II, she balked at turning over the regional disparities "problem" to market forces. No doubt she had to contend with the political realities that government backbenchers continually brought to her attention. Turning regional development to market forces also meant foregoing EEC funds earmarked for Britain's slow growth regions. Political ideology and a strong commitment to neo-conservatism is one thing. Heroism, however, is quite another. Heroism is what is required for a political leader to turn down funds with the risk of seeing them reallocated to a neighbouring country. Such a decision could in the end, for example, serve to strengthen Britany at the expense of England's northeast. Even the most ardent supporter of market forces will insist that all, in particular neighbouring countries, must play by the same rules for the rules to be effective.

Politicians representing highly developed regions are likely to argue that market forces should be unleashed while those representing slow growth ones are more often than not supporters of government intervention in the economy. Indeed, it is difficult to imagine many politicians from slow growth regions supporting pure national efficiency measures at least publicly even if long-term benefits would accrue not only to the national economy but also to his or her own region. The length of political mandates is such that the long term perspective holds little appeal.

Theorists, even those with a prescriptive bend, also paid little attention to the role public bureaucracies would be called upon to play to implement the policies and programs. We have precious little literature on how governments should organize themselves to support regional development policies. A former minister responsible for regional development in Canada once observed that how government organizes itself for promoting regional development is as crucial to the success of regional development efforts as the policy itself. Here, however, we have tried this and that and we are still not satisfied.

A review of the operations of a *newly* created regional development agency conducted in 1990 in Canada called for "a major change in the *culture* of the agency—that is from a pseudo-entrepreneurial organization to one which actively pursues its entrepreneurship. It will be important for the agency personnel to practice what they preach."[9] The agency, it was felt, had after only a few years, already become too "bureaucratic." On this point, the review called on the agency's senior management "to ensure that agency staff are encouraged to take up new challenges, to not stay in one position, in one office or, perhaps, for that matter, with the agency itself for too long...If there is one group of people in Atlantic Canada that should be dynamic at the forefront of new knowledge and outward looking it is ACOA personnel.[10]

It may well be that this issue speaks to a larger problem. There is a growing general disenchantment everywhere with the public bureaucracies. This is true not just in Canada but in most western industrialized countries. President Reagan, for example, declared in his first inaugural speech that he had come to Washington "to drain the swamp."[11] Former Prime Minister Thatcher asked her public servants to read public-choice literature, and Prime Minister Mulroney declared in election speeches that he would hand out "pink slips and running shoes to bureaucrats."[12]

The public bureaucracies stand accused of many things. They are often viewed as large, cumbersome, wedded to the status quo, and expensive. Many, including those who have in the past supported a greater role for government, like J.K. Galbraith, are of the view that public bureaucracies lack creativity and a capacity to challenge the status quo.[13] We have seen a host of measures in recent years designed to modernize public services and make them more "responsive."[14] These measures are designed to remove "administrative" and "creativity" shackles inside the public service. The creativity shackles are, in our views, rooted in the way government is organized. With the aid of hindsight we suspect that the problem is not a recent one. Rather it began in the late 1960s and 1970s, when the public service took in a lot of bright recent university graduates and policy analysts but failed to give them the access, the flexibility, and the tools to do their work properly.

We now see signs everywhere that the passing industrial society will leave in its wake many of the government organization models it engendered. We have organizational models that were structured and designed for the industrial era and for military purposes in a time when wars were fought on the battlefield with what has now become unsophisticated equipment. The models of organization, line, and staff, the way subjects are studied, and the hierarchical nature of government departments and agencies are pure nineteenth-century administrative techniques.

The current structure of government was probably particularly well suited to deliver large-scale services—like the mail and transportation services—in a consistent, objective, and effective fashion. The delivery of large-scale and routine services were the main challenges for government virtually into the 1960s. The 1960s, however, saw the advent of a host of highly "flexible" programs designed to spur economic development at the national, regional, and community levels, to promote adjustment in selected sectors, and to assist disadvantaged groups. Policy-advice and program-evaluation capacities were required to develop and assess these initiatives, but they were simply added on to the existing machinery of government. Meanwhile, central agencies put in place measures designed to keep all these new developments under control, with line departments responding with still more administrative units to keep up with new centrally prescribed procedures and controls.

In addition, many government units, old and new, are organized along the same lines, all are integrated into the departmental structure, and all report through the same channels—through directors, directors-generals and so on. This is even true of new government departments and agencies. Yet it may well be that the delivery of large-scale and routine services and the development and delivery of flexible or open-ended programs (not to mention the requirements for creative thinking about policy and the evaluation of ongoing programs) require quite different organizational structures. The first may best be served by a traditional hierarchical organization and the latter by a new form of government organization capable of encouraging thought-provoking ideas, and even having quick access to political authority for decisions.

Regional development more than any other public-policy field needs a capacity to be creative, to adjust quickly to changing circumstances, to challenge the status quo and often conventional thinking both inside government and in the regions, to deliver initiatives quickly with a minimum of red tape, and to be in the field working with key economic actors and having the authority to make decisions. One hardly thinks of public bureaucracies when one thinks of these requirements. We need to envision different organizational models to get the job done. The decision by the Austin group to involve "practically everyone but the federal government" speaks to this need.

There is a growing consensus that public bureaucracies have not lived up to expectations. John K. Galbraith, among others, argues that public bureaucracies have given the left a bad reputation.[15] Still, with all its shortcomings, we know how government works, how it decides, and why it decides in favour of certain groups over others. We know, however, a great deal less about how large private sector firms make decisions and why they take certain decisions. We know intuitively, for example, that theories outlined in Part I of this book no longer explain how and why firms make investment decisions. The theories hardly mention, for example, the impact of government grants on investment decisions. Yet, we know that very few firms, even those in the service sector, now take investment decisions without first looking at the "juicy morsels" government offer to influence the location of new economic activities. We also know that successful business people will look to "roots" or to their "birthplace" when deciding where to locate new activities. Recent developments in Columbus, Ohio are a case in point.

The point here is that we need a fundamental rethink about how private sector firms make decisions and how government and public bureaucracies could be made more effective in defining and implementing regional development policies. Above all, we need to drop this notion that the public and private sectors can be treated as separate entities making decisions in relative isolation from each other. They no longer do, assuming for a moment they ever did. We believe that theories of regional development that may hold promise, particularly prescriptive ones, will be found in the recognition that it is not possible to separate the public and private sector and in measures designed to "modernize" how the public sector, notably public bureaucracies, work or are allowed to work.

Notes

1. See Benjamin Higgins, "The Task Ahead: The Search for a New Local and Regional Development," (Nagoya: United Nations Centre for Regional Development, undated), p. 6.
2. See Benjamin Higgins and Donald J. Savoie, *Canadians and Regional Development at Home and in the Third World* (Moncton: Canadian Institute for Research on Regional Development, 1988).
3. Joan Robinson, *Economic Philosophy*, (New York: Doubleday, 1964), pp. 63, 73–74.

4. Richard Lipsey quoted in André Raynauld (ed.), *Seminar on Regional Development in Canada: Transcript of the Proceedings* (Montreal: CRDE de l'Université de Montréal, 24 October 1980), p. 105.
5. Quoted in Donald J. Savoie, *Regional Economic Development: Canada's Search for Solutions* (Toronto: University of Toronto Press, 2nd edition, 1990), p. 229.
6. Albert Breton, "The Status and Efficiency of Regional Development Policies," in Donald J. Savoie and Irving Brecher (eds), *Equity and Efficiency in Economic Development: Essays in Honour of Benjamin Higgins* (Montreal: McGill-Queen's University Press), 1992, pp. 161.
7. The Appalachian Regional Commission, *Twenty Years of Progress, 1965–1985* (Washington, D.C., 1985), p. 38.
8. See, for example, Tom J. Courchene, "A Market Perspective on Regional Disparities," *Canadian Public Policy*, vol. vii, no. 4 (1981), p. 513.
9. See Donald J. Savoie, *ACOA: Transition to Maturity* (Moncton: Atlantic Canada Opportunities Agency, 1991), p. 93.
10. *Ibid.*
11. Quoted in Derek Bok, "A Daring and Complicated Strategy," *Harvard Magazine*, May-June 1989, p. 49.
12. Quoted in David Zussman, "Walking the Tightrope: The Mulroney Government and the Public Service," in Michael J. Prince (ed.), *How Ottawa Spends 1986–87* (Toronto: Methuen, 1986), p. 255.
13. See, among others, Donald J. Savoie, *The Politics of Public Spending in Canada* (Toronto: University of Toronto Press, 1990), chapter 9.
14. See *Public Service 2000: The Renewal of the Public Service of Canada* (Ottawa: Minister of Supply and Services, 1990).
15. Quoted in *Dimensions*, winter 1986, 13.

21

Towards a New Political Economy
of Regional Development

So two cheers for Democracy; one because it admits variety and two because it permits criticism. Two cheers are quite enough; there is no occasion to give three. Only Love the Beloved Republic deserves that.

—E.M. Forster

During the last decade, we have learned that, in practice, either a market economy or a socialist one operates in such a way as to create regional imbalances. When these imbalances are accompanied by ethnic, religious, cultural or racial differences, they can tear an existing nation state apart, as they have done in the former Soviet Union and Jugoslavia, and as they threaten to do in Canada. Even where "regional" disparities are not great, as in the United States, economic and social gaps, combined with racial differences, can give rise to violence. After 27 years, the Appalachian Regional Commission has not closed the gaps between their region and others in the United States. Austin, Texas, a prosperous town, seat of a great university and the state government, but home to three distinct racial groups, finds itself confronted with a host of social, economic and cultural problems. Superficially a peaceful, equitable, and harmonious country, Australia, self-styled "the lucky country," nonetheless has extremely high rates of youth unemployment in some regions, which contribute to the world's highest rate of youth suicide. There are no macro-economic policies which can provide solutions to problems like these.

Given the intractable regional differences, in any parliamentary democracy there are bound to be strong political pressures for government intervention to redress them. As Albert Breton has pointed out, in Canada, especially, an influential group of economists has for years been preaching the gospel that policies to assist retarded regions merely reduce mobility, delay adjustment, and cause inefficiency; but the policies continue nonetheless. Occasionally, in some countries, the political pendulum swings far enough to the right to bring to power governments like the Reagan and Bush administrations in the United States and the Hawke government in Australia, whose faith in the market is so strong that they feel no national regional policy is needed. Yet, even Reagan could not persuade Congress to kill the Appalachian Regional Commission, or to kill the Economic Development Administration altogether; and the Labor Party government in Australia, under Keating's leadership, has recently put regional development at the very core of national economic policy. Margaret Thatcher never succeeded in doing away with attempts to reduce regional disparities in Great Britain. In Canada, Prime Minister Brian Mulroney, for all his faith in the market, was not being so foolish as to try to scrap regional development policy altogether. He compromised by decentralizing it and by shifting its forces towards entrepreneurship.

Of course, those economists who think—rightly or wrongly—that regional development policy constitutes dangerous interference with the market, and that enhanced mobility would do a better job of reducing regional gaps, have not only the right but the obligation to say so. And those economists who believe that enforcing the degree of mobility that would be necessary to eliminate regional differences would be so disruptive and so painful for so many people as to be unacceptable to the electorate, and that it would probably fail anyhow, have an equal right and obligation to express and explain their views. To the latter group, which includes the present writers, solving regional problems by mobility summons up a picture of millions of unemployed people forever hitchhiking along the highways, in search of jobs that are not there, leaving behind them broken families, a distorted age structure, abandoned friends, and empty houses, schools and hospitals. Such an exodus can become cumulative, creating ghost towns. In Canada, with unemployment at 9 percent in the province where it is lowest, and where jobs are available only for highly trained and experienced people, "mobility" does not necessarily mean moving from unemployment to employment, and the economic and social costs of movement are extremely high. So why not create jobs for people where they are, and for which they are qualified?

Because of such considerations and fears among the electorate, the industrialized democracies are likely to continue to have some sort of regional development policy. The strength of such policies will wax and wane, as faith of the electorate in the market wanes and waxes. In a democracy, "50% plus 1" of the electorate are always right, no matter what economists say. If the people of any country are prepared to pay for reductions of regional gaps, it cannot be legitimately argued that the policy is "wrong;" economists who oppose such policies can only point out the presumed costs of such policy in terms of efficiency. Those economists who favour such policies can point to the high costs of mobility; and the electorate can make up its mind.

The great strides in information and telecommunication, which make "New York, Tokyo, London and Hong Kong enterprises as close to a hollow in Appalachia as if they were just down the street," together with the continuing managerial revolution, will have an unpredictable effect on regional disparities. They make enterprises much more flexible, mobile, and footloose. They make it more feasible for management teams to seek locations where labour is cheap. In so far as "footloose" enterprises move into retarded regions of the same country, there may be some tendency to reduce regional gaps. But labour must remain cheap in the retarded region, or the enterprises will move out again, so the new flexibility may not help retarded regions after all. And for the R & D phase of the production cycle, enterprises are still likely to go to established metropolitan centres, which may increase regional disparities. If the seekers of cheap labour moved to LDCs, it may reduce national disparities but increase regional disparities.

The main point, however, is that the link between entrepreneurial decisions and social welfare—if it ever existed outside the minds of neoclassical economists—is broken with the new style management. The logic of neoclassical welfare economics requires profit-maximization under reasonably competitive circumstance, so that prices are reasonably close to marginal costs. Only then is the price paid for one good or service a close approximation to the value of other goods and services sacrificed so that the welfare of the person making the purchase is more or less maximized. Then if each person goes on making such purchases to the point where a further purchase would reduce the welfare of someone else, social welfare is said to be maximized. Critics of this theory usually protest that in the real world there is too much monopoly, so that prices are too far from marginal costs and the system breaks down. In our view monopoly power is limited by Schumpeter's "cluster of followers;" and innovation is too quickly followed by other producers of nearly the same thing, for monopoly power to last long. But what if profits are not maximized? What if maximum market share, or maximum rate of growth of the firm, is sought instead? We saw earlier that management teams that are equally well informed and equally rational may make totally different choices as to what to produce, how to produce it, and where to produce it. As regional analysts, we are particularly interested in decisions as to *where* to produce various goods and services. There are, in fact, no rules covering such choices by management teams. Consequently, even if each management team makes rational decisions about location of activity *for itself* (or for a majority of the team, or for its more powerful members) there is no guarantee that the outcome of all these decisions is optimal for society as a whole. The location of industry that comes out of this host of market decisions is almost totally haphazard.

Indeed the growing integration of the world economy is pushing nation states, and large private enterprises, into a borderless world. Capital, goods and services go to places where their home nation states may not like them to go. Some $1 trillion are now traded round the clock on foreign exchange markets—triple the figure of 1986—and Great Britain felt the sting of these markets in the autumn of 1992. Few large, technologically advanced, industrial firms call themselves "national" any more. Ownership of such firms is increasingly spread among several nations and components of major products are manufactured each one in a different country.

Yet at the same time that the world economy is integrating, we see that the attachments to race, religion, language, and culture, and for certain things to the nation state, remain strong, and in many cases are getting stronger. While people may want to break free from shackles that inhibit their ability to buy goods and services from any country they like, and to invest wherever they wish, they continue to rely on race, religion, language, culture, and the nation state for their identity.

Such being the case, the decisions made by governments in a democratic system are the important ones. But what level of government? In the United States, Canada, and Australia, one element in the decisions of management teams as to where to locate is the amount of subsidy offered by various states or provinces. Other things being equal, all enterprises will go to the highest bidder. Now, if the state governments are as omniscient as individual entrepreneurs are assumed to be in neoclassical theory, the highest bidder would be the state where a particular enterprise would be most efficient; so the outcome of a system where location of industry is determined by competition among states would be optimal. But, in reality, state governments are not omniscient, and the highest bidder is likely to be the state with the greatest fiscal capacity, rather than the state where the enterprise concerned will be most productive. Such a system is at least as likely to lead to polarization and increasing regional disparities as it is to reduced regional gaps.

To assure that the social welfare of the whole nation is taken into account in decisions regarding location of industry, it seems that the central government must lay down some rules, and offer some incentives. If indeed enterprises are more flexible and "footloose" than ever before, it should be easier to persuade them to locate in the socially optimal place. Sometimes, no doubt, the optimal location from the standpoint of the management team and the social optimum will coincide, in which case no inducement to locate in a particular region will be necessary. In other cases, it will be almost a matter of indifference to the management where they locate, in which case a very small inducement will suffice to make them choose the location favoured by the government. In many cases, it will be a matter of indifference to the government—and so, presumably, to the society as a whole—where an enterprise locates a certain economic activity, and so the management can be left free to make its own choice.

The general principle should be that decisions or choices should be made by the smallest possible unit: by the individual or household when no other interest is involved; by the neighbourhood when no other interest is involved; by the municipality when no conflict with other municipalities is involved; by the state or province when no possible conflict with another state or province is perceived; and only as a last resort, by the central government, when only it can make sure that the general interest of the whole society is protected.

The disillusionment with aggregative planning, and particularly with planning for steady growth of national income with "trickling down" of benefits; the growing and well-founded dislike and distrust of powerful central governments and their mastodonian bureaucracies; the new insistence on people participating in the decisions which determine their fate; the diminishing faith in both votes with dollars in the market place and with ballots at the polls as devices for getting people what they want; the trend towards "small is beautiful," agropolitan and micropolitan development, and the support for a Basic Needs Approach in advanced countries and less developed countries alike; all these have led to strong arguments for relegating planning, policy formulation, decision-making and implementation to the smallest possible unit, often referred to somewhat ambiguously as "the community." At the same time, it is clear that some aspects of government must remain at the central government level, while others cannot be pushed below the intermediate level—the province, state, or district. Thus, we are confronted with a need to develop split-level systems, involving integrated split-level management.[1]

The purpose of such management is to assure a better allocation of resources than can be obtained by the functioning of a free market alone, or even by a market "patched" by legislation designed to offset or remove some of its defects. In this context "better" means one that brings a higher level of human welfare. The interjection into the process of choice of the special expertise of planners reflects a recognition of some degree of market failure, and a conviction that the flaws cannot be removed simply by "passing laws against them," such as anti-monopoly legislation or laws governing the operation of the banking system. If all markets were functioning perfectly within existing legal and institutional frameworks, so that choices of *individuals* made in their own interest really resulted in a resource allocation optimal for society as a whole, there would be no justification for planners or planning (except within private enterprises), *especially* in the form of evaluation of development projects. If existing market imperfections could be removed by passing new laws, there would still be no need for any planning beyond the isolation of causes of market failure so as to design legislation and institutions to remove them. Once the laws and institutions are in place, resource allocation could be left entirely to the market once again. There would be no thought of planning in the form of *continuous management* of the economy so as to assure a reasonably satisfactory resource allocation. Each intervention in the form of legislation would be regarded as a once-over affair.

Thus, the growing emphasis on continuous management has three sources:

1. A conviction that no once-over intervention can assure satisfactory operation of the market system.
2. The recognition that many of the decisions important for human welfare must be made by collectivities of various types and sizes, rather than by individuals.
3. The conclusion that voting with dollars in the market plus voting with ballots at the polls is not enough to assure an efficient resource allocation.

Reluctance to leave development, and the process of socio-economic evolution, entirely to the market as it exists, may result from any of several quite different perceptions of why the market is imperfect:

1. In most countries there is common agreement that certain activities should be taken over into the public sector, and that the allocation of resources within that sector should not be left to market forces alone: defense, internal security, education, health, environmental protection, etc. There must therefore be another calculus and mechanism for allocating resources to such activities. Providing a rational basis for such allocation is one aspect of management.
2. There may already exist excessive or misguided government intervention in the market. Management then involves reduction and improvement of the role of government in the economy.
3. The conditions for efficient functioning of the market are not fulfilled (pure competition, perfect knowledge and foresight, equal access to information, absence of externalities and indivisibilities, etc.). Here, we should distinguish between imperfections in the form of monopoly control, and inefficient mechanisms resulting in wrong signals, late signals, delayed response, cumbersome and incomplete diffusion of information, etc. Management is necessary to decide whether, how, and to what extent the market can be "patched," and where the market should be replaced by some more direct and more efficient means of allocating resources.
4. More complex problems arise where market signals, no matter how smooth the mechanism, do not provide a good basis for allocating resources because "the rule," marginal cost equals price ($MC = P$), does not really constitute an optimum. The costs and benefits may accrue to groups and collectivities rather than individuals. Money values can be put on such things, but the values are not revealed in any market.
5. If efficiency in terms of welfare is not guaranteed by $MC = P$, the whole process of shadow pricing must be altered.
6. When both analysis and planning are done at the community level, the objectives—that is, the very definition of "development"—are likely to change in ways not revealed by market choices.

By management we mean the systematic application of a range of technical and professional skills to the process of decision-making, with the express purpose of improving resource allocation and income distribution in the interest of defined social groups. In practice the activity of management ultimately boils down to the identification and evaluation of projects, and bundles of projects, which absorb resources and produce results of value to the social group for which the planning is done. As part of the overall process, grand designs for a better future may be proposed, long run projections made, strategies formulated. But if these activities do not ultimately improve resource allocation they are of very limited use.

As much as possible of the basic analysis, formulation of objectives, planning, policy formulation, decision making and implementation should be carried out at the community level, with maximum participation of the target population itself. We shall hold to be self-evident the basic liberal principle that decisions and choices should be made by the smallest possible unit: by the individual, when family or group interests are not involved; by the family or group, when the interests of the neighbourhood are not involved; by the neighbourhood, when the interests of the larger community are not involved; and by the community, when regional interests are not involved. Only as a last resort, where possible conflicts among regional interests must be resolved, or where benefits cannot be subdivided by regions, as in the case of national defence, should choices or decisions be made at a national level.

The essence of management, then, is bringing to bear on choices and decisions, expertise of a sort that the ultimate beneficiary does not normally have, but which is needed to assure that the decision or choice is truly rational, and that the welfare of the beneficiary is protected to the maximum possible degree.

Let us add together the several changes in approach to economic and social policy and planning implicit in the foregoing analysis:

1. In the measurement of benefits and evaluation of projects involving collective choice, market prices of goods and services are replaced by a set of norms or targets relating to major aspects of welfare of target populations in the society concerned. In so far as possible, the selection of norms and their weighting is done by the target populations themselves.
2. Professional planners serve as expert consultants to the target populations rather than as advisors to governments. The government's role is reduced to resolving conflicts (as referee or judge) among various target groups.
3. Decision making by elected representatives of the people is replaced whenever possible by collective decision making by groups of the people themselves.

Obviously, in such a system, regional planners, instead of being on the periphery of the overall process of economic, social, and political development, are at its very core. The implications sound revolutionary, and they are. But they are not quite so revolutionary as they sound. In practice, in non-socialist countries, and even in many socialist ones, allocation of resources to many, even most, fields of economic activity can be left to market forces, if only by default. And mega-decisions on matters of indivisible national interest, such as national defense, monetary policy, and foreign trade policy, would still be left to national governments. In such a system of split-level management, the role of government in the decision-making process would be reduced, the role of individuals as members of social groups increased. The role of private enterprises as producers of goods and services would be substantially unchanged, their role as decision makers in allocating resources perhaps slightly reduced. The most effective way for the target population to weight objectives is by selecting projects, after a full presentation of options and their implications by the experts involved. It does not make much sense to ask a target population, or even their elected representatives, "What relative weights do you attach to education, health and transport?" But they can make a rational choice among a primary school, a clinic and a road, and in so doing are implicitly determining the weights. In other words, the weighting is done by the community itself, towards the very end of the planning process, when all the information and analysis needed for a rational choice can be made available by the planners.

The list of developmental responsibilities which must be handled at the national level is not a very long one. The shift to multi-level decision making could bring a substantial reduction in the size of the civil service of central governments, with no corresponding increase in the bureaucracy of lower levels of government. Moreover, with a much larger share of the planning, policy formulation, and implementation being handled by regional and local authorities, and by social groups outside of government altogether, government as such should seem less remote from the people than it does today.

Pursuing the same principle, there are development activities which cannot be handled exclusively at the local level but which need not go to the national level. These are the proper concern of the regional authorities. For example, communities as we are defining them are too small for all of them to have a good secondary school, let alone a good university. Someone must decide which community will have the regional university and which communities the high schools. For students from communities without educational facilities above the primary level either transport to or lodging in the centres that do have them must be arranged. Similar considerations apply to the hierarchy of clinics, small hospitals and major hospitals, and to the state or provincial road system. There may be some kinds of expertise, such as agricultural extension workers, public health and family planning services which cannot be provided on a permanent, day-to-day basis to all communities and which must, therefore, be allocated by a regional authority.

In terms of technical application of professional skills, it does not seem that the task of the "expert" varies very much from one level to another. What does vary is the relationship between the planner and the people and between the politicians and the people. At the community level, we are envisaging open discussion amongst all interested citizens, leading if possible to unanimous agreement, and if not, to a sense of the meeting. We imagine the experts themselves being available as resource persons to join in such discussions if asked. There is an obvious danger in such a system that the experts may usurp political powers they ought not to have; yet it is essential, given the technological and social complexity of the development process today, that the expertise of the planners should be available to the population to assist them in arriving at their decisions. If there are politicians or bureaucrats from further up the hierarchy of authority whose approval is needed to give effect to decisions taken by the town meeting, they also should be available to hear arguments and answer questions.

What we are suggesting essentially is to remove, as much as possible, the responsibility for planning and implementing regional development measures from the hands of bureaucracies, particularly those in central governments. The past thirty years have taught us that large public bureaucracies are not well suited for formulating and operating regional programs—they do not have the necessary freedom to move quickly, to be flexible, to be creative and to look down to the community level. In the hierarchical world of central bureaucracies, one looks up to serve as best one can political masters, the permanent secretary or other senior permanent officials. There is always a political crisis to manage, a "turf" war to be won and centrally prescribed rules and processes to observe. Looking to community leaders to decide what can work and what cannot involves risks that are not worth taking in the cautious and status quo conscious world of bureaucracies. Looking down to the community invariably entails a loss of control which means risk taking. This is less a criticism of bureaucracy than a recognition that this is what politicians and, ultimately, voters want. There are precious few rewards for risk taking in government bureaucracies and plenty of career punishments for creating or mismanaging a political crisis or a bureaucratic *faux pas*, particularly the ones reported in the media. In short, bureaucracy was designed to give priority to due process, to apply rules and regulations fairly, to respond to political direction from above and to ensure a full public accountability of its decisions and activities. The failures of past regional development efforts, and the reluctance of government to look to theories of regional development for guidance, have more to do with this fact than with the substance of the initiatives themselves. The solution is to push out of government and down to community groups, including local business associations, responsibility for planning and implementing regional development measures.

Global Planning

There is a fourth level of planning which we have not yet mentioned but which is just as fundamental as the others: transnational or global planning. Just as there are some aspects of development which can be handled effectively only at the national level within particular countries, so there are some, such as design of an efficient world monetary system, commodity stabilization, conservation of non renewable resources, protection of the global environment, globalization of world trade, and redistribution of income and wealth among nations, which must be managed at the international level. At this level too, there cannot really be any debate over plan or no plan; the world economy is functioning too badly to contemplate just leaving it alone.

Some progress towards transnational planning is being made through the United Nations and its increasingly influential international civil service. Smaller groupings or nations such as OECD, the Group of 7, the Commonwealth, the Organization of American States, ASEAN, the ANDEAN Group and EEC, also make useful contributions to global management. But much remains to be done.

An increasingly integrated international economy also holds far reaching implications for how nation states or states and provinces should organize to promote regional development. The borderless economy, the pace of change and the intense competition for new economic activities between regions are also rendering the current ways of organizing government departments and agencies obsolete. At the risk of overstating the case, government bureaucracies are by nature and design much too cautious, and too much preoccupied with one process, to be sufficiently flexible to pursue development opportunities that come and go with breathtaking speed, or that require a great deal of creativity and risk taking. What is required now is an ability to think opportunity not process, regions not economic borders and systems and outputs, not government programs and administrative inputs.

All of this to suggest once again that governments should turn over responsibility for promoting economic development to new entities that are not units in government departments and agencies and that have a capacity to bring together the private sector, communities and government representatives. The important point is that the process of economic development cannot any longer fit the narrow focus of a single government agency. Indeed the pressures of the new economy may well force provincial and state governments to look beyond their own borders, including those of their own nation states, to organize for economic development. The need to marshall common strengths and to spend public funds more effectively has already pushed some state government to explore novel ways to organize. For example the Pacific Northwest Economic Region (PNWER) consists of five U.S. states (Washington, Oregon, Montana, Idaho and Alaska) and two Canadian provinces (British Columbia and Alberta) and has a mandate to cooperate across national boundaries in six areas—expanding environmental products and services, creating markets for recycled materials, pooling efforts in tourism promotion, integrating telecommunications services, educating and improving the region's labour force and expanding markets for value-added wood products. In addition, the five states and two provinces have agreed to work towards removing regulatory barriers between states and between nations to strengthen the region's indigenous industries.[2] One can easily speculate whether or not the states and provinces regard their national governments as part of the solution or part of the problem. One could even speculate whether the people involved in the Austin project regarded governments—even the state government—as part of the solution or part of the problem or simply ineffective actors best left on the sidelines. What is much more certain is that the search is on for new ways for regions to organize themselves to promote economic development. All to the good. This study makes clear that developing prescriptive theories of regional economic development or even specific policy measures in isolation of how government is or should be organized to implement them is little more than a costly exercise in futility.

There is no denying that the neo-classical school of thought has been in vogue in most of the countries surveyed in this book during the early 1980s. Thatcher, Reagan and later Bush, Mulroney and even Australia's Labour Prime Minister Bob Hawke adopted right of centre policies or at least preached the gospel of less intervention in the economy. Big government and public spending come under attack as never before and leading economists urged governments to withdraw from a number of policy fields, notably regional development. To be sure, governments, as this study shows, have done stupid things in the name of regional development and wasted public funds. Prescriptive theories and carefully thought out approaches to regional development were either ignored, poorly applied and certainly administered without the proper organization, government or otherwise, in place. We conclude our study, however, with the view that governments should not throw out the proverbial baby with the bath water. Given the challenges of a more integrated international economy, we believe that regional planning holds considerable promise assuming a proper structure in place to encourage creativity and to deliver the measures with both flexibility and speed.

Management and Freedom

We also note that the Friedman school of thought arguing, as others before, like Ludwig Von Mises, did, that there is a conflict between planning and freedom has been in the ascendency of late.[3] We believe that this thinking justifies a frontal attack.

Let us begin by distinguishing between ruthless pursuit of purely selfish interests and true freedom. In their best seller, *Free to Choose*, Milton and Rose Friedman quote with evident relish and approval a famous passage from Adam Smith's *The Wealth of Nations*: "It is not from the benevolence of the butcher, the brewer, or the baker, that we expect our dinner, but from their regard to their own interest. We address ourselves, not to their humanity but to their self-love, and never talk to them of our own necessities but of their advantages. Nobody but a beggar chuses (sic) to depend chiefly upon the benevolence of his fellow citizens."[4]

Adam Smith, as the Friedmans well know, was a moral philosopher. Careful study of his *Theory of Moral Sentiments* makes it clear that in the above passage he is describing the way in which a freely competitive market works, rather than giving his blessing as a philosopher to a society dominated by selfish greed. In the very first sentence of his *The Theory of Moral Sentiments*, Adam Smith wrote: "How selfish soever man may be supposed, there are evidently some principles in his nature, which interest him in the fortunes of others, and render their happiness necessary to him, though he derives nothing from it, except the pleasure of seeing it." We may disapprove of the person who chooses to beg rather than to seek an opportunity to contribute more to the society of which he is a part by producing something himself. But surely, a society in which we could rely for our dinner on the charity of the butcher, the brewer and the baker, while they in turn could rely on our benevolence to help them meet their basic needs, is more admirable than one in which one man's greed is satisfied only by playing upon other men's greed.

A Christian maxim is, "And now abideth these three: faith, hope and charity; and the greatest of these is charity." In more recent translations the word "charity" is sometimes replaced by "love." Now it is obvious that the moment love enters in, the freedom to pursue purely selfish, individualistic ends is limited; and "he who hath children gives hostages to fortune." The freedom to go alone to the marketplace and choose between a bottle of beer and a bottle of wine—even the freedom to go to the polls and choose between candidate White and candidate Black—are less fundamental to a de-cent society than the freedom to make decisions in the interest of the family as a whole, after discussions in which the whole family joins in, and where desirable, obtains expert advice on the issues involved before the final decision is made. The system of multi-level decision making outlined above extends this fundamental principle of the "family-like society" to the neighbourhood, the community, the region, and ultimately to the nation, with the smallest feasible unit always making the decision. Both market signals and votes provide essential inputs into the decision-making process, but the aim is cooperation rather than cutthroat competition. The principle is that collective interests are best met by collective decision making, for each social grouping, of whatever size, on the basis of all the technical knowledge that is required and which can be mustered.

In terms of the centuries-long debate among political theorists, multi-level decision making is a system for assuring that the general will rather than the particular will prevails, while strengthening rather than destroying the associations that stand between the individual and the state. This concept is opposite to that of Rousseau, who argued that such associations are inimical to a healthy society, an idea which, as Frederick Watkins has pointed out, "long continued to inhibit the development of liberal thought."[5]

It is in this context we can best understand the passage of E.M. Forster which begins this chapter. He makes the point, with his inimitable elegance and acuity, that a system of individualism can work well only in a society of true individuals, whole persons, capable of making wise decisions and acting upon them all alone. He goes on: "Alone? As if he (Man) had ever been alone!...Only Heaven knows what Man might accomplish alone!...The service that is perfect freedom perhaps...Perhaps (ultimately) a new creature may appear on this globe, a creature who, we pretend, is here already: the individual. How the globe would get on, if entirely peopled with individuals, it is impossible to foresee. However, Man has another wish, besides the wish to be free, and that is the wish to love, and perhaps something may be born of the union of the two. Love sometimes leads to an obedience which is not servile—the obedience referred to in the Christian epigram...'Even love, the beloved Republic, that feeds upon freedom and lives'...Democracy is not a beloved Republic, really, and never will be. But it is less hateful than other contemporary forms of government, and to that extent it deserves our support..."[6]

In the liberal philosophy of the eighteenth and nineteenth centuries neither the free market, nor parliamentary democracy with sovereignty of strong nation states were presented as ends in themselves. The first was supported as an efficient device for allocating resources, and the second as an efficient device for protecting the individual against maltreatment by the Crown or the State. If a century of two later we find either mechanism to be no longer efficient for the purposes it is supposed to serve, we should modify and improve it, without abandoning the basic virtues of the liberal philosophy itself.

Notes

1. Influenced by Masahiko Honjo (former Director of the United Nations Centre for Regional Development) and others, I have previously used the term "multi-level planning." I have found, however, that despite all protestations to the contrary, this expression summons up pictures of increased government intervention and enlarged bureaucracies. I hope that "split level management" sounds more like the system I actually have in mind.
2. See *Northwest Resources for Regional Cooperation* and *Strategies for the Pacific Northwest Economic Region*, prepared by the Northwest Policy Centre, University of Washington Graduate School of Public Affairs for the Pacific Northwest Legislature Leadership Forum, Seatle, Washington, March 1991.
3. Ludwig Von Mises, *Kritik des Interventionismus Unterschungen und Wirtschafts Ideologie der Gengenwart* (Jena: G. Fisher, 1929) and *Socialism: An Economic Analysis*, translated by J. Kuhane (London: Jonathan Cape, 1951).
4. Milton and Rose Friedman, *Free to Choose: A Personal Statement* (London: Secker & Warburg, 1980), p. 189.
5. Frederick Watkins, *The Political Tradition of the West: A Study in the Development of Modern Liberalism* (Cambridge, Mass.: Harvard University Press, 1948), p. 262.
6. E.M. Forster, *Two Cheers for Democracy* (London: Edward Arnold, 1951 and 1972), pp. 9-10 and 66.

Name Index

Subject Index